Combatting Illicit Trade on the EU Border

Celina Nowak
Editor

Combatting Illicit Trade on the EU Border

A Comparative Perspective

Springer

Editor
Celina Nowak
Institute of Law Studies
Polish Academy of Sciences
Warsaw, Poland

ISBN 978-3-030-51018-3 ISBN 978-3-030-51019-0 (eBook)
https://doi.org/10.1007/978-3-030-51019-0

This Springer imprint is published by the registered company Springer Nature Switzerland AG.
The registered company address is: Gewerbestrasse 11, 6330 Cham, Switzerland

Acknowledgements

This study, conducted at the Centre for Studies on Economic Crime in the Institute of Law Studies, Polish Academy of Sciences, was funded by PMI IMPACT, a grant award initiative of Philip Morris International (PMI). In the performance of its research, the Institute of Law Studies, Polish Academy of Sciences, maintained full independence from PMI. The views and opinions expressed in this document are those of the research team and do not necessarily reflect the views of PMI. Responsibility for the information and views expressed in this collection lies entirely with the Institute of Law Studies, Polish Academy of Sciences. Neither PMI, nor any of its affiliates, nor any person acting on their behalf may be held responsible for any use of the information contained herein.

All errors are those of the authors.

Contents

Part I
Introduction

Introduction: Fighting Against Illicit Tobacco Trade in the Era of Fast Change

Celina Nowak

Contents

Abstract This chapter outlines the framework of the research presented in this volume. It starts with a notion that national criminal policies on illicit tobacco trade are a part of the national tobacco control policy, and at the same time a part of a general national criminal policy and points to the need for an in-depth research of national criminal laws in this regard. It presents the scope of the research, which consists in a comparative analysis about the illicit tobacco trade and about efforts to counteract that trade in six EU Member States—four post-communist states (Lithuania, Poland, Slovakia and Romania), on the Eastern border of the Union and two "old" EU Member States (Germany, Italy).

1 National Criminal Policy as a Part of Tobacco Control Policy: Justification of the Research

Tobacco is the name commonly used to represent some plants in the *Nicotiana* genus, as well as products made with leaves of the tobacco plants. The latter is a substance that is hazardous for human health.

C. Nowak (✉)
Institute of Law Studies, Polish Academy of Sciences, Warsaw, Poland
e-mail: cnowak@inp.pan.pl

C. Nowak (ed.), *Combatting Illicit Trade on the EU Border*,
https://doi.org/10.1007/978-3-030-51019-0_1

Tobacco has been with mankind for millennia. Yet, its expansion as a trade item for personal use dates to the sixteenth century and the arrival of the Europeans to the Americas. In the twentieth century, scientists concluded that tobacco use is detrimental to the health of its users. Tobacco has been identified by the World Health Organisation (WHO) as one of the four major risk factors that contribute to the development of non-communicable diseases. Tobacco "accounts for over 7.2 million deaths every year (including from the effects of exposure to second-hand smoke)".[1] The recent global rise of deaths attributed to non-communicable diseases has motivated international organisations to take action to prevent and control the risk factors.[2] Controlling the production and controlling the use of tobacco have been significant parts of this process.

The relationship between tobacco and individual country policies are complex. On the one hand, states are socially and politically committed to the reduction of tobacco use. On the other hand, states benefit financially from tax revenue from the manufacture and sales of tobacco products. From this perspective, the relationships states have with tobacco are like their relationships with alcohol. Although the use of alcohol and tobacco constitute health hazards, they remain legal, unlike narcotic substances. As von Lampe justly states, "cigarettes are essentially a legal good".[3] However, states are committed to fighting against revenue loss from the manufacture and sale of tobacco products. The manufacture and trade of cigarettes are legal, provided these processes conform to the cigarette taxation rules adopted by states. Cigarette trade is illegal when manufacturers and sellers evade cigarette taxes.

National policies on the tobacco trade struggle to balance states' fiscal interests with their responsibility to protect public health. This balance is mainly struck by pricing tobacco products at high rates. As stated in Article 6.1 of the WHO FCTC, price and tax measures are effective means of reducing tobacco consumption by various segments of the population, young people, in particular. Therefore, tobacco products are legal but taxable with the Value Added Tax (VAT) and excise taxes. Moreover, the EU Member States are obligated to apply the European minimum rates of the excise duty.[4] This application is uniform because, as mentioned in the preamble to the 2011 Directive, "*the level of taxation is a major factor in the price of tobacco products, which in turn influences consumers' smoking habits. Fraud and smuggling undermine tax induced price levels and thus jeopardise the achievement of tobacco control and health protection objectives*".

---

[1]A quote from "GBD 2015 Risk Factors Collaborators (2016), pp. 1659–1724". See https://www.who.int/news-room/fact-sheets/detail/noncommunicable-diseases.

[2]Cf. Resolution adopted on 24 January 2012 by the General Assembly No 66/2. Political Declaration of the High-level Meeting of the General Assembly on the Prevention and Control of Non-communicable Diseases with Annex: Political Declaration of the High-level Meeting of the General Assembly on the Prevention and Control of Non-communicable Diseases.

[3]von Lampe (2011), p. 148.

[4]Cf. the Council Directive 2011/64/EU of 21 June 2011 on the structure and rates of excise duty applied to manufactured tobacco, OJ 5.7.2011, L 176/24.

Despite the relatively uniform application of fiscal policies across the European Union, tobacco products prices vary significantly within and among EU Member States and non-EU Member States. The price difference of a package of cigarettes in the East of the Union may be up to four times lower than in the UK.[5] These price differences encourage the illicit trade of tobacco products in the EU.

Tobacco control policies are a field of a complex dynamics, where governments are under pressure coming from different stakeholders, such as health experts, tobacco industry, NGOs.[6] A tobacco control policy encompasses a variety of measures, as defined in Art. 1(d) of the 2003 WHO Framework Convention on Tobacco Control (FCTC).[7] They cover reduction of the demand of tobacco as well as reduction of the supply of tobacco. In the systematics offered by the FCTC, illicit trade control,[8] which is the focus of this volume, is one of the measures relating to the reduction of the supply.

By one estimate, the EU illicit tobacco trade decreases taxes significantly.[9] It is also likely that illegal tobacco products, manufactured with materials of unknown origin, may be more harmful to consumers' health than legal products; although, interestingly, the content of the legal tobacco products are not verified by national authorities.

States adopt diverse policies to govern the illicit tobacco trade, which is simultaneously recognised a fiscal irregularity and a problem of criminal nature,[10] and as such it is dealt with both by fiscal and criminal policy.[11] Criminal policymaking should however be particularly mindful of the *ultima ratio*, as criminal sanctions are the most powerful tools to address social nuisances. Criminal policy choices should also take into account a variety of social, political, economic and cultural factors as they inherently influence complex and sensitive social relations.

---

[5]See detailed information on pricing policies in different states published in the annual WHO reports on tobacco. Most recent report is "*WHO report on the global tobacco epidemic 2019*", available at: https://www.who.int/tobacco/global_report/en/.

[6]See an interesting recent study on national tobacco policy by Willemsen (2018).

[7]Pursuant to this provision, 'tobacco control' means a range of supply, demand and harm reduction strategies that aim to improve the health of a population by eliminating or reducing their consumption of tobacco products and exposure to tobacco smoke.

[8]Following the wording of Art. 1(a) of the FCTC, illicit trade is to be understood as any practice or conduct prohibited by law and which relates to production, shipment, receipt, possession, distribution, sale or purchase including any practice or conduct intended to facilitate such activity.

[9]The black market for cigarettes in the EU is estimated to have deprived governments of EUR 10 billion in tax revenues in 2017. See KMPG Project Sun. A study of the illicit cigarette market in the European Union, Norway and Switzerland. 2017 Results, https://home.kpmg/uk/en/home/insights/2018/07/project-sun-2017.html.

[10]M. Tonry points out to six "public policy approaches ... available for dealing with crime". They are criminal law enforcement, prevention, harm reduction, regulation, decriminalization, and nonintervention. See Tonry (2011), p. 7.

[11]For M. Delmas-Marty, criminal policy is a set of measures by way of which the social corps organizes responses to the phenomenon of crime. See Delmas-Marty (1992), p. 13.

The national criminal policies on illicit tobacco trade, analyzed in this volume, are just a small part of the national tobacco control policy. At the same time though the criminal policy with regard to illicit tobacco trade is a part of a general national criminal policy and has to correspond and match the goals and specificities thereof. The challenges related to the creation and enforcement of the national criminal policy on illicit tobacco stem from this very double adherence.

The fight against the illicit tobacco trade has become more important in recent years, as this trade has become of increasing interest to organised crime groups. Traditionally, organised crime groups have been involved in a variety of illegal activities, often of a violent nature, such as human trafficking, drugs and extortion. However, in recent years they shifted their interest to tobacco. The danger of being caught is lower, the target market is bigger, and sanctions are less severe than for other types of offences. Interestingly, traditional criminals seeking to diversify their activities and increase their profits, turn to tax crimes. This realization should further justify a need to undertake scientific criminal law research about the illicit tobacco trade.

2 Scope of the Book, Methodological and Terminological Considerations

This research presents the results of comparative analysis about the illicit tobacco trade and about efforts to counteract that trade in six EU Member States. Researchers chose four states (Lithuania, Poland, Slovakia and Romania), based on their geographical location on the Eastern border of the Union. Coincidently, these four states are all post-communist countries, and their penal systems are still coping with the Soviet heritage. Researchers also chose two "old" EU Member States (Germany, Italy) that have struggled with the illicit tobacco trade.

The starting point of the research was the presumption that on the national level, even though the illicit tobacco trade constitutes both a tax irregularity and a criminal offence, the fight against the illicit trade of tobacco products is primarily conducted through the enforcement of criminal law, rather than through tax law. The tax law and criminal law have become more intertwined over recent years,[12] but still, national policymakers evidently consider criminal measures to be more effective in tackling this phenomenon. Therefore, the focus of the research was domestic criminal law—the researchers examined substantive criminal law and procedural criminal law in the study countries. Administrative law (fiscal and tax law) was examined only on subsidiary basis, where necessary to complement the picture of national repressive legal framework. A secondary aim of the research was to assess the enforcement of criminal law measures and, to this end, examine the scope of the illicit tobacco trade and its prosecution in the study countries through a

[12] As confirmed in Alldridge (2017), p. 1 ff.

comprehensive analysis of criminological data. Moreover, since criminal law constitutes an ultimate measure, the research had to control for, where possible, cooperative agreements and practices at transnational and national levels and for administrative instruments adopted by states to prevent and eliminate the illicit tobacco trade.

Studies on illicit tobacco trade published to date[13] has focused to a great extent on criminological and interdisciplinary aspects of this phenomenon and its regulation. The novelty of the research presented in this volume lies in conducting analysis of "hard" criminal legislation in the study countries. Here, the illicit tobacco trade is examined from the perspective of criminal policy—criminalisation, sanctions and enforcement are all examined in detail.

A second novel element of the research at hand lies in a systematic analysis of criminal policies in Central and East European countries which have never been presented in such a comprehensive manner in international publications. The countries chosen for this research—Lithuania, Poland, Slovakia and Romania, located on and responsible for almost all the East border of the EU, with specific geographical and social circumstances, struggling with post-Soviet legacy and mentalities, and often with lack of appropriate financial and human resources, faced with the obligation to implement strict EU rules whereas their neighbouring non-EU countries have more lax policies on tobacco, are at the first line of the fight against illicit tobacco trade in the EU and therefore they deserve more attention.

As a background of the study researchers applied the 2003 WHO Framework Convention on Tobacco Control (FCTC), which had been signed by all six countries covered by this research, and the September 2018 Protocol to Eliminate Illicit Trade in Tobacco Products, signed by half of the examined countries; they also analysed issues related to the European Union response to the illicit tobacco trade.

The research group have analysed national criminal law by reviewing the existing enforcement mechanisms. The research team applied methods traditionally used for comparative legal research—they analysed the national legislation and experiences and challenges related to the fight against the illicit tobacco trade based on the results of a comprehensive and detailed questionnaire. The analysis followed the same structure, which has been subsequently reflected in the chapters on national challenges, and covered all aspects of the fight against illicit tobacco trade and tobacco-related crimes, namely criminalization, administrative regulation, preventive measures and cooperation inside the country and with external partners. National experts wrote the chapters that refer to their states' national policies and practices, also after having consulted legal practitioners and law enforcement officials in the field in their respective countries.

The data and analyses are important for national criminal policy options and best practices in the fight against the illicit tobacco trade. Findings based on the data allowed the researchers to formulate criminal law recommendations for national legislatures and international organisations, which may lead to adoption of new

[13] See e.g. Savona et al. (2017).

mechanisms to effectively combat the illicit tobacco trade. Those recommendations are presented in the final chapter of this collection.

Concerning terminology, one note must be made at the outset of the study. Pursuant to Art. 1(f) of the WHO FCTC, "tobacco products" mean products entirely or partly made of the leaf tobacco as raw material which are manufactured to be used for smoking, sucking, chewing or snuffing. However, in this book the term "tobacco products" and "tobacco" when used in the phase "illicit tobacco trade" are treated as synonyms and will be used to cover traditional types of products manufactured from tobacco, such as cigarettes and fine-cut tobacco, as mainly these two tobacco-made products are subject of illegal trade. It should be mentioned that the research focused on traditional tobacco products, as essentially they are the object of illicit tobacco trade, and issues related to new products, in particular e-cigarettes, have not been addressed.

The research team included researchers from the field of criminal law and criminal procedure. Since a tobacco company funded the research, researchers sought approval for the research plan from the Institute of Law Studies of the Polish Academy of Sciences' Ethical Committee. Only once the Committee approved the plan, we have launched the research. We were also free to draw any conclusions we deemed pertinent for the research.

The negative impact of tobacco products on human health is indisputable. As researchers in the field of criminal law, we focused our research on states' (criminal) tobacco policies, which constitute at the same time an important part of national criminal policies and a part of the national tobacco control policy. The clear health hazards related to tobacco were not subject of this research and are very competently covered by researchers in other disciplines of sciences, in their publications.

3 Research Questions, Structure and Content of the Study

This edited volume constitutes an attempt to address the following research question—how examined countries construct their criminal policies with regard to illicit trade of tobacco products. Additional research questions refer to the characteristics of the national criminal policies and their effectiveness. The researchers aimed at studying what types of behaviours are covered by national law and how they are investigated, prosecuted and sanctioned.

The volume has been divided into three parts. The first one includes a chapter by Celina Nowak devoted to the presentation of the legal framework in international and EU law referring to the fight against illicit tobacco trade. This part constitutes an analysis of a legal background against which the authors of the chapters included into the second part of the volume present their national criminal policies.

The second part is a vertical part of the comparative research and as such it consists of six chapters on national criminal policies with regard to illicit tobacco trade. Each chapter has been elaborated by experts coming from respective examined legal systems. They all address penal, criminological, as well as administrative and social aspects of the fight against illicit trade of tobacco products in the examined country. Some chapters are more detailed (chapter on Germany by Marc Engelhart, chapter on Lithuania by Gintaras Švedas, and chapter on Poland by Konrad Buczkowski and Paweł Dziekański), whereas other are more condense, but they all provide an excellent insight into the national legal systems and national criminal policies with regard to illicit tobacco trade.

They also give an opportunity to appreciate the development of legal reflection and legal research on the examined issues in the respective countries—for instance the chapter on Romania is based on case-law only, as legal doctrine on illicit tobacco trade has not been well developed, whereas other chapters include academic sources as well.

The third part of the book ('Conclusions: criminal policy on illicit trade of tobacco products between Scylla of health concerns and Charybdis of fiscal interests'), authored by Konrad Buczkowski and Celina Nowak, presents results of a comparative analysis of the six legal systems examined in the second part of the book. The ambition of the authors of this chapter was not to plainly juxtapose analysed legal systems or to analyse them in detail, but to indicate some common strategies used by national policymakers as well as common tendencies of national criminal policies with regard to illicit tobacco trade, identified on the basis of a thorough analysis of the national chapters. It also points to the difficult choices faced by national criminal policymakers trying to reconcile health concerns, fiscal interests and specificities of national criminal policies.

Such a horizontal analysis allowed to formulate recommendations the implementation of which could contribute to an increase of effectiveness of the national fight against illicit tobacco trade.

Also, the comparative research does not allow to go into details with regard to specific national provisions, it only can provide an overall picture of the system and the national criminal policy. For this reason, the conclusions drawn on the basis of chapters presented in the second part of this volume also point to directions of the future research concerning national criminal policies with regard to illicit tobacco trade.

References

Alldridge P (2017) Criminal Justice and taxation. OUP

Delmas-Marty M (1992) Les grands systèmes de politique criminelle. PUF

GBD 2015 Risk Factors Collaborators (2016) Global, regional, and national comparative risk assessment of 79 behavioural, environmental and occupational, and metabolic risks or clusters of risks, 1990–2015: a systematic analysis for the Global Burden of Disease Study 2015. Lancet 388(10053):1659–1724. https://www.who.int/news-room/fact-sheets/detail/noncommunicable-diseases

KMPG Project Sun (2017) A study of the illicit cigarette market in the European Union, Norway and Switzerland. 2017 Results, https://home.kpmg/uk/en/home/insights/2018/07/project-sun-2017.html

Savona EU, Kleiman MAR, Calderoni F (eds) (2017) Dual markets. Comparative approaches to regulation. Springer

Tonry M. (2011), Crime and Public Policy, in: The Oxford handbook of crime and public policy, Tonry M. (ed.), OUP

von Lampe K (2011) The Illegal Cigarettes Trade. In: Natarajan M (ed) International crime and justice. Cambridge University Press

"WHO report on the global tobacco epidemic 2019". https://www.who.int/tobacco/global_report/en/

Willemsen MC (2018) Tobacco Control Policy in the Netherlands: between economy, public health, and ideology. Palgrave MacMillan. https://doi.org/10.1007/978-3-319-72368-6

Celina Nowak Ph.D., is Associate Professor and Head of the Institute of Law Studies of the Polish Academy of Sciences. She holds a Ph.D. and habilitation in law, as well as a postgraduate diploma of Université de Paris I – Panthéon–Sorbonne in criminal law and criminal policy in Europe. Her research refers to criminal law, with focus on international, EU and comparative criminal law. In addition, she has extensive experience as an academic teacher at the Kozminski University and the Warsaw University. Prof. Nowak has taken part in a number of comparative law projects, in the national and EU context, either as a project leader, or as a national expert. She has authored 2 monographs, edited and co-edited 10 books. She has written more than three dozen articles and chapters in Polish, English and French, published in Poland and internationally.

International Legal Framework on the Fight Against Illicit Tobacco Trade: An Overview

Celina Nowak

Contents

Abstract This chapter addresses binding legal provisions referring to combating illicit tobacco trade in international law and EU law. Analysis covers first the relevant provisions of the World Health Organisation Framework Convention on Tobacco Control. More detailed provisions in this regard are provided for in the Protocol to Eliminate Illicit Trade in Tobacco Products to the Convention. EU legal instruments as well as other relevant international instruments are also examined, even though they do have a penal character.

1 Introduction

This chapter examines the existing legal framework that has developed on the international level to govern the tobacco trade. Given the overall goal of this research, the analysis will be focused mainly on penal issues.

C. Nowak (✉)
Institute of Law Studies, Polish Academy of Sciences, Warsaw, Poland
e-mail: cnowak@inp.pan.pl

C. Nowak (ed.), *Combatting Illicit Trade on the EU Border*,
https://doi.org/10.1007/978-3-030-51019-0_2

At the outset, it must be noted that international regulations related to tobacco are recent. Even though tobacco has been a part of human life for a long time, it has only lately become known that cigarettes cause diseases. This scientific discovery contributed to the emergence of an international legal framework on tobacco. Therefore, it comes as no surprise that the World Health Organisation (WHO) has engaged in a variety of activities, including the elaboration of a global legal instrument aimed at controlling tobacco,[1] to minimise the use of tobacco worldwide. As a result of multilateral negotiations, on 21st May 2003, the World Health Assembly adopted the WHO Framework Convention on Tobacco Control (WHO FCTC). This global Convention entered into force on 27 February 2005, and it currently has 182 states parties.[2]

The approach taken by the WHO differs from other international legal instruments related to drug control in that it focuses more on the reduction of demand,[3] and less on supply. Also, tobacco use is perceived by the FCTC as a health issue and subsequently, its control is based on the states' right to protect public health.[4] To fulfil their duty to protect citizen health, states have agreed to adopt a twofold approach. On the one hand, they are reducing demand, and on the other, reducing supply.

The FCTC provides for two types of measures aimed at reducing demand. The first category, mentioned in Article 6 FCTC, includes price and tax measures. The rationale behind this approach is straightforward. Price and tax policies should be implemented to reduce tobacco consumption to achieve health goals.

Non-price measures vary. They include protection from exposure to tobacco smoke; regulation of the contents of tobacco products; regulation of tobacco product disclosures; packaging and labelling of tobacco products; education, communication, training and public awareness; tobacco advertising, promotion and sponsorship and demand reduction measures concerning tobacco dependence and cessation.

The second general category of measures provided for by the FCTC to control tobacco refers to the reduction of the tobacco supply. State parties are first obligated to implement provisions on the prohibition of tobacco sales to and by minors, *i.e.* persons under the age of eighteen (Art. 16 WHO FCTC). They are also obligated to provide support for economically viable alternative activities for tobacco workers, growers and individual sellers (Art. 17 WHO FCTC). Finally, they are obligated to fight against the illicit tobacco trade.

---

[1]On the genesis of the WHO FCTC see: Roemer et al. (2005), p. 936.

[2]Including all six Eu member states covered by this study: Germany, Italy, Lithuania, Poland, Romania and Slovakia.

[3]As confirmed by Art. 3 FCTC, "The objective of this Convention and its protocols is to protect present and future generations from the devastating health, social, environmental and economic consequences of tobacco consumption and exposure to tobacco smoke by providing a framework for tobacco control measures to be implemented by the Parties at the national, regional and international levels in order to reduce continually and substantially the prevalence of tobacco use and exposure to tobacco smoke".

[4]As stated in the Preamble to the FCTC.

2 Illicit Trade of Tobacco Products in the Light of the WHO FCTC

The WHO's fight against the illicit tobacco trade honours states' obligation to reduce the supply of tobacco products. Since the illicit tobacco trade is a transnational challenge, states have justly recognized in the Preamble to the WHO FCTC that cooperative action is necessary to eliminate all forms of illicit trade related to cigarettes and other tobacco products, including smuggling, illicit manufacturing and counterfeiting.

Art. 1 WHO FCTC defines illicit trade comprehensively: "any practice or conduct prohibited by law and which relates to the production, shipment, receipt, possession, distribution, sale or purchase including any practice or conduct intended to facilitate such activity". Based on the wording of this provision, states wanted to cover all stages of the illicit trade, from its manufacturing through transfer to acquisition. The definition refers not only to direct participation in the prohibited process but also to the facilitation of the illicit trade.

A substantive provision referring to the illicit trade of tobacco products is provided for in Art. 15 WHO FCTC. According to Art. 15.1, "the elimination of all forms of illicit trade in tobacco products, including smuggling, illicit manufacturing and counterfeiting, and the development and implementation of related national law, in addition to subregional, regional and global agreements, are essential components of tobacco control", thus making the provision at hand a confirmation of the need to tackle illicit tobacco trade. The following provisions in Art. 15 FCTC obligate states to adopt different measures, mainly of legislative, executive and administrative authority, to ensure detailed markings of tobacco products, enabling states to "control the movement of tobacco products and their legal status" (Art. 15.2 FCTC). These measures will be enforced preferably by a tracking and tracing regime. However, states are required only to consider the development of such a system.

It is worth noting that Art. 15 FCTC contains only a few provisions mentioning criminal law measures. The adopted text is the outcome of negotiations over a text that had originally contained more penal provisions.[5] It has been diluted.[6] The states decided against the inclusion of criminal law references in an international treaty on health.

Currently, Art. 15.4 (b) is a primary penal provision of the FCTC, as it stipulates that parties shall "enact or strengthen legislation, with appropriate penalties and remedies, against illicit trade in tobacco products, including counterfeit and contraband cigarettes". The wording of the provision makes it clear that states are must provide an appropriate legislative framework to govern the illicit tobacco trade. This framework must include criminal law sanctions or "penalties". The FCTC also

[5] See Boister and Burchill (2002), p. 44.

[6] Boister and Burchill (2002), p. 47.

mentions confiscation of manufacturing equipment, counterfeit and contraband cigarettes, other tobacco products and proceeds derived from the illicit tobacco trade.

Fragments of Art. 15 FCTC contain the remnants of the draft convention. They refer to cooperation "between national agencies, as well as relevant regional and international intergovernmental organizations as it relates to investigations, prosecutions and proceedings, with a view to eliminating illicit trade in tobacco products".

The WHO FCTC is not a penal treaty. It does not criminalise the illicit tobacco trade. However, its importance lies in the fact that, as a framework convention, it was the first international legal instrument, of binding force, that emphasised the necessity to tackle the illicit tobacco trade, at national and transnational levels.

3 Protocol to Eliminate Illicit Trade in Tobacco Products: General Issues

The WHO FCTC is a general instrument that as a framework convention, has been designed to be complemented by protocols that address specific issues.[7] As described in Annex 2 to the Protocol to Eliminate Illicit Trade in Tobacco Products already in 2006, "at the first meeting of the Conference of the Parties following entry into force of the WHO FCTC, the parties discussed possible protocols to the Convention. One of the areas in which they agreed that a protocol could be established was illicit trade in tobacco products".

Therein lies the origin of the Protocol to Eliminate Illicit Trade in Tobacco Products. It was adopted on 12 November 2012 and entered into force on 25 September 2018. The Protocol currently counts 61 parties.[8]

According to Art. 3, the objective of the Protocol is "to eliminate all forms of illicit trade in tobacco products, in accordance with the terms of Article 15 of the WHO Framework Convention on Tobacco Control".

The Protocol adopted a standard structure of a penal convention in the parts that refer to offences as well as international cooperation. However, its scope goes

---

[7]Such a possibility was foreseen by state parties to the Convention in Art. 33, which stipulates as follows: "1. Any Party may propose protocols. Such proposals will be considered by the Conference of the Parties. 2. The Conference of the Parties may adopt protocols to this Convention. In adopting these protocols every effort shall be made to reach consensus. If all efforts at consensus have been exhausted, and no agreement reached, the protocol shall as a last resort be adopted by a three-quarters majority vote of the Parties present and voting at the session. For the purposes of this Article, Parties present and voting means Parties present and casting an affirmative or negative vote. 3. The text of any proposed protocol shall be communicated to the Parties by the Secretariat at least six months before the session at which it is proposed for adoption. 4. Only Parties to the Convention may be parties to a protocol. 5. Any protocol to the Convention shall be binding only on the parties to the protocol in question. Only Parties to a protocol may take decisions on matters exclusively relating to the protocol in question. 6. The requirements for entry into force of any protocol shall be established by that instrument.".

[8]Including three of the six countries covered by this research: Germany, Lithuania and Slovakia.

beyond criminal law, as it tackles the illicit trade comprehensively. The Protocol also contains provisions on supply chains. Following the *ultima ratio* principle, criminalisation sets in after preventive and administrative measures fail to control illicit tobacco flows.

This two-step perspective is expressed in Art. 4, which lays out a set of obligations for states. One set of obligations is the adoption and implementation of effective measures to control or regulate the supply chain of goods covered by this Protocol. The implementation and control measures should "prevent, deter, detect, investigate and prosecute illicit trade in such goods". The following obligations are intended to increase the effectiveness of national authorities responsible for preventing, deterring, detecting, investigating, prosecuting and eliminating all forms of illicit trade in goods. These obligations also include cooperation with national authorities in other states and regional and international intergovernmental organizations.

Supply chain[9] control includes a range of measures which, ideally, will prevent the illicit trade of tobacco products. National and/or regional tracking and tracing systems and a global information sharing-point located in the Convention Secretariat should exist within 5 years of the Protocol implementation. Other provisions cover licensing, due diligence, record-keeping, security and preventive measures, reflecting the obligations to prevent and detect money laundering. Additional measures refer to Internet and telecommunication-based sales, duty-free sales, free zones and international transit.

4 Protocol to Eliminate Illicit Trade in Tobacco Products: Penal Aspects

In terms of criminal responsibility, Art. 14 of the Protocol seems the most important. It defines several behaviours that are considered unlawful under the national law of the states. It is worth noting though that the parties to the Protocol are at liberty to decide which of the actions described in Art. 14.1 "or any other conduct related to the illicit trade in tobacco, tobacco products and manufacturing equipment shall be criminal offences".[10] Such wording of the provision of Art. 14.2 indicates that states

[9]Which—pursuant to Art. 1 p. 12—is to be understood as 'the manufacture of tobacco products and manufacturing equipment; and import or export of tobacco products and manufacturing equipment; and may be extended, where relevant, to one or more of the following activities when so decided by a Party: (a) retailing of tobacco products; (b) growing of tobacco, except for traditional small-scale growers, farmers and producers; (c) transporting commercial quantities of tobacco products or manufacturing equipment; and (d) wholesaling, brokering, warehousing or distribution of tobacco and tobacco products or manufacturing equipment'.

[10]In other treaties dealing with penal issues one typically finds an obligation bearing on state parties to adopt such legislative and other measures as may be necessary to establish as criminal offences under its domestic law. Also, this is not what was proposed by representatives of the international law doctrine—see Boister and Burchill (2002), p. 48.

may choose not to criminalise behaviours, may criminalise some of them or criminalise all of them. The option to criminalise unwanted behaviours in within states is the main difference between the Protocol and other penal treaties. In this regard, the contents of the Protocol do not necessarily resemble other international legal instruments designed to combat a certain type of offence. Furthermore, if unwanted behaviours are to be considered only unlawful under national laws but not treated as criminal, the responsibility for these actions is watered down considerably and so is the national legislature's responsibility for implementation. Such wording was politically more acceptable for some of the states.[11] However, this wording may lead to an uneven harmonisation of the national legal systems with the Protocol's provision and eventually contribute to ineffective international investigation and prosecution of the illicit tobacco trade.

The catalogue of behaviours prohibited by Art. 14.1 of the Protocol covers very different types of actions. The first prohibited activity, as mentioned in Art. 14.1(a), is of a general character and consists of manufacturing, wholesaling, brokering, selling, transporting, distributing, storing, shipping, importing or exporting tobacco, tobacco products or manufacturing equipment contrary to the provisions of this Protocol.

Art. 14.1 mentions unlawful behaviours related to taxation[12] and custom duties,[13] as well as to forging and falsifying products and markings.[14] This Article clarifies that avoiding transparency in the supply chain process[15] constitutes tax and customs duty evasion.

The Protocol provides detailed rules on using the Internet and any new evolving technology-based sales models, as well as on licensing,[16] thus Art. 14.1 also covers behaviours contrary to the said rules.

---

[11]See Burci (2013), p. 367.

[12]Manufacturing, wholesaling, brokering, selling, transporting, distributing, storing, shipping, importing or exporting tobacco, tobacco products or manufacturing equipment without the payment of applicable duties, taxes and other levies or without bearing applicable fiscal stamps, unique identification markings, or any other required markings or labels.

[13]Any other acts of smuggling or attempted smuggling of tobacco, tobacco products or manufacturing equipment.

[14]Any other form of illicit manufacture of tobacco, tobacco products or manufacturing equipment, or tobacco packaging bearing false fiscal stamps, unique identification markings, or any other required markings or labels; wholesaling, brokering, selling, transporting, distributing, storing, shipping, importing or exporting of illicitly manufactured tobacco, illicit tobacco products, products bearing false fiscal stamps and/or other required markings or labels, or illicit manufacturing equipment.

[15]Mixing of tobacco products with non-tobacco products during progression through the supply chain, for the purpose of concealing or disguising tobacco products; intermingling of tobacco products with non-tobacco products in contravention of Article 12.2 of this Protocol.

[16]Using Internet-, telecommunication- or any other evolving technology based modes of sale of tobacco products in contravention of the Protocol; obtaining, by a person licensed in accordance with Article 6, tobacco, tobacco products or manufacturing equipment from a person who should be, but is not, licensed in accordance with Article 6 of the Protocol.

Art. 14.2 of the Protocol establishes states' obligation to recognise the laundering of proceeds from criminal offences as unlawful. There is a relationship between the illicit tobacco trade and money laundering of proceeds. Therefore, the prohibition of money laundering and criminalization of such activity, curb illicit trade.

Other behaviours that are to be recognised as unlawful by national legal systems apply to public officials in these states. Obstructing any authorized personnel,[17] misleading and misinforming them[18] or hindering controls, including by falsifying documents,[19] should rightly be condemned as facilitating the illicit tobacco trade.

Regarding the modalities of responsibility for unlawful conducts analysed above, Art. 16 of the Protocol provides requires states to ensure that "natural and legal persons held liable for the unlawful conduct including criminal offences established in accordance with Article 14 are subjected to effective, proportionate and dissuasive criminal or non-criminal sanctions, including monetary sanctions". This provision draws from similar provisions in many penal treaties, as well as EU legal instruments. It requires states to provide for effective, proportionate and dissuasive sanctions. However, the Protocol does not require states to institute criminal sanctions. Since states may choose to forego criminalisation of certain behaviours considered unlawful, they may impose non-criminal sanctions on the perpetrators.

The liability of individuals for unlawful conduct mentioned in the Protocol is self-evident. However, it seems important to note that the Protocol also requires the establishment of liability of legal persons. The liability of legal persons varies from one legal system to another. Art. 15 of the Protocol leaves it up to the state parties to determine whether this liability will be criminal, administrative or civil liability.

In addition to the provisions on unlawful conduct and sanctions regarding natural and legal persons, the Protocol contains supplementary provisions referring to penalties and criminal prosecution. The first one tackles the financial side of the illicit tobacco trade, as it obligates states to consider adopting measures "to levy an amount proportionate to lost taxes and duties from the producer, manufacturer, distributor, importer or exporter of seized tobacco, tobacco products and/or manufacturing equipment". This provision covers one of the aspects of the said

---

[17]Obstructing any public officer or an authorized officer in the performance of duties relating to the prevention, deterrence, detection, investigation or elimination of illicit trade in tobacco, tobacco products or manufacturing equipment.

[18]Making any material statement that is false, misleading or incomplete, or failing to provide any required information to any public officer or an authorized officer in the performance of duties relating to the prevention, deterrence, detection, investigation or elimination of illicit trade in tobacco, tobacco products or manufacturing equipment and when not contrary to the right against self-incrimination.

[19]Mis declaring on official forms the description, quantity or value of tobacco, tobacco products or manufacturing equipment or any other information specified in the protocol to: (a) evade the payment of applicable duties, taxes and other levies, or (b) prejudice any control measures for the prevention, deterrence, detection, investigation or elimination of illicit trade in tobacco, tobacco products or manufacturing equipment; failing to create or maintain records covered by this Protocol or maintaining false records.

activity most detrimental to the public finance. It therefore only seems natural that the countries had taken it into consideration when negotiating the Protocol.

Furthermore, international community confirmed the detrimental results of the illicit tobacco trade by agreeing to allow the use of controlled delivery and "other special investigative techniques, such as electronic or other modes of surveillance and undercover operations, by its competent authorities on its territory for the purpose of effectively combating illicit trade in tobacco, tobacco products or manufacturing equipment". Often, the detection of the illicit tobacco trade may be challenging, as the perpetrators are very creative. Therefore, the use of techniques that facilitate the detection and further prosecution may be beneficial. However, while using them, states should be mindful of human rights, including the privacy of the persons concerned.

The last provision, related to the criminal prosecution of illegal trade, refers to the disposal or destruction of illicit tobacco. According to Art. 18, all confiscated tobacco, tobacco products and manufacturing equipment should be destroyed, using environmentally friendly methods to the greatest extent possible, or disposed of according to national law.

5 Protocol to Eliminate Illicit Trade in Tobacco Products: International Cooperation and Jurisdiction

As mentioned above, the Protocol follows the example of other penal treaties and so it contains an elaborate chapter on international cooperation, with solutions like those in other international instruments. It is the longest chapter of the Protocol.

The provisions on international cooperation refer to different measures, from the least to the most advanced form of cooperation. They include general information sharing; enforcement information sharing; assistance and cooperation (training, technical assistance and cooperation in scientific, technical and technological matters, as well as investigation and prosecution of offences); law enforcement cooperation; mutual administrative assistance; mutual legal assistance and extradition.

As with any other penal convention, the Protocol refers to jurisdiction over the criminal offences. They are typical and based on the *aut dedere aut judicare* principle. The mandatory jurisdiction covers the territory of the state party and board of a vessel that is flying the flag of that state or an aircraft that is registered under the laws of that state at the time the offence is committed. Optionally, states may also establish their jurisdiction over offences committed against that state by a national of that state or a stateless person who has his or her habitual residence on its territory or an offence which is one of those established in accordance with Article 14 and is committed outside its territory with a view to the commission of an offence established in accordance with Article 14 within its territory.

6 European Union's Position on Illicit Trade of Tobacco Products

The European Union evolved from the European Economic Community (EEC), which was established as the Economic Cooperation Organisation. Originally, the EEC had shown interest in tobacco only as an element of agriculture and even subsidised tobacco growth. However, in 1985 the European Council adopted two resolutions and established the "Europe against Cancer" program comprised of informational, and later preventive, measures. Since then, the EU's interest in tobacco control has grown.

Historically, the Union's competence on health issues has been contested.[20] However, at present, as stipulated in Art. 168 of the Treaty on the functioning of the European Union, the jurisdiction over and expertise on health issues are shared between the Member States and the Union. It should however be emphasised that this competence refers to public health only and is aimed at "orienting the EU action away from action on health services".[21]

The Union's commitment to tobacco control has been most visible when it has participated in negotiations over the draft FCTC and in its subsequent accession after its adoption in 2005. In 2016 the EU has also confirm its accession to the FCTC Protocol. Yet, the legality of EU's action undertaken with regard to tobacco control has been legally challenged on various occasions,[22] amounting up to the point of annulling a first advertising tobacco directive 20 years ago.[23]

Today, the EU's position on tobacco control is mainly[24] expressed in the Directive 2014/40/EU of the European Parliament and of the Council of 3 April 2014, on the approximation of the laws, regulations and administrative provisions of the Member States concerning the manufacture, presentation and sale of tobacco and related products and repealing Directive 2001/37/EC. The Directive refers to a multitude of measures aimed at controlling tobacco, which, as stated in the Preamble to the Directive, are necessary to implement the WHO Framework Convention on Tobacco Control (FCTC) of May 2003. The provisions are binding on the Union and its Member States. The FCTC provisions on the regulation of the contents of tobacco

---

[20] Mamudu and Studlar (2009), p. 7.

[21] *Everything you always wanted to know about European Union health policies but were afraid to ask*, 2nd ed. European Observatory on Health Systems and Policies, 2019, 63–64, http://www.euro.who.int/en/about-us/partners/observatory/publications/studies/everything-you-always-wanted-to-know-about-european-union-health-policies-but-were-afraid-to-ask-2019.

[22] See more on the limited EU competence in Alemanno and Garde (2015), p. 259 ff.

[23] ECJ, 5 October 2000, *Germany v European Parliament and Council*, C-376/98, EU:C:2000:544.

[24] There are other EU legal instruments relative to tobacco control. One should mention: Council Recommendation of 2 December 2002 on the prevention of smoking and on initiatives to improve tobacco control (2003/54/EC); Directive 2003/33/EC of the European Parliament and of the Council of 26 May 2003 on the approximation of the laws, regulations and administrative provisions of the Member States relating to the advertising and sponsorship of tobacco products; Council Recommendation of 30 November 2009 on smoke-free environments.

products, the regulation of tobacco product disclosures, the packaging and labelling of tobacco products, and the advertisement and illicit trade in tobacco products are particularly relevant.

One of the main features introduced by the 2014 Directive is the EU-wide systems of traceability and security features for tobacco products to address the issue of illicit trade. The systems became operational on 20 May 2019.[25] The special European Commission Implementing Regulation (EU) 2018/574 of 15 December 2017, articulates standards for the establishment and operation of the traceability system for tobacco products.

Neither the Directive nor any other EU legal instrument refers, however, to penal issues. Although, it is conceivable that, if not combatted, over time, the illicit tobacco trade will become such a problem for the Union and EU Member States they will use the clause in Art. 83 TFUE. This clause allows the European Parliament and the Council to establish minimum rules concerning the definition of criminal offences. It also allows the European Parliament and Council to establish sanctions and regular policing, with a cross-border dimension, against serious crime.[26]

Additionally, since the illegal tobacco trade is considered criminal in national policy of the EU Member States, states can cooperate on criminal matters based on the EU general legal framework on cooperation. European institutions may also be involved in the process. Following OLAF Regulation No 883/2013,[27] OLAF may conduct on-the-spot checks and inspections when there is suspicion of activity detrimental to the financial interests of the Union. Also, Europol may enable cooperation of law enforcement institutions from different EU Member States. In addition, the European Public Prosecutor's Office, once operational, may contribute to combatting this type of criminality.

7 Other Relevant Legal Instruments

This chapter examines the existing penal legal framework that has emerged on the international level regarding the illicit tobacco trade. However, one must not forget that the illicit trade of tobacco products is just one part of a wider criminal

---

[25] See more: https://ec.europa.eu/health/tobacco/tracking_tracing_system_en.

[26] Pursuant to Art. 83 TFU, currently these areas of crime are the following: terrorism, trafficking in human beings and sexual exploitation of women and children, illicit drug trafficking, illicit arms trafficking, money laundering, corruption, counterfeiting of means of payment, computer crime and organised crime. However, based on developments in crime, the Council may adopt a decision identifying other areas of crime that meet the criteria specified in this paragraph. It shall act unanimously after obtaining the consent of the European Parliament.

[27] Regulation (Eu, Euratom) No 883/2013 of the European Parliament and of the Council of 11 September 2013 concerning investigations conducted by the European Anti-Fraud Office (OLAF) and repealing Regulation (EC) No 1073/1999 of the European Parliament and of the Council and Council Regulation (Euratom) No 1074/1999. This Regulation is in the proceed of amendments, which are expected to be adopted in 2020.

phenomenon that is addressed by the international community a variety of ways, most notably through binding legal instruments. In this context, one must emphasise that the illicit tobacco trade (which refers to excise fraud, smuggling, illegal manufacturing and counterfeiting) is just one category of crime covered by penal conventions and EU legal acts of general character. When the illicit tobacco trade constitutes a customs violation, the behaviour may also be covered by international and EU legal instruments on administrative cooperation.

Concerning the EU penal legal framework, one should refer to all the legal instruments adopted by the EU Member States regarding police and judicial cooperation in criminal matters, dating back to the III pillar of the EU. This collection covers different and important instruments, starting from the European arrest warrant and joint investigation teams,[28] up to the mutual recognition of decision and the principle of mutual trust.

Concerning international penal instruments, one should mention some notable instruments adopted by the Council of Europe, starting with the 1959 European Convention on Mutual Assistance in Criminal Matters and the 1990 Convention on Laundering, Search, Seizure and Confiscation of the Proceeds from Crime.

Administrative cooperation may seem less spectacular than fighting against criminal behaviours, but it is nonetheless very important. On 25 January 1988, the Council of Europe adopted the Convention on Mutual Administrative Assistance in Tax Matters, which entered into force on 1 April 1995. It was amended by the Protocol to the Convention of 27 May 2010, which entered into force on 1 June 2011. According to this Convention, which binds all six states covered in this research, states must provide administrative assistance to each other in tax matters. Such assistance may involve, where appropriate, measures taken by judicial bodies. Such administrative assistance consists of the exchange of information, including simultaneous tax examinations and participation in tax examinations abroad; assistance in recovery, including measures of conservancy; and service of documents. What is important is that countries must provide administrative assistance whether the person affected is a resident or national or not. According to Art. 2.1b, the excise tax is covered by the scope of the Convention.

Administrative cooperation between EU Member States customs services is regulated by the 1998 Convention based on Article K.3 of the Treaty on European Union. This Convention fosters mutual assistance and cooperation among customs administrations.[29] According to Art. 1 of the Convention, Member States of the European Union provide each other with mutual assistance and cooperate through their customs administrations to prevent and detect infringements on national customs provisions and to prosecute and punish infringements of community and national customs provisions.

The Convention on the Use of Information Technology for Customs Purposes (CIS Convention) is also notable. Also, the system based on the Council Act

[28]Council Framework Decision 2002/465/JHA on joint investigation teams.

[29]Official Journal C 024, 23/01/1998 P. 0002 – 0022.

95/C316/02 of 26 July 1995, draws up the Convention on the use of information technology for customs purposes. A second legal basis for the system is Council Regulation (EC) No 515/97 of 13 March 1997 on mutual assistance between the administrative authorities of the Member States. It also promotes cooperation between the latter and the Commission to ensure the correct application of the law on customs and agricultural matters, as amended by Regulation (EC) No 766/2008 of 9 July 2008. Currently the system operates based on the latter legal act as well as on the Council Decision 2009/917/JHA of 30 November 2009, on the use of information technology for customs purposes. It is calls for a central database and terminal accessible in EU Member States.

A general framework of administrative cooperation between the EU Member States regarding taxation is currently established by the Council Directive 2011/16/EU of 15 February 2011, on administrative cooperation in the field of taxation and repealing Directive 77/799/EEC. However, according to Art. 2.2 of the Directive, the Directive does not apply to value-added tax and customs duties or to excise duties covered by other Union legislation on administrative cooperation between Member States. This approach is due to the fact that these taxes are covered by specific instruments, namely the Council Regulation (EU) No 904/2010 of 7 October 2010, on administrative cooperation and combating fraud in the field of value added tax[30] and the Council Regulation (EU) No 389/2012 of 2 May 2012, on administrative cooperation in the field of excise duties and repealing Regulation (EC) No 2073/2004.[31] Both instruments detail the rules on cooperation and more importantly, the exchange of information among the competent authorities of the Member States to ensure the correct application of legislation on excise duties and VAT.

8 Discussion

Even though tobacco products contain nicotine, which is addictive, and the use of tobacco constitutes a health hazard, tobacco regulation is different from regulation of other addictive substances. Like alcohol, tobacco is a legal addictive, and therefore no one is ready to criminalize the possession or use of tobacco, as has been done with some narcotics. For this reason, both states and international organizations struggle with "tobacco control"' instead of tobacco prohibition.

Tobacco control has been a challenge for the international community. Its conditions are determined, on the one hand, by the interests of consumers, producers (industry)[32] and public finances, and on the other, by the necessity to protect public

[30] OJ L 268, 12.10.2010, pp. 1–18.

[31] OJ L 121, 8.5.2012, pp. 1–15.

[32] Although states are bound based on Art. 5.3 WHO FCTC to protect their public health policies with respect to tobacco control 'from commercial and other vested interests of the tobacco industry in accordance with national law'.

health. Due to the sensitive nature of the issue, international organisations have only recently decided to regulate tobacco, and still to a limited extent.

The tobacco trade relies on a complex system of processes, from manufacturing, transportation to marking and sales marketing. These processes are heavily regulated. Tobacco products are subject to multiple taxes, subject to many customs duties, and are rather pricy for the consumers. Therefore, people are willing to profit by evading taxes on tobacco products. As mentioned by this author in the introduction to this volume, fight against the illicit tobacco trade is just one aspect of a wider process of tobacco control, but an important one. The illicit tobacco trade is detrimental to states, industry and consumers for a variety of reasons: loss of public revenue, loss of private profits and threats to personal health, although consumers are the least committed to combatting the illicit trade.

The international legal framework to combat the illicit tobacco trade is comprised of one international convention (WHO FCTC) and a protocol thereto. As analysed above, the Protocol, which was specifically designed to eliminate this illicit trade, exhaustively tackles the criminal activity, and in this regard, it resembles the more traditional penal international treaties, especially transnational criminal law treaties.[33] As is usual for suppression conventions, the Protocol does not provide for direct criminalisation nor does it contain self-executive norms. However, its provisions impose legislative and practical obligations on states and therefore, require implementation through national legal systems.

As with other penal treaties, it is the level of harmonisation of national law with the conventional standard that poses a real challenge for states. The WHO FCTC has been one of the most eagerly ratified UN conventions and has numerous state signatories. The Protocol has considerably less signatories, however, most likely due to the obligation to establish a costly track and trace system. Yet, it has come into force after just a few years since adoption, although ratification itself does not guarantee compliance of the national law and practice with the convention requirements. Some authors have already expressed doubts about the practical implementation of the FCTC by national legislatures as well as the WHO's capacity to survey the states in this regard.[34] Similarly, the monitoring mechanisms set forth by the Convention and the Protocol, which encompass respectively the Conference of the Parties and the Meeting of the Parties, even though typical for international treaties,[35] seem too weak to ensure a proper implementation of both these treaties into the national law. It remains to be determined the extent to which state signatories to the Convention and the Protocol will be ready to comply with their provisions.

The situation is less controversial regarding the EU law, as the EU deals with the administrative aspects of tobacco control in a limited capacity. Also, its supranational status empowers the EU to enforce Member States' compliance with the 2014 Directive and other legal instruments. The impact of the EU legislation on

[33]On the notion of transnational criminal law, see Boister (2012).

[34]See Hoffman and Rizvi (2012), p. 727.

[35]See Boister (2012), p. 261 ff.

administrative cooperation between the Member States is praiseworthy. Moreover, the developing institutional framework for combatting crimes that are detrimental to the EU financial interests, embodied by the newly established European Public Prosecutor's Office (expected to start its operations in the nearest future), deserve attention in future research. For one may expect that this institution, as well as already existing bodies, will contribute to the improvement of investigation and prosecution of economic crimes, including illicit trade of tobacco products.

References

Alemanno A, Garde A (2015) European Union. In: Regulating Tobacco, alcohol and unhealthy foods. The legal issues. Routledge

Boister N (2012) An introduction to transnational criminal law. Oxford University Press

Boister N, Burchill R (2002) Stopping the smugglers: proposals for an additional protocol to the World Health Organization's framework convention on Tobacco control. Melb J Int Law 3 (33):44

Burci GL (2013) Protocol to Eliminate Illicit Trade in Tobacco products. Int Legal Mater 52:367

Everything you always wanted to know about European Union health policies but were afraid to ask, 2nd edn. European Observatory on Health Systems and Policies, 2019. http://www.euro.who.int/en/about-us/partners/observatory/publications/studies/everything-you-always-wanted-to-know-about-european-union-health-policies-but-were-afraid-to-ask-2019

Hoffman SJ, Rizvi Z (2012) WHO's undermining tobacco control. The Lancet 380:727

Mamudu HM, Studlar DT (2009) Multilevel Governance and Shared Sovereignty: European Union, Member States, and the FCTC. Governance 22(1):73–97. https://doi.org/10.1111/j.1468-0491.2008.01422.x, p 7

Roemer R, Taylor A, Lariviere J (2005) Origins of the WHO Framework Convention on Tobacco control. Am J Public Health 95(6)

Celina Nowak Ph.D., is Associate Professor and Head of the Institute of Law Studies of the Polish Academy of Sciences. She holds a Ph.D. and habilitation in law, as well as a postgraduate diploma of Université de Paris I – Panthéon–Sorbonne in criminal law and criminal policy in Europe. Her research refers to criminal law, with focus on international, EU and comparative criminal law. In addition, she has extensive experience as an academic teacher at the Kozminski University and the Warsaw University. Prof. Nowak has taken part in a number of comparative law projects, in the national and EU context, either as a project leader, or as a national expert. She has authored 2 monographs, edited and co-edited 10 books. She has written more than three dozen articles and chapters in Polish, English and French, published in Poland and internationally.

Part II
Criminal Policy with Regard to Illicit Tobacco Trade: National Experiences and Challenges

Between Taxes, Criminal Law and Health Care: The Fight Against Illicit Tobacco Trade in Germany

Marc Engelhart

Contents

M. Engelhart (✉)
Max Planck Institute for the Study of Crime, Security and Law, Freiburg, Germany

C. Nowak (ed.), *Combatting Illicit Trade on the EU Border*,
https://doi.org/10.1007/978-3-030-51019-0_3

Abstract The German chapter deals with illicit trade of tobacco goods in Germany, its regulation by law, the authorities responsible for preventive and repressive aspects of fighting illicit trade and the procedures that apply as well as the relevance of illicit trade in practice. Repressive regulations in the field can mainly be found in tax criminal law. The specific area of tobacco tax criminal law (Tabaksteuerstrafrecht) is a special matter of excise tax criminal law (Verbrauchssteuerstrafrecht). Tax criminal law follows the general criminal law rules and therefore the criminal courts are responsible, which means that their point of view can differ from that of the fiscal courts. The main offense in tax criminal law is § 370 AO (tax evasion), which is accompanied by special regulations in the Tabaksteuergesetz (Tobacco tax law—TabStG). In practice, besides the criminal justice authorities the custom authorities play a major role in investigating tobacco crimes, mainly the Customs Criminal Investigation Office (Zollkriminalamt—ZKA) and its local offices.

1 Substantive Law Issues

1.1 Legal Architecture Related to the Illicit Trade of Tobacco Products

1.1.1 Relevant Offences and Their Features

Illicit trade of tobacco goods is covered in Germany mainly by tax criminal law. The specific area of tobacco tax criminal law (Tabaksteuerstrafrecht) is a special matter of excise tax criminal law (Verbrauchssteuerstrafrecht) being a special matter of tax criminal law. This means it is a highly specialized field of law only few experts are familiar with but not the common criminal lawyer. This creates problems, e.g., when prosecutors, judges and the defense have to deal with a case in the ordinary criminal proceedings. Tax criminal law is criminal law in regard to a specific protected good, public taxes and duties. Because of the specifics of taxes and duties the offences are not part of the Criminal Code (Strafgesetzbuch—StGB), but are included in the German Fiscal Code (Abgabenordnung—AO). But, tax criminal law follows the criminal law rules and therefore the criminal courts take their own stand on interpretation etc., which means that their point of view can differ from that of the fiscal courts (dealing with the tax issues).[1]

The main offense in tax criminal law is § 370 AO (tax evasion). The offense applies to all taxes and duties as it only speaks of taxes etc. This means, the offense presupposes the details of taxation that are regulated by tax law. In regard to tobacco goods the main legislation is the Tabaksteuergesetz (Tobacco tax law—TabStG).

[1]See for such a dispute between criminal and fiscal courts Weidemann (2014), p. 433.

German law makes a difference between the "Verbringung" as the transfer of goods from a EU Member State to Germany and the "Einfuhr" as the import from a third country to Germany. Hence, the illegal *transfer* of tobacco goods from one EU Member State to Germany (see § 23 TabStG) is to be distinguished from the direct *import* of tobacco products from a third country into German territory (see § 21 TabStG). Following the distinction made by Art. 15 of the WHO FCTC the reports deals with smuggling, illicit manufacturing and counterfeiting separately. In addition to the in the following mentioned offenses, e.g. § 34 Gesetz über Tabakerzeugnisse und verwandte Erzeugnisse (TabakerzG) as a criminal offense and § 35 TabakErzG as an administrative offense (Ordnungswidrigkeit) cover illegal methods of production and distribution.[2]

1.1.1.1 Smuggling

*1.1.1.1.1 Furnishing Authorities with Incorrect or Incomplete Particulars, § 370 (1) No. 1 German Fiscal Code (*Abgabenordnung: *AO)*

For § 370 (1) No. 1 AO it is necessary that taxes are reduced by *incorrect statements* to the tax authority (or other authorities) upon transfer or import. Anyone who unjustly achieves refunds or the remission of tax claims in terms of the remission and reimbursement procedure regulated in §§ 48 et seq. of the Regulation on the implementation of the Tobacco tax law (Verordnung zur Durchführung des Tabaksteuergesetzes—TabStV), reduces taxes and therefore fulfils § 370 (1) No. 1 AO.[3] The offender who has entrusted the customs formalities to bona fide haulers who have delivered incomplete customs declarations so that no or incorrect import duties have been fixed must be penalized as an indirect offender as of § 25 (I) Alt. 2 StGB.[4]

The most important case of violation of § 370 (1) No. 1 AO occurs, when illicit tobacco products are concealed as regular cargo or camouflaged by other goods without having been declared orderly as stipulated by tax or customs law. If the *transferor* makes no statements at all, he cannot state anything incorrectly. Thus, he avoids the perpetration of § 370 (1) No. 1 AO.[5] However, if he fails to comply with the tax code or makes willingly misleading declarations, he is punishable according to § 370 (1) No. 1 AO.

However, this does not apply to the *import* of tobacco goods: In the *Papismedov* judgment, the European Court of Justice ruled that the duty to present goods to customs (*Gestellungspflichten*) as laid down in Art. 139 (1) Regulation (EU) No

[2]For a typical case of organized tobacco trading and applicable offenses see Calderoni et al. (2013), p. 51.

[3]Weidemann and Weidemann (2005), p. 207.

[4]Bundesgerichtshof (BGH), *Strafbarkeit des Zigarettenschmuggels* (2007) 5 StR 461/06 wistra 2007, 262.

[5]Instead, § 370 (1) No. 2 AO applies.

952/2013 (Union Customs Code) does not only require the informal notification, that the goods have arrived, but also the declaration of all relevant information which enables the tariff classification and calculation of import duties to be made.[6] As a result, criminal liability has shifted from the *omission* of § 370 (1) No. 2 AO to the offence of *commission* of § 370 (1) No. 1 AO, when illicit tobacco products are not presented to customs.[7]

1.1.1.1.2 Omission of the Tax Declaration, § 370 (1) No. 2 AO

Anyone who refrains from declaring taxes in front of the tax authority (other authorities are not mentioned), contrary to an obligation is liable under § 370 (1) No. 2 AO. The offence of omission is a crime that can only be committed by the tax debtor.[8] It has to be clarified as to which of those involved in the offence were obliged to submit a corresponding tax declaration.[9]

Transfer to Germany from Another EU Member State: Making the Delivery or Holding the Tobacco Goods If tobacco goods without the use of German tax marks (see § 17 (1) TabStG) are transferred from the tax-free circulation of another member state to the German tax territory for commercial purposes or if they are sent there, the tax debtor has to submit a tax return on the tobacco goods without delay (§ 23 para (1) Sentence 1 and (3) TabStG).

According to § 23 (1) Sentence 2 of the Tobacco tax law the person liable for the tax (*Erklärungspflichtiger*) is the person who makes the delivery or holds the tobacco goods and the recipient as soon as he has acquired possession of the tobacco goods. With regard to the characteristic "who makes the delivery", a certain domination over the goods is required when they are brought to Germany. This is an equivalent to the term "*Verbringer*" in the customs jurisdiction of the EUCJ.[10] The decisive criterion in this respect is the domination of the vehicle upon import. Not only the driver has control over the transport vehicle, but possibly (by virtue of their authority to issue instructions) the organizers of the transport as well. At least, if they can rule over the driver in his decision-making before and during the journey, e.g. in terms of route, place and time.[11] Especially when crossing the green border, criminal

[6]Europäischer Gerichtshof (EuGH), *Papismedov* (2005) C-195/03 Slg 2005, I-1667 31.

[7]Bender (2006), p. 44; Bundesgerichtshof (BGH) *Steuerhinterziehung durch Unterlassen* (2007) 5 StR 372/06 NJW 2007, 1294.

[8]It is insofar limited to a specific group of persons ("eingeschränktes Jedermannsdelikt"), see Weidemann (2018), p. 13.

[9]Bundesgerichtshof (BGH), *Steuerhinterziehung durch Unterlassen* (2013) 1 StR 586/12 BGHSt 58, 218.

[10]Bauer (2018), p. 85.

[11]BGH NJW 2007, 1294 (n 7).

liability[12] depends essentially on the type and manner of import as well as on the type and degree of control over the specific import procedure.[13]

On the one hand, the drivers of the transport vehicles are usually regarded as acting in bad faith because they have imported goods from the third country territory into the customs territory of the European Community bypassing the customs offices.[14] On the other hand, the question of criminal liability of the indirect perpetrators is not so clear if the goods subject to import duties were imported into the customs territory of the EU by drivers who had no knowledge of the smuggled goods. According to the traditional dogma of omission offences, however, criminal liability for tax evasion as a perpetrator requires that the persons behind the offence themselves had a duty to act. According to the prevailing opinion, the offender of a tax evasion by omission (§ 370 (1) No. 2 AO) can only be the person who has a special duty to inform the tax authorities.[15] Insofar, the people behind the transport might only be liable to prosecution by omission as instigators or assistants of tax evasion.[16]

An important extension is that not only the driver, because he drives the vehicle, and his companions in the vehicle have control over the transport vehicle, but by virtue of their authority to issue instructions also those organizers of the transport who have a controlling influence on the driver by taking the decision to carry out the transport and determining the details of the journey (e.g. route, place and time of importation). This has been now clarified in the UCC (see Art. 79 and 139 UCC),[17] following the jurisdiction of the ECJ.[18]

Import to Germany from a Non-EU Country As a consequence of the *Papismedov* judgment, the import of tobacco products is not punishable under § 370 (1) No. 2 AO.

Receiving Tobacco Goods § 370 (1) No. 2 AO applies to the *receiver* of tobacco goods imported as a tax debtor in terms of § 23 (1) Sentence 2 TabStG.[19] Yet, The mere participation in the reloading of cigarettes is in any case not sufficient to justify

---

[12]The import duties resulting from irregular introduction pursuant to Art. 79 Union Customs Code were not fixed and thus reduced due to violation of the obligation to present the imported cigarettes (Art. 139 Union Customs Code) resulting in a violation of § 370 (1) No. 2 AO.

[13]BGH NJW 2007, 1294 (n 7).

[14]BGH NJW 2007, 1294 (n 7).

[15]BGHSt 58, 218 (n 9).

[16]Jäger (2015), § 370 AO para. 456.

[17]Art. 38, 40 Council Regulation (EEC) No 2913/92 of 12 October 1992 establishing the Community Customs Code, Official Journal L 302, 19/10/1992, p. 1 were not clear on that point.

[18]See Europäischer Gerichtshof (EuGH) *Viluckas & Jonusas* (2004) C-238/02 und C-246/02, C-238/02, C-246/02 Slg 2004, I-2141, 4.3.2004, wistra 2004, 376; see also EuGH-Judgement of 23 September 2004 - C-414/02 "Spedition Ulustrans".

[19]Bundesfinanzhof (BFH) *Tabaksteuerschuldnerschaft des Zwischenhändlers* (2014) VII R 44/11 BFHE 248, 271.

an obligation to declare taxes as the "recipient" of the tobacco products,[20] nor can a person who has acquired possession of the tobacco products after the transfer or dispatch process.[21]

1.1.1.1.3 Omission of the Use of Tax Stamps, § 370 (1) No. 3 AO

Those who do not use tax characters in accordance with their obligations are penalized according to § 370 (1) No. 3 AO. The non-use of tax stamps is only punishable if tax stamps are mandatory.[22] According to § 17 (2) TabStG, only manufacturers, importers and equals are required to obtain tax stamps. Thus, § 370 (1) No. 3 AO does not apply to the transferor.[23] Tobacco tax stamps are the only remaining examples of application for this statutory offence.[24] So, in the event that German tax stamps are not used when untaxed tobacco goods are brought from another EU Member State to Germany for commercial purposes, the importer as the tax debtor of the tobacco tax (cf. § 23 (1) Sentence 2 TabStG) is a suitable perpetrator of a tax evasion pursuant to § 370 I No. 3 AO. He must ensure that German tax marks are used for the tobacco products when they enter the tax territory of the Federal Republic of Germany.

§ 370 (1) No. 3 AO is deemed to have been committed if the tax debtor does not immediately submit a tax return for tobacco products imported without a German tax mark. In such cases, the relationship of the acts of evasion pursuant to § 370 I No. 2 AO and § 370 I No. 3 AO is disputed.[25] But, with regard to the criminal liability associated with the violation of different duties to act, both offences can be committed side by side and do not exclude each other in fact. Hence, the criminal provision of § 370 I No. 3 AO is not merely a catch-all offence which, as a subsidiary offence, takes precedence over the offences of § 370 I No. 1 and 2 AO.[26]

1.1.1.1.4 Illegal Import, Export, or Transit of Goods, § 372 (1) AO

Criminal liability for illegal import, export, or transit of goods can results from § 372 AO (so-called "Bannbruch"), if no other specific law criminalizes the behavior.

[20]Bundesgerichtshof (BGH) *Hinterziehung von Tabaksteuer durch Unterlassen* (2015) 1 StR 521/14 wistra 2016, 74.

[21]Bundesgerichtshof (BGH) *Erklärungspflicht durch Besitzerwerb* (2010) 1 StR 635/09 NStZ 2010, 644.

[22]Weidemann (2018), p. 18.

[23]Weidemann (2018), p. 47, although the issue is disputed, see also Leitner et al. (2017), § 370 AO para. 124.

[24]Weidemann (2017), p. 136. § 370 (1) No. 3 AO was introduced at a time when the TabStG did not contain any declaration obligations and therefore the tobacco tax reduction was not covered by the declaration facts of § 370 (1) No. 1, 2 AO. Insofar the legitimacy of § 370 (1) No. 3 AO has become doubtful, see Weidemann (2017), p. 140.

[25]Weidemann (2017), p. 136.

[26]See for details Jäger (2015), § 370 AO para. 391-395.

The provision is—however—pre-eminently considered irrelevant,[27] because nowadays, special laws, such as the TabStG, regulate the actions previously covered conclusively, see § 372 (2) AO.[28]

1.1.1.1.5 Receiving, Holding or Selling Goods Obtained by Tax Evasion, § 374 (1) AO

According to § 374 (1) AO it is punishable, among other things, buying, procuring (or helping to procure) himself (or a third party) goods which excise duties or import duties have been evaded, or who sells or helps to sell them with the intention of enrichment. This offense covers the handling of goods that result from tax or custom offenses and follows the same structure as § 259 StGB (Handling stolen goods) in regard to goods that stem from theft offenses.

Transfer to Germany from Another EU Member State If goods are transferred into Germany via another EU member state and not imported, no import duties are payable and consequently no import duties can be evaded. Instead, the transfer tax will be reduced, and—by import into the third country—the import tax on tobacco, which is also a punishable offence under § 374 (4) AO.

Already with the procurement or purchase of cigarettes in other European countries, which were evaded with their import into the customs territory of the EU import duties, the elements of crime of tax fraud are fulfilled.[29] In order to complete the offence, the elements of "selling" and "sales assistance" presuppose the success of the sale following the case law on § 259 StGB (Handling of stolen goods), as it is considered an *Erfolgsdelikt*.[30]

The entry into purchase negotiations can be considered as *unmittelbares Ansetzen*[31] according to § 22 StGB to tax fraud in the form of "procurement", but only if the transfer can and should follow immediately after agreement on the price.[32]

If it is certain that the import procedure was already completed in the other EU Member State according to the criteria described above. The persons only involved in the onward transport to Germany, in addition to evasion of the German tobacco tax, also carry out the tax fraud pursuant to § 374 AO (with regard to import duties). The evasion of import duties in violation of the duty to present goods to customs (*Gestellungspflichten*) as laid down in Art. 139 (1) Regulation (EU) No 952/2013

---

[27]Küchenhoff (2018), p. 92 f. regards the offense still necessary in cases of the withdrawal of non-EU goods from customs supervision.

[28]See Wegner (2015a), § 372 AO para. 1–3.

[29]Bundesgerichtshof (BGH), *Steuerstrafrecht* (2008) 1 StR 443/08 wistra 2008, 470.

[30]Weidemann (2018), pp. 74–76.

[31]The courts accepts an unmittelbares Ansetzen according to § 22 StGB if the (direct) delivery to a third party recipient is agreed, but the planned subsequent handover—even if to be carried out over a long distance—fails because the goods are stolen or confiscated on their way to the recipient.

[32]Bundesgerichtshof (BGH), *Steuerhehlerei* (2007) 5 StR 371/07 NStZ 2008, 409.

(Union Customs Code) or the evasion of tobacco tax in violation of the obligation to submit a tax return is only completed when the tobacco goods have been brought to safety and have "come to rest".[33] This is the case when the tobacco goods have crossed the border and the transferor completed his business.[34]

Import into Germany from a Non-EU-State Since § 374 (4) AO refers to the entire section (6) of § 370 AO, the evasion of domestic *excise duties of other member states* is also a suitable predicate offence for § 374 AO. If the goods were not imported but, for example, manufactured in Poland with the consequence that domestic tobacco tax (Polish excise duty) is incurred, this would be a suitable predicate offence for tax evasion, whereas anyone importing untaxed cigarettes into Poland from the Ukraine is liable to prosecution for evasion of customs duties, import turnover tax and Polish import tobacco tax.[35]

1.1.1.2 Illicit Manufacturing

1.1.1.2.1 Omission of the Tax Declaration, § 370 (1) No. 2 AO

§ 17 (3) TabStG imposes a tax declaration obligation on the unlawful manufacturer according to § 15 (2) No. 2 and (6), so that in the absence of a declaration only § 370 (1) No. 2 AO (and not No. 1) must be taken into consideration.

The manufacturer fulfils § 370 (1) No. 2 AO by evading the taxes, provided that the conduct towards the authorities of another member states violated obligations within the meaning of § 370 (1) AO and leads to the presumed tax evasion. The courts have to investigate this, taking into account that obtaining an expert opinion on foreign law is permitted. The courts of fact (*Tatsachengerichte*) have to differentiate between import and transfer from other Member States: The shortened tax from the predicate offence must be determined correctly because of its importance for the sentence.

If the warehouse keeper fails to oblige to bookkeeping and recording orders issued by the Main Customs Office (*Hauptzollamt*) in accordance with § 10 (2) Sentence 2 TabStV, he fulfils the omission of § 370 I No. 2 AO. The quasi-causal success in the form of the shortening of the period of assessment exists if the main customs office, if the books had been kept correctly, would have fixed the tobacco tax arising from withdrawal or consumption.[36]

---

[33]Bundesgerichtshof (BGH) *Erklärungspflicht durch Besitzerwerb* (2010) 1 StR 635/09, NStZ 2010, 644 (n 21).

[34]As a rule of thumb, tax evasion will therefore only be completed once the tobacco goods have reached their destination. If, on the way there, the tobacco products are merely reloaded in an interim storage facility, they have not "come to rest". See Bauer (2018), p. 85.

[35]Weidemann (2018), p. 75.

[36]Weidemann and Weidemann (2005), p. 207.

1.1.1.2.2 Omission of the Use of Tax Stamps, § 370 (1) No. 3 AO

Those who do not use tax characters in accordance with their obligations are penalized according to § 370 (1) No. 3 AO.[37] Following § 17 (2) TabStG, the offence applies to manufacturers, who do not use the previously acquired tax marks in terms of affixing them to the tobacco products they have manufactured, once they are removed from the tax warehouse.[38]

1.1.1.2.3 Illicit Manufacturing and Distribution of Tobacco Products, § 34 (1) TabakErzG

In addition, § 34 (1) TabakErzG criminalizes various ways of producing and distributing tobacco products in violation of the conditions set out in the TabakErzG.

1.1.1.3 Counterfeiting

1.1.1.3.1 Forgery of Stamps, §§ 369 (1) No. 3 AO; 148 StGB

If the illicit manufacturer counterfeits *tax stamps*, he commits forgery of stamps in the sense of §§ 369 (1) No. 3 AO, 148 StGB. The rare offence has seen a new popularity due to German tax stamps which have been counterfeited in Eastern Europe and occasionally found on smuggled cigarette packets. The counterfeits are easily detectable[39] in forensic laboratories.[40] The mere preparation of forgery can already be punishable, see § 149 (1) StGB, as well as the attempt to falsify the tax stamp according to § 148 (3) StGB.

1.1.1.3.2 Punishable Infringement of a Community Trade Mark, § 143a Trade Mark Act

§ 143a Trade Mark Act (Gesetz über den Schutz von Marken und sonstigen Kennzeichen—MarkenG) punishes the intentional infringement of a Union trade mark and supplements the penal provision applicable to infringement of national trade marks (§ 143 MarkenG) in this respect.[41]

§ 143a No. 1-3 MarkenG lists possible acts of infringement. § 143a (1) No. 1 MarkenG penalizes the identical use of the Union trade mark for identical goods and services (criminal identity protection). § 143a (1) No. 2 MarkenG makes the use

---

[37]Weidemann (2018), p. 14.

[38]Schmitz and Wulf (2015), § 370 AO para. 352.

[39]The German legislator has just reformed § 7 of the Tabakerzeugnisgesetz in order to require unforgeable stamps to be applied to tobacco products, see Erstes Gesetz zur Änderung des Tabakerzeugnisgesetzes of 29. April 2019, BGBl. I p. 514. See also BT-Drs. 19/4461.

[40]Harder (2014), Chapter 22 para. 106.

[41]Kutschke (2018), § 143a MarkenG para. 1 ff.

of signs identical with or similar to the Union trade mark for identical or similar goods punishable if this creates a likelihood of confusion on the part of the public (criminal protection against confusion); however, uses of a trade mark which is identical with or similar to an established mark in the Union for identical or similar goods or services are not sanctioned by § 143a(1) No. 1-3 MarkenG, but covered by civil law.[42] § 143a (1) MarkenG also presupposes that the offender has used the Union trade mark despite a prohibition. The absolute prohibition of the use of the Union trademark, is a consequence of its publication.[43] Criminal liability is limited to the use in commercial transactions with the pursuit of a business purpose.

The reference in § 143a (2) MarkenG to § 143 (2) MarkenG ensures that the scope of criminal protection of the Union trade mark corresponds in all other respects to that of the national trade mark. Thus, the reference to § 143 (2) MarkenG increases the penalty for a commercial or gang offence. Moreover, the punishability of the attempt is given by the reference to § 143 (3) MarkenG. As can be seen from the reference to § 143 (4), the infringement of a Union trade mark is in principle only prosecuted upon a request to prosecute, unless the prosecution authority considers that there is a special public interest. In addition, due to the reference § 143 (5) MarkenG goods in question can be confiscated. Also, the publication of the conviction can be ordered in the case of a conviction, see § 143 (6) MarkenG.

1.1.1.4 Administrative Offenses

Besides the aforementioned criminal offenses a large number of administrative offenses (Ordnungswidrigkeiten) exist in regard to the evasion of taxes and other fiscal duties. These offenses are mainly regulated either in §§ 377-384a AO or in the TabStG and the TabStV. The offenses follow the general rules set out in the Ordnungswidrigkeitengesetz (OWiG) that are comparable to the criminal law standards. The main administrative tax offense is § 378 AO, the reckless understatement of tax. The offense requires as actus reus the same elements of crime as § 370 AO but as mens rea element negligence in the form of recklessness is sufficient. Insofar intent makes the behavior a crime under § 370 AO, recklessness an administrative offense under § 378 AO.

§ 379 AO covers general minor tax fraud, especially using or producing incorrect documents, making incorrect statements or not timely providing notifications or reports. § 380 covers failing to comply at all, in full or in time with an obligation to withhold or remit to revenue authorities tax amounts which are due. § 381 AO sanctions the endangerment of excise taxes in combination with other regulations that require a specific behavior. Such regulations are § 36 TabStG and § 60 TabStV in the field of tobacco trading. They cover a wide range of formal requirements, e.g. in regard to documentation, presentation and notification.

---

[42]See Art. 9 (2) lit. c of Regulation (EU) No. 1001/2017.

[43]Fezer (2009), § 143a MarkenG para. 6.

In addition, specific provisions sanction further behavior. Among these is § 37 TabStG that criminalizes the purchase of cigarettes without a valid tax stamp insofar as not more than 1000 cigarettes are concerned. This regulation privileges the purchase of small amounts, it also declares §§ 369-374 AO inapplicable. Moreover, anyone who is unable to rebut the assumption that illegal goods or equipment in terms of § 12e (1) Sentence 1 Zollverwaltungsgesetz (ZollVG) are carried in cross-border traffic with the intention of committing a tax offence under § 369 AO, can be fined according to § 31a (1) No. 5 ZollVG.

1.1.2 Fiscal Responsibility for Illicit Trade

1.1.2.1 Smuggling

1.1.2.1.1 Transfer

For cigarettes, which have been imported or manufactured illegally in another member state of the EU and subsequently introduced into German tax territory, the following taxes and duties are imposed:

- the German tobacco tax as excise duty for transfer (§ 23 TabStG),
- duties already levied by the other EU member state.

1.1.2.1.2 Import

When importing goods into Germany from non-EU-countries the following taxes arise:

- the German tobacco tax as excise duty for import (§ 21 TabStG),
- customs duties in accordance with the regulations of the European Union, and
- the national import turnover tax.[44]

1.1.2.1.3 Description of the Taxes

Tobacco Tax: General The German tobacco tax is collected, if either § 21 TabStG (Import) or § 23 TabStG (Transfer) is fulfilled. The calculation of the German tobacco tax is determined in accordance with § 2 TabStG irrespective of whether the tobacco tax is levied directly in Germany similar to an import tax or when smuggled in or only when brought into the German tax territory from another member state of the EU. In order to calculate the tobacco tax, it is necessary to calculate the so-called retail selling price, i.e. the price determined by the manufacturer or importer as the retail price for cigarettes per unit (§ 3 (1) TabStG). If there is no regular legal retail selling price based on taxed cigarettes in Germany, it has to be

---

[44] Jäger (2009), p. 452.

estimated on the basis of the average retail selling price of branded cigarettes in the lower price segment.[45] The (possible) black market price is not to be used, as this would unfairly favor the smugglers.[46]

Tobacco Tax: § 23 TabStG (Transfer) If tobacco products, to which no German tax stamps are attached,[47] are brought into the German tax territory or dispatched for commercial purposes from the tax-free free circulation of another EU member state, the tobacco tax arises when the tobacco products are held in Germany for the first time for commercial purposes (§ 23 (1) Sentence 1 TabStG). Pursuant to § 23 (1) Sentence 2 TabStG, the tax debtor is a person who conducts the delivery or holds the tobacco goods in possession as well as the recipient as soon as he has acquired possession of the tobacco goods. The tax debtor has to submit a tax return immediately in accordance with § 23 (1) Sentence 3 TabStG in conjunction with § 17 (1) TabStG.[48] The requirement for immediate action demands the visit of the nearest main customs office as the competent tax authority (§ 6 (2) No. 5 AO) and that a tax return be submitted there.[49] It is not necessary for the transferor to be aware of the existence of excise goods.[50]

The transferor has no choice as to whether he uses tax stamps or whether he declares the tobacco tax to the customs authorities immediately after the transfer. If he does not want to be criminally liable under § 370 (1) No. 3 AO, he must use tax stamps *before* bringing the tobacco goods to Germany. For the registration in the case of § 23 (1) Sentence 3 TabStG does not serve to clear the tobacco goods for free circulation; it is intended solely to guarantee the levying of the tobacco tax incurred pursuant to § 23 (1) Sentence 2 TabStG as well as, if tobacco goods are not properly released for free circulation, the securing (§ 215 AO) and the confiscation of the tobacco goods (§ 375 II AO).[51]

If the goods cross the German border, the offence of tax evasion with regard to the German tobacco tax (excise duty) pursuant to § 370 (1) No. 2 AO in conjunction with § 23 (1) Sentence 3 TabStG will also be realized if the goods are brought tax-free into the Federal Republic of Germany from another EU member state without the corresponding tax mark.

With regard to the characteristic "who conducts the delivery", a certain domination over the goods is required when they are brought to Germany. The decisive sign

[45]Bauer (2018), p. 88.

[46]Bundesgerichtshof (BGH) *Steuerhinterziehung* (2004) 5 StR 554/03, wistra 2004, 348.

[47]§ 23 TabStG does not cover tobacco products bearing German tax stamps, for example because a manufacturer authorized to obtain tax stamps in accordance with § 17 (2) TabStG is a consignor and has used the tax stamps.

[48]Bundesgerichtshof (BGH) *Strafverfahren wegen Steuerhinterziehung* (2014) 1 StR 240/14, wistra 2014, 486.

[49]Jäger (2015), § 370 AO para. 386.

[50]Bundesfinanzhof (BFH) *Tabaksteuerschuldnerschaft für versteckte Waren* (2007) VII R 49/06, BFHE 218, 469.

[51]Jäger (2015), § 370 AO para. 390.

in this respect is the domination of the vehicle upon import. As mentioned, not only the driver has control over the transport vehicle, but also the organizers of the transport by their authority to issue instructions who have control over the driver by making the decision to carry out the transport and determine the details of the journey (e.g. route, place and time of import). Yet, again, the mere participation in the reloading of cigarettes is not sufficient to justify an obligation to declare taxes as the "recipient" of the tobacco products.

For *private purposes*, the transfer by private individuals is tax-free according to § 22 (1) TabStG, provided it is for their own use (i.e. not for other persons, not even as a gift) and the goods are transferred to the tax territory by the recipient himself (not, for example, by other persons or by mail). The quantities are determined according to § 39 TabStV (currently 800 pieces for cigarettes). Excessive quantities are assumed to have been transferred on a commercial basis. For tax purposes, this is to be understood as a legal fiction (unlike the provision in § 22 (4) TabStG, which speaks of a rebuttable presumption).

Also, a "private individual" can easily become a *commercial transferor* simply by bringing tobacco goods with him for third parties. In such cases, there will often be an error about "the tax claim", as the common opinion is that there is free movement of goods within the EU.[52] Since, furthermore, according to § 1 (2) ZollVG, customs must also monitor the movement of excise goods across the internal border, § 32 (1) ZollVG (Non-Prosecution of Trifles under 250 €) must be applied mutatis mutandis in this context, insofar as the transfer is not duty-free. The distinction from commercial use is made by taking into account the "criteria" mentioned in § 22 (2) No. 1-4 TabStG. For certain quantities, a (rebuttable) presumption of commercial use exists for tax purposes. In criminal proceedings, however, commercial use must be proven to the satisfaction of the court for the conviction.[53] Any person who holds the tobacco products for commercial purposes, even if he was not the first owner in the Member State of destination, is to be regarded as the owner.[54]

Tobacco Tax: § 21 TabStG (Import) The tax debtor is the person required under customs legislation to declare the tobacco products or on whose behalf the tobacco products are declared or any other person involved in an illegal import (§ 21 (2) Sentence 1 TabStG). This concerns the person who has control over the transfer, either as the transferor or the recipient of the goods.[55] If tobacco products are imported into the territory of the EU and are transported through several member states, the state's right of collection ends as soon as the goods leave its territory.[56] This does *not* alter the punishment for tax evasion by omission according to § 370 (1) No. 2 AO, if a tax

---

[52]Weidemann (2018), p. 41.

[53]Weidemann (2018), p. 41.

[54]BFHE 248, 271 (n 19); Europäischer Gerichtshof (EuGH) *Gross* (2014) C-165/13, wistra 2014, 433.

[55]BGH, NJW 2007, 1294 (n 7); EuGH, wistra 2004, 376 (n 18).

[56]BGH, wistra 2016, 74 (n 20).

return is not submitted immediately after crossing the German border, § 23 (1) Sentence 3 TabStG.[57]

Taxes by Other Member States There are particular difficulties when it comes to penalizing the evasion of national turnover and tobacco tax from another member state. The foreign legal situation must be clarified ex officio, making a foreign legal advisory opinion necessary on a regular basis. In cases where the determination of the foreign duties is too complicated, prosecution in respect to the reduced duties may be limited pursuant to §§ 154, 154a Code of Criminal Procedure (*Strafprozessordnung*—StPO) to customs evaded upon importation into another Member State and/or German tobacco tax evaded upon introduction into the German excise territory.[58] This is intended to save the courts from having to make difficult findings about foreign tobacco tax law.[59] Insofar, goods should not be subject to the excise duties of several Member States. This is also the principle underlying the possibility of refunding excise duty levied in other Member States.[60] Furthermore, any (even "neutral") help carried out in Germany to acts in other EU countries is punishable by law.[61]

Import Tax In the case of cigarette smuggling, the incurrence of a customs debt is governed by Article 79 (1) of Regulation (EU) No 952/2013 (Union Customs Code—UCC) by unlawful introduction, i.e. the disregard of the customs regulations applicable to the registration of goods. This implies

- breaches of transport obligations under Art. 135 (1), (2) Union Customs Code;
- failure to present goods contrary to Art. 139 Union Customs Code;
- no or insufficient applications for temporary storage of goods contrary to Art. 145 Union Customs Code.[62]

For the calculation of the customs debt, the customs value is the relevant starting point. The customs value for imported goods is generally determined in accordance with Art. 70 UCC according to the so-called transaction value, i.e. according to the price actually paid or payable for the imported goods in the case of a sale for export to the customs territory of the Community, or after adjustment in accordance with Art. 71, 72 UCC. The transaction value is therefore generally determined by the gross settlement price to be paid or already paid to the seller. It does not matter whether the agreed sum is to be paid directly to the seller or indirectly by payment to a third party. If the customs value cannot be determined according to Art. 70 UCC or according to the alternative methods according to Art. 74 (1, 2) UCC, it must be

57 Weidemann (2018), p. 48.

58 BGH NStZ 2010, 644 (n 21).

59 Weidemann (2018), p. 48.

60 BGH NStZ 2010, 644 (n 21).

61 BGH (Bundesgerichtshof) *Neutrale Beihilfe zur Steuerhinterziehung in Polen* (2017) 1 StR 56/17, NStZ 2018, 328.

62 Europäischer Gerichtshof (EuGH), Papismedov (2005) C-195/03 Slg 2005, I-1667 31.

determined on the basis of Art. 74 (3) UCC (so-called final method). In his reasoning the judge must state whether and, if so, on what basis he has made an estimate of the tax base. If no valuation bases are available for the imported cigarettes, the estimate to be made can in turn be based on the usual import price for branded cigarettes in the lower price segment. The resulting customs value must finally be multiplied by the customs rate in order to determine the specific customs debt.[63]

In the event of a breach of duty relating to the introduction, the person liable to pay customs duty under Article 79(3)(a) UCC is the person who had the obligation to bring the goods properly into the customs territory:

- *Transferor*, i.e. the actual carrier: The customs obligation of the transferor may be transferred to another person after introduction into the customs territory of the Union. If it turns out that, contrary to Art. 135 UCC, the goods were transported after the introduction, the person liable for customs duty is the person who was responsible for the transport at the relevant time. If it is not clear who was responsible at the time of the breach of duty, it is to be assumed that this is the transferor.[64]
- *Representative*: Pursuant to Article 79(3)(b) UCC, the representative also becomes a customs debtor.
- *Other persons* involved in the unlawful removal (e.g. co-drivers, participants or helpers): Any person who initiates or supports the breach of duty through his or her conduct is generally involved in the breach of duty. This can be done, for example, by giving the actor appropriate instructions or assistance for his actions. Personal presence is not required.[65] This also applies to anyone who provides storehouses where the goods can be unloaded from the means of transport used for the irregular introduction, provided that this was already clear beforehand (prior promise of a later use).[66]
- *Owner* or acquirer of the goods: Finally, a person who acquired the goods by legal transaction after the transfer and thus after the customs debt was incurred (purchase is sufficient) or acquired possession of the goods otherwise (directly or indirectly) is a customs debtor. The "consignee" is the person who receives untaxed tobacco products in the tax territory by establishing his actual dominion (sovereignty) over them.[67] The purpose of determining the person liable for the payment of the excise duty is to be able to claim the benefit of the person in whose immediate custody a product subject to excise duty is located and who can therefore be easily identified on the basis of objective circumstances and made liable for paying taxes.[68]

---

[63]Bauer (2018), p. 88.

[64]Zoll (2019).

[65]Europäischer Gerichtshof (EuGH) *Spedition Ulustrans* (2004) C-414/02, Slg 2004, I-8633.

[66]Bundesfinanzhof (BFH) *Beteiligung am Verbringen* (2006) VII R 24/04, BFHE 213, 473.

[67]Bundesfinanzhof (BFH) *Steuerschuldnerschaft als Empfänger* (2012) VII R 50/11, BFHE 237, 554.

[68]Müller (2018), p. 2667.

It is irrelevant whether the *transferring person* knew of the irregular conduct. However, it is a prerequisite for the customs debt of the *representative*, *participant* and the *owner or acquirer* of the goods, that they know or should reasonably have known about the breach of duty. In this respect, the point of view of the informed and carefully acting economic operator is decisive.[69] The act is completed as soon as the goods have crossed the EU external border in violation of the duty to present goods to customs (*Gestellungspflichten*) as laid down in Art. 139 (1) UCC.

No customs debt is incurred on importation and therefore no punishment for tax evasion can be meted out if it is unclear whether the cigarettes were brought into the customs territory of the Union or manufactured in the territory of a Member State.[70] Consequently, no import duties arise on counterfeited cigarettes which may also have been manufactured in the customs territory of the Union. The burden of ascertaining that goods have been brought into the customs territory of the Union in contravention of the regulations is with the tax authority.[71]

According to Art. 87 (1, 2) UCC, the customs debt is incurred where the customs offence is fulfilled, i.e. when goods are imported from outside a Member State. Art. 87 (4) UCC contains an exception for smaller amounts (customs debt under 10.000 €): The customs debt is "deemed" to have arisen where it is established, i.e., if the customs authorities establish that a customs debt has arisen in another member state, the place of origin is deemed to be the place where it was established. This legal fiction serves to facilitate collection and is therefore a rule for establishing the jurisdiction for the customs administration of the Member State in which the customs debt was incurred. This rule does not apply to excise duties and import turnover tax.[72]

National Import Turnover Tax, § 21 UStG The provisions for customs duties apply mutatis mutandis to import turnover tax (§§ 21 (2) Value Added Tax Act—Umsatzsteuergesetz—UStG). The (German) import turnover tax is calculated by multiplying the relevant tax base by the German tax rate (19%).[73] If cigarettes smuggled into the customs territory of the Union and seized in Germany were brought into the German tax territory via a particular other Member State, the German customs administration shall, in addition to the customs duty and the tobacco tax applicable to the tobacco goods, also determine the import turnover tax if the customs debt is less than € 5,000.[74] In that case, the import turnover tax arises after the tobacco products have been unlawfully brought into the German tax

---

[69] Europäischer Gerichtshof (EuGH) *Jestel* (2011) C-454/10, Slg 2011, I-11725 ().

[70] FG Hamburg *Einfuhrabgaben bei gefälschten Zigaretten* (2017) 4 K 217/16.

[71] Weidemann (2018), p. 55.

[72] Deimel (2019), Art. 87 UZK para. 18.

[73] Bauer (2018), p. 88.

[74] BFHE 237, 554 (n 67).

territory, so that the resulting tobacco tax must be added to the basis of assessment for the import turnover tax.[75]

1.1.2.2 Illicit Manufacturing

1.1.2.2.1 Furnishing Authorities with Incorrect or Incomplete Particulars, § 370 (1) No. 1 AO

According to § 10 (2) and (3) TabStV the warehouse keeper has to keep a stock book in which he has to record the entries and exits. If he keeps the books incorrectly and submits these records to the main customs office, he fulfils the elements of crime of § 370 I No. 1 AO by providing incorrect information.[76]

1.1.2.2.2 Omission of the Use of Tax Stamps, § 370 (1) No. 3 AO

The non-use of tax stamps is only punishable if tax stamps are mandatory.[77] Tobacco tax must be paid using tax stamps by invalidating and affixing them to the retail sales packages (at the latest) at the time the tax arises (§ 17 (1) TabStG).[78] According to § 17 (2) TabStG, manufacturers, importers and equals are entitled to obtain tax stamps from the main customs office in Bielefeld (§ 32 (1) TabStV).

The main purpose for the use of tax stamps lies in their publicity effect. They must therefore already be used before the tax arises, i.e. before they are released into free circulation, even if they only then develop their tax effect.[79] At the time of tax emergence, the tobacco tax claim is met immediately within one logical second with the consequence of extinction. Illicit tobacco products, for which no tax stamps have been used are "taxed" even if they have been subject to tax evasion, because the use of tax stamps concerns only the collection of tobacco tax.

The tax arises when tobacco products are released for consumption, unless it is followed by a tax exemption (§ 15 (1) of the TabStG). If the tobacco tax arises, the tax mark must be affixed (§ 17 (1) Sentence 3 TabStG). Tobacco products are released for free circulation through

- withdrawal from a tax warehouse, unless followed by another procedure of tax suspension (consumption in the tax warehouse is equivalent to withdrawal, § 15 (2) No. 1 TabStG);
- production without permission according to § 6 TabStG (§ 15 (2) No. 2 TabStG);
- an irregularity under § 14 TabStG during carriage under suspension of excise duty (§ 15 (2) No. 4 TabStG).

---

[75]BFHE 237, 554 (n 67).

[76]Weidemann and Weidemann (2005), p. 207.

[77]Weidemann (2018), p. 30 f.

[78]Jäger (2015), § 370 AO para. 377.

[79]Jäger (2015), § 370 AO para. 378.

Tobacco products from other EU member states may be obtained from registered consignees under tax suspension (§§ 12 (1) No. 2 lit. b, 7 TabStG). The tobacco tax then arises when the tobacco is withdrawn from the procedure under tax suspension when it is admitted into the business of the registered recipient (§ 15 II No. 3 TabStG). At this time, the tax characters must be used (§ 17 I 3 TabStG).[80]

1.1.3 Relation Between Criminal and Administrative/Fiscal Responsibility

Under German law fiscal responsibilities to pay taxes and duties exist besides any criminal or administrative liability. In case of tax evasion this means that taxes and duties that apply must be paid following taxation rules. In addition, criminal and/or administrative sanctions can apply. This means taxation and criminal/administrative sanctions are seen as different measures so that no "ne bis in idem principle" applies. In regard to the relationship between criminal and administrative offences, criminal liability prevails if offenses cover the same conduct (see § 21 Ordnungswidrigkeitengesetz—OWiG).

There is a mandatory procedural obstacle according to § 32 ZollVG for tax offences under § 369 AO (and also tax administrative offenses under § 377 AO) in cross-border travel (i.e. no illegal border crossing and no connection with commercial traffic in goods are covered.[81] This requires that the reduction in import, export or excise duties attributable to goods in excess of the duty-free quantity[82] does not exceed 250 € in total.

1.2 Relations Between Criminalization of Illicit Trade of Tobacco and Other Types of Economic Crimes

Illicit trade of tobacco often goes along with money laundering pursuant to § 261 StGB and forgery of stamps in the sense of §§ 369 (1) No. 3 AO; 148 StGB.[83] The provision on money laundering in § 261 StGB plays a particular important role, because it permits the prosecution of those who have participated in the deferral and distribution of the illegally obtained proceeds, such as the managing directors of fictitious companies or the relatives of the smugglers.[84] Additionally, organized smuggler gangs can be regarded as criminal associations according to §

[80] Jäger (2015), § 370 AO para. 379.

[81] Harder (2014), Chapter 22 para. 111–112.

[82] BayObLG *Hinterziehung von Zollabgaben* (2000) 4St RR 98/2000, 4St RR 98/00, BayObLGSt 2000, 121.

[83] Knickmeier (2016), p. 431.

[84] Koziolek (2015a), p. 215.

129 StGB.[85] Even though the reasoning is usually difficult and the requirements of the jurisdiction are high, § 129 StGB served as a justification for the implementation of surveillance measures against smuggling gangs until § 100a (2) No. 2 StPO was amended in 2008.[86]

Also, there is a liability for assistance after the fact. According to §§ 369 (1) No. 4 AO; 257 StGB (Assistance after the fact) it is punishable to assist the offender of an unlawfully committed tax offence as of § 369 (1) No. 1-3 AO in order to secure the benefits he has obtained from such a tax offence. In practice, advantages within the meaning of the preferential treatment lie in the occurring reduction of taxes.[87] In the case of tax evasion, the benefit is complete if the assistance provided makes it impossible to enforce the tax claim or at least makes it even more difficult than it has already been due to the evasion.[88] In this sense, the prevailing opinion is that the offence must be objectively suitable and subjectively intended to secure the advantages of the tax offence committed against confiscation for the offender.[89]

In most cases the illicit trade of tobacco does not fulfill the elements of fraud (§ 263 StGB) as this requires deceiving someone who then acts because of an error and creates some damage based on the deception. Although tobacco companies suffer some damage if falsified products with their name or logo etc. are sold,[90] often there is no deception of the consumer or an error on side of the consumer.

1.3 Aggravating Cases of Illicit Trade of Tobacco Products

1.3.1 Professional, Violent or Organized Smuggling, § 373 AO

Anyone who evades import or export duties on a commercial basis or who illegally imports, exports or transports goods on a commercial basis in contravention of monopoly regulations on a commercial basis shall be punished under the aggravated offense of § 373 (1) AO, providing to a sentence of at least 6 months of imprisonment up to 10 years of imprisonment. This also applies to any person who

- evades import or export duties or illegally imports, exports or transports goods, and in committing these acts he or another participant carries a firearm (§ 373 (2) No. 1 AO),

[85] Koziolek (2015a), p. 215.

[86] Bauer (2018), p. 87.

[87] Bundesgerichtshof (BGH) *Begünstigung bei Steuerhinterziehung* (1998) 5 StR 746/97, wistra 1999, 103; Jäger (2000), pp. 346–347.

[88] Bundesgerichtshof (BGH) *Begünstigung bei Steuerhinterziehung* (n 87); *Beihilfe zur Steuerhinterziehung* (2000) 5 StR 624/99, BGHSt 46, 107.

[89] BGHSt 46, 107 (n 88).

[90] Hefendehl (2015) § 263 StGB para. 493.

- evades import or export duties or illegally imports, exports or transports goods, and in committing these acts he or another participant carries with him a weapon or some other tool or means to prevent or overcome the resistance of another person by violence or by the threat of violence (§ 373 (2) No. 2 AO), or
- as a member of a group formed for the purpose of repeatedly evading import or export duties or of illegally importing, exporting or transporting goods, commits such an act (§ 373 (2) No. 3 AO).

§ 373 AO is applicable instead of § 370 AO as a qualifying offence in the case of a reduction of import duties, but not in cases of a reduction of taxes arising within the country or from transfers from other member states. The offence is deemed to have been committed when tobacco products (under the abovementioned qualification) are moved from a third country to the EU without presentation. In contrast to § 370 (6) sentence 1 and § 374 (2) AO, import duties administered by another Member State of the European Union are not covered by the facts of § 373 AO. Therefore, import duties within the meaning of § 373 AO are only the customs duties administered by Germany for the EU[91] as well as German import turnover tax and tobacco tax. It must be observed that only in cases in which tobacco products are imported directly from a non-EU-country into Germany (e.g. by air or via a free port such as Hamburg and Bremerhaven) the German tobacco tax arises with the import turnover tax and the customs duty as import duty (cf. § 53 (3) AO). Accordingly, § 373 AO does not cover the German tobacco tax as import duty if the cigarettes are not brought directly from a non-member state of the European Union to Germany.[92]

§ 373 AO is therefore only relevant if the goods are transported *directly to Germany from outside the EU*. The import duties, customs duty, import turnover tax, import tobacco tax (but not, for example, domestic tobacco tax) are then reduced. If, on the other hand, the goods are initially moved from the third country to another Member State and from there to Germany, the import duties are reduced when the goods cross the EU external border and the German border, the transfer tobacco tax. In this case both measures constitute a criminal offense.

If, e.g., cigarettes originating from Asia are transported by ship to Germany hidden under goods to be cleared and imported via the free ports, this constitutes commercial and gang smuggling in the sense of § 373 (1), (2) No. 3 AO in conjunction with § 370 (1) No. 1 AO.[93]

It is important that the criminal court judge considers the legal qualification that both commercial conduct (§ 373 (1) AO) and gang membership (§ 373 (2) No. 3 AO) are special personal characteristics within the meaning of § 28 (2) StGB with

[91]Bender (2001), p. 166; BGH (Bundesgerichtshof) *Hinterziehung von Eingangsabgaben* (1987) 3 StR 146/87, ZfZ 1987, 345.

[92]BGH, NJW 2007,1294 (n 7). When the transport (e.g. by land) into the German territory takes place via another EU member state, *Tatmehrheit* (§ 53 StGB) between § 373 AO (related to the import duties administered by the EU member state) and § 370 Paragraph 1 No. 2 AO (related to the German tobacco tax) must be assumed, cf. Bauer (2018), p. 85.

[93]BGH wistra 2007, 262 (n 4).

the consequence that a party to the offence who does not possess the personal characteristics can only be punished for participating in the basic offence (§ 370 AO).

1.3.2 § 370 (3) AO

In § 370 (3) AO the law provides for aggravating cases of tax evasion mentioned in § 370 (1) AO. The nature of these "Strafzumessungsregeln" (sentencing rules) only affects the applicable sentence but does not change the nature of the offense (so that the cases that are covered do not qualify as a qualified offense).[94] If the criteria of § 370 (3) AO are met, in general the higher sentencing range of imprisonment from 6 months to 10 years applies. Yet, if there is a non-average case, the rules do not have to be applied. Insofar, the judge has some discretion to apply the higher sentencing range or not. The most important constellations under § 370 (3) AO are:

- tax evasion on a large scale (No. 1), whereas the courts regard evaded taxes or import duties etc. of at least 50.000 EUR to be large scale;[95]
- abuse of the authority or position as a public official (No. 2) and making use of this abuse (No. 3);[96]
- repeated use of falsified or forged documents (No. 4);
- commission of the offense as a gang member (No. 5).[97]

If a case falls under § 370 (3) AO a special limitation period of 10 years applies (see § 376 AO), whereas for a normal case under § 370 (1) AO the normal limitation period of 5 years (see § 78 StGB) applies.[98]

1.4 Legal Responsibility of Individuals for Illicit Trade of Tobacco Products

The main responsibility for the trade in tobacco products is of an administrative nature. Especially the "Gesetz über Tabakerzeugnisse und verwandte Erzeugnisse (TabakerzG)" and the "Verordnung über Tabakerzeugnisse und verwandte Erzeugnisse (TabakerzV)" set out the basic framework how to deal with tobacco products. In addition, the trading of tobacco products is an important fiscal issue so that the TabStG and the TabStV provide for further obligations. These obligations have to be observed independent of any specific state of mind of the person affected.

---

[94]Hadamitzky and Senge (2018), § 370 AO para. 87.

[95]Hadamitzky and Senge (2018), § 370 AO para. 88.

[96]Hadamitzky and Senge (2018), § 370 AO para. 90b; see also Jäger (2015), § 370 AO para. 577.

[97]Jäger (2015), § 370 AO para. 579–584.

[98]Budde (2019), p. 28.

If obligations are not observed the public authorities have the power to enforce them in administrative or fiscal proceedings.

In addition, the breach of main obligations is sanctioned in the respective legislation either as a criminal or (if regarded less important) as an administrative offense. In these cases individual responsibility requires the existence of a subjective element, especially intention or negligence. Important criminal offenses such as §§ 370, 372, 373, 374 AO require intent. Nonetheless they cover a large number of criminal behavior as they regulate conduct prior to the commission of fraud offenses and insofar are "Vorfeldtatbestände". In contrast administrative offenses can often be committed intentionally and negligently, although in the majority of administrative tax offenses a special form of negligence is needed, the so-called "Leichtfertigkeit".[99] Normal negligence is not sufficient, there must be a higher degree of guilt.[100] It is comparable to the Anglo-American concept of recklessness.

1.5 Sanctions Applicable for Illicit Trade of Tobacco Products (Individuals)

1.5.1 Taxes

Any person who evades taxes or receives, holds or sells goods obtained by tax evasion or participates in such an act is liable for the taxes understated or the tax advantages wrongfully granted (§ 71 AO). Also, interest has to be paid on evaded taxes (§§ 235, 238 AO). These payments are not regarded as sanctions as they are only intended to reimburse the state for the damage caused.

1.5.2 Criminal Sanctions

As criminal sanctions for criminal offenses fines and imprisonment apply, depending on the offense committed. Fines are determined by the general rules in §§ 40, 41 StGB. They are calculated by multiplying the number of daily units (ranging from 5 to 360 depending on individual guilt) with the daily amount (from 1 to 30,000 EUR depending on the individual income). The maximum term of imprisonment depends on the offense committed. Often these offenses provide for a maximum sentence of 5 years of imprisonment such as the main tax crimes in §§ 370, 372, 374 AO. In addition to at least 1 year's imprisonment § 375 (1) AO provides in regard to the most important tax offenses for the possibility to disqualify someone from holding public office and acquiring rights from public elections.

---

[99]Heuel (2016), § 378 AO para. 54 ff.

[100]See BGH of 29.4.1959—2 StR 123/59, DStZ/B 1959, 351 (352).

1.5.3 Forfeiture

In cases of criminal offenses the forfeiture of instrumentalities and proceeds is possible in addition to a criminal sanction but also instead of a criminal sanction (§§ 73-75 StGB). § 375 (2) AO allows the confiscation of the products, goods and other items used for or obtained by tax evasion and amends the general rules in §§ 73-75 StGB. E.g. according to § 73 (1) StGB, objects, which the perpetrator "obtained through" the unlawful act, are to be confiscated. In the case of tax evasion, this is the monetary advantage in the form of the tax owed. Since the collection of this "something" is not possible due to its nature, the court orders the collection of an amount of money corresponding to the tax reduction (value replacement) according to § 73c sentence 1 StGB. Pursuant to § 459h (2) StPO, the proceeds from the realization of the proceeds are paid "to the injured party who has a claim to compensation for the value of the proceeds from the offence". The injured party may also be the tax authorities. The public prosecutor's office, as the executing authority, decides on the claim to which the injured party is entitled. Only the amount corresponding to the tax claim may be paid out.[101]

In more detail: The goods "to which the evasion of excise duties relates" are not obtained through tax evasion as such. They are therefore not directly subject to forfeiture pursuant to § 73 StGB. However, they can still be confiscated because of the specific regulation under § 375 (2) Sentence 1 No. 1 AO. If the perpetrator has sold the goods before the decision, it lies within the discretionary power of the court to order that some compensation (*Wertersatz*) be paid up to the amount which corresponds to the value of the object pursuant to § 74c StGB.[102]

The confiscation of the means of transport used for the offence is permitted according to § 375 (2) Sentence 1 No. 2 AO. This includes preceding or following escort vehicles.[103] The reference in § 375 (2) Sentence 2 AO to § 74a StGB enables the confiscation of objects if the person who owns or is entitled to them has at least recklessly ("leichtfertig") contributed to the fact that the object or the right was the instrument or object of the act or its preparation.[104] According to § 369 (2) AO, the general provisions on confiscation of crime products, means of crime and objects of crime (§§ 74 ff. StGB) apply additionally, unless § 375 (2) AO provides otherwise. This is the case for those items which fulfil only the general characteristics of § 74 (1) StGB, i.e. which were the result of an intentional—at least attempted and as such punishable—offence or were used or intended for its commission or preparation.

---

[101]Bauer (2018), pp. 89–90; see also Weidemann (2018), pp. 49–50.

[102]Jäger (2017), pp. 522–523.

[103]Bundesgerichtshof (BGH) *Einziehung des Sicherungsfahrzeuges* (1952) 2 StR 354/52, BGHSt 3, 355.

[104]Bundesgerichtshof (BGH) *Einziehung von Transport- und Begleitfahrzeugen* (2016) 1 StR 118/16, NStZ 2016, 731.

Only objects which were created directly through the act (producta sceleris) are produced by the act (§ 74 (1) Alt. 1 StGB). Proceeds from the sale of goods do not fall under this category, so that this alternative has no practical significance in criminal tax law apart from § 150 StGB and § 375 (2) AO.[105] Objects which were used or intended to be used as a means or tools for the commission of an offence or its preparation and which have promoted or should have promoted the offence (instrumenta sceleris), e.g. a mobile telephone, are used (§ 74 (1) Alt. 2 StGB) or intended to be used (§ 74 (1) Alt. 3 StGB) for the commission of an offence are also covered. However, even if it is proven that a telephone was used during the crime, the confiscation order is not possible if the content of the call cannot be clarified in detail.[106] Objects which were used after the crime had been committed but before it ended, e.g. suitcases for transporting the smuggled goods after crossing the border, can also be confiscated under certain conditions.[107] According to § 150 StGB it is compulsive to confiscate false or devalued tax stamps and the respective counterfeit means in case of tax stamp offences (§§ 148, 149 StGB).[108]

1.5.4 Sanctions for Administrative Offences

For administrative offenses the only sanction is a fine (§ 1 OWiG). If the specific offense does not provide otherwise, intentional conduct is fined by a maximum of 1000 EUR and negligent conduct by a maximum of 500 EUR (§ 17 OWiG). Tax offences in most cases provide for a higher sentence as an exception to this general rule: § 378 AO (up to 50,000 EUR), § 379 AO (up to 25,000 EUR), § 381 AO in connection with § 60 TabStV or § 36 TabStG (up to 5,000 EUR). Confiscation in cases of administrative offenses is only possible if there is a referral to the general rules in the OWiG (§§ 22-29a OWiG), which is not the case for §§ 378-383 AO as well as for § 60 TabStV and § 36 TabStG. But it applies to § 37 (3) TabStG in the case of confiscation of no more than 1000 cigarettes per act traded on the black market. [109]§ 375 AO is not applicable to administrative offences.

1.5.5 Other Sanctions

In addition to these consequences further administrative measures with a sanctioning effect can apply. Among these are the withdrawal of licenses for exercising a trade (§

[105]Wegner (2015b), § 375 AO para. 31.

[106]Wegner (2015b), § 375 AO para. 32.

[107]Bundesgerichtshof (BGH) *Einziehung von Tatwerkzeugen* (2004) 2 StR 362/04, StV 2005, 210 3.

[108]Hilgers-Klautzsch (2017), § 375 AO para. 40.

[109]Hilgers-Klautzsch (2017), § 375 AO para. 39–40.

35 (1) GewO), the withdrawal of firearms licenses or the refusal to issue a hunting license (§ 17 BJagdG).[110]

1.6 Liability and Sanctions for Illicit Trade of Tobacco Products (Legal Persons)

German criminal law does not provide for corporate criminal liability in the criminal code. Yet, legal entities can be subject to criminal confiscation orders under § 73b StGB (e.g., if a company obtained some gain from smuggling committed by its staff). Also, the OWiG provides for a corporate fine in case of violations of criminal and administrative offences by senior staff of the legal entity (§ 30 OWiG). The company is responsible if a senior staff member commits either a criminal or an administrative offense in his capacity as a corporate member. In these cases fines up to € 10 million for intentional crimes or up to €5 million in negligence cases are possible. As the illegal gain can be added to this, confiscation can be part of an overall fine. In the Volkswagen (VW) emission case, VW was fined €1 billion, consisting of €5 million for the punitive part and €995 million for the confiscation part. Although Germany in this regard has a corporate liability system, there is a vigorous debate to modernize the system and increase the pressure on companies. The state of Northrhine-Westfalia[111] has proposed a respective bill in 2013, the federal government is currently working on a proposal that includes increased sanctions and new rules for internal investigations, cooperation with authorities, and compliance.

1.7 Disposal or Destruction of Confiscated Tobacco Products

Illegal tobacco products can often be secured and transferred to the ownership of the federal government (see e.g. § 23 (1) Sentence 5 TabStG in conjunction with §§ 215, 216 AO, see also § 111b StPO). In cases of a criminal offense the StGB allows for the confiscation of the goods (that normally have been secured before brought into public custody). According to § 75 StGB the state becomes owner of the confiscated goods when the confiscation order is final. Illegal goods are then regularly destroyed.

[110]Jäger (2018), § 370 AO para. 348–349.

[111]Land Nordrhein-Westfalen (2013). See Zieschang (2014), p. 91; Schlagowski (2018).

1.8 WTO FCTC and the 2012 Protocol

Germany has signed and ratified the FCTC[112] and the 2012 Protocol.[113] The FCTC was mainly implemented by implementing Directive 2014/40/EU and its following European legislation.[114] It has been disputed if Art. 13 FCTC has been sufficiently implemented as Germany does not completely ban tobacco advertising, promotion and sponsorship.[115] Yet, as the obligation leaves some discretion in regard to the implementation strategy the German approach is to be seen still in line of the minimum requirements.[116] In regard to Art. 14 of the 2012 Protocol German law basically covers the mentioned acts especially under its main criminal and administrative tax offenses, §§ 370-374 AO and §§ 378, 381 (in conjunction with § 60 TabStV and § 36 TabStG) AO.[117] The requirement of corporate criminal liability (Art. 15 of the 2012 Protocol) is fulfilled by the regulation in § 30 OWiG.[118]

2 Procedural Law Issues

As tax criminal law is criminal law the normal criminal procedure rules apply, apart from some specialties mainly in regard to custom duties.[119] As custom duties are an exclusive legislative competence of the federal government (Art. 105 (1) GG) all fiscal authorities in the customs area (so-called customs administration) are federal

---

[112]"Gesetz zu dem Rahmenübereinkommen der Weltgesundheitsorganisation vom 21. Mai 2003 zur Eindämmung des Tabakgebrauchs (Gesetz zu dem Tabakrahmenübereinkommen)" of 19 November 2004, BGBl. II p. 1538.

[113]"Gesetz zu dem Protokoll vom 12. November 2012 zur Unterbindung des unerlaubten Handels mit Tabakerzeugnissen" of 17 July 2017, BGBl. II p. 1538.

[114]See the relevant legislation: Gesetz zur Umsetzung der Richtlinie über Tabakerzeugnisse und verwandte Erzeugnisse of 4 April 2016, BGBl. I p. 569; Verordnung zur Umsetzung der Richtlinie über Tabakerzeugnisse und verwandte Erzeugnisse of 27 April 2016, BGBl. I p. 980; Erste Verordnung zur Änderung der Tabakerzeugnisverordnung of 21 June 2016, BGBl. I p. 1468; Zweite Verordnung zur Änderung der Tabakerzeugnisverordnung of 17 May 2017, BGBl. I p. 1201; Dritte Verordnung zur Änderung der Tabakerzeugnisverordnung of 2 May 2019, BGBl. I p. 547.

[115]Critical on the issue, e.g. several parliamentary members of the Green Party, see the parliamentary document BT-Drs. 17/2036 (of 10 June 2010). For a general ban see the parliamentary motion in BT-Drs. 19/2539 (of 6 June 2018).

[116]See Streinz (2017).

[117]See also the evaluation of the Government on the implementation status of the protocol under German law in BT-Drs. 18/11868, pp. 40 ff. Within the scope of this report it is not possible to evaluate Art. 14 of the 2012 protocol and its implementation status in detail.

[118]See BT-Drs. 18/11868, p. 41.

[119]See Harder (2014), Chapter 22 para. 1 ff.; Krause and Prieß (2014), § 34 para. 1 ff.; Retemeyer and Möller (2015), Chapter 20 para. 1 ff.

authorities that are assigned to the Federal Ministry of Finance.[120] The customs administration, the main customs offices (Hauptzollamt) and the customs investigation service (Zollfahndungsdienst), have been separate branches until 2015, but since then and the reorganization of the customs administration are combined under the single umbrella of the General Customs Directorate (Generalzolldirektion) as the supreme authority. However, the 43 main customs offices and the eight customs investigation offices remained unchanged as local authorities.[121] The Customs Criminal Investigation Office (Zollkriminalamt—ZKA), as the central office of the Customs Investigation Offices, was integrated as Directorate in the General Customs Directorate. The directorate of the ZKA and the customs investigation offices have a considerable number of staff.[122]

The main customs offices are tasked besides the prosecution services with the investigation of and partly the prosecution of criminal and administrative customs offenses.[123] The customs offices are responsible if the case only involves customs offenses. If not, the prosecution is responsible (but can ask the custom offices for assistance). The custom authorities have a similar power as the tax authorities in regard to taxes. Insofar as these independently conduct a customs criminal procedure, they, like the tax authorities, have individual public prosecutorial powers.[124] Particularities arise from the extensive competences in preliminary investigations at the borders, where, in principle, the investigations are carried out by border customs officers assigned to the main customs offices.[125] Here, controls without suspicion are possible as part of the regular customs supervision, but which can as well lead to criminal proceedings (for example due to customs offenses or money laundering).

An example of the powers at the borders is the 2017 introduced § 12e (1) ZollVG, which allows the seizure (Sicherstellung) of excise goods, in particular cigarettes, and raw materials (e.g. tobacco) and machinery suitable for their manufacture, as well as the associated containers and enclosures until the end of the fifth working day after their discovery.[126] These measures are intended to verify the lawfulness of the use of the goods. The only requirement is that an assumption has to be established that these goods are transferred with the intention of committing a tax offence under § 369 AO. This makes it possible to temporarily stop such goods at the border, without regard to the threshold of an initial suspicion in a normal criminal proceedings.[127]

---

[120]See § 1 Gesetz über die Finanzverwaltung (FVG).

[121]See Gesetz zur Neuorganisation der Zollverwaltung v. 3.12.2015, BGBl. I S. 2178.

[122]In 2017 the ZKA employed 944 persons and the eight customs investigation offices 2435 persons, see Generalzolldirektion, Der Zoll. Jahrestatistik 2017, p. 19.

[123]§ 386 Abs. 1 AO. For an overview of the agencies involved see Calderoni et al. (2013), pp. 48 ff.

[124]Vgl. Krause and Prieß (2014), § 34 para. 153.

[125]Wirth (2005), pp. 31 ff.

[126]Weerth (2018), pp. F19–F20.

[127]Häberle (2018), § 12e ZollVG para. 1.

The customs investigation service, which includes the ZKA and the customs investigation offices (§ 1 ZFdG), also has its own special investigative powers. Even though the latter is not himself a law enforcement agency, in practice the facts (as in the case of the tax investigation department, the Steuerfahndung) are regularly completely determined by the agency and then sent to the main customs office for a decision.[128] The Customs Criminal Office takes over the investigation only in exceptional cases and mainly supports the work of the customs investigation offices by providing information and coordinating the case.[129] The customs investigation has police powers (such as the Steuerfahndung) in the customs area under the AO and StPO.[130]

Like the Steuerfahndung, the customs investigation department has the competence to conduct preliminary investigations in the customs procedure which it also has to carry out.[131] Insofar, in addition to prosecution tasks, it is assigned extensive preventive tasks, too, and has in this regard, numerous powers, in particular for information acquisition and processing.[132] Prevention and repression go hand in hand as "preventing and prosecuting crimes and offenses" as well as "uncovering unknown crimes" and "preparing for future criminal cases".[133]

The ZKA manages and manages an extensive collection of data.[134] In that regard, the ZKA is similar to the Federal Police Office (Bundeskriminalamt—BKA) in terms of the breadth of tasks and the nature of an information administration office. The collection includes both preventive and repressive data.[135] The ZKA has special powers, e.g., it may preventively monitor telecommunication in the event of suspicion of the preparation of certain crimes.[136] This data may in principle be used for both preventive and repressive purposes.[137] In general, § 393 (3) Sentence 1 AO allows that lawfully obtained findings of tax authorities or the public prosecutor's office in the course of criminal investigations may also be used in taxation proceedings.

Besides the aforementioned examples "normal" investigation measures can also be referred to. Pursuant to § 100a (2) No. 2 a, b StPO it is possible to monitor electronic communications of suspects in the case of serious tax crimes (especially in gang cases or where a commercial conduct is given).[138] Furthermore, investigative

---

[128] Krause and Prieß (2014), § 34 para. 152.

[129] See on the tasks §§ 3 ff., 24 f. ZFdG and Linke (2004), pp. 143 ff.

[130] See for details Harder (2014), Chapter 22 para. 30 ff.

[131] Krause and Prieß (2014), § 34 para. 155 ff.; Fehn (2006), Chapter B para. 8 ff.

[132] See §§ 7–23g, 26–38 ZFdG.

[133] See § 24 Abs. 2 ZFdG.

[134] §§ 7-13 ZFdG.

[135] For detail see Lenz (2006), Chapter C para. 173 ff.

[136] See §§ 23a ff. ZFdG (covering offenses against the German Weapons Control Act); critical Wachner (2006), Chapter H para. 194 ff.

[137] § 23d ZFdG.

[138] Bauer (2018), p. 87; Bittmann (2010), p. 125.

measures may include long-term observation ("controlled transport") according to § 163f StPO or the use of undercover investigators under § 110a (1) No. 3, 4 StPO. §§ 110a et seq. StPO allows covert investigations. Of particular importance is the provision of § 100g StPO for obtaining information on telecommunications connections.[139]

In order to safeguard the enforcement of monetary claims German law provides for several measures. Among these are § 111b StPO that allows objects to be secured by seizure until a final decision on forfeiture. § 324 AO allows a freezing injunction for movable or immovable assets where there are reasons to fear that recovery for tax monetary claims will otherwise be thwarted or seriously hindered.

From a legal perspective in the custom offense cases the determination of the course of the transport process is particularly important for the distinction between §§ 370, 373 AO on the one hand and § 374 AO (*Steuerhehlerei*) on the other during the investigation procedure. Especially the question of whether the import operation (from a non-EU-country) has already been completed at the time of participation is decisive for the question of criminal liability. This is important for perpetrators, who obtain tobacco products which have previously been imported into the EU by third parties in another EU Member State for the purpose of further transfer to the Federal Republic of Germany. Then, the offences of evasion of import duties or the evasion of tobacco tax is only completed when the tobacco goods have been brought to safety and "come to rest".[140] Yet, in practice in many cases, the smuggled goods are only seized and secured by customs authorities in Germany without investigating the question of how long the imported goods had already been (temporarily) stored in the other EU member state. This is unfortunate if it is ascertainable that the import procedure was already completed in the other EU member state because the persons involved in the onward transport to Germany also carry out tax fraud with regard to import duties (in accordance with § 374 AO) in addition to the evasion of the German tobacco tax (§§ 370, 373 AO).[141]

The jurisprudence also tries to facilitate speedy proceedings. E.g., in order to save the courts from having to make difficult findings about foreign tobacco tax law, the Federal Court, the BGH, permits the courts to restrict prosecution under §§ 154; 154a StPO to the German transfer tobacco tax (in addition to the import turnover tax and customs duty) and not to extend it to the transfer tax incurred in other Member States.[142]

Altogether, dealing with custom offenses requires formidable resources since the costs for personnel deployment and especially technical investigation measures such as telephone surveillance are enormous. This is especially true in cross-border investigations. Especially in such investigations resource inadequacies are taken advantage of by perpetrators in a targeted manner. Enhanced cooperation and

[139]Koziolek (2015a), p. 211.

[140]BGH, wistra 2016, 74 (n 20).

[141]Bauer (2018), p. 85.

[142]BGH, NStZ 2010, 644 (n 21).

Table 1 Number of economic and tax crime cases in 2017[a]

Economic- and tax crime cases, money-laundering cases	135,836
Economic crime cases (according to § 74c GVG)	5007
Other economic crime cases	65,792
Tax crime cases	21,012
Money laundering cases (§ 261 StGB)	41,049
Other cases within § 74c Abs. 1 GVG	2976

[a]Statistisches Bundesamt (Destatis), Rechtspflege: Staatsanwaltschaften 2017: Fachserie 10 Reihe 2.6 Statistisches Bundesamt (Destatis) (2018a), p. 22

networking of police, customs and prosecution services involved in the fight against illicit trade is therefore to be aimed at, also it might be effective to establish central offices or include these offenses in the mandate of the European Public Prosecutor's Office.[143]

3 Criminological Data

Sound information on the scope, the investigation and the adjudication of the illicit trade of tobacco products in Germany is scarce as there is often only information available on criminal offenses (and not on administrative offenses) and on tax offenses in general (but not on the percentage of custom offences etc.). The main resources for statistical data are the police statistics (Polizeiliche Kriminalstatistik) and the tables for the judiciary (Rechtspflegestatistik). In addition, some authorities such as the customs offices provide further information. In the following, only the available data is presented. The tables referred to in the text are part of the annex.

3.1 Investigation of Illicit Trade of Tobacco Products

The general statistics of the judiciary give a general overview on the number of economic and tax crime cases investigated (see Table 1).

115.857 cases were initiated in 2017 by the tax investigation department (Steuerfahndung) and the customs investigation service (Zollfahndungsdienst) in regard to all subject matters these authorities are responsible for.[144]

The number of cases investigated by the tax investigation department (Steuerfahndung) in the field of tax and custom offences is quite considerable with

[143]See Koziolek (2015a), p. 211.

[144]Statistisches Bundesamt (Destatis), Rechtspflege: Staatsanwaltschaften 2017: Fachserie 10 Reihe 2.6 (Statistisches Bundesamt (Destatis) 2018a, p. 20).

Table 2 Completed investigations of the tax investigation department (Steuerfahndung) from 2000 to 2016[a]

Year	No. of completed investigations
2000	48,638
2001	45,792
2002	46,729
2003	42,393
2004	37,370
2005	36,195
2006	35,666
2007	36,309
2008	31,537
2009	31,878
2010	34,186
2011	35,592
2012	31,655
2013	34,183
2014	40,241
2015	36,708
2016	36,667

[a]Figures by the Federal Ministry of Finance, Verfolgung von Steuerstraftaten und Steuerordnungswidrigkeiten (various monthly reports), www.bundesfinanzministerium.de

Table 3 Completed investigations of custom investigation service (*Zollfahndungsdienst*) from 2011 to 2018[a]

Year	No. of completed investigations
2011	2057
2012	1935
2013	1342
2014	1306
2015	1217
2016	1149
2017	995
2018	1261

[a]Figures provided by Generalzolldirektion—Zollkriminalamt, Fachgebiet B.322 (Bekämpfung der Tabakwarenkriminalität)

36,667 cases in 2016 (see Table 1). Yet, it has generally decreased since 2000, when there were 48,638 cases (see Table 2).

The figures of the customs investigation service (Zollfahndungsdienst) on customs offenses investigations also shows a decrease in numbers in recent years (see Table 3).

This means that the overall number of cases (1.261 cases in 2018, see Table 2) is much lower than the ones of the Steuerfahndung, although this data does not include the investigations by the 43 principal customs offices (Hauptzollämter). The German government stated in 2018 (based on information by the custom offices) that within the last 12 months 3826 investigations took place in regard to tax crimes in connection cigarettes and another 1108 investigations in regard to illegal tobacco products (including cigarettes) were initiated.[145]

Additional information stems, e.g., from the Federal Criminal Police Office (*Bundeskriminalamt*—BKA) that listed 48 investigations of tax and custom offences in regard to organized crime in 2017 (decrease of 15.8% compared to 2016).[146] 8.4% of these organized crime offences concerned taxes and customs.[147] An illustrative example is provided by the city of Berlin that lists 741 cases of suspected violations of the AO in the context of illicit trade of cigarettes in 2016.[148] The police imposed 570 measures implying restrictions of freedoms. Among them were 19 arrest warrants.

3.2 *Prosecution/Convictions in Cases of Illicit Trade of Tobacco Products*

There is hardly any information on the number of prosecutions in cases of illicit trade of tobacco products. Information available is, e.g., on preliminary proceedings in the area of organized crimes, that includes organized crime in regard to tax and custom offences. The numbers have steadily declined between 2000 (854) and 2017 (572) (see Table 4).

In regard to adjudicated cases information is available in regard to the specific offenses in the AO (see Table 5). In 2002 there were altogether 11,288 judgements and 10,161 convictions for offenses in the AO.[149] In 2017 the number has increased to 12,551 judgements and 11,051 convictions with the large majority of cases being tax evasion according to § 370 AO.

There is no specific data on penalties in regard to customs offenses or the illicit traffic of tobacco goods. The information on sanctions for all offenses in the AO

145 Deutscher Bundestag (BT), 'Steuerschäden durch Tabak- und Zigarettenschmuggel: Antwort der Bundesregierung auf die Kleine Anfrage der Abgeordneten Markus Herbrand, Christian Dürr, Dr. Florian Toncar, weiterer Abgeordneter und der Fraktion der FDP – Drucksache 19/6263 –', 19 December 2018, BT-Drucksache 19/6644.

146 Bundeskriminalamt, Organisierte Kriminalität, Bundeslagebild 2017, Wiesbaden April (2018), pp. 5, 33–34.

147 Bundeskriminalamt, Organisierte Kriminalität, Bundeslagebild 2017, Wiesbaden April (2018), p. 5.

148 See the answer to a parliamentary request in 2017: Abgeordnetenhaus Berlin, 'Schriftliche Anfrage des Abgeordneten Peter Trapp (CDU) vom 29. Mai 2017 (Eingang beim Abgeordnetenhaus am 30. Mai 2017) zum Thema Illegaler Zigarettenhandel in Berlin im Jahr 2016 und Antwort vom 12. Juni 2017 (Eingang beim Abgeordnetenhaus am 14. Juni 2017)' Drucksache 18/11328, p. 2.

149 Statistisches Bundesamt (Destatis), 'Rechtspflege: Strafverfolgung: Fachserie 10 Reihe 3' (2002), table 2.1. The table does not yet go into more details.

Table 4 Preliminary proceedings in the area of organized crime from 2000 to 2017

Year	Total	Initial reports	Pending cases
2000	854	473	381
2001	787	389	398
2002	690	338	352
2003	637	327	310
2004	620	307	313
2005	650	345	305
2006	622	308	314
2007	602	295	307
2008	575	271	304
2009	579	305	274
2010	606	318	288
2011	589	318	271
2012	568	278	290
2013	580	298	282
2014	571	299	272
2015	566	281	285
2016	563	275	288
2017	572	274	298

Table 5 Adjudicated offenses of the AO[a]

Type of offense	No. of judgements	No. of convictions
All tax- and custom offenses in the AO	12,551	11,051
§ 370 (1) AO	11,808	10,443
§ 370 (3) AO	243	225
§ 372 (2) AO	23	21
§ 373 (1) AO	20	17
§ 374 (1) AO	240	209
§ 374 (2) AO	68	62
Other offenses in the AO	149	74

[a]Statistisches Bundesamt (Destatis), 'Rechtspflege: Strafverfolgung: Fachserie 10 Reihe 3' Statistisches Bundesamt (Destatis) (2018b), p. 86

shows that in the majority of cases a fine is the only sanction. Forfeiture orders did apply in 6.8% of the cases (see Table 6).

In about 11% of the cases an imprisonment sanction has been referred to, in most cases for a period between 9 months and 2 years (see Table 7).

No detailed information on the number of legal persons convicted in regard to illicit trade of tobacco products exists. The overall number of convicted legal persons according to § 30 OWiG (and insofar in conjunction with all criminal and administrative offenses) ranges between about 2000 and 4000 per year (see Table 8).

Table 6 Sanctions for offenses in the AO[a]

Offenses	Total no. of convictions	Fines	Convictions with imprisonment	Forfeiture
All Tax- and custom offenses in the AO	11,051	9812	1239	749
§ 370 (1) AO	10,443	9514	929	638
§ 370 (3) AO	225	45	18	17
§ 372 (2) AO	21	17	4	3
§ 373 (1) AO	17	4	13	3
§ 374 (1) AO	209	138	71	65
§ 374 (2) AO	62	27	35	14
Other offenses in the AO	74	67	7	9

[a]Statistisches Bundesamt (Destatis), 'Rechtspflege: Strafverfolgung: Fachserie 10 Reihe 3' (Statistisches Bundesamt (Destatis) 2018b)

3.3 *Financial Impact of Illicit Trade of Tobacco Products*

There are no exact figures on the financial impact of illicit trade of tobacco products. An assessment by *Bräuninger/Stiller* of the Hamburg Institute of International Economics (HWWI) estimates that in recent years, about 20% of cigarettes consumed in Germany have not been taxed in Germany.[150] This corresponds to a volume of approx. 23 billion units, whereof at least seven billion are estimated to have been brought illegally to Germany. The resulting tax loss amounts to at least 4.0 billion EUR, and the additional damage to industry and trade amounts to at least 1.2 billion EUR.

According to the Project SUN by the professional service company KPMG, 4.2 billion of smuggled or counterfeited tobacco products constitute an estimated tax loss (VAT and tobacco tax) of 845 million EUR in 2017, provided that all those tobacco products would have been purchased legally otherwise.[151]

The German Cigarette Association ("*Zigarettenverband*") assumes that in 2011, 23.5 billion untaxed cigarettes were smoked. 19.9 billion out of 23.5 billion cigarettes (85%) were bought in another member state of the European Union or as duty-free goods. The association estimates tax losses of 5.5 billion € (for 23.5 billion cigarettes).[152] According to the association the estimated market share of untaxed cigarettes fluctuates between 16.1% (2005) and 22.1% in 2011, and in recent years very stable at about 18 % (see Table 9), while the value of cigarettes sold in Germany

[150]Bräuninger and Stiller (2010), p. 21.

[151]KPMG (2017).

[152]See the press release Deutscher Zigarettenverband (15 Feb. 2012) Neuer Rekord beim Zigarettenschmuggel: Deutsche rauchen über 23 Milliarden Zigaretten am Fiskus vorbei! https://www.zigarettenverband.de/pos-data/page_img/Publikationen/Pressemitteilungen/2012-15-02-PM-Schmuggelzahlen.pdf. Accessed 15 May 2019.

Table 7 Imprisonment sanctions for offenses in the AO[a]

Offenses	Convictions with imprisonment	Under 6 months (ms)	6 months	6–9 months	9–12 months	1–2 years	2–3 years	3–5 years	5–10 years
All Tax- and Custom Offenses in the AO	1239	23	48	179	400	476	58	45	10
§ 370 (1) AO	929	20	39	132	322	347	36	26	7
§ 370 (3) AO	18	–	3	15	39	90	15	16	2
§ 372 (2) AO	4	–	–	–	1	3	–	–	–
§ 373 (1) AO	13	1	–	1	4	7	–	–	–
§ 374 (1) AO	71	2	4	15	26	18	4	2	–
§ 374 (2) AO	35	–	1	14	6	9	3	1	1
Other offenses in the AO	7	–	1	2	2	2	–	–	–

[a]Statistisches Bundesamt (Destatis), 'Rechtspflege: Strafverfolgung: Fachserie 10 Reihe 3' (Statistisches Bundesamt (Destatis) 2018b)

Table 8 Corporate fines according to § 30 OWiG[a]

Year	Total no. of fines per years
2000	3295
2001	4067
2002	2286
2003	4745
2004	2804
2005	1911
2006	2222
2007	2487
2008	2483
2009	2617
2010	2871
2011	2273
2012	3035
2013	2871
2014	3243
2015	4647
2016	2907
2017	3065

[a]Figures by the Federal Office of Justice (Bundesjustizamt): Übersicht über die Eintragungen im Gewerbezentralregister (Teilregister juristische Personen und Personenvereinigungen), 2000–2017, Table 1

Table 9 Estimated market share of untaxed cigarettes[a]

Year	Germany	West	East	
2005	16.1	11.6	30.6	in %
2006	19.9	15.7	33.6	in %
2007	20.3	15.5	36.1	in %
2008	19.9	13.8	39.7	in %
2009	20.1	13.5	41.6	in %
2010	21.2	14.0	45.2	in %
2011	22.1	14.5	47.6	in %
2012	20.6	14.3	44.5	in %
2013	21.7	15.4	45.2	in %
2014	18.9	13.2	41.6	in %
2015	17.6	12.3	37.1	in %
2016	18.0	12.2	39.5	in %
2017	17.9	12.0	39.4	in %

[a]Information provided by the German Cigarette Association (Deutscher Zigarettenverband) on the basis of studies by the market research institute Ipsos GmbH (Hamburg), see https://www.zigarettenverband.de/de/18/Themen/Zahlen_&_Fakten/Nicht_Versteuerter_Zigarettenabsatz (as of 15 May 2019)

Table 10 Value of cigarettes sold in Germany[a]

Year	Revenue ("Kleinverkaufswert") in Million EUR
1979	9,181.60
1985	11,397.40
1991	15,888.80
2000	19,175.90
2005	19,532.50
2006	19,913.35
2007	19,992.47
2008	19,424.98
2009	19,624.97
2010	19,199.77
2011	20,643.15
2012	20,106.01
2013	20,147.18
2014	20,461.55
2015	21,696.76
2016	20,520.88
2017	21,377.47
2018	21,659.30

[a]Statistisches Bundesamt: Fachserie 14: Finanzen und Steuern, Reihe 9.1.1: Absatz von Tabakwaren. A compilation is found on the Website of the German Cigarette Association (Deutscher Zigarettenverband), see https://www.zigarettenverband.de/pos-data/page_img/Grafiken/Infografik/Tab_Absatz_Umsatz_Steuer_2018.pdf (as of 15 May 2019)

varies between 19,532.5 million (2005) and 21,696.76 million (2015), being 21,377.47 million in 2017 (see Table 10).

Although these figures indicate a very high level of tax losses in Germany, it is not possible to validate their accuracy. Reliable dark field studies are not available,[153] and bright field data can only stem from known financial effects. Especially there exist no reliable information on how big the market share of untaxed cigarettes (compared to all consumed cigarettes) in Germany is.[154]

A first impression gives the amount of confiscated illegal goods (of all sorts) at the border: In 2018 in 37,698 cases more than five million goods with an estimated value of more than 196 million EUR were confiscated (see Table 11, also for the development since 2011). Custom authorities confiscated 62 million cigarettes in 2018, much less than 10 years ago when they confiscated 291 million (see for the years 2008–2018 Table 12). Also, the numbers of confiscated cigarettes by the custom investigation office have dropped significantly since 2010 (see Table 13).

---

[153]See for a critical assessment of the existing studies Adams and Effertz (2011), p. 705; Gallagher et al. (2018), p. 1; Mersmann (2015), pp. 187–192; Stoklosa (2016), p. 360; Taschowsky (2015), p. 28.

[154]See BT-Drucksache 19/6644 (n 146).

Table 11 Confiscation of illegal goods by customs[a]

Year	No. of cases of confiscation of illegal goods at the borders	No. of illegal goods confiscated in 1.000	Value of illegal goods confiscated in million EUR
2011	23,635	2,534.6	82.60
2012	23,883	3,202.8	127.40
2013	26,127	3,926.9	134.00
2014	45,738	5,926.8	137.70
2015	23,338	4,025.9	132.30
2016	21,229	3,640.1	180.04
2017	21,506	3,295.6	196.16
2018	37,698	5,066.3	196.70

[a]Statista, Anzahl der vom Zoll in Deutschland durchgeführten Beschlagnahmungen von gefälschten Waren sowie Anzahl und Wert der beschlagnahmten Waren von 2012 bis 2018, https://de.statista.com/statistik/daten/studie/155571/umfrage/wert-durch-den-zoll-beschlagnahmter-waren/ (as of 15 May 2019)

Table 12 Amount of confiscated cigarettes by customs from 2008 to 2018[a]

Year	Confiscated cigarettes (in million)
2008	291
2009	281
2010	157
2011	160
2012	146
2013	147
2014	140
2015	75
2016	121
2017	77
2018	62

[a]Statista, Anzahl der durch den Zoll in Deutschland sichergestellten Zigaretten von 2008 bis 2018 (in Millionen Stück), https://de.statista.com/statistik/daten/studie/29364/umfrage/sicherstellung-von-zigaretten-in-deutschland/ (as of 15 May 2019)

Concerning the respective tax losses, the investigated tax losses amounted to 153 million EUR in 2010 and dropped to around 38 million EUR in 2018 (see Table 14). The German government received an additional tax revenue of about 3.000 million EUR due to investigations by tax investigation department (Steuerfahndung) from 2002 to 2016 in general including illicit trade of tobacco (see Table 15).

A bright field quantification of tax losses according to the federal ministry of finance on the basis of information from investigation proceedings conducted by the customs offices shows the following development of the tax losses of the past 5 years in regard to tobacco products: 130 million EUR (2014); 120 million EUR (2015);

Table 13 Amount of confiscated cigarettes by custom investigation service (Zollfahndungsdienst) from 2010 to 2018[a]

Year	Cigarettes/piece	Tobacco/kg
2010	156,958,482	14,536
2011	145,040,585	15,579
2012	132,473,470	1,719
2013	135,623,466	22,760
2014	126,138,076	5,274
2015	68,226,603	1,013
2016	121,357,257	150,604
2017	77,132,481	96,017
2018	61,845,268	404,481

[a]Figures provided by Generalzolldirektion – Zollkriminalamt, Fachgebiet B.322 (Bekämpfung der Tabakwarenkriminalität)

Table 14 Additional tax revenue in million EUR due to investigations by tax investigation department (Steuerfahndung) from 2002 to 2017[a]

Year	Additional tax revenue in million EUR
2002	1,540.9
2003	1,628.7
2004	1,613.4
2005	1,658.0
2006	1,433.6
2007	1,603.8
2008	1,474.5
2009	1,565.8
2010	1,745.7
2011	2,228.6
2012	3,079.6
2013	2,051.2
2014	2,451.2
2015	3,025.3
2016	3,179.7
2017	2,897.9

[a]Statista, Steuermehreinnahmen in Folge von Ermittlungen der Steuerfahndung in Deutschland von 2002 bis 2017 (in Millionen Euro), https://de.statista.com/statistik/daten/studie/257517/umfrage/anzahl-der-abgeschlossenen-ermittlungen-der-steuerfahndung/ (as of 15 May 2019)

73 million EUR (2016); 89 million EUR (2017); 28 million EUR (first 9 months of 2018).[155]

[155]See BT-Drucksache 19/6644 (n 146).

Table 15 Investigated tax loss from 2010 to 2018[a]

Year	Investigated tax losses in EUR
2010	153.798.581
2011	102.186.648
2012	93,4 Mio.
2013	174,7 Mio.
2014	121.216.538
2015	114.968.018
2016	56.994.476
2017	81.816.215
2018	37.781.680

[a]Figures provided by Generalzolldirektion—Zollkriminalamt, Fachgebiet B.322 (Bekämpfung der Tabakwarenkriminalität)

3.4 Exemplary Cases

On March 13, 2018, customs discovered 10.4 million cigarettes in a refrigerated truck during a check on the harbor city of Kiel's eastern shore. They were hidden behind cargo (ice). The truck from Estonia should have contained frozen fish. If the cigarettes had been sold in Germany, the treasury would have lost about two million EUR.[156]

Five prosecuted members of gang were convicted for gang and commercial smuggling of cigarettes.[157] On the basis of the joint plan they carried at least 76,500 kg of smoking tobacco ("fine cut" of processed tobacco, which can be used without significant intermediate steps for cigarette production), with the incorrect declaration as "tobacco waste" from April to June 2005 via Antwerp into the European Union. It was used for the illegal production of cigarettes in Greece. As a result, import duties of around 424,000 euros were evaded. Also, from July 2005 to February 2011 the gang imported smoking tobacco declared as "tobacco waste" via Klaipeda (Lithuania) to the European Union. As a result, import duties of more than EUR 45 million were withdrawn. The non-duty-paid and untaxed smoking tobacco was used by the group for illegal cigarette production in Poland and Moldova. Their profit from the sale of only the cigarettes produced in Poland between the beginning of 2006 and July 2010 amounted to approximately 54 million euros.

In the so-called "Hydra" case two Joint Investigation Teams (JITs) were set up between the Hanover Customs Office and the customs authorities in Athens and Thessaloniki on the basis of the Naples II Agreement.[158] These joint investigations required a large number of meetings between the investigators and the implementation of covert action in Greece. In the course of the procedure, OLAF therefore supported this investigation with the financing of flights and provided surveillance

[156]Norddeutscher Rundfunk (2018).

[157]Bundesgerichtshof (BGH) *Selbstgeldwäsche* (2018) 5 StR 234/18, NJW 2019, 533.

[158]Koziolek (2015a), p. 211. See also with more details and on the previous case "Boomerang" Koziolek (2015b), p. 719.

technology to the Greek authorities. As a result of intensive German-Greek investigations, including telephone surveillance measures, it was possible to secure a production facility hidden in a cow barn near Thessaloniki in 2009. A professional assessment of the machine by experts of the Customs and cigarette companies could show a connection between the plant and cigarettes seized in 23 cases throughout Europe. The total volume of cigarette counterfeiting produced on this production line was estimated at more than 300 million cigarettes.

In the so-called "woodworm" (Holzwurm) case, the perpetrators in Russia, the Baltic States, Germany and overseas had founded a large number of companies in tax havens, some of which were also used for legal freight forwarding.[159] These companies supplied wooden pallets from Russia via Austria and Germany back to the Baltic States and for this purpose issued each other with delivery notes and invoices. In fact, however, only boards prepared with cigarettes were brought to Western Europe. In the case of a single delivery check, this was hardly noticeable, since seemingly proper freight documents appeared in each case. Only an intensive examination and overall consideration of the documents revealed not only the economic folly of these transactions but also considerable discrepancies regarding individual freight times and delivery locations. Also, none of the companies involved in Western Europe had employees or storerooms for the wood. It was rather pure letterbox companies. With the support of OLAF, several meetings of the investigators were coordinated in 2010, which brought the investigations forward decisively. Investigations included day-to-day co-ordination of arrests and search warrants in a total of five European countries through mutual assistance.

3.5 *Features of Illicit Trade of Tobacco Products*

The illegal cross-border distribution covers a number of illegal activities, mainly illegal import or export of original cigarettes or counterfeit products, the purchase of unbranded, illegally manufactured products or "cheap whites" and also bootlegging.[160]

Main routes for smuggling to the Germany are the land route from Asia via eastern European countries (Baltic countries, Poland, Romania) or via south-eastern European countries (Greece, Bulgaria), by sea from Asia, the United Arab Emirates, Dubai and South America to harbors (mainly Hamburg) and by air, often used to smuggle tobacco products from within the European Union. The routes by land, by sea and partly by air change regularly dependent on the less risky way to their European destination.

[159] Koziolek (2015a), p. 211.

[160] The following information is mainly based on the reports of Maffei and Markopoulou (2014a), pp. 43 ff.; Maffei and Markopoulou (2014b), pp. 35 ff. See also Sinn (2016), pp. 51 ff.; Sinn (2018b). See also Koziolek (2015a), p. 211.

A very large number of the cigarettes smuggled to Germany are purchased on the Vietnamese markets in the Czech Republic.[161] Whereas in the past often counterfeit cigarettes from Asia were discovered in Germany in recent years more often legally produced cigarettes similar to well-known brands are found, often arriving from the United Arab Emirates, Dubai and Singapore. On the land routes cigarette smuggling is often carried out in trucks declared as empty or loaded with camouflage cargo, other methods include manipulated transit procedures, supposed travel and also the unlawful removal from a bonded warehouse or during a transit procedure.[162] Increasingly vans as smaller, quicker and more flexible vehicles are use, as the damage in cases of detection is not as high as if a truck is confiscated. At the Polish-German border also a substantial number of pedestrians smuggle cigarettes.

Retail selling occurs at different places, for example in the street, at flea markets, in public parks, near supermarkets, rarely in shops next to legal products. Germany is still one of the main destination countries for Jin Ling cigarettes. The Vietnamese cigarettes market and other Eastern European flea markets in Berlin now exist for decades, but trade places have been reduced substantially. Groups who involved in the smuggling trade are well-organized, often working together in loose criminal networks. The (street) vendors are acting very carefully and inconspicuously, which makes investigations difficult. They often only carry a small number of cigarette cartons at one time, so that only a few cartons are usually confiscated if they are detected.

The illegal market also includes the smuggling of branded products, the sale of cheapwhites, and the manufacture and sale of counterfeit cigarettes. The so-called *bootlegging* describes the purchase of cigarettes in a low-tax country, which are introduced beyond the permissible free allowance for personal use into another country usually with a higher tax rate such as Germany, and/or the imported cigarettes are resold in another country, without the on-site pay taxes due.[163]

Illicit trading of tobacco products has a close relationship to organized crime.[164] Among all tax and custom offence activities of groups involved in organized crime, they have been most engaged in illicit trade of tobacco products. Although customs and tax offences are not the main field of organized criminal activity (around 10%), customs and tax offences account for the highest amounts of losses for the treasury.[165] Especially in regard to illicit whites organized crime groups play a major role as these cigarettes are produced on industrial scale in large production sites, connected to sophisticated logistics and distribution channels.[166]

---

[161] Sinn (2018b).

[162] Müller (2018), p. 2667.

[163] Knickmeier (2016), pp. 430–431.

[164] See Sinn (2018a), pp. 17 ff.; Sinn (2018b).

[165] Bundeskriminalamt, Organisierte Kriminalität, Bundeslagebild 2017, Wiesbaden April (2018).

[166] Sinn (2018b).

3.6 Characteristics of Perpetrators of Illicit Trade of Tobacco

There is not much data available on the characteristics of perpetrators. Official statistics provide the nationality, the sexe of the perpetrator and if prior convictions exist. In regard to offenses of the AO the perpetrator is in 72% of the cases male, in 67% a German national and has in 26% of the cases a prior conviction (of any kind).[167]

Additional information stems from research studies. Perpetrators of illicit trade of tobacco can be subdivided as follows:[168] small smugglers (e.g. tourists who carry cigarettes beyond their own needs or for resale across national borders with them), smugglers in groups working together across borders without a permanent connection (and were relations are formed through family or friends or through business relationships, often with close ties to the home country) and organized smugglers organized hierarchically into well-organized and profitable networks.

The trafficking of cigarettes involves very divers actors, from private travelers to professional distributors.[169] According to a study in the 1990s on 216 offenders in Berlin, 93.4% were non-German nationals (mainly Vietnamese nationals on retail level and Polish nationals within the supply chain).[170] Only 11.7% of all suspects were women.[171] The average age was 27.[172] The offenders' previous criminal records were not of a severe nature.[173] To them, illicit trade in tobacco was more of an additional income than an alternative to legal employment.[174] The information was gathered in the city of Berlin, which implies factors that only come to play in this specific region.[175]

3.7 Trends in Illicit Trade of Tobacco Products

In the last years a significant cutback in the amount of confiscated cigarettes can be seen (see Tables 10 and 11). This goes along with a steady decrease in tobacco consumption since 2000, indicating that tobacco control policies have been successful.[176]

[167] Statistisches Bundesamt (Destatis) (2018b).
[168] Knickmeier (2016), p. 430.
[169] See von Lampe (2011), p. 151.
[170] von Lampe (2005), p. 222.
[171] von Lampe (2005), p. 222.
[172] von Lampe (2005), p. 222.
[173] von Lampe (2005), p. 222.
[174] von Lampe (2005), p. 222.
[175] von Lampe (2005), p. 221.
[176] Kuntz et al. (2017), p. 82.

In the fight against contraband legal cigarettes legal provisions for supply chain security and track-and-trace systems were successful. Yet, illicit whites evade such regulations.[177] The challenge of the fight against illicit whites is their raison d'être—namely illicit trade.[178] These cigarettes are manufactured outside legal frameworks and do not enter regulated markets. This means, that they are not subject to production standards, consumer protection regulations or tobacco regulations. Insofar, police and criminal investigations seem to be the most effective measures in that regard.

Also, the organized crime dimension has become a major factor in this regard. The globalization of organized crime and the "professionalization" of respective groups enable large-scale counterfeit and contraband of various goods, in particular easily tradeable goods such as cigarettes.[179] This means that organized crime is not just a specific form of participation in crime, but mainly an international and major threat to public security. This is especially true when established structures are used to broaden the scope of business, e.g., by also smuggling drugs or other substances. Insofar, more attention and emphasis needs to be put on the fight against structures of organized crime.

4 Preventive Measures

German prevention strategy against illicit trade of tobacco products mainly builds on criminalizing illicit tobacco trade as a tax offense and by providing the respective authorities (mainly the custom authorities) with financial and staff resources that in many aspects go beyond normal police resources.[180] Insofar the authorities already mentioned (see supra B.) in regard to repressive measures are also entrusted with the prevention of illicit trading. Yet, the main strategy in recent years is to reduce tobacco consumption as a whole and thus reduce the incentives for illicit trading because of a decreased number of consumers. Tobacco consumption is regarded as a serious health risk and legal measures limit advertising tobacco products and provide for special notifications on health risks,[181] although the German legislator is rather reluctant to proactively take measures.[182]

In order to better fight illicit trading the German legislator has transposed Regulation (EU) 2018/574, Delegated Regulation (EU) 2018/573 and Commission

[177] Sinn (2018b).

[178] Sinn (2018b).

[179] Sinn (2018b).

[180] Allen (2013).

[181] Meyer (2006), p. 217; Mons and Pötschke-Langer (2010), p. 144; Runkel, (2018), p. 232; Schaller and Mons (2018), p. 1429.

[182] See Schaller and Mons (2018), p. 1429.

Implementing Decision (EU) 2018/576 into German law in April 2019.[183] This has laid down basic rules for a system of traceability and security features by labeling tobacco products with an individual identification feature and a forgery-proof security feature. The traceability system aims to track the movement of these products so that they can be tracked across the European Union. In addition, the introduction of security features shall make it easier to verify that tobacco products are genuine.

5 Cooperation

Close cooperation between the authorities is the key element for successfully fighting illicit trade of tobacco goods. This means first hand that the custom offices at the borders and the custom investigation service have to work closely together. With the reform of the customs administration under the roof of the General Customs Directorate in 2015 steps have been taken that an effective cooperation can take place.

In regard to other authorities (such as the state and federal police offices and prosecution services) a close cooperation is especially enabled by the legal institution of administrative assistance. This institution shall enable the efficient handling of cases where tasks and powers have been distributed among different authorities. Specific aspects, especially the exchange of information are regulated explicitly in the respective legislation (e.g. §§ 6-16 ZFdG). These rules amend the basic regulations.[184] There exist also special data banks such as the custom investigation information system (Zollfahndungsinformationssystem, see § 11 ZFdG), enabling a central storage of vital information for investigations. In general, authorities questioned to provide information or help have an obligation to cooperate with the requesting authority.

As in all border cases a close cooperation with neighboring countries (such as Poland) is vital and has been intensified in recent years in regard to mutual information and assistance.[185] Especially organized crime cases cannot be conducted without investigations abroad. In regard to this cooperation with foreign countries, international institutions mainly the European ones have become indispensable:[186] Interpol, Europol, Eurojust and above all OLAF are of particular importance for

[183] Erstes Gesetz zur Änderung des Tabakerzeugnisgesetzes of 29. April 2019, BGBl. I p. 514.

[184] See art. 35 para. 1 GG (administrative assistance between federal and state authorities) as well as § 4 of the federal administrative procedure act (Bundesverwaltungsverfahrensgesetz) and the similar regulations in the state administrative procedure acts (Landesverwaltungsverfahrensgesetze).

[185] See e.g. on form of cooperation von Lampe and Zurakowska (2017), p. 403; see also Calderoni et al. (2013), pp. 49 f.

[186] Koziolek (2015b), p. 719. See also Mersmann (2015), pp. 202 ff.

anti-trafficking cases.[187] Without the logistical support of these authorities a successful fight against organized crime would not have been possible, such as the above mentioned cases show (supra C. IV.).

Weaknesses in practice exist in the areas of resources, communication, organization and technology.[188] Mobilization of personnel is often a problem in larger investigations (especially in regard to complex organized crime cases), worsened if disputes among the authorities over competencies exist.[189] Communication is often not fast or comprehensive enough, sometimes with problems because of differing technical equipment or technical standards.

6 General Aspects and Conclusion

Regulating the illicit trade of tobacco products is closely connected to the regulation of the legal market. The relationship of the markets are not exactly clear, but there is on overlap of the legal and illegal market insofar as changes in the condition of the legal market has effects on the illegal one (and to a certain extent vice versa).[190] One aspect to influence the market is taxing tobacco products. This is generally regarded to be among the most efficient instruments against tobacco consumption.[191] Insofar raising taxes reduces overall consumption as some give up smoking completely or at least reduce consumption,[192] especially in regard to vulnerable groups such as teenagers or pregnant women.[193] Besides this effect consumers refer to cheaper product or alternative tobacco products not taxed equally.[194] Referring to alternative products of course only works as long as their taxes are not raised, too.[195] In addition, to a certain extent people refer to the illegal market,[196] although it is unclear how big this effect is.[197] From a fiscal point of view the effect on raising

[187]Koziolek (2015a), p. 211.

[188]Hoser (2013), p. 8.

[189]Hoser (2013), p. 8.

[190]Mersmann (2015), p. 82.

[191]Effertz and Schlittgen (2013), pp. e95–e100; Hanewinkel and Isensee (2003a), p. 395; Hanewinkel and Isensee (2003b), p. 168; Hanewinkel and Isensee (2007), p. 26; Isensee and Hanewinkel (2004), p. 771; see also Bräuninger and Stiller (2010), p. 21.

[192]Hanewinkel and Isensee (2005), pp. 9, 13; Schwarz (2009), p. 235.

[193]Richter and Klopprogge (2018), p. 400.

[194]Schwarz (2009), p. 235.

[195]Schwarz (2009), p. 235; Wigger (2011), pp. 39–40.

[196]Groneberg and Haustein (2008), p. 646; Schwarz (2009), p. 235.

[197]Major effects are seen by Bräuninger and Stiller (2010). No effect see: Effertz and Schlittgen (2013). See also Mersmann (2015), pp. 91 ff. on the complex relationship between tax and illegal market, that has not been taken into account in major studies (ibid 187–198), concluding that in some cases tax increases can also reduce illegal market activities.

taxes is quite neutral.[198] From a criminal law/policy perspective the effect on the illegal market is at least not substantial (if not even neglectable).[199] There is no general substitution effect of smokers turning from consumption of legal cigarettes to smuggled ones. Insofar higher taxes are a suitable element in reducing tobacco consumption and do not foster a major criminal market.[200] Altogether, the existing German tobacco tax regime is quite successful in achieving several (tax) aims simultaneously: falling consumption with steady tax revenues and also a tackling the consumption of non-domestic taxed tobacco, especially smuggled goods.[201]

Nonetheless, there is an illegal market and tax changes may have some minor effects on it, so that illicit trade of tobacco products needs to be addressed by the legislator. Current German legislation with its criminal and administrative offenses insofar appears to cover the phenomena sufficiently. In practice, the fight against smuggling with intensified efforts in recent years, has been more successful than years before.[202] For the future a constant high level of controls in border regions is necessary in order to continue this successful path, what also means in lack of institutionalized border controls within the EU/Schengen area that alternative control mechanism have to developed further. Special attention has to be put to organized crime, although this is no specific problem of illicit trade in tobacco products. Insofar, the coordination of custom authorities with their special focus on taxes and customs and general police and prosecution authorities (covering the general phenomena of organized crime) could be improved especially when organized crime groups cover several areas of business (from tobacco trading over counterfeiting other products to smuggling drugs and persons), some of them also partly legal.[203] Also, international cooperation should be improved in order to allow timely cross-border investigations.[204] The legislator could involve tobacco producers and sellers more in compliance efforts, but should refrain from further integrating them into law enforcement efforts as long as there is a suspicion of them being involved in such illegal activities.[205]

---

[198] Schwarz (2009), p. 242.

[199] A pure speculation (and not empirically founded) is the assumption by Bräuninger and Stiller (2010), pp. 21–22 that the expansion of the consumption of cigarettes not taxed has a self-reinforcing effect insofar as a higher proportion of illegal cigarettes increases the acceptance of consumptions. Vice versa decreases the illegality of a certain behavior its general social acceptance.

[200] Effertz and Schlittgen (2013); Groneberg and Haustein (2008), pp. 646–647.

[201] See Steidl and Wigger (2018), p. 331 seeing even a decrease in smuggled goods and pointing out that is central that the tax allows for a differentiation so that a price differential arises between high and low price cigarettes and fine-cuts taxation does not come close to cigarette taxation as in this way, low-priced cigarettes and fine cuts remain an alternative to non-domestically-taxed cigarettes (and also promote supplier competition and product diversity).

[202] Only see Steidl and Wigger (2018), p. 321 who state that the proportion of smuggled cigarettes has dropped since 2009. More cautios is the evaluation by Calderoni et al. (2013), pp. 45 ff.

[203] For the importance of cooperation see also Calderoni et al. (2013), pp. 81, 85.

[204] Hoser (2013), p. 4.

[205] See e.g. Richter and Klopprogge (2018), p. 400; Evans-Reeves et al. (2015), pp. e168–e177.

In order to further address the problem of illicit trading tobacco products harmonizing taxes (and selling prices) within the European Union could reduce cross-border-shopping and also smuggling activities.[206] A larger effect would be achieved by generally reducing consumption, what equally affects the legal and illegal market. In this regard health measures are of great importance.[207] Banning smoking in public places (such as restaurants), restricting advertising and sponsoring and increasing awareness in regard to the risk of smoking have helped reducing consumption and as consequence the legal and illegal market already substantially, although Germany's efforts are not more than average.[208] Insofar, further public health legislation would probably be the most effective measure to address this specific criminal phenomenon.

References

Adams M, Effertz T (2011) Tabaksteuern, Schmuggel und unversteuerte Zigaretten: Zur Glaubwürdigkeit der "Entsorgungsstudie" der Tabakindustrie. Gesundheitswesen 73 (10):705–712

Allen E (2013) Illegaler Handel mit Tabakprodukten: und wie man ihn bekämpft. International Tax and Investment Center, Almaty

Bauer C (2018) Praktische Fragen im Zusammenhang mit dem organisierten "Schmuggel" von Tabakwaren. NZWiSt (Neue Zeitschrift für Wirtschafts-Steuer- und Unternehmensstrafrecht):85–90

Bender P (2001) Rechtsfragen um den Transitschmuggel mit Zigaretten. wistra (wistra-Zeitschrift für Wirtschafts- und Steuerstrafrecht):161–167

Bender P (2006) Der EuGH und das Zollstrafrecht. wistra (wistra-Zeitschrift für Wirtschafts- und Steuerstrafrecht):41–45

Bittmann F (2010) Telefonüberwachung im Steuerstrafrecht und Steuerhinterziehung als Vortat der Geldwäsche seit dem 1-1-2008. wistra (wistra-Zeitschrift für Wirtschafts- und Steuerstrafrecht):125–130

Bräuninger M, Stiller S (2010) Ökonomische Konsequenzen des Konsums von nicht in Deutschland versteuerten Zigaretten. HWWI Policy Paper 1-28. Hamburgisches WeltWirtschaftsInstitut (HWWI), Hamburg

Budde S (2019) Anmerkung zu einer Entscheidung des BGH, Beschluss vom 19.12.2017 (1 StR 56/17) - Zur Strafbarkeit der neutralen Beihilfe bei Steuerstraftaten. NZWiSt (Neue Zeitschrift für Wirtschafts-Steuer- und Unternehmensstrafrecht):27–28

Bundeskriminalamt (2018) Bundeslagebild Organisierte Kriminalität 2017. https://www.bka.de/SharedDocs/Downloads/DE/Publikationen/JahresberichteUndLagebilder/OrganisierteKriminalitaet/organisierteKriminalitaetBundeslagebild2017.pdf?__blob=publicationFile&v=3. Accessed 15 May 2019

Calderoni F et al (2013) Factbook zum illegalen Handel mit Tabakerzeugnissen: Deutschland. http://www.transcrime.it/wp-content/uploads/2013/11/Germany-Factbook-on-the-ITTP-German.pdf. Accessed 15 May 2019

206 Wigger (2011), p. 40.

207 See, e.g., Wimmer (2013), pp. 111 ff.; Deutsches Krebsforschungszentrum (2010).

208 Calderoni et al. (2013), pp. 31 ff. See also the rating with Germany on 33th place among 35 European countries, https://www.tobaccocontrolscale.org/results-last-edition/.

Deimel K (2019) Art. 87 UZK. In: Dorsch E, Rüsken R (eds) Zollrecht. Recht des grenzüberschreitenden Warenverkehrs. Kommentar. Loose-leaf commentary, 161st supplementary delivery. Accessed 15 May 2019. Stollfuß, Bonn

Deutsches Krebsforschungszentrum (ed) (2010) Illegaler Zigarettenhandel und seine wirksame Bekämpfung zum Gesundheitsschutz der Bevölkerung. Deutsches Krebsforschungszentrum, Heidelberg

Effertz T, Schlittgen R (2013) Zigarettenpreise, Tabaksteuern und der Anteil an Schmuggelzigaretten in Deutschland. Gesundheitswesen 75(6):e95–e100

Evans-Reeves KA, Hatchard JL, Gilmore AB (2015) 'It will harm business and increase illicit trade': an evaluation of the relevance, quality and transparency of evidence submitted by transnational tobacco companies to the UK consultation on standardised packaging 2012. Tob Control 24(e2):e168–e177

Fehn BJ (2006) Überblick über das Steuerstrafverfahren (Zoll). In: Wamers P, Fehn BJ (eds) Handbuch Zollfahndung. Otto Schmidt, Köln. Chapter B

Fezer K-H (2009) Markenrecht. Beck'sche Kurz-Kommentare, 4th edn. Beck, München

Gallagher AWA et al (2018) Tobacco industry data on illicit tobacco trade: a systematic review of existing assessments. Tob Control:1–12. https://doi.org/10.1136/tobaccocontrol-2018-054295

Groneberg JDA, Haustein K-O (eds) (2008) Tabakabhängigkeit: Gesundheitliche Schäden durch das Rauchen, 2nd edn. Springer-Verlag, Berlin

Häberle P (2018) § 12e ZollVG. In: Erbs/Kohlhaas (ed), Strafrechtliche Nebengesetze. Loose-leaf commentary, 221 supplementary delivery (August 2018). C.H.Beck, München.

Hadamitzky A, Senge L (2018) § 370 AO. In: Erbs, Kohlhaas (eds) Strafrechtliche Nebengesetze. Loose-leaf commentary, 221st supplementary delivery (August 2018). C.H.Beck, München

Hanewinkel R, Isensee B (2003a) Der Zusammenhang zwischen Preis und Konsum von Zigaretten: Eine Analyse vorliegender Studien und Implikationen für die Tabakkontrollpolitik. In: Rumpf H-J (ed) Alkohol und Nikotin: Frühintervention, Akutbehandlung und politische Maßnahmen. Lambertus-Verlag, Freiburg im Breisgau, pp 395–411

Hanewinkel R, Isensee B (2003b) Umsetzung, Akzeptanz und Auswirkungen der Tabaksteuererhöhung in Deutschland vom 1.Januar 2002. SUCHT 49(3):168–179

Hanewinkel R, Isensee B (2005) Umsetzung, Akzeptanz und Auswirkungen der Tabaksteuererhöhung vom 1. Dezember 2004: Untersuchung im Auftrag des Bundesministeriums für Gesundheit und Soziale Sicherung (Juli 2005)

Hanewinkel R, Isensee B (2007) Auswirkungen von Tabaksteuererhöhungen in Deutschland. Public Health Forum 15(1):26–28

Harder M (2014) Kapitel: Zoll. In: Wabnitz H-B, Janovsky T (eds) Handbuch des Wirtschafts- und Steuerstrafrechts, 4th edn. Beck, München, p 22

Hefendehl R (2015) 263 StGB. In: Joecks W, Schmitz R (eds) Münchener Kommentar zum Strafgesetzbuch, 2nd edn. Beck, München

Heuel I (2016) § 378 AO. In: Kohlmann G (ed) Steuerstrafrecht §§ 377-412 AO. Loose-leaf commentary, 54th supplementary delivery (April 2016). Otto Schmidt, Köln

Hilgers-Klautzsch B (2017) § 375 AO. In: Kohlmann G (ed) Steuerstrafrecht: Kommentar zu den §§ 369 - 412 AO 1977. Otto Schmidt, Köln

Hoser M (2013) Bekämpfung der Organisierten Kriminalität: Unter besonderer Berücksichtigung der Rolle des Zigarettenschmuggels. Tagungsbericht, Bildungszentrum Wildbad Kreuth 13. bis 15 November 2013, Hanns-Seidel-Stiftung. https://www.hss.de/fileadmin/media/downloads/Berichte/131113_TB_Kriminalitaet.pdf. Accessed 15 May 2019

Isensee B, Hanewinkel R (2004) Evaluation der Tabaksteuererhöhung vom 1. Januar 2003 (2004). Bundesgesundheitsblatt - Gesundheitsforschung - Gesundheitsschutz 47(8):771–779

Jäger M (2000) Voraussetzungen der Strafbarkeit von Bankangestellten wegen Beihilfe zur Steuerhinterziehung durch Mithilfe beim anonymen Kapitaltransfer von Kunden. wistra (wistra-Zeitschrift für Wirtschafts- und Steuerstrafrecht):344–348

Jäger M (2009) Die Auswirkungen der Osterweiterung der Europäischen Union auf das deutsche Steuerstrafrecht. In: Böse M, Sternberg-Lieben D (eds) Grundlagen des

Straf- undStrafverfahrensrechts. Festschrift für Knut Amelung zum 70. Geburtstag. Duncker & Humblot GmbH, Berlin, pp 447–472
Jäger M (2015) § 370 AO. In: Joecks W, Jäger M, Randt K (eds) Steuerstrafrecht: Mit Zoll- und Verbrauchsteuerstrafrecht; Kommentar §§ 369 - 412 AO, § 32 ZollVG, 8th edn. C.H. Beck, München
Jäger M (2017) Aus der Rechtsprechung des Bundesgerichtshofs zum Steuerstrafrecht: Teil 2/2. NStZ (Neue Zeitschrift für Strafrecht):517–523
Jäger M (2018) § 370 AO. In: Gersch E-M et al (eds) Abgabenordnung: Einschließlich Steuerstrafrecht, 14th edn. C.H. Beck, München
Knickmeier S (2016) Der Zigarettenschmuggel, das Recht und die Moral. In: Neubacher F, Bögelein N (eds) Krise - Kriminalität – Kriminologie. Forum Verlag Godesberg GmbH, Mönchengladbach, pp 429–439
Koziolek M (2015a) Zigarettenschmuggel. Kriminalistik:211–217
Koziolek M (2015b) Zigarettenschmuggel und Organisierte Kriminalität: Ein positives Beispiel deutsch-griechischer Zusammenarbeit. Kriminalistik:719–726
KPMG (2017) Project SUN: a study of the illicit cigarette market in the European Union, Norway and Switzerland 2017 results
Krause DM, Prieß H-J (2014) § 34 Zollstrafrecht. In: Volk K (ed) Münchener Anwalts-Handbuch Verteidigung in Wirtschafts- und Steuerstrafsachen, 2nd edn. C.H. Beck, München
Küchenhoff B (2018) Strafbares Entziehen aus der zollamtlichen Überwachung - die Renaissance des Verbotsbannbruchs. NZWiSt (Neue Zeitschrift für Wirtschafts-Steuer- und Unternehmensstrafrecht):90–95
Kuntz B et al (2017) Zeitliche Entwicklung des Absatzes von Tabakwaren in Deutschland. J Health Monit:82–89
Kutschke P (2018) § 143a MarkenG. In: Kur A, von Bomhard V, Albrecht F (eds) Markenrecht: Markengesetz, Verordnung über die Unionsmarke (UMV): Kommentar, 2nd edn. C.H. Beck, München
Land Nordrhein-Westfalen (2013) Entwurf eines Gesetzes zur Einführung der strafrechtlichen Verantwortlichkeit von Unternehmen und sonstigen Verbänden. https://www.landtag.nrw.de/portal/WWW/dokumentenarchiv/Dokument/MMI16-127.pdf. Accessed 15 May 2019
Leitner W et al (eds) (2017) Wirtschafts- und Steuerstrafrecht. Nomos, Baden-Baden
Lenz J (2006) Datenschutz. In: Wamers P, Fehn BJ (eds) Handbuch Zollfahndung. Otto Schmidt, Köln. Chapter C
Linke H-D (2004) Das Zollkriminalamt: Eine geheimnisvolle, unsichtbare und mächtige Strafverfolgungsbehörde? Lang, Frankfurt am Main
Maffei S, Markopoulou L (2014a) FIDUCIA - New European crimes and trust-based policy, vol 2. ISBN 978-618-81128-4-1
Maffei S, Markopoulou L (2014b) FIDUCIA - New European crimes and trust-based policy, vol 3. ISBN 978-618-81128-8-9
Mersmann H (2015) Die ökonomische Analyse des Zigarettenschmuggels. Dissertation, Universität Hamburg.
Meyer K (2006) Takakprävention. Prävention und Gesundheitsförderung 1(4):217–218
Mons U, Pötschke-Langer M (2010) Gesetzliche Maßnahmen zur Tabakprävention. Bundesgesundheitsblatt - Gesundheitsforschung - Gesundheitsschutz 53(2):144–151
Müller V (2018) Zigarettenschmuggel. In: Möllers HW, Kastner M (eds) Wörterbuch der Polizei, 3rd edn. Beck, München, pp 2667–2668
Norddeutscher Rundfunk (2018) Bislang größter Zigarettenschmuggel aufgeflogen (18 April 2018). https://www.ndr.de/nachrichten/schleswig-holstein/Bislang-groesster-Zigarettenschmuggel-aufgeflogen,zoll818.html. Accessed May 2019
Retemeyer A, Möller T (2015) Kapitel 20: Zölle und Marktordnungen. In: Adick M, Bülte J (eds) Fiskalstrafrecht: Straftaten gegen staatliche Vermögenswerte. Müller, Heidelberg, pp 554–597

Richter UH, Klopprogge M (2018) Unternehmensverantwortung in der Tabakindustrie: Strategische Herausforderungen und Lösungsansätze. In: Bungard P (ed) CSR und Geschäftsmodelle. Springer, Berlin, pp 393–406
Runkel K (2018) Stolpersteine der Tabakwerbung. IPRB (Der IP-Rechts-Berater):232–235
Schaller K, Mons U (2018) Tabakprävention in Deutschland und international. Bundesgesundheitsblatt - Gesundheitsforschung - Gesundheitsschutz 61(11):1429–1438
Schlagowski J (2018) Originäre Verbandsstrafbarkeit. Nomos, Baden-Baden
Schmitz R, Wulf M (2015) 370 AO. In: Joecks W, Schmitz R (eds) Münchener Kommentar zum Strafgesetzbuch, 2nd edn. Beck, München
Schwarz P (2009) Optionen einer rationalen Regulierung des Tabakkonsums: Die Vorteile eines liberalen Paternalismus. Perspektiven der Wirtschaftspolitik 10(2):235–251
Sinn A (2016) Organisierte Kriminalität 3.0. Springer, Berlin
Sinn A (2018a) Wirtschaftsmacht Organisierte Kriminalität: Illegale Märkte und illegaler Handel. Springer, Berlin
Sinn A (2018b) The link between illicit tobacco trade and organised crime (Fighting illicit tobacco, European Commission, Brussels, 23 March 2018). https://www.eesc.europa.eu/en/news-media/presentations/link-between-illicit-tobacco-trade-and-organised-crime. Accessed 15 May 2019
Statistisches Bundesamt (Destatis) (2018a) Rechtspflege: Staatsanwaltschaften: Fachserie 10 Reihe 2.6
Statistisches Bundesamt (Destatis) (2018b) Rechtspflege: Strafverfolgung: Fachserie 10 Reihe 3
Steidl F, Wigger BU (2018) Optimale Besteuerung von Tabakwaren. List Forum für Wirtschafts- und Finanzpolitik 44(3):311–333
Stoklosa M (2016) Is the illicit cigarette market really growing?: The tobacco industry's misleading math trick. Tob Control 25(3):360–361
Streinz R (2017) "Gutachten zur Frage der Verpflichtung der Bundesrepublik Deutschland aus Artikel 13 des Rahmenübereinkommens der WHO zur Eindämmung des Tabakgebrauchs (FCTC) zum Erlass der im Entwurf eines Gesetzes zur Änderung des Tabakgesetzes vorgesehenen Ausweitung der Werbeverbote und –beschränkungen für Tabakerzeugnisse und verwandte Erzeugnisse, soweit Verfassungsrecht nicht entgegensteht" (of 27 September 2017), https://www.bmel.de/SharedDocs/Downloads/Ernaehrung/Gesundheit/Tabakrichtlinie/Gutachten_BMEL_Art13_FCTC.pdf?__blob=publicationFile. Accessed 15 May 2019
Taschowsky P (2015) Illegale Aktivitäten in den Volkswirtschaftlichen Gesamtrechnungen: Möglichkeiten und Grenzen der Erfassung von Zigarettenschmuggel und Drogen. WISTA (Wirtschaft und Statistik):28–41
von Lampe K (2005) Explaining the emergence of the cigarette black market in Germany. In: van Duyne PC (ed) The organised crime economy: managing crime markets in Europe. Wolf Legal Publication, Nijmegen, pp 209–229
von Lampe K (2011) The illegal cigarette trade. In: Natarajan M (ed) International crime and justice. Cambridge University Press, Cambridge, pp 148–154
von Lampe K, Zurakowska A (2017) German-polish cross-border police cooperation: the many faces of crime for profit and ways of tackling it. In: van Duyne PC et al (eds) The many faces of crime for profit and ways of tackling it. Wolf Legal Publishers, Nijmegen, pp 403–423
Wachner P (2006) AWG/KWKG/CWÜ. In: Wamers P, Fehn BJ (eds) Handbuch Zollfahndung. Otto Schmidt, Köln. Chapter H
Weerth C (2018) Bekämpfung des Verbrauchsteuerschmuggels mit § 12e ZollVG, BDZ-Fachteil 4/2018: F19-F20. https://www.econstor.eu/bitstream/10419/177388/1/Weerth_Verbrauchsteuerschmuggel_BDZ-Fachteil_4_2018.pdf. Accessed 15 May 2019
Wegner C (2015a) § 372 AO. In: Joecks W, Schmitz R (eds) Münchener Kommentar zum Strafgesetzbuch, 2nd edn. Beck, München
Wegner C (2015b) § 375 AO. In: Joecks W, Schmitz R (eds) Münchener Kommentar zum Strafgesetzbuch, 2nd edn. Beck, München

Weidemann J (2014) Anmerkung zu EuGH, Urteil vom 03.07.2014 – Rs. C-165/13: Steuerschuldnerschaft bei Tabaksteuer. wistra (wistra-Zeitschrift für Wirtschafts- und Steuerstrafrecht):433–434

Weidemann J (2017) § 370 Abs. 1 Nr. 3 AO im funktionalen Zusammenhang mit dem Erklärungsdelikt des § 370 Abs. 1 Nr. 2 AO. wistra (wistra-Zeitschrift für Wirtschafts- und Steuerstrafrecht):136–140

Weidemann J (2018) Tabaksteuerstrafrecht: Die Tabaksteuer als harmonisierte Verbrauchsteuer. https://www.jura.rub.de/sites/default/files/2018-06/Tabaksteuerstrafrecht_OnlineVersion.pdf. Accessed 15 May 2019

Weidemann J, Weidemann A (2005) Handeln und Unterlassen im Steuerstrafrecht: Warum der Begehungstatbestand der Steuerhinterziehung (§ 370 Abs. 1 Nr. 1 AO) fast leer läuft. wistra (wistra-Zeitschrift für Wirtschafts- und Steuerstrafrecht):207–211

Wigger BU (2011) Zur schrittweisen Erhöhung der Tabaksteuer. Wirtschaftsdienst 91(1):39–41

Wimmer T (2013) Rauchen, ein ganz normales Konsumverhalten? Perspektiven und Analysen zur Erklärung des Zigarettenkonsums. Springer VS, Wiesbaden

Wirth J-C (2005) Verdachtslose Ermittlungen nach Zollverwaltungsgesetz. Lang, Frankfurt am Main

Zieschang F (2014) Das Verbandsstrafgesetzbuch. GA (Goltdammer's Archiv für Strafrecht):91–106

Zoll (2019) Pflichtverstöße, die das Verbringen betreffen - Art. 79 Abs. 1 a) UZK. https://www.zoll.de/DE/Fachthemen/Zoelle/Zollschuldentstehung/Pflichtverstoesse-Verbringen/pflichtverstoesse-verbringen_node.html. Accessed 15 May 2019

Marc Engelhart currently holds a deputy professorship for criminal law and digitalization at the Ludwig-Maximilians-University Munich (winter term 2019/20 and summer term 2020). He is also a senior researcher at the Max Planck Institute for the Study of Crime, Security and Law in Freiburg i. Br. (Germany) where he is head of the section for business and economic criminal law and of the Max Planck Research Group on "The Architecture of Public Security Regulation". His main research focus is on business and economic criminal law, European and international criminal law, the law of criminal procedure, security studies and comparative criminal law.

The Italian National Legal Framework Related to Illicit Trade in Tobacco Products

Daniele Negri

Contents

Abstract The chapter firstly examines the Italian legal background in the field of illicit trade of tobacco products, both in a substantive and procedural criminal law perspective, highlighting the complexity of the normative scenario and trying to identify the main existing best practices. Empirical data referred to the level of asset recovery in the fight against illicit trade of tobacco are also provided, as well as with regard to the main criminological aspects of smuggling cases investigated and prosecuted in Italy.

Finally, the author presents his conclusion by highlighting the theoretical adequacy of the national legal framework in ensuring effective instruments for contrasting the illegal trade of tobacco products, but also underlining the lack of stable communicative channels for the exchange of information between the public authorities involved.

D. Negri (✉)
University of Ferrara, Department of Law, Ferrara, Italy
e-mail: daniele.negri@unife.it

C. Nowak (ed.), *Combatting Illicit Trade on the EU Border*,
https://doi.org/10.1007/978-3-030-51019-0_4

1 Substantive Law Issues

In general terms, the Italian national legal framework related to the illicit trade in tobacco products appears to be quite complex, being characterized by old and heterogeneous sources, amended by subsequent normative changes, which make it often difficult to individuate the specific provisions applicable to each particular case. Historically, the provisions dedicated to combatting the illicit trade in tobacco products are mainly the result of the implementation of supranational obligations. This might suggest that—differently from other criminal acts, such as drug trafficking—the phenomenon is not regarded too seriously by the national legislator.[1]

The illicit trade in tobacco products is punished in Italy on two levels: criminal and administrative sanctions might be applicable depending on the seriousness of the offence.

Firstly, it must be stressed that all criminal offences only punished by fine have been recently decriminalised by legislative decree n. 8/2016. For this reason, many violations originally regarded as criminal are now qualified as merely administrative breaches.[2]

More particularly, coming to the analysis of the relevant provisions, Law n. 907 of 17 July 1942 regulates illicit trade in national tobacco products.

Article 64 of the aforementioned Law prohibits the conduct of growing tobacco plants without the prescribed authorisations. The same article prohibits the manufacturing, preparation and sale of tobacco and its derivates without the State's authorisation.

Article 65 forbids the introduction into the State's territory of tobacco products in violation of provisions established by law.

Finally, Art. 66 punishes whoever carries, holds, sells or simply handles illicit national tobacco products.

As said, after the decriminalisation effected by legislative decree n. 8/2016, most of these violations are now considered as administrative offences, punished with only a fine. However, the sanctions remain substantially unchanged. According to Art. 75 et seq. of Law n. 907/1942 and Art. 1 of Law n. 27 of 3 January 1957, all these crimes are punished with a financial penalty depending on the relevant quantity of illicit tobacco (from €387 to €1162 for each kg). However, due to Art. 1, par. 6 of legislative decree n. 8/2016, the fine imposed for such breaches cannot be lower than €5000 nor greater than €50,000.

By contrast, illicit trade in national tobacco products above the quantity of 15 kg still constitutes a criminal offence, punished with imprisonment of up to 2 years in addition to the aforementioned financial penalty.

Even the illicit trade of tobacco under 15 kg committed by someone who has already been convicted for smuggling offences—even if not related to tobacco

[1]For a general overview of the criminal provisions applicable, Cerqua and Pricolo (2002), p. 1072 f.; Velani (2002), p. 659 f.; Scafati (2013).

[2]Bolis (2016), p. 1 f.

products—still constitutes a criminal offence, punished with a fine determined as above and detention of up to 6 months. The detention is furthermore increased from half to two-thirds of the penalty if a repeat offender commits another violation (Art. 82 of Law n. 907/1942).

At the same time, aggravated illicit trade in tobacco pursuant to Art. 81 of Law n. 907 of 17 July 1942 is punished with a fine and imprisonment from 6 months to 3 years—and thus still constitutes a criminal offence—when:

(a) the culprit was armed;
(b) three or more culprits obstructed police activities;
(c) the offence is connected with other crimes against public faith or public administration;
(d) the offence has been committed by participants in a criminal association of illicit traders.

All the crimes described are punishable only if intentional. On the other hand, administrative breaches are punishable if consciousness and willingness of the negligent conduct is ascertained, locating the burden of proof for the lack of responsibility on the perpetrator.[3]

Article 87 of Law n. 907/1942 imposes mandatory confiscation of the instruments used to commit violations constituting criminal offences, and of the object, the product and the income of such unlawful acts. During criminal proceedings the same items may also be seized.

Illicit trade in foreign tobacco products is regulated in Presidential Decree n. 43 of 23 January 1973 (so-called customs law).[4] These provisions are deemed to be applicable also to the so-called "cheap white" cigarettes (or "illicit whites"), that is, cigarettes legally produced outside the EU by authorised manufacturers but with low quality standards.

In order to apply the provisions of Presidential Decree n. 43/1973, the foreign tobacco products must be materially introduced into the State's territory, even if only temporarily (see Court of Cassation, III criminal division, n. 7619/2012).

According to the customs law, the introduction into the State's territory, the sale, the transportation and the possession of foreign tobacco products whose excise duties have not been properly paid is punished with a fine of €5.16 for each gram of tobacco (Art. 291 *bis*, par. 2).

If the quantity of illicit tobacco is below 10 kg, the violation constitutes an administrative breach, and the fine imposed cannot be lower than €5000 nor greater than €50,000.

If the quantity is above 10 kg, the conduct constitutes a criminal offence, and imprisonment between 2 and 5 years is applied in addition to the aforementioned fine (Art. 291 *bis*, par. 1, of Presidential Decree n. 43/1973).

---

[3]See, among others, Court of Cassation, civil section n. III, n. 26306/17.

[4]Di Paola (2012), p. 575 f.

Illicit trade under 10 kg committed by a repeat offender constitutes a criminal offence punished with a fine and imprisonment of up to 1 year (Art. 296).

Article 291 *ter* contains some aggravating circumstances of the conduct of illicit trade described by Art. 291 *bis*. Namely, the fine increases to €25.82 per gram and imprisonment from 3 to 7 years is applied if:

(a) the culprit holds weapons while committing the crime;
(b) after committing the crime, the culprit with two or more persons obstructed police activities;
(c) the offence is connected with other crimes against public faith or public administration;
(d) special means of transport were used;
(e) legal persons or money coming from States which did not ratify the Convention on Laundering, Search, Seizure and Confiscation of the Proceeds made in Strasbourg on the 8/11/1990 were used in committing the crime.

Finally, Art. 291 *quater* of Presidential Decree n. 43/1973 punishes the promotion, constitution, direction, organisation and financing of a criminal organisation of three or more persons for the commission of the offences described in Art. 291 *bis*. The penalty established is one of imprisonment from 3 to 8 years. The mere participation in such organisations is punished by 1 to 6 years of imprisonment. If the organisation owns weapons or if the circumstances described by Art. 291 *ter* d) or e) are present, the imprisonment is from 5 to 15 years, and 4 to 10 years for mere participation in the organisation.

All the crimes described are punishable only if intentional. By contrast, administrative breaches are punishable if consciousness and willingness of the conduct is ascertained, locating the burden of proof for the lack of responsibility on the perpetrator (Court of Cassation, civil section n. III, n. 26306/17).

According to Art. 338 of the Customs Law, excise duty for illicitly traded tobacco must be paid in any case in addition to the financial penalty, except if the goods were seized.

Article 301 of the Customs Law provides for mandatory confiscation of the articles used to commit violations constituting criminal offences and of the object, the product or the income of such unlawful acts. Additionally, vehicles used for smuggling activities are subject to mandatory confiscation. It is worth noting that this kind of confiscation is substantially harsher than ordinary criminal confiscation established by Art. 240 C.P., which only establishes the *possibility* of confiscating the same goods considered by Art. 301.

Article 3 of Law n. 92/2001 states that when confiscation of tobacco products ordered by a judicial authority becomes definitive, the same judicial authority orders its destruction, taking one or more samples of the goods destroyed. Such samples can be passed to national or foreign producers for analytical verification. According to Art. 301 *bis* of the Customs Law, vehicles seized or confiscated can be turned over to police forces or other public entities, and used for law enforcement, environmental protection or civil protection activities; otherwise, they are destroyed.

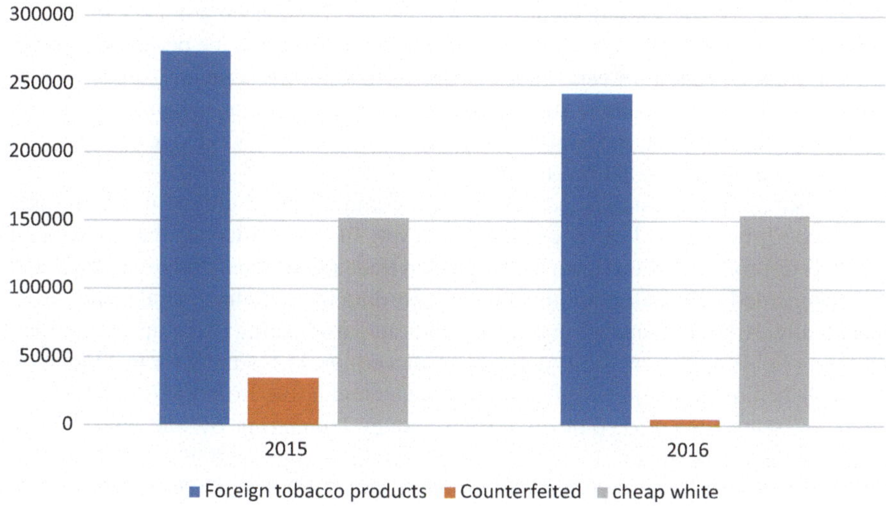

Fig. 1 Kg of tobacco seized by the Guardia di Finanza in years 2015 and 2016, source Guardia di Finanza

Article 2, par. 7 of Law n. 92/2001 provides that administrative confiscation of illicit tobacco products must be always ordered in the event of breaches of the relevant provisions.

The quantity of seized/confiscated tobacco products in Italy appears to be quite large. The level of asset recovery by Guardia di Finanza from illicit trade in tobacco products for the years 2015–2016 is shown by Fig. 1.

The same data related to the activities of the National Customs Agency (A.A.M.S.) show for year 2017 the seizure of 71,455 kg of tobacco, corresponding to 1,899,979 packs of cigarettes.[5]

In addition to the provisions specifically related to illicit trade, other norms also should be considered.

If the standard of tobacco products does not meet the minimum requirements set out by EU directive n. 2014/40, implemented in Italy by legislative decree n. 6/2016, the manufacturer and the importer are indeed subject to the administrative financial sanctions established by Art. 25 of the aforementioned legislative decree, from €30,000 to €150,000. The administrative sanction from €500 to €5000 is in the same case applicable against the retailer of such products. An administrative breach occurs only if the conduct does not constitute a crime. Administrative sanctions from €20,000 to €120,000 are also applicable if the manufacturer or the importer do not respect the provisions regarding information and labelling of tobacco products.

Illicit trade in tobacco might raise fiscal responsibility issues. Beside the evasion of excise duties, punished as above according to Law n. 907/1942 or Presidential

[5]See "Yearly Report of the Agency for 2017", p. 41, at: https://www.adm.gov.it/portale/documents/20182/536133/ADMLibroBlu-2017-v2.pdf/0c4b31c2-46c9-4473-b5a5-b792a32da6ea.

Decree n. 43/1973 depending on the origin of the goods, tobacco products are indeed subject to VAT, and thus, if the relevant rules are not observed, the perpetrator might be subject to the sanctions established by law. The relevant breaches can be merely administrative (see legislative decree n. 471/1997) or criminal, when no VAT tax return is submitted (Art. 5, legislative decree n. 74/2000), or VAT over €250,000 is not duly paid (Art. 10 *ter* d.lgs. n. 74/2000).

No specific link is established between the commission of unlawful acts in trade in tobacco products and other crimes. However, in general terms, the disposal of products or profits deriving from illicit tobacco trade (as from any other criminal act) can be regarded as an autonomous offence according to the Italian Penal Code. More specifically, Art. 648 punishes one who—without participating in the upstream illicit activity—holds money or goods deriving from a crime. The penalty for this violation is established as imprisonment from 2 to 6 years and a fine from €516 to €10,329.

At the same time, Art. 648 *bis* forbids money laundering by one who did not participate in the upstream illicit activities. In this case, the sanction is imprisonment between 4 and 12 years, together with a fine from €5000 to €25,000.

The mere use in economic or financial activities of money or goods deriving from criminal acts is also punished by Art. 648 *ter* and Art. 648 *ter*.1. If the perpetrator did not take part in the upstream illicit activity, the penalty is established as imprisonment between 4 and 12 years and a fine from €5000 to €25,000. If the culprit participated in the crime which generated the profit, the sanction for money laundering depends on the seriousness of the upstream criminal activity. Generally, the punishment is determined as imprisonment between 2 and 8 years with a fine from €5000 to €25,000. If the upstream crime is punished by not more than a maximum of 5 years imprisonment, the sanction is imprisonment from 1 to 4 years and a fine from €2500 to €12,500.

Criminological surveys show that the incomes derived from illicit tobacco trade are usually an important financing source for criminal organisations, including mafia-type groups and terrorist organisations. However, no specific legal provision exists to sanction these kinds of conduct.

Italian statutory law does not explicitly deal with the problem of the relation between criminal and administrative responsibility. More particularly, the principle of *ne bis in idem* between the two types of sanctions is not formally enshrined in legal sources, and Italian courts are traditionally reluctant to recognize this rule. However, in 2014, the European Court of Human Rights, in the case *Grande Stevens v. Italy*, stated that—with a view to Art. 4 of Protocol No. 7 of the ECHR—one cannot be punished twice for the same conduct, even if one of the proceedings brought against the accused is of a formal administrative nature, but has to be regarded as substantially criminal due to the seriousness of the penalties imposed.

Afterwards, this judgment was partially overruled by another verdict of the Grand Chamber of the ECHR (*A.B. v. Norway*, 15 November 2016), in which the judges mitigated the conclusions reached in *Grande Stevens v. Italy*, stating that European rules are not violated if there is a "sufficiently closely connected in substance and in time [between the criminal and the administrative sanctions]. In other words, it must be shown that they have been combined in an integrated manner so as to form a coherent whole. This implies not only that the purposes pursued and the means used to achieve them should in essence be complementary and linked in time, but also that the possible consequences of organizing the legal treatment of the conduct concerned in such a manner should be proportionate and foreseeable for the persons affected" (§130).

This approach is adopted by the Italian Court of Cassation, which recognises the possibility of applying criminal and formally administrative sanctions for the same facts, on condition that the penalty as a whole is proportionated to the seriousness of the facts.[6] No specific case-law is available with regard to the application of the *ne bis in idem principle* in the field of sanctions against illicit tobacco trade. This is probably because administrative and criminal sanctions imposed for these illicit activities constitute alternatives depending on the quantity of tobacco illegally traded, so that no combined application of penalties for the same conduct is practically foreseeable.

No *ad hoc* provisions are established for the conduct of counterfeiting tobacco products, with the result that the general norms of Articles 473 and 474 of the Penal Code will be applicable. More specifically, Art. 473 punishes whoever counterfeits or alters trademarks or other distinctive signs of industrial products with imprisonment from 6 months to 3 years and a fine from €2500 to €25,000. The same penalties are established for one who uses altered or counterfeited trademarks. Article 474 punishes whoever introduces into the State's territory industrial products with altered trademarks or other distinctive signs with imprisonment from 1 to 4 years and fine from €3500 to €35,000. The same article also establishes imprisonment of up to 2 years and a fine of up to €20,000 for the seller of such products. Finally, Art. 474 *bis* introduces mandatory confiscation of items used to commit the crimes punished by Art. 473 and 474, and of the object, product, price and income of the offence. According to Art. 474 *bis*, par. 2 of the Penal Code, when it is impossible to effect confiscation of such goods, value confiscation can be ordered.

Article 1, par. 7 of Law n. 80/2005 establishes an administrative sanction between €500 and €10,000 for those who purchase or accept goods that, for their quality, for the condition of the seller or for their price allow one to suspect that the provisions regulating the origin and provenience of the products have been breached. Those who in any way participate in the purchase are also punished with the same sanction. When the breach is committed by an importer or by a commercial operator the sanction is from a minimum of €20,000 up to €1 million. Administrative confiscation of the purchased goods is always ordered.

With regard to criminal or even administrative responsibility of legal persons, corporate liability is established by Art. 10, par. 2 of Law n. 146/2006 only for the crime of transnational criminal association for illicit tobacco trading *ex* Art. 291 *quater* of the Customs law. According to Art. 3 of Law n. 146/2006, the association is transnational when—alternatively—the crime is committed in more

[6]Among others, Criminal Court of Cassation, ses. V, 16 July 2018, n. 45,829, in *www.penalecontemporaneo.it*, with specific regard to the market abuse sanctioning system.

than one State, if it is committed in one State but a substantial part of its organization, direction or control takes part in another State, it is involved an organized criminal group which operates in more than one State, or if it is committed in one State but has substantial effects in another State. The corporation is subject to an administrative sanction of between €103,200 and €1,549,000. Disqualification penalties for a duration of at least 1 year are also applied. These are: disqualification from social activity; suspension or revocation of public authorisations necessary to commit the offence; ban from contracting with public authorities; exclusion or revocation of financing; ban on advertising. If the sole or main scope of the corporation is the illicit trade of tobacco, it can be permanently dissolved.

More generally, the system of corporate liability in Italy is regulated by Legislative Decree n. 231/2001. Formally, this kind of responsibility is qualified as administrative by the law, however, what gives rise to the liability is the commission of a criminal offence by one of the employees of the corporation in order to benefit the legal person. In addition, pursuant to Art. 34 and Legislative Decree n. 231/2001, the accused corporation shall face a criminal trial.

However, save for the aforementioned case of transnational criminal association of illicit trade in tobacco, corporations cannot be held liable for other violations related to illicit trade in tobacco products and, in the event of breaches of the relevant provisions, only the individual (natural person) will be charged under the conditions set out by law.

Italy is a party to the WTO FCTC, having signed the Convention on 16 June 2003, later ratified by Law n. 75 of 18 March 2008. Italy did not sign the FCTC Protocol of 2012. However, the unlawful conduct described by Art. 14 of the Protocol seems to be already envisaged as illicit in the domestic system. As pointed about above, no specific corporate liability is established in Italy for illicit trade in tobacco products except for a transnational organization of illicit traders of tobacco products pursuant to Art. 291 *quater* of the Customs Law and Art. 10, par. 2 of Law n. 146/2006.

2 Procedural Law Issues

Guardia di Finanza and the National Customs Agency (A.A.M.S.) are the main authorities involved in the investigation and prosecution of illicit trade in tobacco products, and of economic-tax crimes in general.

Guardia di Finanza is a police body dependant on the Ministry of Economy, and one of the Armed Forces of the Italian State. More particularly, the Central Service for the Investigation of Organized Crime (S.C.I.C.O.) is a specialised body of the Guardia di Finanza appointed for the prevention and repression of illicit activities, including illicit trade in tobacco products.

The Guardia di Finanza has administrative and criminal competences. It acts as customs police, with the power to control and inspect persons, bags and vehicles according to Art. 19 et seq. of Presidential Decree n. 43/1973, usually through the use of scanners and x-ray devices, at least in the preliminary phase of the inspection.

In addition, the Guardia di Finanza may generally act as a criminal investigation division. In this case, the provisions of the Code of Criminal Procedure must be applied, and the personnel of the Guardia di Finanza is subject to the authority of the Public Prosecutor (Art. 59 of the Code of Criminal Procedure). However, it has some autonomous powers, especially in discovering and investigating criminal activities (Art. 55 of the Code of Criminal Procedure).

Personnel of the National Customs Agency (A.A.M.S.) is endowed with the same administrative tasks of control and inspection of persons and vehicles for the investigation of illicit trade in tobacco (Art. 19 et seq. Presidential Decree n. 43/1973). It is an administrative agency, whose investigative competence is limited to administrative breaches.

Article 325 of the Customs Law establishes that if a criminal violation is discovered, either by the Guardia di Finanza or A.A.M.S., written reports must be transmitted to the competent Public Prosecutor. By contrast, if an administrative breach is ascertained, a report will be forwarded to the Head of the Customs Office, which is the authority competent for the application of administrative sanctions (see also *infra*).

The Guardia di Finanza and A.A.M.S. operate together closely. No specific rules are present in the legal framework with regard to cooperation between the two bodies; their relationship is regulated by internal agreements, protocols and memoranda, mainly aimed at permitting access to databases and information. Offices of integrated analysis are established in the main ports of the country with the joint participation of A.A.M.S. and Guardia di Finanza. These offices conduct risk assessment activities in order to individuate the cargos to be controlled (usually through the use of x-ray scanning devices in order to reduce physical inspections) and, to this end, personnel of the Guardia di Finanza have access to the databases of the National Customs Administration.

The procedural rules for investigating and prosecuting illicit trade in tobacco depend on the nature of the relevant breach.

If administrative violations occur, the provisions applicable are those of the Legislative Decree n. 472/1997 regarding administrative sanctions for fiscal violations and, only subordinately, those of Law n. 689/1981, which regulates in general the procedure for applying administrative sanctions.[7]

In this case, the procedure is very simple. The authority competent for applying administrative sanctions is the National Customs Agency, which determines the sanction after verifications and inspections conducted according to Art. 19 et seq. of the Customs Law. The decision to apply an administrative sanction can be appealed before the Tribunal.

---

[7]Note of the A.A.M.S., 24 May 2016, n. 55,383, available on-line at: https://www.adm.gov.it/portale/documents/20182/1296686/20160524-N.55383.pdf/3c2973eb-e00b-49d6-8539-b6bab95a0383.

Alternatively, it is possible to extinguish a violation by paying a reduced fine. For violations originally regarded as criminal, but recently depenalised by Legislative Decree n. 8/2016, half of the sanction applied can be paid within 60 days of verification for breaches committed before 6 February 2016 (Art. 9, par. 5 of Legislative Decree n. 8/2016). For decriminalised offences committed after that date, it is possible to pay one-fourth of the sanction applied within 60 days of verification (Art. 16 and 17 of Legislative Decree n. 472/1997).

Article 2 of the Law n. 92/2001 establishes that offences of smuggling of tobacco products under the amount of 10 kg only punishable with financial penalties can be extinguished by paying one-tenth of the sanction within 30 days of the notification of the breach.

According to Art. 13, par. 2 of Law n. 689/1981, it is possible to seize the items subject to confiscation following the rules of the Code of Criminal Procedure (see *infra*). Due to Art. 295 *bis* of the Customs Law, confiscation *ex* Art. 301 of the things used to commit violations constituting criminal offences and of the object, the product or the income of such unlawful acts is also applicable to administrative violations.

If the offence is qualified as a crime, the general rules of the Code of Criminal Procedure must be observed. No specific procedural provisions for illicit trading or tax crimes exists in the Italian legislative system.

Given that, the investigation shall be conducted by the Public Prosecutor, who directs the activity of the criminal investigation police (in this field, mainly the Guardia di Finanza). The investigative phase lasts 6 months, prolongable for a maximum of 18 months. During this period, evidence to ascertain the violation are collected and—if they are sufficient to support the accusation—the public prosecutor must proceed with the indictment of the suspected person. During the investigation, the prosecutor—sometimes with the authorization of the judge for preliminary investigation—can engage in a wide range of activities, such as inspections, searches and seizures when there is the suspect that items related to the commission of a criminal offence are being hidden in a certain place or on someone's body. Such measures are normally ordered by the Public Prosecutor, but, in case of urgency, they can be conducted directly by the police and subsequently validated by the prosecutor. Also, telephone wiretaps can be used under conditions set out by law, namely with the authorisation of the investigative judge when there is strong evidence suggesting the commission of a crime. Even operations not explicitly taken into consideration by the Code of Criminal Procedure can be performed. These include investigations involving new technologies (such as the use of GPS tracking or video surveillance). By contrast, the use of malware for the purpose of interception of communications has been recently regulated, and it is considered always admissible for the investigation of organised crime offences, including those punished by Art. 291 *quater* of the Customs Law. However, in general terms, it is unclear if malware could be used even for real time monitoring of non-communicative activities of the target of the investigation or just for the interception of communications.

Illicit trade in tobacco products is not included in the list of offences which can be also investigated through undercover operations (Art. 9 of Law n. 146/2006).

Article 332 of Presidential decree n. 43/1973 addresses a special case of arrest of a person accused of illicit trade in foreign tobacco products, who can be arrested if his identity is not known and cannot be released until it has not been verified.

After the indictment, the trial phase is opened before the court. As a general rule, evidence collected during the investigation cannot be used against the defendant, as the Italian criminal procedure system is inspired by the adversarial model. However, that evidence which cannot be presented again at trial is usable against the accused person.

Before the trial phase, the defendant can conclude a plea with the Public Prosecutor. The agreement must be subsequently approved by the judge. In this case the penalty can be reduced by one-third.

Also, probation is generally admissible and, if the defendant respects the obligations imposed, the crime is extinguished before the term of the verdict.

Special procedural rules are established only with regard to the investigation of the crime punished by Art. 291 *quarter* of the Customs Law, that is, a criminal organisation for illicit trade in foreign tobacco products. In this case, competence for conducting the preliminary investigation is enjoyed by the district public prosecutor. At the same time, investigations can last up to 2 years instead of 18 months.[8] Special evidentiary rules are applicable in this case; namely, examination of witnesses can be admitted only if it is not possible to produce minutes of earlier examinations of the witnesses in different proceedings in the presence of the defendant, or if the examination is necessary on the basis of specific needs (Art. 190 *bis* Code of Criminal Procedure).

Special rules for the phase of execution of the sentence are established for persons convicted of the crime punishable under Art. 291 *quarter* of the Customs Law. In general, they cannot be sentenced to measures alternative to detention. Such measures may be only applied if the convicted person becomes a cooperating witness, or—if cooperation is impossible—only if the absence of any link between the convicted person and criminal organisations is demonstrated.

3 Criminological Data

Table 1 shows the number of smuggling crimes investigated in Italy for each year of reference (data are lacking from 2000 to 2005). All the provided data originates from the archives of the National Institute for Statistics.

Please be aware that the provided data refers only to criminal offences, with the exclusion of merely administrative violations, for which no statistical data appears to be available. In addition, please also note that the data refers to smuggling offences

---

[8] Also for the case of aggravated illicit trade of foreign tobacco products *ex* art. 291 *ter* letters a), d) and e) the duration of investigations is extended to 2 years.

Table 1 Number of smuggling crimes investigated in Italy per year

2006	1150
2007	1096
2008	1062
2009	1132
2010	1067
2011	1034
2012	1284
2013	1254
2014	1231
2015	1106
2016	408
2017	360

2006	1150
2007	1096
2008	1062
2009	1132
2010	1067
2011	1034
2012	1284
2013	1254
2014	1231
2015	1106
2016	408
2017	360

(table 1) - number of smuggling crimes investigated in Italy per year

Fig. 2 Amount of tax loss in million € resulting from illicit trade in tobacco products

in general, including goods different from tobacco products. Data specifically related to illicit trade in tobacco seems to be unavailable.

Figure 2 shows the amount of tax loss in million € resulting from illicit trade in tobacco products in Italy (source: "Project SUN" by KPMG, available online at: https://public.tableau.com/profile/project.sun#!/vizhome/ExecutiveSummary2017/ProjectSun-ExecutiveSummary2017?publish=yes).

Table 2 shows the number of definitive convictions for smuggling since 2000 divided into male and female offenders. All the provided data originates from the archives of the National Institute for Statistics.

Please be aware that the data provided refers only to criminal offences, with the exclusion of merely administrative violations, for which no statistical data appears to be available. In addition, please also note that the data refers to smuggling offences in general, including goods different from tobacco products.

Table 2 Number of definitive convictions for smuggling divided into male and female offenders

Sex	Male	Female	Total
Period			
2000	11,244	531	11,775
2001	8654	468	9122
2002	6323	393	6716
2003	9809	449	10,258
2004	14,494	965	15,459
2005	14,338	1108	15,446
2006	8508	557	9065
2007	3836	267	4103
2008	3990	324	4314
2009	2449	195	2644
2010	1754	163	1917
2011	1286	155	1441
2012	1284	180	1464
2013	1639	219	1858
2014	2133	216	2349
2015	2555	268	2823
2016	2017	234	2251
2017	1320	140	1714

Table 3 Number of definitive convictions for smuggling divided into male and female, foreign offenders

Sex	Male	Female	Total
Period			
2000	3401	103	3504
2001	3224	66	3290
2002	1152	25	1177
2003	1736	32	1768
2004	1973	26	1999
2005	1568	17	1585
2006	1190	20	1210
2007	994	34	1028
2008	1020	50	1070
2009	759	67	826
2010	830	95	925
2011	830	99	929
2012	747	93	840
2013	659	70	729
2014	642	85	727
2015	750	80	830
2016	691	100	791
2017	522	70	592

Table 4 Number of definitive convictions for smuggling of tobacco products divided into offenders with and without prior criminal record

	Without prior criminal record	With prior criminal record	Total
Period			
2000	435	769	1328
2001	506	925	1623
2002	350	760	1252
2003	349	619	968
2004	264	454	718
2005	285	403	738
2006	279	251	545
2007	308	254	604
2008	491	304	836
2009	619	308	969
2010	700	288	1017
2011	676	333	1099
2012	651	380	1031
2013	627	502	1129
2014	698	843	1541
2015	840	1246	2086
2016	652	996	1648
2017	475	846	1321

Table 3 shows the number of definitive convictions for smuggling since 2000, divided into male and female, for foreign offenders. All the provided data originates from the archives of the National Institute for Statistics.

Please be aware that the data provided refers only to criminal offences, with the exclusion of merely administrative violations, for which no statistical data appears to be available. In addition, please also note that the data refers to smuggling offences in general, including goods different from tobacco products.

Table 4 shows the number of definitive convictions for smuggling of tobacco products since 2000, divided into offenders with and without prior criminal record at the moment of conviction. All the provided data originates from the archives of the National Institute for Statistics.

Please be aware that the provided data refers only to criminal offences, with the exclusion of merely administrative violations, for which no statistical data appears to be available.

Table 5 shows the duration of imprisonment imposed for the smuggling of tobacco products. All the provided data originates from the archives of the National Institute for Statistics.

Please be aware that the provided data refers only to criminal offences, with the exclusion of merely administrative violations, for which no statistical data appears to be available.

Table 5 Duration of imprisonment imposed for the smuggling of tobacco products

	Less than 1 month	1 to 3 months	3 to 6 months	6 months to 1 year	1 to 2 years	2 to 3 years	3 to 5 years	5 to 10 years	More than 10 years	Total
Period										
2000	5	6	144	516	251	6	7	1	0	936
2001	5	4	153	568	262	6	3	0	0	1001
2002	3	2	125	433	267	7	3	0	0	840
2003	5	10	69	289	237	24	1	1	0	636
2004	4	3	39	214	178	9	1	0	0	448
2005	12	9	28	156	152	5	0	0	0	362
2006	6	3	15	94	99	10	0	0	0	227
2007	5	3	13	68	104	12	0	0	0	205
2008	2	4	6	69	100	8	1	0	0	190
2009	1	3	10	87	91	6	2	2	0	202
2010	0	5	6	32	55	14	1	0	0	113
2011	1	2	2	30	35	11	9	0	0	90
2012	3	4	6	21	39	4	3	0	0	80
2013	0	4	2	34	47	2	0	1	0	90
2014	4	3	2	24	28	5	2	1	0	69
2015	2	5	5	33	54	7	0	1	0	107
2016	3	17	8	21	48	13	3	0	0	113
2017	36	50	26	30	61	5	1	0	0	209

Table 6 Main security measures applied in addition to the principal penalty for smuggling crimes

Security measure	Confiscation	Confiscation and destruction of seized goods	Hospital for criminally insane	Penal labour	Probation	Expulsion	Others
Period							
2000	6915	0	0	34	22	5	0
2001	5756	0	0	14	33	3	0
2002	4904	0	0	15	34	2	0
2003	6606	3	0	18	43	0	0
2004	12,224	1	0	25	27	1	0
2005	13,266	2	1	11	13	1	0
2006	8170	1	0	3	26	4	0
2007	3009	673	0	1	34	2	0
2008	2245	1737	0	1	11	1	0
2009	1625	740	0	1	32	3	0
2010	992	742	0	0	18	1	0
2011	340	899	0	1	7	0	0
2012	271	1031	0	1	5	0	1
2013	412	1248	0	1	5	0	1
2014	373	1763	0	0	16	0	0
2015	277	2321	0	0	7	1	0
2016	315	1764	0	0	17	0	0
2017	214	1358	0	2	11	0	0

Table 7 Age at the time of the crime of perpetrators convicted with a definitive verdict for the smuggling of tobacco products

	Less than 15 years	16–17 years	18–24 years	25–34 years	35–44 years	45–54 years	55–64 years	More than 65 years	Total
Period									
2000	0	1	196	524	322	136	50	8	1237
2001	0	8	268	682	443	199	55	9	1664
2002	0	5	208	489	355	153	59	16	1285
2003	2	1	212	436	316	141	54	12	1174
2004	0	0	101	286	261	147	62	5	862
2005	0	1	101	288	229	120	47	12	798
2006	0	0	73	204	178	113	42	17	627
2007	0	1	76	237	195	99	35	5	648
2008	0	0	110	298	248	184	60	14	914
2009	1	0	105	391	352	220	65	20	1154
2010	0	0	106	367	326	195	70	19	1083
2011	0	0	126	340	348	193	61	22	1090
2012	0	0	143	363	321	200	72	29	1128
2013	0	0	163	398	319	253	76	21	1230
2014	0	0	256	522	450	273	112	26	1639
2015	0	0	316	692	622	417	173	27	2247
2016	0	0	227	522	558	354	136	40	1837
2017	0	0	112	372	408	307	141	34	1374

Table 6 shows the main security measures applied in addition to the principal penalty for smuggling crimes. All the provided data originates from the archives of the National Institute for Statistics.

Please be aware that the provided data refers only to criminal offences, with the exclusion of merely administrative violations, for which no statistical data appears to be available. In addition, please also note that the data refers to illicit trade offences in general, including goods different from tobacco products. Data specifically related to illicit trade in tobacco seems to be unavailable.

Table 7 shows the age at the time of the crime of perpetrators convicted with a definitive verdict for the smuggling of tobacco products by offenders with prior criminal records. All the provided data originates from the archives of the National Institute for Statistics.

Please be aware that the provided data refers only to criminal offences, with the exclusion of merely administrative violations, for which no statistical data appears to be available.

Table 8 shows the number of convictions for the smuggling of tobacco products pronounced in combination with other crimes. All the provided data originates from the archives of the National Institute for Statistics.

Table 8 Number of convictions for the smuggling of tobacco products pronounced in combination with other crimes

Number of concurring offences	1	2	3	4 or more	Total
Period					
2000	509	604	64	27	1204
2001	664	712	40	15	1431
2002	452	609	32	17	1110
2003	528	415	21	4	968
2004	424	276	14	4	718
2005	453	221	14	0	688
2006	430	89	8	3	530
2007	400	134	14	14	562
2008	659	105	13	18	795
2009	756	120	18	33	927
2010	880	62	21	25	988
2011	946	43	13	7	1009
2012	951	53	15	12	1031
2013	1071	44	5	8	1128
2014	1482	34	9	17	1542
2015	1943	79	43	21	2086
2016	1521	83	22	22	1648
2017	1276	31	9	5	1321

Please be aware that the data provided refers only to criminal offences, with the exclusion of merely administrative violations, for which no statistical data appears to be available.

No specific data is available with regard to the number of smuggling cases that have been prosecuted in Italy, neither with regard to illicit manufacturing nor counterfeiting activities.

The main trends deriving from the analysis of the data collected can be summarised as follows.

The collected data show a significant decrease in the number of smuggling cases investigated since 2016. However, the estimated tax loss remains substantially unchanged even for 2016. This may be evidence of a change in the phenomenological aspects of the illicit trade, which may progress from numerous minor offences to bigger trafficking activities.

The number of convictions for smuggling and illicit trade in tobacco products remains substantially unchanged in the period under consideration; nonetheless, a significant decrease of convictions for smuggling cases in general is observable. This suggests that smuggling of tobacco products has a significant bearing on smuggling activities in general and continues to be the main smuggling activity.

Confiscation and destruction of goods appear to be the most frequent security measures applied for the smuggling of tobacco products.

The involvement in smuggling crimes of offenders with prior criminal records appears to be very frequent. This suggests that such offences are often committed by persons already integrated into a criminal environment.

The conviction for smuggling of tobacco products is almost always accompanied by a conviction for at least another criminal offence.

Among the forms of illicit trade described by Art. 15, par. 1 of the WHO FCTC, the most common in Italy can, of course, be identified in the smuggling of foreign tobacco products. Such conduct has been widespread in Italy since the 1970s years, as a source of self-financing and money laundering for mafia-type organisations. The most common mode of smuggling in that period was by sea, mainly along the Adriatic coast, avoiding customs controls.

At present, smuggling maintains strong links with organised crime (mafia-type and human trafficking organisations[9]) and often takes place through the presentation of goods for customs controls, hiding illicit tobacco products so as to hinder inspections (so-called "intra-inspective" smuggling).

Smugglers continue to use sea routes for extra-inspective smuggling (particularly for products coming from North African regions). Alternatively, they use overland transportation, mainly for products coming from eastern market (Poland, Russia, etc.).

4 Preventive Measures

As mentioned above, the EU Directive n. 2014/40 on the approximation of the laws, regulations and administrative provisions of the Member States concerning the manufacture, presentation and sale of tobacco and related products has been implemented in Italy through Legislative Decree n. 6/2016.

The national legislation regulates all the preventive measures mentioned in the European legislation and—more specifically—introduces specific prescriptions for the labelling of tobacco products with health warnings (Art. 9–13), establishes a system of tracking and tracing of products which must be marked with a unique identification sign (Art. 16). Moreover, each package shall be provided with a tamper-proof security feature (Art. 17) and new tobacco products must be notified to the Italian Ministry of Health and to the Ministry of Economics (Art. 20).

According to Legislative Decree n. 6/2016, it is also forbidden to label tobacco products in order to encourage their consumption, presenting the relevant products as less harmful than other similar ones, recalling tastes or aromas which are not present in the product, suggesting that the product is environmentally friendly or presenting it as similar to foods or cosmetics (Art. 14).

---

[9]See, among others, the *Report to the Ministry of Interiors by the Central "anti-mafia" Investigative Bureau* for the 1st semester 2018, available on-line at: http://direzioneinvestigativaantimafia.interno.gov.it/semestrali/sem/2018/1sem2018.pdf, p. 745 ss.

It must be also stressed that, according to Art. 1, par. 50 *bis* and 50 *ter* of Law n. 296/2006, the National Customs Agency can restrict access to web pages through which foreign tobacco products are illegally sold or advertised, such activities being forbidden.

In addition to the provisions related to the prevention of illicit trade in tobacco products, the Italian legal system is characterized by general preventive mechanisms.

Firstly, the criminal police divisions (mainly the Police, Carabinieri and Guardia di Finanza) and the Public Prosecutor itself may—on their own initiative—investigate violations even before a formal criminal offence report is submitted.

The Guardia di Finanza and the National Customs Agency may also undertake controls to ascertain investigative violations, mainly through static and dynamic surveillance at ports, airports and borders, and also through online monitoring of websites.

Moreover, a system of preventive measures is established by Legislative Decree n. 159/2011 (so-called anti-mafia code). According to its provisions, a wide range of personal and patrimonial measures can be applied to those who, although not convicted of a criminal offence, are deemed to be "dangerous" to public order. Such dangerousness might be "generic", referring to those usually involved in criminal activities or who live from profits derived from criminal activities (Art. 1 of Legislative Decree n. 159/2011). Preventive measures can also be applied—among others—against those suspected to be part of an organisation of illicit traders of foreign tobacco products punished by Art. 291 *quater* of the Customs Law (Art. 4 of Legislative Decree n. 159/2011 in conjunction with Art. 51, par. 3 *bis* of the Code of Criminal Procedure).

The most important and afflictive personal preventive measure is "special surveillance", which establish various restrictions on personal freedom, related mainly to places one cannot frequent and persons one cannot meet.

The main patrimonial preventive measures are seizure and confiscation of goods which appear to be disproportionate with regard to the income of the person suspected, as well as of goods which appear to be the product of illicit activities.

Both personal and patrimonial preventive measures must be applied by a court, upon proposal of the Police Commissioner, the competent Public Prosecutor or the Director of the Anti-Mafia Investigative Bureau.

No particular practices or strategic policies with regard to the prevention of illicit trade in tobacco products different from those generally referred to other forms of criminality are made available to the public.

5 Cooperation

Administrative cooperation between European national institutions in the field of illicit trade in tobacco products is regulated in Italy by the "Convention drawn up on the basis of Article K.3 of the Treaty on European Union, on mutual assistance and cooperation between customs administrations" (Napoli II Convention), ratified through Law n. 217/2008.

This legal instrument establishes mutual assistance instruments to prevent, investigate, prosecute and punish violations of customs laws—thus including illicit trade in tobacco products—providing three different forms of mutual assistance.

Firstly, assistance can be provided on request of a Member State to another Member State. Such a request may concern a request for information, for surveillance or for enquiries (Art. 8–14 of the Convention).

Spontaneous assistance through surveillance or sharing of information is also possible (Art. 15–17).

The Convention also regulates "special forms of cooperation". Namely, officers of the customs administration of one of the Member States pursuing in their country an individual observed in the act of committing one of the infringements referred to in Article 19(2) of the Convention which could give rise to extradition, or participating in such an infringement, shall be authorised to continue pursuit in the territory of another Member State even without prior authorisation in case of urgency (Art. 20).

In addition, officers of the customs administration of one of the Member States who are keeping under observation in their country persons in respect of whom there are serious grounds for believing that they are involved in one of the infringements referred to in Article 19(2) shall be authorised to continue their observation in the territory of another Member State where the latter has authorised cross-border observation in response to a request for assistance which has previously been submitted (Art. 21).

Covert investigations (art. 23) and setting up joint investigation teams (art. 24) are also regulated in the Convention.

Therefore, at least with regard to assistance on request of a Member State, it seems there exists a duty to cooperate pursuant to the conditions set out by the Convention, without prejudice to the exemptions of Art. 28, according to which the Convention shall not oblige the authorities of Member States to provide mutual assistance where such assistance would be likely to harm the public policy or other essential interests of the State concerned, particularly in the field of data protection, or where the scope of the action requested, in particular in the context of the special forms of cooperation, is obviously disproportionate to the seriousness of the presumed infringement. In such cases, assistance may be refused in whole or in part or made subject to compliance with certain conditions. Refusals to give assistance shall be in any case duly motivated.

The Convention regulates national coordination offices with the task of coordinating received requests for mutual assistance. Such an office has been appointed in Italy through the Decree of 10 May 2018.

Within the framework of European cooperation, Italy is a party to the "Convention on the Use of Information Technology for Customs Purposes" (CIS Convention), which has been ratified through Law n. 291/1998. The text established a common action of the customs administrations of the Member States, and procedures to exchange data and information regarding suspect activities. The National

Customs Administration is identified as the national authority responsible for the system. Both the Guardia di Finanza and National Customs Administration have access to the CIS database.

With specific regard to EU Law, particular mention should be made of Council Regulation n. 515/97 of 13 March 1997 on mutual assistance between the administrative authorities of the Member States and cooperation between the latter and the Commission to ensure the correct application of the law on customs and agricultural matters, as amended by Regulation (EU) 2015/1525 of the European Parliament and of the Council of 9 September 2015 amending Council Regulation (EC) No 515/97 on mutual assistance between the administrative authorities of the Member States and cooperation between the latter and the Commission to ensure the correct application of the law on customs and agricultural matters. The two sources further strengthen the customs cooperation system, attributing a central role to coordination by the European Commission and establishing the possibilities for joint customs operations between different Member States.

The Italian Customs Administration has also concluded various cooperation agreements with non-European third countries (Albania, Algeria, Argentina, Azerbaijan, Belarus, Croatia, Ethiopia, Russia, Finland, Japan, Jordan, Iran, Israel, Yugoslavia, Macedonia, Morocco, Norway, United States of America, Tunisia, Turkey, Ukraine, Uzbekistan, Vietnam), mainly aiming at ensuring the exchange of documents and information regarding suspect customs operations.

Italy has signed the "International Convention on mutual administrative assistance for the prevention, investigation and repression of Customs offences" concluded in Nairobi on 9 June 1977 and entered into force on 21 May 1980, within the framework of the World Customs Organization (WCO).

In the field of police cooperation, one of the most relevant instruments is Framework Decision n. 2002/465/GAI, implemented in Italy through Legislative Decree n. 34/2016, on joint investigation teams. The framework decision establishes a special form of cooperation which facilitates the formation of investigative teams comprising public prosecutors and the police forces of multiple Member States when there is a need to investigate serious crimes in territory under a different national jurisdiction, or when investigative coordination is necessary. In Italy, a joint investigation team can be constituted to investigate crimes punishable by at least 5 years of imprisonment, or for specified offences including that of criminal association for smuggling of foreign tobacco products punished under Art. 291 *quater* of Presidential Decree n. 43/1973.

Italy cooperates within the framework of Europol and Interpol through the Service for International Police Cooperation established at the Ministry of Interior.

Finally, the role of OLAF should also be given consideration. According to Art. 3 of EU Regulation n. 883/2013 (so-called OLAF Regulation), the Office is entitled to conduct "external investigations" and carry out on-the-spot checks and inspections in the Member States and, in accordance with the cooperation and mutual assistance agreements and any other legal instrument in force, in third countries, to combat illegal activities affecting the financial interests of the European Union. During such activities, OLAF is subject to the rules and practices of the Member

State concerned, and the competent authorities shall provide for the assistance needed in order to carry out its tasks effectively.

6 General Issues

Likely one of the most important social factors contributing to the growth of illicit trade in tobacco products in Italy may be found in the significant tax burden related to these goods. More than 70% of the price of tobacco products is comprised of fiscal duties. More specifically, concerning cigarettes, the final price of each package is composed as follows: 59.1% of the final price—excise duties; 22% of the final price—VAT (Excise duties + VAT cannot be lower than €175.74 per kg of tobacco); 10%—dealer fee. The remaining portion of the price constitutes the income of the producer. Therefore, it is easy to understand that illicit products are offered at prices which are substantially lower than those distributed via the regular market, making them attractive especially for low-income consumers and incentivizing the activities of illicit traders.

The strong presence of criminal organisations (mainly mafia-type organisations but recently also smaller organisations of foreigners) is favourable to the illicit trade in tobacco products, which still represents an important form of self-financing for such criminal groups.

Another important factor is represented by the migrant flows impacting Italy. Human traffickers, often belonging to criminal organisations also active in the field of illicit trade, use the same routes and means of transportation to carry migrants and tobacco products, thus maximizing their profits derived from these activities.

Italy's geographical position also contributes to the growth of the illicit trade in tobacco products. Italy has large coastal areas with important commercial ports. The country sometimes represents the final destination of smuggled products, and it is also sometimes a transit location for the subsequent movement of goods to mainly northern European countries.

7 Conclusion

The national operators involved in the fight against illicit trade in tobacco products almost unanimously recognize the adequacy of the relevant legal framework existing in Italy. Italian legislation punishes—either criminally or administratively—all the relevant forms of conduct through which this illicit trade is performed, sometimes also imposing very afflictive sanctions such as value confiscation.

However, the establishment of stable communication channels for the exchange of information between the public authorities involved and also between public actors and private stakeholders (such as tobacco manufacturers) could further improve the efficacy of strategies to combat illicit trade, monitoring relevant trends in the licit and illicit markets so as to immediately adopt an adequate strategy to limit the illicit trade.

Given the increasing importance of online platforms, it is worth noting the possibility to prohibit access to web pages through which foreign tobacco products are illegally sold or advertised as ensured by Art. 1, par. 50 *bis* and 50 *ter* of Law n. 296/2006; this law was established in Italy following experience in the fight with illicit gambling.

The strong controls existing in Italy with regard to the authorized network of retailers of tobacco products and the prohibition of online purchases prevents the infiltration of illicit products into the regular market, limiting the distribution of such goods, which are therefore sold via alternative channels.

Each of these actions could in principle be exported to different legal systems, if they have not yet been adopted, thereby contributing to the fight against illicit trade.

On an operational level, no specific best practices in the fight against illicit trade in tobacco products have been made available to the public.

References

Bolis S (2016) Depenalizzazione del contrabbando e attenuata tutela degli interessi finanziari dell'Unione. www.penalecontemporaneo.it: 1–26

Cerqua LD, Pricolo CM (2002) Modifiche alla legge sulla repressione del contrabbando di tabacchi lavorati esteri. Diritto penale e processo: 1072–1076

Di Paola S (2012) In tema di condotta di contrabbando di tabacchi lavorati esteri. Foro italiano: 575–576

Scafati I (2013) Reati tributari e doganali. Giuffrè, Milano

Velani LG (2002) L. 19 marzo 2001, n. 92 - Modifiche alla normativa concernente la repressione del contrabbando di tabacchi lavorati. La legislazione penale: 659–664

Daniele Negri received his Ph.D. at the University of Bologna, and is currently Full Professor of criminal procedure and Dean of the Faculty of Law at the University of Ferrara. He authored two monographs (*Fumus commissi delicti: la prova per le fattispecie cautelari*, Torino, Giappichelli, 2004 and *L'imputato presente al processo: una ricostruzione sistematica*, Torino, Giappichelli, 2014), together with many articles and essays published in specialized peer-reviewed journals. He has been involved, both as participant and as principal investigator, in the staff of different national and international research projects. Among his main research interests, it is included the study of the principle of strict legality in criminal procedure, in the light of the latest developments related to the influence of European sources.

Prevention of Illicit Trade in Tobacco Products: Experience of Lithuania

Gintaras Švedas

Contents

G. Švedas (✉)
Department of Criminal Justice, Faculty of Law, University of Vilnius, Vilnius, Lithuania
e-mail: gintaras.svedas@tf.vu.lt

C. Nowak (ed.), *Combatting Illicit Trade on the EU Border*,
https://doi.org/10.1007/978-3-030-51019-0_5

Abstract The chapter deals with Lithuanian legal framework related to illicit trade in tobacco products, criminological data and preventive measures on illicit trade in tobacco products in Lithuania. Also, various aspects of cooperation matters concerning control and prevention of the illicit trade of tobacco products in Lithuania.

1 National Legal Framework Related to Illicit Trade in Tobacco Products

1.1 Substantive Law Issues Concerning Illicit Trade in Tobacco Products

The Seimas (Parliament) of Lithuania ratified the WHO Framework Convention on Tobacco Control (hereinafter—FCTC) on 28 September 2004 m. by the Law on Ratification of the WHO Framework Convention on Tobacco Control No. IX-2460 (The Parliament of the Republic of Lithuania 2004b). Furthermore, the WHO FCTC Protocol to Eliminate Illicit Trade in Tobacco Products (hereinafter—Protocol) was ratified on 3 November 2016 by the Law on Ratification of the WHO Framework Convention on Tobacco Control Protocol to Eliminate Illicit Trade in Tobacco Products No. XII-2732 (The Parliament of the Republic of Lithuania 2016b). The Protocol has not come into force in Lithuania yet. An expert assessment of national laws leads to the general conclusion that all acts mentioned as unlawful in the WHO Framework Convention on Tobacco Control and its Protocol to Eliminate Illicit Trade in Tobacco Products are recognised as illegal under the Criminal Code of Lithuania (The Parliament of the Republic of Lithuania 2000b) (hereinafter—CC) and Code of Administrative Offences (The Parliament of the Republic of Lithuania 2015) (hereinafter—CAO) in the Lithuanian legal system. In Lithuania, all illegal acts, depending on factual circumstances, may be qualified as (a) smuggling (administrative offence[1] or crime[2]), (b) deceit of

[1]Smuggling is an administrative offence when a person "transporting across the state border of Lithuania items, money, works of art or other goods (except movable cultural properties or antiques, substances indicated in the laws on control of certain doping substances, firearms, ammunition, explosives, explosive, radioactive materials or other strategic goods, toxic, highly active, narcotic or psychotropic substances or precursors of narcotic or psychotropic substances) which must be declared at customs and whose value does not exceed 150 BAPP, fails to go through customs control or otherwise avoids this control or transports the mentioned products across the state border of Lithuania without authorisation".

[2]Smuggling is a crime when "a person who, when transporting across the state border of Lithuania items which must be declared at customs and whose value exceeds the amount of 150 BAPP, fails to go through customs control or otherwise avoids this control or transports the mentioned objects across the state border of the Republic of Lithuania without authorisation".

customs (crime),[3] (c) unlawful possession of goods subject to excise duties (administrative offence[4] or crime[5]), (d) unlawful failure to bring goods or products outside the Republic of Lithuania (crime),[6] (e) unauthorised engagement in economic, commercial, financial or professional activities (crime),[7] unlawful activities of a legal person (crime),[8] use of another's trademark or service mark (crime),[9] etc. It should be noted that the Lithuanian legal system, while establishing liability for the above-mentioned acts, does not exclude tobacco products as an object of administrative offences or crimes.

Liability for the smuggling (of tobacco products) may be administrative or criminal. The specific kind of liability depends on the value of smuggled tobacco products, which shall be calculated according to their customs value, including taxes to be paid (Art. 212, CC and Art. 208, CAO). It should be noted that according to a resolution of the Government of Lithuania, passengers arriving to Lithuania by air are allowed to legally import 200 cigarettes, and those arriving not by air/by land from third countries—40 cigarettes (The Government of the Republic of Lithuania 2004). Furthermore, the value of smuggled tobacco products is also a basis for the differentiation of criminal and administrative liability. The threshold separating administrative and criminal liability is 150 basic units of punishment and penalty

[3]Deceit of customs is a crime when "a person who brings items from a Member State of the European Union (EU) into Lithuania, which must be declared at customs and whose value exceeds the amount of 150 BAPP, and fails to go through the customs control of Lithuania or another Member State of the EU or otherwise avoids this control".

[4]Unlawful possession of goods subject to excise duties is an administrative offence when "the acquisition of excise goods (except for energy products and electricity), storage, transport, use or disposal in violation of established procedures, trade in excise goods without stamps or other special marks, or stamps of the old model when illegally acquired, held, transported, used or the value of the goods sold does not exceed 150 BAPP".

[5]Unlawful possession of goods subject to excise duties is a crime when "a person who, in violation of the established procedure, acquires, stores, transports, forwards, uses or handles the goods subject to excise duties whose value exceeds the amount of 150 BAPP".

[6]Unlawful failure to bring goods or products outside the Republic of Lithuania is a crime when "a person who unlawfully fails to bring beyond the state border of Lithuania goods or products whose value exceeds the amount of 150 BAPP, but does not exceed the amount of 250 BAPP, and which ought to have been brought outside Lithuania according to transit or export documents".

[7]Unauthorised engagement in economic, commercial, financial or professional activities is a crime when "a person who undertakes economic, commercial, financial or professional activities in the form of business or, on a large scale, without holding a licence/authorisation to engage in activities for which it is required or by other unlawful means, also a person who engages in prohibited economic, commercial, financial or professional activities".

[8]Unlawful activities of a legal person is a crime when "a person who, on a large scale, engages in activities not provided for in the founding documents of a public legal entity, also a person who establishes or is in charge of a legal entity used as a cover for unlawful activities".

[9]Use of another's trademark or service mark is a crime when "a person who, without holding authorisation, identifies a large or small quantity of goods with another's trademark or presents them for trade or makes use of another's service mark and thereby causes major or small damage".

(hereinafter—BAPP):[10] criminal liability arises when the value reaches the indicated amount. Administrative liability is differentiated:

- when the value is up to 5 BAPP (Part 1, Art. 208, CAO): fine from €200 to €1120;
- when the value is from 5 to 50 BAPP (Part 2, Art. 208, CAO): fine from €1820 to €4000;
- when the value is from 50 to 150 BAPP (Part 3, Art. 208, CAO): fine from €3500 to €6000.

Criminal liability is also differentiated:

- when the value is from 150 up to 250 BAPP (Part 1, Art. 199, CC), smuggling is considered a general *corpus delicti* (less serious crime), punishable by a fine from 100 up to 4000 BAPP (€5000–€200,000) or custodial sentence up to 4 years;
- when the value exceeds 250 BAPP (Part 3, Art. 199, CC), smuggling is considered a qualified *corpus delicti* (serious crime), punishable by a fine from 150 to 6000 BAPP (€7500–€300,000) or custodial sentence up to 8 years.

Liability for unlawful possession of goods subject to excise duties also may be administrative or criminal. Responsibility arises depending on the customs value of cigarettes, which does not include the legally held quantity of tobacco products (The Supreme Court 2007b). According to the rules approved by the Minister of Economy, natural persons may legally hold and transport [...] tobacco products if they: keep imported tobacco products in Lithuania in quantities not exceeding: (a) 100 packets of cigarettes, 400 cigarillos, 200 cigars, 1 kg of smoking tobacco when goods are imported from Member States of the EU; (b) 10 packets of cigarettes, 100 cigarillos, 50 cigars, 0.5 kg of smoking tobacco when goods are imported from other countries than Member States of the EU (The Minister of Economy 2004). The threshold separating administrative and criminal liability is 150 BAPP: criminal liability arises when the value reaches the indicated amount. Administrative liability is differentiated:

- when the value is up to 2 BAPP (Part 1, Art. 209, CAO): a fine from €40 to €200; in case of a repeat offence (Part 2, Art. 209, CAO)—fine from €200 to €1000;
- when the value is from 2 to 10 BAPP (Part 3, Art. 209, CAO): a fine €400 to €1900; in case of a repeat offence (Part 4, Art. 209, CAO)—a fine from €1950 to €5590;
- when the value is from 10 to 50 BAPP (Part 5, Art. 209, CAO): a fine from €2000 to €5590; in case of a repeat offence (Part 6, Art. 209, CAO)—a fine from €5460 to €6000;
- when the value is from 50 to 150 BAPP (Part 7, Art. 209, CAO): a fine from €5200 to €6000; in case of a repeat offence (Part 8, Art. 209, CAO)—a fine from €5760 to €6000.

[10] 1 BAPP is equal to €50 (The Government of the Republic of Lithuania 2017).

Criminal liability is also differentiated:

- when the value is from 150 to 250 BAPP (Part 1, Art. 199^2, CC), the unlawful possession of goods subject to excise duties is considered a general *corpus delicti* (less serious crime), punishable by a fine from 100 to 4000 BAPP (€5000–€200,000) or a custodial sentence up to 4 years;
- when the value exceeds 250 BAPP (Part 3, Art. 199^2, CC), the unlawful possession of goods subject to excise duties is considered a qualified *corpus delicti* (serious crime), punishable by a fine from 150 to 6000 BAPP (€7500–€300,000) or a custodial sentence up to 8 years.

Liability for deceit of customs (Art. 199^1, CC) and unlawful failure to bring goods or products outside the Republic of Lithuania (Art. 200, CC) may be only criminal. Criminal liability is differentiated:

- when the value is from 150 to 250 BAPP, deceit of customs and unlawful failure to bring goods or products outside the Republic of Lithuania (Para 1, Art. 199^1 and 200, CC) are considered a general *corpus delicti* (less serious crime), punishable by a fine from 100 to 4000 BAPP (€5000–€200,000) or a custodial sentence up to 4 years;
- when the value exceeds 250 BAPP, deceit of customs and unlawful failure to bring goods or products outside the Republic of Lithuania (Part 2, Art. 199^1 and 200, CC) are considered a qualified *corpus delicti* (serious crime), punishable by a fine from 150 to 6000 BAPP (€7500–€300,000) or a custodial sentence up to 8 years.

Liability for unauthorised engagement in economic, commercial, financial or professional activities (Art. 202, CC), unlawful activities of a legal person (Art. 203, CC), use of another's trademark or service mark (Art. 204, CC) may be only criminal.

According to the Union Customs Code (2013), the Law on excise duties (The Parliament of the Republic of Lithuania 2010) and the Law on Value Added Taxes (The Parliament of the Republic of Lithuania 2002a), as well as the jurisprudence of the Supreme Administrative Court of Lithuania (The Supreme Administrative Court 2012) and regional administrative courts (Kaunas Region Administrative Court 2012), when smuggled tobacco products are seized in Lithuania, additional financial sanctions—custom duties, excise duties and VAT—are applied. It should be noted that liability under financial law (above-mentioned financial sanctions) can and must be imposed with both criminal and administrative liability for committed crimes (smuggling, deceit of customs, unlawful possession of goods subject to excise duties) or administrative offenses (smuggling or unlawful possession of goods subject to excise duties).

The Constitution, the CC, the CAO and the Code of Criminal Procedure (The Parliament of the Republic of Lithuania 2002b) (hereinafter—CCP) determine the principle of *non bis in idem*, which means the prohibition of punishing a person for the same violation of law twice. When explaining this constitutional principle, the Constitutional Court of Lithuania has noted in several cases that the prohibition on punishing twice for the same (criminal) act "means a prohibition on punishing twice for the same act that is contrary to law, i.e. for the same crime, as well as for the same violation of law which is not a crime. The above-mentioned constitutional principle does not mean that different kinds of liability may not be applied to the person for the violation of law. In itself, the constitutional principle *non bis in idem* does not deny the possibility of applying more than one sanction of the same kind (i.e. defined by the norms of the same branch of law) to a person for the same violation, i.e. the main and additional punishment or the main and additional administrative penalty" (The Constitutional Court 2001). Furthermore, the Constitutional Court of Lithuania has emphasized that "the constitutional principle *non bis in idem* also means, inter alia, that if a person who has committed an act which is contrary to law has been held administratively but not criminally liable, i.e. a sanction was imposed on him/her – a penalty not for a crime but for an administrative violation of law – he/she cannot be held criminally liable for the said act" (The Constitutional Court 2005). Thus, the principle of *non bis in idem* refers only to the relationship between criminal and administrative offenses law.

Statistics of criminal cases and the opinions of experts[11] show that smuggling, unlawful possession of goods subject to excise duties and unlawful failure to bring goods or products outside the Republic of Lithuania are, as a rule, committed in conjunction with the bribery (passive corruption) of a customs official (Art. 225, CC), abuse of office of a customs official (Art. 228, CC), forgery of a document or possession of a forged document (Art. 300, CC), illicit enrichment (Art. 189^1, CC), money laundering (Art. 216, CC), etc. Smuggling, unlawful possession of goods subject to excise duties and unlawful failure to bring goods or products outside the Republic of Lithuania are most commonly committed in complicity in the forms of a group of accomplices and organized group (in some instances—criminal association). It should be noted that criminal association consists of separate *corpus delicti* of the crime, provided for in Art. 249, CC.

When the illicit trade in tobacco products is committed as a part of a larger-scale crime, the situation, according to the jurisprudence of the Supreme Court of Lithuania, should be defined as a concurrence of criminal acts (real concurrence). Real concurrence of criminal acts occurs if the offender performs more than one criminal act provided for in the same or different articles of the Special Part of the CC by committing more real acts. The Lithuanian criminal law provides special sentencing rules when several criminal acts (concurrence of criminal acts) have been committed. It should be noted that in this situation, the final combined punishment may consist of two punishments. Where several criminal acts are committed, a court shall impose a punishment for each criminal act separately and subsequently—a final combined punishment.

[11]Prosecutor (Prosecutor General Office), pre-trial investigator (Customs Criminal Service) and representative of the criminal intelligence unit (Customs Criminal Service).

1.2 Administrative Penalties and Administrative Measures for Illicit Trade in Tobacco Products

The CAO provides that in case of violation of the procedure for providing information on tobacco products or related products (Art. 70, CAO), purchase or other transfer of tobacco products to minors (Art. 77, CAO), violation of the licensing procedure for the production, import and marketing of tobacco or related products (Art. 132, CAO), violation of trade in tobacco products by trade and public catering companies (Art. 170, CAO), smuggling (Art. 208, CAO), acquisition of excise goods (except for energy products and electricity), storage, transport, use or disposal in violation of established procedures (Art. 209, CAO), violation of restrictions of consumption or possession of tobacco products or related products (Art. 492, CAO), etc. an administrative penalty—administrative fine from €200 up to €6000—must be imposed. Additionally, in the case of smuggling (Art. 208, CAO), acquisition of excise goods (except for energy products and electricity), storage, transport, use or disposal in violation of established procedures (Art. 209, CAO), violation of restrictions of consumption or possession of tobacco products or related products (Art. 492, CAO), etc., an administrative measure—administrative confiscation of property (smuggled goods, excise goods used or disposed in violation of established procedures, tobacco products, etc.)—also must be imposed; in case of violation of rules on trade in tobacco products by trade and public catering companies (Art. 170, CAO)—administrative confiscation of the tobacco products may be imposed. Furthermore, in the case of smuggling (Art. 208, CAO) and acquisition of excise goods (except for energy products and electricity), storage, transport, use or disposal in violation of established procedures (Art. 209, CAO), administrative confiscation of transport or other means for smuggling or transport or other means for transportation of excise goods must be imposed.

Article 25 of the CAO states that a fine is a pecuniary administrative penalty imposed in the cases provided for in the Special Part of the CAO. According to the CAO, the minimum amount of a fine shall be not less than €10, and the maximum amount of a fine shall be not more than €6000. Sanctions of the Articles of the Special Part of the CAO provide the minimum and maximum amounts of fines imposed following an administrative offence. In the cases and procedures provided for in the CAO, a fine or a part thereof may be replaced by community service.

Administrative confiscation of property is an administrative measure, which may be imposed together with an administrative penalty by the court or the administrative case investigating authority (official). The confiscation of property subject to legal registration under Lithuanian legislation may be ordered only by a court. According to Art. 29 of the CAO, the "confiscation of property shall be the compulsory uncompensated taking into the ownership of the state of any form of property subject to confiscation and held by the offender or other persons".

An instrument or a means used to commit an administrative offence, including the object and result of such an act, shall be considered as property subject to confiscation. Property of any form directly or indirectly obtained from an act prohibited by the CAO shall be considered as the result of the act. Confiscation of property may be imposed in the cases provided for in the article of the Special Part of the CAO which establishes administrative responsibility for an act committed by a person. Items that are banned from circulation are confiscated in all cases. Only items that are the property of the offender may be confiscated. This general rule has an exception according to which, in the case of administrative offences provided for in a special list (which includes, *inter alia,* smuggling (Art. 208, CAO), acquisition of excise goods (except for energy products and electricity), storage, transport, use or disposal in violation of established procedures (Art. 209, CAO), etc.), property subject to confiscation may be confiscated irrespective of whether the natural or legal person is owner of that property, in cases where: (1) when transferring the property to the offender or other persons, he/she was or ought to have been aware that this property would be used for the commission of the administrative offence; (2) the property has been transferred thereto under a fictitious transaction; (3) the property has been transferred thereto as to a family member or close relative of the offender; (4) the property has been transferred to him/her as to a legal person, and the offender, his/her family members or close relatives is/are the legal person's manager, a member of its management body or participants holding at least 50% of shares in the legal person (member shares, contributions, etc.); (5) when acquiring the property, he/she or the persons holding managerial positions in the legal person and being entitled to represent it, to make decisions on behalf of the legal person or to control the activities of the legal person was/were or ought to and could have been aware that the property is an instrument or a means used to commit an administrative offence, and/or the object or result of such an act.

1.3 Punishments and Penal Measures for Illicit Trade in Tobacco Products

Lithuanian criminal law foresees three forms of implementation of criminal liability of a natural or legal person for the commission of a criminal act: (1) imposition of a punishment; (2) release from criminal liability with application of penal or reformative measures or without them; (3) suspension (partial suspension) of the execution of arrest or imprisonment or release from the execution of punishment with application of penal or reformative measures or without them.

The CC provides that:

(a) simple smuggling (Part 1, Art. 199, CC), simple deceit of customs (Part 1, Art. 199^1, CC), simple unlawful possession of goods subject to excise duties (Part 1, Art. 199^2, CC) shall be punished by a fine (from 100 to 4000 BAPP) or by a custodial sentence for a term of up to 4 years;
(b) qualified smuggling (Part 3, Art. 199, CC), qualified deceit of customs (Part 2, Art. 199^1, CC), qualified unlawful possession of goods subject to excise duties

(Part 2, Art. 199^2, CC) shall be punished by a fine (from 150 to 6000 BAPP) or by a custodial sentence for a term of up to 8 years;

(c) simple unlawful failure to bring goods or products outside the Republic of Lithuania (Part 1, Art. 200, CC), prohibited activities (Part 2, Art. 202, CC) shall be punished by a custodial sentence for a term of up to 4 years;
(d) qualified unlawful failure to bring goods or products outside the Republic of Lithuania (Part 2, Art. 200, CC) shall be punished by a custodial sentence for a term of up to 8 years;
(e) unauthorised engagement in economic, commercial, financial or professional activities (Part 1, Art. 202, CC) shall be punished by community service or a fine (from 100 to 4000 BAPP), or by restriction of liberty, or by a custodial sentence for a term of up to 4 years;
(f) unlawful activities of a legal entity (Part 1, Art. 203, CC) shall be punished by a fine, by arrest or by a custodial sentence for a term of up to 1 year; qualified unlawful activities of a legal person (Part 2, Art. 203, CC) shall be punished by a fine (from 50 to 2000 BAPP), by arrest or by a custodial sentence for a term of up to 2 years;
(g) use of another's trademark or service mark (Part 1, Art. 204, CC) shall be punished by a fine (from 50 to 2000 BAPP), by restriction of liberty, or by a custodial sentence for a term of up to 2 years.

A fine is a pecuniary punishment imposed by a court in the cases provided for in the Special Part of the CC. Article 47 of the CC provides that a fine is calculated in BAPP. The maximum amount of a fine shall be determined as follows: (1) for a misdemeanour—from 15 to 500 BAPP; (2) for a minor crime—from 50 to 2000 BAPP; (3) for a less serious crime—from 100 to 4000 BAPP; (4) for a serious crime—from 150 to 6000 BAPP; (5) for a negligent crime—from 20 to 750 BAPP. A minor may be subject to a fine in an amount from 5 to 50 BAPP. A fine may be imposed only against a minor already employed or possessing his/her own property. The concrete amount of a fine for a committed criminal act shall be specified by the court when imposing the punishment.

Where a person does not possess sufficient funds to pay a fine imposed by a court, the court may (with the convict's consent) replace this punishment with community service. Where a person evades voluntary payment of a fine and it is not possible to recover it, a court may replace the fine with restriction of liberty.

Arrest shall mean a short-term custodial sentence served in a short-term detention facility. Article 49 of the CC provides that arrest shall be imposed by a court in the cases provided for in the Special Part of the CC. Arrest shall be imposed for a period from 15 to 90 days for a crime and from 10 to 45 days for a misdemeanour. The term of arrest for a criminal act shall be specified by the court when imposing the punishment. Arrest shall not be imposed upon pregnant women and may be not imposed upon persons raising a child under the age of 3 years, taking into consideration the interests of the child.

Fixed-term imprisonment is compulsory isolation of the offender from society in special state institutions. Article 50 of the CC provides that fixed-term imprisonment may be imposed by a court in the cases provided for in the Special Part of the CC. Fixed-term imprisonment may be imposed for a period from 3 months to 20 years. In the case of imposition of such a punishment, when a new crime is committed before a sentence for a previous crime is served, imprisonment for a period of up to 25 years may be imposed. In the event of imposition of imprisonment upon a minor, the minimum punishment shall be equal to one-half of the minimum punishment provided for by the sanction of the article of the Special Part of the CC under which the minor is prosecuted. The maximum period of imprisonment in respect of a minor may not exceed 10 years.

It should be noted that in the case of simple smuggling (Part 1, Art. 199, CC), simple deceit of customs (Part 1, Art. 199^1, CC), simple unlawful possession of goods subject to excise duties (Part 1, Art. 199^2, CC), simple unlawful failure to bring goods or products outside the Republic of Lithuania (Part 1, Art. 200, CC), prohibited activities (Part 2, Art. 202, CC), unauthorised engagement in economic, commercial, financial or professional activities (Part 1, Art. 202, CC) unlawful activities of a legal entity (Part 1, Art. 203, CC), use of another's trademark or service mark (Part 1, Art. 204, CC), the offender may be released from criminal liability (with application or without application of penal measures). Release from criminal liability means that a natural or legal person which has committed a criminal act is released from the main consequences of criminal liability (e.g. imposition of the punishment). Chapter VI "Release from Criminal Liability" and Chapter XI "Peculiarities of Criminal Liability of Minors" of the General Part of the CC provides for adults 7 types of release from criminal liability, which may be conditional or unconditional, and 1 type of unconditional release from criminal liability for minors.

Furthermore, in the case of the above-mentioned crimes the court may order the suspension (partial suspension) of the execution of a punishment (arrest or fixed-term imprisonment). Article 75 of the CC provides rules concerning suspension of the execution of a punishment. First of all, where a person is subject to arrest, the court may suspend the execution of the imposed sentence for a period ranging from 3 months to 1 year and impose intensive supervision. Secondly, where a person is subject to a custodial sentence for a term of up to 6 years for one or several crimes committed through negligence or to a custodial sentence for a term of up to 4 years for the commission of one or several premeditated crimes (except for grave crimes), the court may suspend the execution of the imposed sentence for a period ranging from 1 to 3 years. Thirdly, where a person is subject to a custodial sentence for a term of more than 6 years for crimes committed through negligence, or to a custodial sentence for a term of more than 5 years for minor or less serious premeditated crimes, or to a custodial sentence for a term of up to 5 years for a serious crime, the court may impose a partial suspension of the execution of the sentence for a period ranging from 1 to 3 years. The execution of the sentence may be suspended (partially suspended) where the court rules that there is a reasonable ground for believing that the purpose of the punishment will be achieved without the sentence actually being served. In suspending the execution of the sentence, the court shall impose upon the convict one or more mutually compatible penal measures and/or obligations: (1) to offer an apology to the victim; (2) to provide assistance to the victim during the victim's medical treatment; (3) to undergo treatment for addiction to diseases, where the convict agrees; (4) to educate and take care of his/her minor children, to take care of their health, to maintain them; (5) to take up employment or studies, or continue employment or studies; (6) to participate in a programme addressing behaviour; (7) house arrest, unless the need to leave is related to work or studies; (8) not to leave the city/district of the place of residence without the authorisation of the institution supervising the convict; (9) to refrain from visiting certain places or to refrain from communicating with certain persons or groups of persons; (10) to refrain from using psychoactive substances; (11) to refrain from possessing, using or acquiring certain items or from engaging in certain activities.

The court may impose, at the request of the person concerned or other participants of criminal proceedings, also at its own discretion, other obligations not provided for by the criminal law which, in the court's opinion, would have a positive impact on the conduct of the convict. In imposing such penal measures and/or obligations, the court shall specify the time limit for complying therewith.

According to the CC, an adult person released from criminal liability for the commission of a misdemeanour, negligent crime, minor or less serious crime or punishment may be subject to the following penal measures: (1) prohibition on exercising a special right; (2) deprivation of public rights; (3) deprivation of the right to be employed in a certain position or to engage in a certain type of activity; (4) compensation for or remediation of property damage; (5) unpaid work; (6) payment of a contribution to a fund for victims of crime; (7) confiscation of property; (8) the obligation to reside separately from the victim and/or prohibition on approaching the victim closer than a prescribed distance; (9) participation in programmes addressing violent behaviour; and (10) extended confiscation of property.

Prohibition to exercise a special right, deprivation of public rights, deprivation of the right to be employed in a certain position or to engage in a certain type of activity, payment of a contribution to a fund for crime victims, confiscation of property, the obligation to reside separately from the victim and (or) prohibition on approaching the victim closer than a prescribed distance, participation in programmes addressing violent behaviour and extended confiscation of property may be imposed jointly with a punishment.

When imposing two or more penal measures, the compatibility of the measures and the possibility of their corrective effect upon the convicted person must be taken into consideration.

Deprivation of public rights is provided for in Art. 68^1 of the CC, which states that "deprivation of public rights shall be deprivation of the right to be elected or appointed to an elected or appointed position at state or municipal institutions and agencies, undertakings or non-state organisations". The court shall impose deprivation of public rights in cases when a criminal act is committed in abuse of public rights. Public rights may be deprived for a period from 1 to 5 years. When imposing deprivation of public rights, the court shall indicate the right which is being deprived and a specific term for this penal measure.

Deprivation of the right to be employed in a certain position or to engage in a certain type of activity is provided for in Art. 68^2 of the CC, which states that "the court shall order deprivation of the right to be employed in a certain position or to engage in a certain type of activity in cases when a person commits a criminal act in the field of his occupational or professional activities or where, having regard to the nature of the criminal act committed, the court comes to the conclusion that the person may not preserve the right to be employed in a certain position or to engage in a certain type of activity". This penal measure may be imposed for a period from 1 to 5 years. When ordering deprivation of the right to be employed in a certain position or to engage in a certain type of activity, the court shall indicate the right which is being deprived and a specific term for this penal measure.

Payment of a contribution to a fund for crime victims is provided for in Art. 71 of the CC, which states that "a court may order payment of a contribution in the amount from 5 up to 125 BAPPs for an adult person and from 100 up to 2000 BAPPs for a legal person to a fund for crime victims. The contribution must be paid within a time limit (not to exceed 3 years) laid down by the court.

Confiscation of property is provided for in Art. 72 of the CC, which states that "confiscation of property shall be the compulsory uncompensated taking into the ownership of the state of any form of property subject to confiscation and held by the offender or other persons". An instrument or a means used to commit an act prohibited by the CC or the result of such an act shall be considered as property subject to confiscation. Property of any form directly or indirectly obtained from an act prohibited by the CC shall be considered as the result of the act.

Property held by the offender and being subject to confiscation must be confiscated in all cases.

Property held by another natural or legal person and being subject to confiscation shall be confiscated irrespective of whether the person has been convicted of the commission of an act prohibited by the CC, where: (1) when transferring the property to the offender or other persons, he/she was or ought to have been aware that this property would be used for the commission of the act prohibited by the CC; (2) the property has been transferred thereto under a fictitious transaction; (3) the property has been transferred thereto as to a family member or close relative of the offender; (4) the property has been transferred to it as to a legal person, and the offender, his/her family members or close relatives is/are the legal person's manager, a member of its management body or participants holding at least 50% of shares in the legal person (member shares, contributions, etc.); (5) when acquiring the property, he/she or the persons holding management positions in the legal person and being entitled to represent it, to make decisions on behalf of the legal person or to control the activities of the legal person was/were or ought to and could have been aware that the property is an instrument or a means used to commit an act prohibited by the CC or the result of such an act.

Where the property which is subject to confiscation has been concealed, consumed, belongs to third parties or cannot be taken for other reasons or confiscation of this property would not be appropriate, the court shall recover from the offender or other persons a sum of money equivalent to the value of the property subject to confiscation.

When ordering confiscation of property, the court must specify the items subject to confiscation or the monetary value of the property subject to confiscation.

Extended confiscation of property is provided for in Art. 72^3 of the CC, which states that "extended confiscation of property shall be the taking into ownership of the State of the property of the offender or part thereof disproportionate to the legitimate income of the offender, where there are grounds for believing that the property has been obtained by criminal means".

Extended confiscation of property shall be imposed provided that all of the following conditions are met: (1) the offender has been convicted of a less serious, serious or grave premeditated crime from which he/she obtained or could have obtained material gain; (2) the offender holds the property acquired during the commission of an act prohibited by the CC, after the commission thereof or within a period of 5 years prior to the commission thereof, whose value does not correspond to the offender's legitimate income, and the difference is greater than 250 BAPP, or transfers such property to other persons within the period specified in this point; (3) the offender fails, in the course of criminal proceedings, to provide proof of the legitimacy of acquisition of the property. This property, if it has been transferred to another natural or legal person, shall be confiscated from this person where at least one of the following grounds exists: (1) the property has been transferred under a fictitious transaction; (2) the property has been transferred to the offender's family members or close relatives; (3) the property has been transferred to a legal person, and the offender, his/her family members or close relatives is/are the legal person's manager, a member of its management body or participants holding at least 50% of shares in the legal person (member shares, contributions, etc.); (4) the person whereto the property has been transferred or the persons holding managing positions in the legal person and being entitled to represent it, to make decisions on behalf of the legal person or to control the activities of the legal person was/were or ought to and could have been aware that the property has been obtained by criminal means or with illicit funds of the offender.

Where the property or part thereof which is subject to confiscation has been concealed, consumed, belongs to third parties or cannot be taken for other reasons or confiscation of this property would not be appropriate, the court shall recover from the offender or other persons a sum of money equivalent to the value of the property subject to confiscation.

When ordering extended confiscation of property, the court must specify the items subject to confiscation or the monetary value of the property or part thereof subject to confiscation.

1.4 Criminal and Administrative Liability of Legal Persons for Illicit Trade in Tobacco Products

The CC of Lithuania provides criminal liability for a legal person, while special laws provide administrative responsibility (economic sanctions) for a legal person having committed an administrative offence.

Corporate criminal liability was introduced in 2002 for several crimes when Lithuania ratified the Council of Europe Criminal Law Convention on Corruption (1999). The prerequisites for the criminal liability of legal persons stem directly from the aforementioned Convention and EU legal acts. It should be noted that the Constitutional Court, by its decision of 8 June 2009 (The Constitutional Court 2009), has recognised that corporate criminal liability does not expostulate with the Constitution of Lithuania. Also, the Constitutional Court has recognised that corporate criminal liability derives from the liability of a natural person, and this leads to the conclusion that a legal person and a natural person may be subject to criminal liability only for one and the same crime, committed by a natural person (Švedas 2011, p. 98).

A legal person shall be held liable solely for the criminal acts the commission whereof is subject to liability of a legal person as provided for in the Special Part of the CC. Currently, there are up to 110 criminal acts provided for in the CC for which legal persons may be punished. This list has been composed mostly as a result of the national implementation of international treaties and EU secondary law requirements. This list includes smuggling (Art. 199, CC), deceit of customs (Art. 199^1, CC), unlawful possession of goods subject to excise duties (Art. 199^2, CC), unlawful failure to bring goods or products outside the Republic of Lithuania (Art 200, CC), unauthorised engagement in economic, commercial, financial or professional activities (Art. 202, CC), unlawful activities of a legal entity (Art. 203, CC), use of another's trademark or service mark (Art. 204, CC), etc.

The CC provides two grounds for the criminal liability of a legal person—mandatory and discretionary. A legal person shall be held mandatorily liable for criminal acts committed by a natural person solely where the criminal act was committed for the benefit or in the interests of the legal person by a natural person acting independently or on behalf of the legal person provided that he/she, while occupying a management position in the legal person, was entitled: (1) to represent the legal person, or (2) to take decisions on behalf of the legal person, or (3) to control the activities of the legal person.

The discretionary ground of the criminal liability of a legal person may be realised in two instances. First, a legal person may be held liable for criminal acts also where they have been committed by an employee or authorised representative of the legal person as a result of insufficient supervision or control by the person occupying a management position in the legal person. Second, a legal person also may be held liable for a criminal act committed by another legal person representing him/her or being under its control, when the criminal act was committed for the benefit of the above-mentioned legal person as a result of an order or permission, or insufficient supervision or control by a person occupying a management position in the legal person. In these cases, a legal person may be prosecuted only when it is held that such liability is reasonable. The prosecutor and the court, when ascertaining whether it is possible to prosecute, should take account of the entity's organizational culture, management principles applicable to the prevention of criminal acts, acceptance of the consequences of the criminal act, the relationship between the legal person and the employee who has committed the criminal act, indicating whether the criminal act and consequences may be associated with the legal person, etc. It should be noted that the Constitutional Court has stressed that, although the legal person's guilt is closely related to the individual's guilt, they are not identical. This separation of guilt allowed the Constitutional Court to conclude that the legal person's guilt should be established by law and recognised by an effective court judgement. The Supreme Court of Lithuania has also emphasised that a legal person's guilt should be proved by the methods mentioned in the CCP (The Supreme Court 2010a). In order to hold a legal person guilty, two elements should be present: (1) a relationship between the criminal act of the head of the legal person and the legal person's business strategy (for example, all appropriated money was used for unreported payments, etc.) and (2) the legal person's owner, who is responsible for formulation of strategy and compliance with the duty of care, should promote the illegal conduct, be aware of or at least tolerate such behaviour (for example, recognise the results of the crime *ex post facto*, etc.) (Švedas 2011, p. 100).

Criminal liability of a legal person does not release from criminal liability a natural person who has committed, organised, instigated or assisted in the commission of the criminal act, nor does the fact that a natural person shall be released from criminal liability or not be held liable for any other reason.

The State, a municipality, a State or municipal institution or agency (for example, the Ministry of Foreign Affairs, Prison Department under the Ministry of Justice, etc.) as well as international public organisation (for example, EU, Council of Europe, etc.) shall not be held liable under the CC of Lithuania.

Article 43 of the CC provides that the following punishments may be imposed upon a legal person for the commission of a criminal act: (1) a fine; (2) restriction of operation of the legal person; (3) liquidation of the legal person. Having imposed a punishment upon a legal person, a court may also decide to announce this judgement in the media.

According to Art. 47 of the CC, the amount of the fine imposed on a legal person shall be from 200 to 100,000 BAPP. The specific amount of the fine for a committed criminal act shall be specified by the court when imposing the punishment.

Restriction of operation of a legal person is one of the medium-stringency punishments that may be imposed on a legal person. Article 52 of the CC provides that "when imposing the restriction of operation of a legal person, a court shall prohibit the legal person from engaging in certain activities or order it to close a certain division of the legal person". Scholars of Lithuanian criminal law have emphasised that the restriction of operation of a legal person may not be applicable to an internal division of a legal person which is designated to serve the legal person (for example, finance or human resources department, etc.) (Švedas (Ed.) 2004, p. 300). Operation of a legal person may be restricted for a period from 1 to 5 years.

Liquidation of a legal person is the most severe punishment applicable to a legal person. Scholars of Lithuanian criminal law have emphasised that this punishment should be imposed in exceptional cases, where a legal person, for example, acts as a cover for criminal activity (Švedas (Ed.) 2004, p. 301). Article 53 of the CC provides that "when imposing the liquidation of a legal person, a court shall order the legal person to terminate, within the time limit laid down by the court, the entire economic, commercial, financial or professional activity and to close all divisions of the legal person".

It should be noted that according to the CC, a legal person may also be subject to payment of a contribution to a fund for crime victims, confiscation of property or extended confiscation of property.

Article 26 of the Law on Control of Tobacco, Tobacco Products and Related Products (The Parliament of the Republic of Lithuania 2003) provides administrative responsibility (economic sanctions) for legal persons and branches of foreign legal persons who commit various infringements of the provisions of the above-mentioned law. Economic sanctions consist of a fine from €289 to €8688 and may also include withdrawal of licences. For example, legal persons and branches of foreign legal persons who infringe the prohibitions on sales, storage or shipment of tobacco products and the requirements on the traceability of tobacco products, provided that this does not give rise to criminal liability, shall be subject to a fine in an amount between €2896 and €8688 together with the withdrawal of the licence, etc. Moreover, according to Art. 25 of the Law on Control of Tobacco, Tobacco Products and Related Products, confiscated tobacco products shall be destroyed in accordance with the procedure laid down by the Government. The description of the procedure for the destruction of seized tobacco products (The Government of the Republic of Lithuania 1999) determines that seized tobacco products are burned in specially designated places.

1.5 Procedural Law Issues

The main institution responsible for the pre-trial investigation of crimes involving illicit trade in tobacco products is the Customs Criminal Service (hereinafter—CCS). It should be noted that customs units of the Customs Department are the main institution for the investigation of administrative offences involving illicit trade in tobacco products. Moreover, the State Border Protection Service (hereinafter—SBPS) also has responsibility for the pre-trial investigation of crimes involving illicit trade in tobacco products. The main tasks of the CCS and SBPS (which are both law enforcement agencies) in the area of their competence are: (1) to collect criminal intelligence for disclosing smuggling, deceit of customs, unlawful possession of goods subject to excise duties, unlawful failure to bring goods or products outside Lithuania, and illegal migration; (2) to disclose and investigate crimes and other violations of legal acts related to customs or state border protection service activities; (3) to collect, analyse and evaluate information on the development of trends in the illicit trade in tobacco products, economical, social and criminogenic reasons for the existence and development of illicit trade in tobacco products; and (4) to carry out international and interdepartmental cooperation in the prevention and pre-trial investigation of crimes involving illicit trade in tobacco products or illegal migration, etc.

According to the CCP and Prosecutor General's recommendation "On the distribution of the pre-trial investigation between the institutions of the pre-trial investigation" (Prosecutor General 2003a), pre-trial investigation of smuggling (Art. 199, CC), deceit of customs (Art. 199^1, CC), unlawful possession of goods subject to excise duties (Art. 199^2, CC), and unlawful failure to bring goods or products outside the Republic of Lithuania (Art. 200, CC) is entrusted to the CCS and SBPS. It should be noted that the prosecutor may entrust a pre-trial investigation institution with the investigation of another criminal act even though the pre-trial investigation of such criminal acts is not within the competence of this institution. Furthermore, if necessary, the prosecutor may set up a joint investigation group involving officials of the different pre-trial investigation institutions.

The Lithuanian criminal procedure foresees that all criminal acts (including crimes involving illegal trade of tobacco—smuggling (Art. 199, CC), deceit of customs (Art. 199^1, CC), unlawful possession of goods subject to excise duties (Art. 199^2, CC), and unlawful failure to bring goods or products outside the Republic of Lithuania (Art 200, CC), etc.) are investigated and prosecuted following the same procedures. The legality principle applies to pre-trial investigations and prosecutions in Lithuania, since, in accordance with Art. 2 of the CCP, a prosecutor and a pre-trial investigator must institute criminal proceedings in every case in which the elements of a criminal act come to light and shall take all measures to conduct, as soon as possible, the pre-trial investigation to uncover the criminal act. The CCP specifies that any pre-trial investigation shall be commenced: (1) upon the receipt of a complaint, application or report about a criminal act; (2) upon the receipt of a victim's complaint; and (3) upon establishing elements of a criminal act and the drawing up of an official notice by a prosecutor or pre-trial investigator. When the prosecutor receives a complaint, an application or communication about a criminal act or where the prosecutor himself/herself ascertains the elements of a criminal act, he/she shall initiate a pre-trial investigation at the earliest opportunity. After the start of the pre-trial investigation, the prosecutor either performs the actions of the pre-trial investigation himself/herself or directs a pre-trial investigation institution to perform them. Following the receipt of a complaint, an application or a report, and, where necessary, its updated version, the prosecutor or pre-trial investigator may refuse to commence a pre-trial investigation only where the facts stated in the complaint, application or the report about the criminal act are obviously irrelevant, or circumstances which are set out in the law of the criminal procedure and make the criminal procedure unavailable are evident. It should be noted that in the course of updating a complaint, an application or a report, the prosecutor or pre-trial investigator may gather additional information, for example, by asking the person who filed the complaint, by taking documents from state institutions, etc.

A pre-trial investigation must be carried out in an expedited manner and not later than: (1) 3 months for the investigation of a misdemeanor; (2) 6 months for the investigation of negligent, minor and less serious crimes; (3) 9 months for the investigation of serious and grave crimes. These terms may be extended by the decision of a superior prosecutor due to the complexity, importance or other relevant circumstances of the case. The pre-trial investigation must be a priority in cases where suspects are arrested, as well as cases in which the suspects or victims are minors. The pre-trial investigation may be closed under the condition that all necessary pre-trial investigation actions provided for by the CCP have been conducted, and the case has been sufficiently clarified that the prosecutor may decide (a) to file an indictment, or (b) to terminate the pre-trial investigation, or (c) to suspend the pre-trial investigation (the suspension of a pre-trial investigation means a temporary pause of the pre-trial investigation that is not included in the term of the pre-trial investigation[12]).

The CCP provides an exhaustive list of admissible means of proof (kinds of evidence): testimony of the suspect and the accused; testimony of the victim; testimony of the witness; expert report; specialist conclusion; item as evidence; document as evidence.

The Lithuanian criminal procedure provides only one type of prosecution, i.e. state prosecution. State prosecution is pursued by the state prosecutor. Where the prosecutor is satisfied that sufficient evidence has been gathered during the pre-trial investigation as to the culpability of the suspect for committing a criminal act, he/she shall notify the suspect, his/her defence counsel, the victim, the plaintiff and the accused in a civil action and their representatives that the pre-trial investigation is finished and that they have a right to examine the case file and make motions for additional pre-trial investigation actions. The prosecutor must issue a reasoned decision on any motions for additional pre-trial investigation actions. Where the pre-trial investigation or the majority of its actions was conducted by a pre-trial investigation institution, the prosecutor may order that the pre-trial investigation institution submit a short written report about the pre-trial investigation it carried out (Prosecutor General 2003b). Afterwards, the prosecutor shall draft an indictment. The indictment shall state: (1) the name of the court which will hear the criminal case; (2) the name, surname, date of birth, marital status, profession, workplace of the suspect and, at the prosecutor's discretion, any other personal information; (3) a brief description of the criminal act: the place, time, forms, motives, consequences and other important circumstances; information about the victim; extenuating or aggravating circumstances for the suspect; (4) the basic information on which the prosecution is based; (5) the article (paragraph and subparagraph) of the CC establishing liability for the committed act; etc. (Prosecutor General 2015).

The Lithuanian legal system distinguishes two forms of secret data collection. Secret data collection may be performed by state authorities for the purposes of criminal proceedings and for the purposes of national security. Secret data collection for the purposes of national security is regulated by the Law on Intelligence (The Parliament of the Republic of Lithuania 2000a). Meanwhile, secret data collection

---

[12]The Lithuanian criminal procedure currently provides one discretionary ground for the suspension of a pre-trial investigation according to which, when all the necessary pre-trial investigation actions have been carried out and all possibilities to determine the offender have been exhausted, but that person's identity has not been established, a pre-trial investigation may be suspended by the reasoned decision of the prosecutor.

for the purposes of criminal proceedings is provided for in the Law on Criminal Intelligence (The Parliament of the Republic of Lithuania 2012) and CCP. According to the Law on Criminal Intelligence, an investigation involving criminal intelligence shall be started before a pre-trial investigation if: (1) there is information about the preparation of or commission of a serious or grave crime, or of a less serious crime specified in a special list (which includes all crimes involving illegal trade in tobacco—smuggling (Art. 199, CC), deceit of customs (Art. 199^1, CC), unlawful possession of goods subject to excise duties (Art. 199^2, CC), unlawful failure to bring goods or products outside the Republic of Lithuania (Art. 200, CC); (2) the suspect, accused or convicted is in hiding; (3) the person has disappeared; (4) the protection of individuals from criminal activity is carried out. During a criminal intelligence investigation, state authorities may apply such methods of secret data collection as: (a) questioning; (b) controlled delivery; (c) actions simulating a criminal act; (d) covert surveillance; (e) secret operation; (f) use of technical means, etc. If a criminal intelligence investigation reveals the *corpus delicti* signs of a criminal act, a pre-trial investigation is immediately initiated (Prosecutor General 2013). The Supreme Court of Lithuania has noted that criminal intelligence must be turned into a pre-trial investigation as soon as possible since the CCP requires the pre-trial investigation and disclosure of the criminal act to be carried out in the shortest time (The Supreme Court 2016).

When the pre-trial investigation is started, the pre-trial judge or prosecutor may order the application of covert (secret) investigative actions provided for in the CCP. The CCP lists these covert (secret) investigative actions: actions of the officers of a pre-trial investigation institution without disclosing their identity (Art. 158, CCP), simulation of a criminal act (Art. 159, CCP) and covert surveillance (Art. 160, CCP). According to the CCP, a prosecutor, upon receiving information from about plans to commit a crime or to participate in such a crime, may file an application with a pre-trial judge to authorise the person to commit actions simulating a criminal act in order to detect persons committing crimes. This measure may be applied only for the crimes provided for in the CC. When performing actions simulating a criminal act, it is prohibited to incite another person to commit a criminal act (The Supreme Court 2007a). This measure is performed by an officer of the pre-trial investigation institution. In special cases, when there are no other possibilities for detecting persons engaged in the commission of crimes, this measure may also be conducted by persons who are not officers of a pre-trial investigation institution. When authorising actions simulating a criminal act, the pre-trial judge must make a ruling specifying the following: (1) the person authorised to commit actions simulating a criminal act; (2) the person against whom such actions are to be performed; (3) information about the criminal act of that person; (4) the authorised actions; (5) the result sought. According to the CCP, actions of the officers of a pre-trial investigation institution without disclosing their identity shall be authorised by a ruling of the pre-trial judge and on condition that there is sufficient information about the criminal activities of the person who is subject to the pre-trial investigation. These officers may also engage in conduct simulating a criminal act. If such actions restrict the inviolability of the home or the secrecy of correspondence, they may be applied only when investigating less serious, serious and grave crimes. Officers of a pre-trial investigation institution conducting actions without disclosing their identity shall be prohibited from inciting or inducing a person to commit a criminal act (The Supreme Court 2010b), nor may they resort to procedural coercive measures in relation to which a separate decision or a ruling has not been made. This measure is performed by an officer of the pre-trial investigation institution. In special cases when there are no other possibilities to detect the persons committing crimes, this measure may be also performed by persons who are not officers of a pre-trial investigation institution. A prosecutor must apply for authorisation of this measure. The pre-trial judge's ruling authorising officers of a pre-trial investigation institution to perform actions without disclosing their identity must be written and reasoned, and must indicate the following: (1) the persons who will perform the undercover actions; (2) the person against whom undercover actions are to be performed; (3) information about the person's criminal act; (4) the authorised actions; (5) the result sought; (6) the duration of the undercover actions. The CCP provides that a pre-trial judge, upon receiving an appropriate application from a prosecutor, may order (acoustic and visual) covert surveillance of a person or a motor vehicle or other object (e.g. houses, flats, administrative premises, etc. (Goda et al. 2011, p. 278). An official who has taken part in secret surveillance may be questioned as a witness. If necessary, the rules of non-disclosure of the identity of a witness (official) may be applied. The ruling of a pre-trial judge or the decision of a prosecutor or a pre-trial investigator for surveillance of a person, a motor vehicle or an object must specify the following: (1) the person, the motor vehicle or the object of the surveillance; (2) the reason for such a measure; (3) the duration of the surveillance. If a video or audio recording or filming is sought (intended) during the surveillance, this must also be provided for in the ruling of the pre-trial judge, or the decision of the prosecutor or the pre-trial investigator. In cases of utmost urgency, all these covert (secret) investigative actions may also be applied by the decision of a prosecutor or a pre-trial investigator; however, if this is the case, the consent of the pre-trial judge must be sought within 3 days of the commencement of these actions. If such consent is not forthcoming, any actions that have been initiated must be terminated and all collected information must be destroyed. A record of actions simulating a criminal act, actions of the officers of a pre-trial investigation institution without disclosing their identity and secret surveillance shall be made and must be added to the case file.

During a pre-trial investigation, a pre-trial investigator and a prosecutor may carry out procedural coercive measures and investigative actions provided in the CCP. The CCP establishes an exhaustive list of these procedural coercive measures and investigative actions, which means that the pre-trial investigator, prosecutor, pre-trial judge and the court may apply only those actions. This list provides such procedural coercive measures and investigative actions as provisional arrest, committal of the suspect to a medical institution, detention, taking of samples for comparative analysis, search, seizure, temporary limitation of property rights, temporary removal from office, the prosecutor's right to request information, taking photographs, filming, taking measurements, fingerprints and samples for genetic dactiloscopy, actions of the officers of a pre-trial investigation institution without disclosing their identity, simulation of a criminal act, covert surveillance, etc.

The CCP provides that the prosecutor who acts as the prosecuting party during the trial must bring a civil action, if it has not yet been brought, where injury to the State has been caused by a criminal act. Furthermore, when a civil action is brought at the pre-trial investigation stage, the pre-trial investigator and prosecutor must collect information proving the legal ground and value of the civil action. During the criminal procedure, a pre-trial investigator, prosecutor or the court must invoke remedies for the pending civil action: to discover property belonging to the suspect or the accused, or a person who bears material responsibility for the actions of the suspect or the accused and to impose a temporary limitation of property rights.

A temporary limitation of the property rights of a suspect or a natural person who is financially responsible for the actions of the suspect, or of another natural person who has possession of property received or acquired by criminal means, may be imposed by the decision of a prosecutor. The temporary limitation of the property rights of a legal entity also may be imposed with a view to securing a civil claim or the confiscation of property. According to scholars of the Lithuanian criminal procedure (Bilius and Stonys 2016, p. 389), a temporary limitation of property rights is a procedural coercion measure, which fulfils a preventive function. A temporary limitation on property rights may be imposed together with or separately from a seizure or search. A temporary limitation of property rights shall be revoked by the decision of a prosecutor or a court ruling where the measure is no longer necessary. A prosecutor's decision on a temporary limitation of property rights may not be for longer than for a period of 6 months. This term may be extended, but for not more than two periods of 3 months by a ruling of a pre-trial judge. However, the number of extensions in cases involving serious and grave crimes or when a suspect is in hiding shall not be subject to any limits. Where a temporary limitation is imposed on bank deposits, all transactions involving them shall be suspended if the decision on a temporary limitation of property rights does not provide otherwise. A person on whom a temporary limitation of rights of property has been imposed shall be entitled to appeal against the decision of the prosecutor to the pre-trial judge. Such an appeal must be reviewed by the pre-trial judge within 3 days from the receipt of the appeal. The decision of the pre-trial judge may be appealed against to a higher court, the decision whereof shall be final and not subject to appeal.

2 Criminological Data

2.1 General Data on Registered Crimes of Illicit Trade in Tobacco Products

The crime rate during 2005–2016 shows a constantly growing number of registered crimes of illicit trade in tobacco products (smuggling (Art. 199, CC), unlawful possession of goods subject to excise duties (Art. 199^2, CC), customs deceit (Art. 199^1, CC) and unlawful failure to bring goods or products outside the Republic of Lithuania (Art. 200, CC)), of cases involving illicit trade in tobacco products decided in court, and of sentenced persons (see Table 1).[13] It should be noted that this data is of a general nature; illicit trade in tobacco products is not distinguished from illicit trade of other kinds of products. On the other hand, statistical data and scientific research show that, for example, about 80% of smuggling cases consist of cigarette smuggling (Bikelis et al. 2017, p. 40). Data on the number of registered crimes of illicit trade in tobacco products shows that the largest proportion of these crimes is constitutes by smuggling, the highest number of which was recorded in 2013, at 599. The next most frequently registered crime of this type is unlawful possession of goods subject to excise duties, the highest number of which was reported also in 2013, at 394. Meanwhile, the highest number of other registered crimes of this type, deceit of customs, was registered in 2011 (8 cases), while the highest number of cases (14) of unlawful failure to bring goods or products outside the Republic of Lithuania was registered in 2010. It should be noted that in the opinion of experts (confirmed by trends in illicit trade in tobacco products), tobacco smuggling and other crimes of illicit trade in tobacco products are likely to remain at the same level in the nearest future.

The biggest number of cases decided in court involving smuggling was in 2014, at 220, while cases of unlawful possession of goods subject to excise duties was in 2015, at 230. In addition, the highest number of persons sentenced (acquitted) for smuggling was in 2014—277 (13), and of unlawful possession of goods subject to excise duties was in 2015—328 (10).

Data on the value of seized illegal goods (which is of a general nature; illicit trade in tobacco products is not distinguished from illicit trade of other kinds of products) shows that the highest value of seized goods was in 2014, and amounted to €42.9 million (see Table 2).[14] Meanwhile, the largest number of seized cigarettes was in 2016—238 million packs—and the highest volume of seized tobacco was in 2011—69,000 kg.

Moreover, data on losses caused by tobacco products detected during the period of 2010–2018 shows that the greatest damage was caused in 2016—€29.2 million, while the lowest was caused in 2013—€10.2 million[15] (see Table 3). In Lithuania, 570 million smuggled cigarettes were consumed in 2017. According to the "Project Sun" survey, it is estimated that the country's budget lost €62 million of potential income due to the shadow tobacco market. Growth of the illicit market for tobacco

[13]Data on the number of registered crimes, decided cases in courts and sentenced (acquitted) persons was collected from the databases of the Statistics Department, the National Court Administration and Yearly Reports of the Prosecutor General.

[14]Data on the number of detected administrative offences, initiated pre-trial investigations, value of seized illegal goods, number of seized cigarettes (in packs), number of seized tobacco (in kilos) and number of detected and closed illegal factories for counterfeiting cigarettes was collected from the databases of the Customs Criminal Service.

[15]Data received from the Customs Department.

by 1% generates about €3 million in losses for the state budget. According to the Nielsen Empty Packet Survey, illegal cigarettes accounted for 16.5% of the Lithuanian market in 2018 (for example, in 2017, illegal cigarettes in Lithuania accounted for 19.6% of the market) (Ignotas 2018).

2.2 *Data on Punishments and Measures (Penal and Others) Applied with Regard to Offenders of Illicit Trade in Tobacco Products*

Lithuanian statistics on imposed punishments and penal measures did not provide separate data on punishments and penal measures for the illicit trade in tobacco products. The number of persons serving imprisonment for smuggling (Art. 199, CC) decreased from 79 in 2012 to 47 in 2017. Moreover, 26 persons were newcomers to prison sentenced for smuggling and 26 persons who had been sentenced for smuggling were released from prison in 2017 (see Table 4).[16] The average court-imposed term of imprisonment increased from 6 years 2 months and 2 days in 2012 to 6 years 7 months and 16 days in 2016; while the average of actually served terms of imprisonment increased from 2 years 3 months and 5 days in 2012 to 2 years 9 months and 10 days in 2017 (see Table 5).[17] It should be noted that the average term of imposed and actually served terms of imprisonment for smuggling was significantly longer than the general average, which consisted of 7 years and 10 days and 4 years 3 months and 19 days in 2017 respectively (see Table 5).[18] Moreover, the average term of actually served imprisonment for smuggling increased significantly from 2 years 2 months and 17 days in 2012 to 4 years 3 months and 19 days in 2017.

Notably, the number of suspected (accused) legal persons was relatively high, and ranged from 110 in 2010 to 29 in 2016. On the other hand, few of them were suspected (accused) of smuggling—only 1 in 2008 and 2010–2012 (see Table 6).[19]

It is worth mentioning the results of a scientific study on cigarette smuggling in Lithuania that was published in 2017 (Bikelis et al. 2017). According to the study, during 2009–2013, about 80% of all convicts at the time of commission of their

---

[16]Data on newcomers to correctional institutions sentenced for smuggling, persons imprisoned for smuggling and persons released from prison who were sentenced for smuggling was collected from the databases of the Prison Department.

[17]Data on the general average of court-imposed and actually served terms of imprisonment was collected from the databases of the Statistics Department.

[18]Data on the average of court-imposed and actually served terms of imprisonment for smuggling was collected from the databases of the Prison Department.

[19]Data on the number of suspected and sentenced legal persons was collected from the databases of the Statistics Department. It should be noted that this data is of general nature; illicit trade in tobacco products is not distinguished from other kinds of crimes. Data on the number of legal persons suspected of smuggling was collected from the databases of the Ministry of the Interior.

crimes did not have a criminal record (previous conviction) (Bikelis et al. 2017, p. 68; see Table 7). It should be noted that 57.6% of persons convicted for smuggling and unlawful possession of goods (cigarettes) subject to excise duties remanded for imprisonment had a criminal record (previous conviction), and only 8.7% convicted and ordered to pay a fine had a criminal record (previous conviction) (Bikelis et al. 2017, p. 68).

During 2009–2013, imprisonment for smuggling (Para 1, Art. 199, CC) was imposed on 80 persons: up to 6 months—17, from 6 to 12 months—13, from 12 to 18 months—7, from 18 to 24 months—12, from 24 to 30 months—12, from 30 to 36 months—9 and more than 36 months—10. Meanwhile, a fine for smuggling (Para 1, Art. 199, CC) during 2009–2010 was imposed on 97 persons, and in 2012—on 105.

During 2009–2013, imprisonment for unlawful possession of goods (cigarettes) subject to excise duties (Art. 199^2, CC) was imposed on 56 persons: up to 6 months—7, from 6 to 12 months—13, from 12 to 18 months—9, from 18 to 24 months—12 and more than 24 months—15. Meanwhile, a fine for unlawful possession of goods (cigarettes) subject to excise duties (Art. 199^2, CC) during 2009–2010 was imposed on 161 persons, and 2012–2013—279.

Moreover, imprisonment was imposed in most cases for persons who committed crimes in complicity—15.5% in cases of a group of accomplices and 18.1% in cases of an organised group (on the distribution of persons sentenced to imprisonment or a fine according to the form of complicity (2009–2013) see Table 8).

Also, it should be noted that young people under 25 years of age dominate among those sentenced to imprisonment for smuggling, and persons under 34 years of age constitute over 90% (Bikelis et al. 2017, p. 71). Meanwhile, among those sentenced to imprisonment for unlawful possession of goods (cigarettes) subject to excise duties acts and smuggling (so-called "truck drivers" cases), prisoners under the age of 25 did not appear at all (on the distribution of persons sentenced to imprisonment by age and by crime qualification (in per cent) (2009–2013) see Table 9).

Official data on estimated the financial impact of prosecuted cases of illicit trade in tobacco products and the total amount and share of asset recovery related to illicit trade in tobacco products is not collected in Lithuania.

2.3 *Short Description of the Most Interesting and/or Exemplary Case Studies with Regard to Illicit Trade in Tobacco Products*

One of the biggest smuggling case in Lithuania was the case in which M.T. and 32 other people were accused of more than 150 crimes committed in a criminal association. For example, this criminal association was accused on cigarette smuggling, when in Lithuania alone 19 trucks with smuggled cigarettes from Russia and Belarus were seized with a value of approx. 23 million litas. Another 12 cargoes (value of approx. 10 million litas) were detained in Latvia, Estonia, Poland and Germany. The criminal association operated until 2011 in Lithuania, Latvia, Belarus, Russia, the Netherlands and Germany. According to prosecutors, from the beginning of 2008 until the end of 2011, members of the association bought several cargo haulage companies, several dozen trucks and semi-trailers with cigarette shelters. Cigarettes were purchased from special criminal funds in Russia and Belarus. Smuggling of cigarettes was organised by the continual use of transportation schemes and other means of transportation, routes and hiding places, falsified car indentification numbers; some cigarettes were transported by using timber cargo mulches; semi-trailers and their registration numbers were changed at intermediate locations of cigarette transportation; in some cases, unhindered transportation of cigarettes through the Lithuanian state border was secured by bribed customs officials, etc. Prosecutors also brought charges claiming that members of the association in Lithuania produced at least 1200 kg of first-class precursors of narcotic and psychotropic substances, which they sold to other persons for at least €1.5 million (Sinkevičius 2015).

Another large-scale smuggling case investigated in Lithuania, in which former police officer V. K. was accused with other persons of having formed a criminal association and having organized a cigarette smuggling ring valued at millions of euros in Russia, Belarus, Poland and Germany. The prosecutor claimed that cigarettes were brought to Lithuania from Belarus in 2009–2010 and transported from Lithuania to Germany via Poland. In addition, the prosecutor's accusation states that smugglers gave bribes worth approx. €50,000–80,000 to customs officials (Steniulienė 2019).

Main types of smuggling in Lithuania:

- carriage of tobacco products which are hidden among other goods in trucks;
- carriage of tobacco products which are indicated in documents as other goods in trucks;
- "open" carriage of tobacco products in small transport vehicles (e.g. Ford Transit, Fiat Ducato, Volkswagen Transit, etc.) with the expectation that customs officials will not carry out an inspection (as a rule, on the border between Lithuania and Latvia);
- waterway transport of tobacco products over the Nemunas River by so-called ichtiandrs, sometimes even underwater transhipment (as a rule, on the border between Lithuania and Russia (Kaliningrad);
- first attempts for the carriage of tobacco products by railway transport were detected in 2018;
- physical carriage by natural persons of tobacco products through the state border (usually in the forest between Lithuania and Belarus).

Also, there are other qualitative differences between the small and large-scale illegal trade in cigarettes. Small-scale consumers are residents of Lithuania, while large-scale illegal trade in cigarettes usually is dedicated to transit from cheap illegal (or legal) cigarette factories in Belarus and Russia to Western European countries (Germany, United Kingdom, Ireland, Sweden, Norway, etc.), which, due to economic and geographic peculiarities, form a "trade belt" of networks dealing in illegal trade in cigarettes (Bikelis et al. 2017, p. 55).

2.4 Characteristics of Perpetrators of Illicit Trade in Tobacco Products in Lithuania (Age, Gender, Education, Nationality/Citizenship, Prior Criminal Record, Other Information)

The results of the above-mentioned study on cigarette smuggling in Lithuania show that during 2009–2013, in the case of administrative offenses, a significant proportion of the offenders (especially in the case of illegal possession of cigarettes) consisted of women, whereas criminal cases of smuggling were dominated by men (Para 1, Art. 199, CC), as was unlawful possession of goods subject to excise duties (Art. 199^2, CC). Out of 1165 persons prosecuted under the above-mentioned articles of the CC, men accounted for as much as 97.4% (1135), while only 2.6% (30) were women (Bikelis et al. 2017, p. 59).

The dominance of men can be explained by the specificity of these crimes. First of all, such crimes often require male physical strength since cigarettes, which must be in large amounts, should be loaded, reloaded, transported, etc. Moreover, such dominance is also explained by men's skills and knowledge about the transport and technical means necessary to commit these criminal acts. Analysis of the age distribution of men convicted for smuggling shows that more than half (57.2%) were particularly young ($\leq$24 years of age). Meanwhile, slightly older men (35–44 years of age) were mostly (33.1%) convicted for the unlawful possession of goods subject to excise duties. Men of this age group also constituted the largest share (38.8%) among convicts under both articles of the CC (Bikelis et al. 2017, p. 59).

The age of convicted persons is also determined by the fact that persons convicted of smuggling were usually unmarried (68%). At that time, the proportion of those who had already been convicted of unlawful possession of goods (cigarettes) subject to excise duties was equal (42% and 41% respectively) (see Table 10). It should be noted that the data on the distribution of age and marital status reflect the general family situation in society, i.e. the largest number unmarried convicts are under 24 years of age, from 25 to 44 years old, divorced and widowed from 44 years of age (Bikelis et al. 2017, p. 60).

The analysis of the education of convicts shows that persons convicted under Art. 199^2 of CC and under both articles of CC (53.2% and 67.3% respectively) had at least secondary education. Meanwhile, even 47.6% of convicted persons for the smuggling (Para 1, Art. 199, CC) had not yet been acquired the secondary education (see Table 11). This tendency can also be determined by the young age of convicts for smuggling (Bikelis et al. 2017, p. 61).

The data shows that, at the time of commission of the crime, there were more unemployed than those in work among persons convicted for a single crime (see

Table 12). In contrast, when a person was convicted of both crimes (Para 1, Art. 199 and Art. 199^2, CC), the number of employed was, on the contrary, higher than that of unemployed. It is likely that this group of convicts consisted mostly of truck drivers trying to make a profit from illegal activity—smuggling of cigarettes and their further transport in the territory of Lithuania (when a truck is detained at a border customs post, the driver's activity is usually qualified as concurrence of two crimes (Art. 199 and 199^2, CC) (Bikelis et al. 2017, pp. 62–63).

The distribution of convicts by citizenship shows that the vast majority of persons convicted only under one of the articles (Art. 199 or Art. 199^2, CC) were citizens of Lithuania. Among the persons convicted under both articles of CC, citizenship varied, as there were more frequent cases committed not only by citizens of Lithuania, but also of neighbouring countries (citizens of Belarus, Poland and Russia) (see Table 13). Most of them were truck drivers detained crossing the Lithuania state border with hidden cigarettes (Bikelis et al. 2017, p. 63).

Official data from the databases of the Ministry of the Interior on the distribution of those suspected of smuggling (Art. 199, CC) by gender, education (see Table 14), occupation (see Table 15) and citizenship (see Table 16) does not show a greater difference in the period of 2014–2018.

It should be noted that crimes involving illicit trade in tobacco products are most commonly committed in complicity through the forms of a group of accomplices and organized group (and only in some instances—criminal association, which is the most dangerous form of organised crime). Usually, smuggling (Art. 199, CC) is committed by a group of accomplices or by an organized group (see Table 17). Meanwhile, unlawful possession of goods (cigarettes) subject to excise duties (Art. 199^2, CC) or both crimes are usually committed by a single truck driver. If the cargo is seized at a border crossing point during routine customs checks (without criminal intelligence), it is very difficult to the establish driver's relationship with the organizers and other accomplices. The driver does not usually provide the identities of accomplices, assumes the guilt and presents unconvincing stories that he/she is the organizer and perpetrator of the crime. It should be noted that data on complicity was not even obtained; the circumstances of many cases indirectly indicated that the driver was not alone (for example, a large quantity of cigarettes and bad financial situation of the driver may give rise to doubts as to his/her ability and possibility to obtain a large quantity of cigarettes, as well as to transport them independently, etc.). If detection is the result of a criminal intelligence investigation, the cigarette transport scheme and accomplices are more often identified (Bikelis et al. 2017, p. 58).

According to the data, the organizers were mostly 25–34 years old (50% of all convicts). Persons aged less than 25 years old and over 44 years old people among the organizers constituted only 22%. Married persons accounted for 52% of the organizers, while two-thirds of them were officially employed. Higher education was held by 24, while 56.5% had a secondary education. A total of 24% of organizers had a criminal record. Although the social portrait of these individuals was quite positive, in smuggling cases, as many as 38% (unlawful possession of goods (cigarettes)—

15%) of organizers were sentenced to real imprisonment (Bikelis et al. 2017, pp. 64–65).

Meanwhile, convicted accomplices make up a vast majority of the perpetrators—84.3%. Two groups of perpetrators can be distinguished—the so-called "mules" carrying cigarettes on their person (in 90% of all cases—through a "green zone") and drivers. The "mules" constituted 58% of all perpetrators. According to the data, "mules" were mostly young men: under 25 years old—63%, younger than 34 years old—82%. Only 13% of them were married; 25% were officially employed; 11% had completed tertiary education (57% did not even have secondary education). Of the "mules", 24% had a criminal record, while 27% of them had been imprisoned (Bikelis et al. 2017, p. 66). The social portrait of the second group, drivers (not truck drivers), exhibits many similarities to the "mules", but was a little "brighter". Drivers are somewhat older, although a large proportion of them (50%) consisted of young people under 25 years of age; 43% were married; 43% were officially employed; 8% had completed higher education (51.4%—did not have secondary education). A criminal record was found for 22% of drivers. Only 19.5% of drivers had been sentenced to real imprisonment (Bikelis et al. 2017, p. 66).

Another group of perpetrators consists of truck drivers carrying illegal (usually hidden) cigarette loads through customs posts. This group of perpetrators dominates among those convicted under both articles (Para 1, Art. 199 and Art. 199^2, CC). The age of these convicts is older: the predominant age groups were 35–44 years (43%) and 25–34 years (33%). A large majority of them were officially employed; two-thirds were married. There was no criminal record for 97% of them. Of these persons, 71% were convicted of the carriage of cigarette loads of a very high value. Most of them were citizens of foreign countries (Russia, Belarus) (Bikelis et al. 2017, pp. 66–67).

Moreover, accessories are usually members of lower social class and are local residents of border villages. In smuggling cases, 71% of them were under 24 years of age. These statistics do not include children, who are sometimes involved in cigarette smuggling. Other social data was "poor"—only 27% were officially employed; 11%—married; 40%—without secondary education. Of the accessories in smuggling cases, 20% had a criminal record. Despite their relatively small role, 13% of accessories were sentenced to real imprisonment (Bikelis et al. 2017, p. 68).

3 Preventive Measures

Lithuania has implemented certain measures in compliance with FCTC and the Protocol, as well as the Tobacco Directive (Directive 2014/40/EU of the European Parliament and of the Council), which are covered by the above-mentioned Law of Control of Tobacco, Tobacco Products and Related Products:

3.1 Measures Relating to Track and Tracing System

Requirements for a "track and tracing" system were added to the Law on Control of Tobacco, Tobacco Products and Related Products on 9 June 2016 by amending law No. XII-2419 (The Parliament of the Republic of Lithuania 2016a). These requirements came into force on 20 May 2019. In accordance with the above-mentioned Law, on 16 November 2018, the head of the State Tax Inspectorate under the Ministry of Finance adopted Order No. VA-90 "On the Establishment of a Procedure for Marking and Registration of Wholesale Tobacco Packaging as referred to in Article 14(1) of the Law on Control of Tobacco, Tobacco Products and Related Products" (State Tax Inspectorate under the Ministry of Finance of the Republic of Lithuania 2018), which states that the wholesale packaging of tobacco products shall be marked and registered in accordance with the procedure laid down in the European Commission (hereinafter—EC) Implementing Regulation (EU) 2018/574 of 15 December 2017 technical standards for the establishment and operation of the traceability system for tobacco products (The European Commission 2017). Thus, the Lithuanian system of national regulation on the "track and tracing" system of tobacco products is fully compliant with EC standards as well as the requirements of the Protocol.

3.2 Measures Relating to the Reduction of Demand for Tobacco

Price and tax measures were taken to reduce the demand for tobacco products (as in Art. 6, FCTC)—during the last few years prices of all tobacco products have increased; in only the last year the price of electronic cigarettes liquid fillings increased twice due to new excise duty rates which had not been previously applied to electronic cigarettes; the rates of excise duties have increased again since March 2019, raising tobacco product prices even higher.

Non-price measures to reduce the demand for tobacco products (as in Art. 7, FCTC) include education on the effects of short and long-term passive and active smoking on one's health in schools, medical institutions, etc. Other measures include various legal restrictions: it is forbidden to sell tobacco products in vending machines, in pharmaceutical companies, health care, education, cultural institutions, Internet cafes (online clubs, etc.); locations for sale of tobacco products are restricted to specialised kiosks—it is forbidden to place and sell any tobacco products at checkouts or anywhere in stores next to other products. It is also forbidden to give away free samples of tobacco products, include them in sets with other products, add them as a present or a prize in lotteries or games, exchange them for coupons, etc., affect buyers by showing discounts for tobacco products, sell any other products whose design imitates tobacco products or marking them with their signs.

Protection from exposure to tobacco smoke (as in Art. 8, FCTC). It is forbidden to smoke inside cafés and, currently, even though smoking is not strictly forbidden in the outdoor areas of cafés, café managers must ensure that customers are not forced to breathe in tobacco smoke. A new legislative amendment has been registered which aims to completely ban smoking in outdoor cafés as well as on balconies and terraces of apartment buildings if at least one resident of the building is opposed to smoking, as well as at public transport stops (pavilions), playgrounds and leisure venues where sporting events or other events take place.

Regulation of the contents of tobacco products (as in Art. 9, FCTC and Art. 3, Tobacco Directive) include standards for maximum amount of released substances: 10 mg of resins, 1 mg of nicotine, 10 mg of CO (carbon monoxide) per cigarette. In order to reduce the addictiveness of the product, it is forbidden to place tobacco products on the market which have, for example, added flavours or smells which would hide the natural taste, smell, strength of tobacco, as well as any vitamins, caffeine, taurine or other components associated with energy, healthy lifestyle (or give the impression that particular cigarettes are somehow less detrimental to health). Also, there cannot be any tobacco, nicotine, or flavouring in cigarette filters, paper, capsules or any other technical element of a cigarette. It is prohibited to sell oral, chewing and snuff tobacco in Lithuania.

Regulation of tobacco product disclosures (as in Art. 10, FCTC)—manufacturers and/or importers of tobacco products have to submit a specified form of report to the Drug, Tobacco and Alcohol Control Department that includes a list of components, their quantity and other features of all tobacco products in accordance with legal regulations as well as sales volumes of each product. The gathered information is publicly accessible online.

Packaging and labelling of tobacco products is specific (as in Art. 11, FCTC and section II, Tobacco Directive): every package of cigarettes must be marked with certain warning signs which inform users about the health risks of the product—texts about the health risks of smoking or pictures showing diseases caused by smoking—that must fill at least 50% of the package surface (if composed of combined text and picture—65%, other tobacco products—at least 30%), they cannot be covered in any way (with extra packaging, stickers, prices, etc.) and must be in Lithuanian. It is also forbidden to include any elements on the package which make a false impression that the product is somehow less harmful to one's health (statements, markings, etc.). The package must include a unique identifier allowing to determine the production date, place, transfer routes, etc. as well as to carry a tamper-proof security feature composed of visible and invisible elements.

Education, communication, training and public awareness (as in Art. 12, FCTC)—schools that deliver formal education incorporate issues about the health damage caused by the use of tobacco products, a health-friendly environment preventing damage from smoking, and a healthy lifestyle into the general education curriculum. Information and a list of ingredients of each tobacco product containing tar, nicotine and carbon monoxide are available and distributed to consumers by all appropriate means.

Tobacco advertising and promotion in mass media (open or hidden) is forbidden, as well as sponsorship (as in Art. 13, FCTC). At retail outlets, only certain formal and brief information on equipment intended to accommodate tobacco products is allowed.

Demand reduction measures concerning tobacco dependence and cessation (as in Art. 14, FCTC): smoking is prohibited in all educational, social service institutions providing social care and/or social care services for children, health care institutions and their premises; workplaces in enclosed spaces (except special facilities (places) where smoking is allowed if they comply with requirements), in common dwellings, other common areas where non-smokers may be forced to breathe in smoke-polluted air; all types of public transport, except long-distance trains, which must include separate wagons for non-smokers and smokers, as well as aircraft with separate seats for non-smokers and smokers; restaurants, cafes, bars, other catering establishments, clubs, discos, Internet cafes (internet clubs, etc.), gambling houses (casinos), vending machines or bingo halls, other leisure facilities, sports facilities or other events, and other facilities for serving people, except specially equipped cigar and/or pipe clubs. Municipal councils have the right to prohibit smoking in public places (parks, squares, etc.) and other areas within their competence. Management bodies of a legal person must ensure that employees of legal persons, serviced customers and visitors are not forced to breathe in air contaminated with tobacco smoke, and that special warning rooms (places) and smoking rooms are provided in visible places with placards or signs pointing to them.

3.3 Measures Relating to the Reduction of the Supply of Tobacco

Illicit trade in tobacco products (as in Art. 15, FCTC) is controlled by preventive, administrative and criminal legal measures. The main national institutions responsible for the prevention of illicit trade in tobacco products are, *inter alia*, the Customs Department and Drug, Tobacco and Alcohol Control Department. The Customs Department carries out risk assessment using all available information sources; creates risk profiles, which automatically notify customs officers about risks occurring at the borders; performs its own risk profiling at central and regional levels, etc. The Drug, Tobacco and Alcohol Control Department (established in 2011) participates in forming and implementing state policy on drug, tobacco and alcohol control and use prevention; cooperates with the European Monitoring Centre for Drugs and Drug Addiction and other EU institutions, international partners and with non-EU countries, etc.

Sales to and by minors (as in Art. 16, FCTC)—it is forbidden to sell any tobacco or tobacco-related products (including electronic cigarettes and refill containers) to anyone under 18 years old. It is prohibited for persons under 18 years of to smoke or consume tobacco products age. Tobacco products cannot be sold in any places where at least 50% of products are intended for children. Every point of sale for tobacco products must display warning signs that tobacco products are not sold to anyone under 18. If a person looks young, the cashier has to ask for a document to check the buyer's age. It is prohibited to create and publish commercials in which tobacco products are promoted by underage persons.

It should be noted that there are no official statistics on the impact of the above-mentioned measures on illicit trade in tobacco products in Lithuania. Meanwhile, the latest Nielsen Empty Packet Survey (2018) shows that illegal cigarettes still make up 16.5% of the Lithuanian market (in 2017 this was 19.6% of the Lithuanian market). Moreover, some experts have emphasised that increasing excise duties on cigarettes may have the same impact as increased excise duties on alcohol: a significant increase of excise duties resulted in a significant increase in alcohol smuggling in 2018. However, not all scientific research shows that increased excise duties on cigarettes have an unambiguous and clear influence on the growth of smuggling (Misiūnas and Rimkus 2007, pp. 45, 47; Bikelis et al. 2017, pp. 12–15, etc.).

4 Cooperation

Laws on national institutions responsible for the fight against illicit trade in tobacco products (CCS, SBPS, Police Department, etc.) provide that these institutions have the right to cooperate with other national and foreign institutions. There is a different legal framework for state authorities to provide information on cooperation by other national institutions. For example, Art. 11 of the Law on Customs (The Parliament of the Republic of Lithuania 2004a) provides that "the Customs, having information about suspected violations of legal acts, the prevention or investigation of which belongs to other law enforcement institutions of Lithuania, shall immediately submit it to these law enforcement authorities within its competence". Meanwhile, the Law on State Border Protection (The Parliament of the Republic of Lithuania 2017) provides the general right for the SBPS to provide gathered information to other state institutions. Only Art. 23 of the above-mentioned Law sets out special obligation for the SBPS to inform customs immediately about illegal transport of goods and cargo not passing through border control points. It should be noted that in order to make cooperation among different state institutions more effective at central and operational levels, the Interagency Cooperation Agreement between Police, Customs and State Border Guard Service (20 May 2002) was signed. Pursuant to the provisions of this agreement, working groups are formed and contact persons appointed at central, regional and local levels of the police, customs and SBPS, cooperation forms are established, forms of sharing criminal intelligence and other data from institutional databases have been defined, etc. Moreover, such bilateral and multilateral national cooperation agreements concluded by the Customs

Department as the Agreement between the Criminal Intelligence Institutions, the Prosecutor General's Office of the Republic of Lithuania and the District Courts on sanctioning of means of criminal intelligence in the criminal intelligence telecommunications network (2018), Agreement between the Criminal Intelligence Institutions and the Prosecutor General's Office on Co-operation and Coordination of Criminal Intelligence (2017), Cooperation agreement between the Customs Department, State Border Protection Service, Financial Crime Investigation Service and Police Department (2010), Cooperation agreement between the Customs Department and Police Department (2005), etc could be mentioned. In addition, it should be noted that criminal intelligence activities and institutional cooperation on investigation of crimes of illicit trade in tobacco products, in accordance with the Law on Criminal Intelligence, must be coordinated and ensured by the prosecutor.

Assessment of the legal regulation and the opinions of experts allow for the conclusion that the legal framework for interinstitutional cooperation and the division of competences are appropriate and accurate, while practical cooperation and exchange of criminal intelligence (though improved over the past 5–8 years) could be more effective. Nevertheless, experts have pointed out that the main difficulty (or even challenge) is mutual trust, which determines effective day-to-day cooperation (especially exchange of information of criminal intelligence) between different institutions.

Cooperation of the Customs Department and CCS in administrative matters with institutions of other EU Member States is based on the Convention on mutual assistance and cooperation between customs administrations (1998), drawn up on the basis of Article K.3 of the Treaty on European Union. Moreover, the Customs Department has concluded bilateral cooperation treaties with the competent institutions of other EU Member States, for example, the Consortium agreement between the Customs Department of Lithuania and National Board of Customs of Finland (2011), the Agreement between the Customs Department under the Ministry of Finance of Lithuania, the Estonian Tax and Customs Service, the State Tax Service of Latvia and the National Tax Administration of Poland on the exchange of information between automated identification systems (2017), etc. Mutual assistance in criminal matters is carried out by competent prosecutors on the basis of the Convention on Mutual Assistance in Criminal Matters between the Member States of the EU (2000), established by the Council in accordance with Article 34 of the Treaty on European Union, and other EU legal acts on legal cooperation (for example, European Investigation Order according to the Directive for a European Investigation Order, etc.), etc.

The assessment of legal regulation, practice of cooperation and opinions of experts allow for the statement that cooperation on all administrative matters mostly takes place with Latvia, Estonia, Germany, Poland, the United Kingdom and the Scandinavian countries, and it is sufficiently effective. Particular emphasis is placed on the effectiveness of cooperation with Germany and the United Kingdom through liaison officers. Moreover, a few negative aspects of cooperation in criminal matters were highlighted: (a) quite significant differences in national legal regulation, particularly of the means and grounds of criminal intelligence, and (b) quite significant differences of state institutions responsible for the fight against illicit trade in tobacco products (for example, some of them are law enforcement agencies and have the right to collect criminal intelligence, while others do not, etc.).

Customs Department and CCS cooperation in administrative matters with the institutions of non-EU Member States (Russia, Belarus, Ukraine, Georgia, USA, etc.) is based on mutual agreements, for example, the Joint declaration between the Customs Department of Lithuania and US Justice department (2010), etc. Mutual assistance in criminal matters is carried out through competent prosecutors only on the basis of the conventions of the Council of Europe (for example, Convention on Extradition and its additional protocols, Convention on Mutual Assistance in Criminal Matters and its additional protocols, etc.), as well as mutual treaties on legal assistance in Lithuanian criminal matters (for example, Lithuania has concluded such treaties with Russia, Belarus, Ukraine, China, USA, etc.). Experts drew attention only to the complicated cooperation with Russia, because the execution of requests takes a long time and quality is poor. This situation may be explained, *inter alia*, by the fact that Russia (and Belarus, Ukraina, Moldova, etc.) receives substantial income to the state budget from factories producing cheap legal cigarettes, so these countries are not too interested in controlling and cooperating (especially regarding exchange of information) in matters concerning trade in tobacco products.

Furthermore, Lithuanian Customs officers participate in the activities of the Operating Committee of the Task-Force of the Baltic Sea Region on fighting organized crime (Denmark, Estonia, Finland, Germany, Iceland, Latvia, Lithuania, Norway, Poland, Russia and Sweden). The Operating Committee is tasked with facilitating cooperation and promoting the exchange of information on joint operational measures and actions between member states.

Representatives of Lithuanian Customs take part in the activities of the EU Council's working groups, the High Level Working Party of Directors General and expert working groups on Customs Union and Customs Cooperation, as well as in the EU Council's Internal Security Committee (COSI). Experts from Lithuanian Customs participate in the activities of the EC's Committees and Expert Groups. It should be noted that Lithuanian Customs, according to Council Regulation (EC) No 515/97, exchange information with the competent authorities by means of the Anti-Fraud Information System (AFIS), personal data contained in the Export Control System (ECS) and New Computerized Transit Information System (NCTS) with a view to identifying fraud cases. Lithuanian Customs also take part, through competent prosecutors or other officials, in cooperation with special agencies of the EU—EUROPOL, EUROJUST, OLAF.

5 General Issues

5.1 Rates of Excise Duties on Cigarettes, Cigars, Cigarillos and Smoking Tobacco

According to the Law on Excise Duties (The Parliament of the Republic of Lithuania 2018), the rates of excise duties on cigarettes, cigars, cigarillos and smoking tobacco from 1 March 2019 in Lithuania are: (a) for cigarettes—€62.25 per 1000 cigarettes (€65.7 from 1 March 2020 and €69.4 from 1 March 2021); (b) a combined excise duty for cigarettes—of at least €102 per 1000 cigarettes (€108.5 from 1 March 2020 and €115.5 from 1 March 2021); (c) for cigars and cigarillos—€42 per kilogram of product (€48 from 1 March 2020 and €55 from 1 March 2021); (d) smoking tobacco—€68.6 per kilogram of product (€78.5 from 1 March 2020 and €90 from 1 March 2021). Meanwhile, in retail stores the official price of the most popular cigarettes "Marlboro" ranges from €3.65 to €3.87 per pack.

By comparison, currently, one pack of the most popular smuggled cigarettes from Belarus, "Minsk", "Fest" and "NZ" on the black market in Lithuania costs around €2 (buying up to 10 packs the price is around €2.20/€2.30 per pack, and in larger quantities (for example, more than 1000 packs)—the price of one pack should be around €1.70/€1.80 per pack).

5.2 Main Social, Political and Geographical Factors Which Contribute to the Illicit Trade in Tobacco Products in Lithuania

Scientific research, statistical data and the opinions of experts show that the low incomes of residents of some border regions in Lithuania, high differences of prices of tobacco products when comparing Lithuania with neighbouring countries (for example, one pack of cigarettes is 7 times more expensive in Lithuania than in Belarus), and traditional close social contacts (or even family relations) with Belarus are the main social factors which contribute to the illicit trade in tobacco products in Lithuania. Scientific research and statistical data also show a correlation between unemployment and decrease in the consumption of legal cigarettes which was observed in 2008–2010, when rising unemployment significantly reduced consumption of legal cigarettes (Bikelis et al. 2017, p. 18). Furthermore, sociological surveys also show that one of the social factors is the favorable attitude of Lithuanians towards smuggling and the use of smuggled cigarettes (31% of Lithuanian residents have justified smuggling and illegal use of goods in 2017). Another interesting trend is that the smuggling of tobacco products has been targeted at emigrants from

Lithuania and other states of the former Soviet Union living in Germany, Norway, Sweden, etc. Also, criminal groups which organize smuggling of tobacco products mostly consist of members from Lithuania or the former Soviet Union. Some experts also have pointed to increased rates of excise duties on cigarettes (even beyond EU requirements), but this factor should be analysed more deeply.

Scientific research (Šatienė et al. 2011, pp. 19–28) and the opinions of experts indicate that among the main political and institutional factors which contribute to the illicit trade in tobacco products in Lithuania are corruption (of customs officials), an insufficient number of officials with the necessary qualifications and practical experience, and the lack of a sufficient number of appropriate technical means (for example, X-ray machines, drones, border protection technologies, etc.). Some experts have pointed out that for a more effective fight against the illicit trade in tobacco products, the following would be beneficial: (i) increase in the number of qualified officials; (ii) increased funding for salaries and (iii) additional technical equipment and modern border surveillance technologies, etc. Moreover, some new investigative rights of CCS (such as the right to receive information constituting a commercial secret from commercial contracts between economic entities) should be considered.

In the opinion of experts, the long border and convenient location as a transit country are the main geographical factors which contribute to the illicit trade in tobacco products in Lithuania. Lithuania shares borders with Latvia (land border—588 km, sea border—22 km), Belarus (border—677 km), Poland (border—104 km) and Russia (Kaliningrad) (land border—255 km, border in Curonian sea—18 km, sea border—22 km). The EU external border section in Lithuania accounts for 61% of the total length of the state border (Kazakevičius 2018).

Scientific research (Bikelis et al. 2017, p. 20) also indicates among geographical factors the fact that the Lithuanian (and EU external) border is very close to cheap (legal) cigarette production factories, which are located also in low-taxing states, such us Belarus and Russia.

6 Conclusion. Identification of Best Practices at the National Level

The following items can be attributed to the best practices of Lithuanian institutions:

- sufficiently criminal intelligence effective activity. It may be mentioned that in 2018, as much as 81% of all illicit tobacco products were detained by SBPS on the ground of information received through criminal intelligence activity;
- sufficiently effective activity of the analytical unit of the Customs Department, on the basis of which a list of potentially dangerous carriers and other legal entities is

formed. Carriers and other legal persons included in this list are subject to additional, more frequent or more stringent inspections by officials of the Customs Department;

- cooperation with other countries through liaison officers;
- further installation of a guard fence (44.64 km of which is already installed) in the state border section with Russia. Moreover, the portion of the EU's external border (Lithuania) monitored by modern border surveillance technologies is expected to increase to 53% by the end of the year 2018 (in 2015 it was 32%, while in 2016—33%) (Giriūnaitė 2018).

Annex: Tables

Table 1 Data on number of registered crimes, on number of decided cases in courts and on number of sentenced (acquitted) persons

Number of registered crimes Number of decided cases in courts Number of sentenced/acquitted persons											
2005	2006	2007	2008	2009	2010	2011	2012	2013	2014	2015	2016
1. Smuggling (art. 199, CC)											
93	79	122	108	138	179	228	314	599	336	306	449
74	74	90	62	70	93	105	147	166	220	168	142
–	–	–	–	–	–	130	238/9	205/6	277/13	238/7	213/3
2. Unlawful possession of goods subject to excise duties (art. 199^2, CC)											
54	70	100	69	108	174	161	215	394	273	241	195
–	543	18	46	77	129	164	147	212	224	230	176
–	–	–	–	–	–	191	264/6	275/4	299/7	328/10	269/9
3. Customs deceit (art. 199^1, CC)											
3	1	0	1	1	5	8	4	7	6	3	0
–	0	0	2	1	2	4	2	2	3	2	6
–	0	0	–	–	–	1	3	2	4	4	2/1
4. Unlawful failure to bring goods or products outside the Republic of Lithuania (Art. 200, CC)											
8	5	1	3	1	14	7	12	2	3	10	3
4	7	7	0	3	2	3	1	0	2	1	3
–	–	–	0	–	–	0	9	0	1	1/1	1

Table 2 Data on number of detected administrative offences, on number of initiated pre-trial investigations, value of seized illegal goods, on number of seized cigarettes, on seized tobacco and on number of detected and closed illegal factories for counterfeiting cigarettes

Year	2005	2006	2007	2008	2009	2010	2011	2012	2013	2014	2015	2016	2017
Number of detected administrative offenses	272	170	241	266	326	No data	No data	No data	No data	No data	No data	No data	No data
Number of initiated pre-trial investigations	77	74	76	53	149	179	218	186	316	328	286	No data	No data
Value of seized illegal goods	9 mln. litas	6.8 mln. litas	No data	No data	27 mln. litas	66.7 mln. litas	56 mln. litas	No data	32.7 mln. eur	42.9 mln. eur	30.6 mln. eur	No data	No data
Number of seized cigarettes (in packs)	No data	2 mln.	1.5 mln.	1.9 mln.	3.85 mln.	9.7 mln.	3.3 mln.	6.7 mln.	4.2 mln.	5.2 mln.	No data	238 mln.	128 mln.
Number of seized tobacco (in kilos)	No data	5300	3000	198	No data	10,000	69,000	No data	No data	No data	No data	No data	No data
Number of detected and closed illegal factories for counterfeiting of cigarettes	2	–		1	–	1	–	No data	No data	No data	No data	No data	No data

Table 3 Data on damage caused by detected tobacco products

Year	2010	2011	2012	2013	2014	2015	2016	2017	2018
Damage caused by detected tobacco products (in millions euros)	15.4	12.7	11.4	10.2	12.4	24.1	29.2	15.8	20.7

Table 4 Data on newcomers to correctional institutions sentenced for smuggling, imprisoned persons for smuggling and persons released from prison who were sentenced for smuggling

Year	2010	2011	2012	2013	2014	2015	2016	2017
Newcomers to prison sentenced for smuggling (Art. 199, CC)	42	24	37	30	27	30	30	26
Persons imprisoned for smuggling	74	75	79	69	54	45	44	47
Persons released from prison who were sentenced for smuggling	25	20	32	45	45	37	29	26

Table 5 Data on general average of court-imposed and actually served terms of imprisonment

Year	2012	2013	2014	2015	2016	2017
Average of court-imposed term of imprisonment for smuggling (Art. 199, CC)	6 y 6 m 29 d	4 y 11 m 3 d	6 y 1 m 20 d	6 y 11 m 6 d	6 y 7 m 4 d	7 y 10 d
Average of actually served term of imprisonment for smuggling (Art. 199, CC)	2 y 2 m 17 d	2 y 11 m 17 d	2 y 9 m 15 d	2 y 8 m 29 d	3 y 3 m 4 d	4 y 3 m 19 d
Average of court-imposed term of imprisonment	6 y 2 m 2 d	No data	6 y 3 m 12 d	6 y 5 m 28 d	6 y 7 m 16 d	No data
Average of actually served term of imprisonment	2 y 3 m 5 d	No data	2 y 7 m 23 d	2 y 8 m 9 d	2 y 9 m 26 d	2 y 9 m 10 d

Table 6 Data on number of suspected and sentenced legal persons

Year	2005	2006	2007	2008	2009	2010	2011	2012	2013	2014	2015	2016
Number of suspected (accused) legal persons	22	47	86	119	112	110	89	47	63	33	35	29
Number of suspected legal persons for smuggling (Art. 199, CC)	0	0	0	1	0	0	1	1	1	0	0	0
Number of sentenced legal persons	22	18	37	56	67	56	49	33	–	30	18	18

Table 7 Data on convicts who had or did not had previous convictions at the time of crime commission

	Art. 199, para 1, CC	Art. 199^2, CC	Art. 199, para 1 and Art. 199^2, CC
Had previous conviction	21.3	15.5	3.3
Did not had previous conviction	78.7	84.5	96.7

Table 8 Distribution of persons sentenced to imprisonment or a fine according to form of complicity (2009–2013)

	Single crimes	Group of accomplices	Organised group
Imprisonment	6.8	15.3	18.1
Fine	93.2	84.7	81.9

Table 9 Distribution of persons sentenced to imprisonment by age and by crime qualification

	≤24 y/o	25–34 y/o	35–44 y/o	45–54 y/o	≥55 y/o
Art. 199. para 1	63.3	27.8	5.1	3.8	0.0
Art. 199^2	43.1	15.7	27.5	11.8	2.0
Art. 199. para 1 and Art. 199^2	0.0	44.4	44.4	11.1	0.0

Table 10 Distribution of convicts by age and marital status

	Married	Unmarried	Divorced	Widow/ widower	Unspecified
Art. 199, para 1	21%	68%	8%	1%	1%
Art. 199^2	42%	41%	13%	1%	3%
Art. 199 para 1 and Art. 199^2	60%	26%	11%	0%	3%

Table 11 Distribution of convicts by education

	Without secondary education	Secondary education	More than secondary education	Unspecified
Art. 199, para 1	47.6%	41.3%	9.8%	1.3%
Art. 199^2	22.9%	53.2%	18.1%	5.9%
Art. 199, para 1 and Art. 199^2	10.0%	67.3%	16.6%	6.2%

Table 12 Distribution of convicts by employment

	Employed	Unemployed	Studying	Other	Unspecified
Art. 199, para 1	39.0%	46.7%	10.8%	1.6%	1.9%
Art. 199^2	40.4%	50.1%	3.4%	4.6%	1.4%
Art. 199, para 1 and Art. 199^2	66.8%	29.9%	1.9%	0.5%	0.9%

Table 13 Distribution of convicts by citizenship

	Lithuania	Russia	Poland	Belarus	Latvia	Ukraine	Other
Art. 199 para 1	91.7%	5.1%	0.3%	2.5%	0.0%	0.0%	0.3%
Art. 199^2	93.1%	0.2%	3.6%	1.4%	0.3%	0.3%	0.7%
Art. 199 para 1 and Art. 199^2	43.1%	14.2%	17.1%	19.0%	2.8%	3.3%	0.5%

Table 14 Distribution of those suspected of smuggling by gender and education

Year	2014	2015	2016	2017	2018
Suspected persons for smuggling (Art. 199, CC)	290	222	173	266	188
Men	277	220	159	254	183
Women	13	2	14	12	5
Without secondary education	18%	11%	18%	21%	17%
Secondary education	60%	64%	62%	56%	62%
More than secondary education	22%	25%	20%	23%	21%

Table 15 Distribution of those suspected of smuggling by occupation

Year	2014	2015	2016	2017	2018
Employed	59%	53%	50%	49%	43%
Unemployed	33%	41%	43%	36%	35%
Studying	8%	6%	7%	15%	22%

Table 16 Distribution of those suspected of smuggling by citizenship

Year	2014	2015	2016	2017	2018
Foreigners suspected of smuggling (Art. 199, CC); of them:	60	68	56	54	44
Belarussian	20	28	26	24	12
Russian	21	25	13	19	20
Polish	9	4	5	–	2
Latvian	–	–	4	4	2

Table 17 Distribution of crimes committed as a single crime or in the forms of a group of accomplices and organised group

	Art. 199, para 1	Art. 199^2	Art. 199 para 1 and Art. 199^2
Single crimes	10.8	46.8	57.3
Group of accomplices	44.1	46.8	25.1
Organised group	45.1	6.4	17.5

References

International and European Union Legal Acts, National Laws and Other Legal Acts

Convention on mutual assistance and cooperation between customs administrations (1998) Convention drawn up on the basis of Article K.3 of the Treaty on European Union. OJ C 24, 23.1.1998, pp. 2–22. Official Gazette *Valstybės žinios*, 2004, Nos. 67-2355; 112-4180

Convention on Mutual Assistance in Criminal Matters between the Member States of the European Union (2000) Established by the Council in Accordance with Article 34 of the Treaty on European Union. Official Gazette *Valstybės žinios*, 2004-10-21, No. 154-5599

Directive 2014/40/EU of the European Parliament and of the Council of 3 April 2014 on the approximation of the laws, regulations and administrative provisions of the Member States concerning the manufacture, presentation and sale of tobacco and related products and repealing Directive 2001/37/EC

Prosecutor General (2003a) Recommendation "On the Distribution of the Pre-Trial Investigation Between the Institutions of the Pre-Trial Investigation". Official Gazette *Valstybės žinios*, No. 39-1805

Prosecutor General (2003b) Order "On the Compilation of the Recommendation on the Report to be Submitted Upon Completion of a Pre-Trial Investigation (Article 218 of the Code of Criminal Procedure)". Official Gazette *Valstybės žinios*, No. 39-1805

Prosecutor General (2013) Order "On Approval of the Recommendations on the Law on Criminal Intelligence, Application of the Norms of the Code of Criminal Procedure and Use of Criminal Intelligence Information in Criminal Proceedings". Official Gazette *Valstybės žinios*, No. 2-83

Prosecutor General (2015) Order of the Prosecutor General "On the Recommendation on the Compilation and Transmission of an Indictment to a Court". Register of Legal Acts, No. 2015-08536

State Tax Inspectorate under the Ministry of Finance of the Republic of Lithuania (2018) Order "On the Establishment of a Procedure for Marking and Registration of Wholesale Tobacco Packaging as referred to in Article 14(1) of the Law on Control of Tobacco, Tobacco Products and Related Products". Register of Legal Acts, No. 18573

The Council of Europe Criminal Law Convention on Corruption (1999) Strasbourg, 27 January 1999. Official Gazette *Valstybės žinios*, 2002, No. 23-851; 23-853

The European Commission (2017) The European Commission Implementing Regulation (EU) 2018/574 of 15 December 2017 on technical standards for the establishment and operation of a traceability system for tobacco products

The Government of the Republic of Lithuania (1999) Description of the procedure for destruction of tobacco products confiscated and transferred to the state. Official Gazette *Valstybės žinios*, No. 85-2537

The Government of the Republic of Lithuania (2004) Resolution of the Government "Exemption of Goods Imported by Travelers from VAT and Excise Duties on Imports". Official Gazette *Valstybės žinios*, No. 58-2049

The Government of the Republic of Lithuania (2017) Regarding the Government of the Republic of Lithuania October 14 Resolution no. 1031 "On the Basic Approval of the Amount of Punishment and Penalties". Register of Legal Acts, No. 14215

The Minister of Economy (2004) Order of the Minister of Economy No. 4-200 "On Approval of the Rules for the Transport and Storage of Alcohol Products and Tobacco Products Applicable to Natural Persons in the Territory of the Republic of Lithuania". Official Gazette *Valstybės žinios*, Nos. 4-759, 92-4590

The Parliament of the Republic of Lithuania (2000a) The Law on Intelligence. Official Gazette *Valstybės žinios*, No. 64-1931

The Parliament of the Republic of Lithuania (2000b) The Criminal Code of the Republic of Lithuania (2000). Official Gazette *Valstybės žinios*, Nos. 89-2741, 112-4973

The Parliament of the Republic of Lithuania (2002a) Law on Value Added Tax. Official Gazette *Valstybės žinios*, No. 35-1271

The Parliament of the Republic of Lithuania (2002b) The Code of Criminal Procedure of the Republic of Lithuania. Official Gazette *Valstybės žinios*, No. 37-1341

The Parliament of the Republic of Lithuania (2003) Law on Control of Tobacco, Tobacco Products and Related Products. Official Gazette *Valstybės žinios*, No. 117-5317

The Parliament of the Republic of Lithuania (2004a) Law on Customs. Official Gazette *Valstybės žinios*, No. 73-2517

The Parliament of the Republic of Lithuania (2004b) The Law on Ratification of the WHO Framework Convention on Tobacco Control No. IX-2460. Official Gazette *Valstybės žinios*, No. 152-5529

The Parliament of the Republic of Lithuania (2010) Law on Excise Duty. Official Gazette *Valstybės žinios*, No. 45-2174

The Parliament of the Republic of Lithuania (2012) Criminal Intelligence Act. Official Gazette *Valstybės žinios*, No. 122-6093

The Parliament of the Republic of Lithuania (2015) Code of Administrative Offenses of the Republic of Lithuania. Register of Legal Acts, No. 2015-11216

The Parliament of the Republic of Lithuania (2016a) Law on Amending the Law on Control of Tobacco, Tobacco Products and Related Products. Register of Legal Acts, No. 2016-17405

The Parliament of the Republic of Lithuania (2016b) Law on the Ratification of the Protocol to Eliminate Illicit Trade in Tobacco Products. Register of Legal Acts, No. 26439

The Parliament of the Republic of Lithuania (2017) Law on State Border Protection. Register of Legal Acts, No. 12168

The Parliament of the Republic of Lithuania (2018) Law amending Article 26 of the Law on Excise Duties No. IX-569. Register of Legal Acts, No. 20967

The Union Customs Code (2013) Regulation (EU) No 952/2013 of the European Parliament and of the Council of 9 October 2013 laying down the Union Customs Code. – OJ L 269, 10.10.2013, pp. 1–101

Jurisprudence of the Constitutional Court of Lithuania, Supreme Court of Lithuania and Other Courts

Kaunas Region Administrative Court (2012) Decision of 22 October 2012 in admnistrative case No. Ik-124-505/2012

The Constitutional Court (2001) Ruling of 7 May 2001 "Dėl Lietuvos Respublikos administracinių teisės pažeidimų kodekso 130(2) straipsnio atitikties Lietuvos Respublikos Konstitucijai". Official Gazette *Valstybės žinios*, No. 39-1373

The Constitutional Court (2005) Ruling of 10 November 2005 "Dėl Lietuvos Respublikos administracinių teisės pažeidimų kodekso 163(2) atitikties Lietuvos Respublikos Konstitucijai". Official Gazette *Valstybės žinios*, No. 134-4819

The Constitutional Court (2009) Ruling of 8 June 2009 "Dėl Lietuvos Respublikos baudžiamojo kodekso 20 straipsnio 1, 2, 3 dalių, 20 straipsnio 5 dalies, 43 straipsnio 4 dalies atitikties Lietuvos Respublikos Konstitucijai". Official Gazette Valstybės žinios, No. 69–2798

The Supreme Administrative Court (2012) Ruling of 25 January 2012 in administrative case No. A143-250/2012

The Supreme Court (2007a) Ruling of 3 April 2007 in criminal case No. 2K-251/2007

The Supreme Court (2007b) Ruling of 13 November 2007 in criminal case No. 2K-P-549/2007

The Supreme Court (2010a) Ruling of 27 April 2010 in criminal case No. 2K-269/2010

The Supreme Court (2010b) Ruling of 31 May 2010 in criminal case No. 2K-313/2010
The Supreme Court (2016) Ruling of 23 February 2016 in criminal case No. 2K-7-85-696/2016

Special Literature

Bikelis S, Giedraitytė-Mačiulienė R, Mickėnienė I, Venckevičienė J (2017) Cigarečių neteisėta apyvarta: kompleksinė reiškinio ir kontrolės priemonių analizė. Eugrimas, Vilnius
Bilius M, Stonys J (2016) Laikino nuosavybės teisių apribojimo problematika baudžiamajame procese: optimalaus sprendimo beieškant. In: Švedas G (ed) Baudžiamoji justicija ir verslas. Vilniaus universiteto leidykla, Vilnius
Goda G, Kazlauskas M, Kuconis P (2011) Baudžiamojo proceso teisė. Registrų centras, Vilnius
Misiūnas A, Rimkus V (2007) Preconditions and consequences of illegal goods traffic. Intelektinė ekonomika, No. 2(2)
Šatienė G, Baltrūnienė J, Jokšas L (2011) Kontrabandos ir korupcijos kaip socialinių reiškinių santykis. Ekonomika ir vadyba: aktualijos ir perspektyvos, 3(23)
Švedas G (ed) (2004) Lietuvos Respublikos baudžiamojo kodekso komentaras. Bendroji dalis (1-98 straipsniai). Teisinės informacijos centras, Vilnius
Švedas G (2011) Kai kurie probleminiai juridinio asmens baudžiamosios atsakomybės aspektai Lietuvos konstitucinėje jurisprudencijoje ir baudžiamosios justicijos doktrinoje. In: Švedas G (ed) Lietuvos Respublikos baudžiamajam kodeksui – 10 metų. Registrų centras, Vilnius

Online Sources

Giriūnaitė A (2018) Nepajėgiant užsukti kontrabandos čiaupų Lietuvoje skelbiama apie naujas priemones. https://www.lrytas.lt/verslas/rinkos-pulsas/2018/12/16/news/nepajegiant-uzsukti-kontrabandos-ciaupu-lietuvoje-skelbiama-apie-naujas-priemones-8378251. Accessed 16 Apr 2020
Ignotas P (2018) Tabako gamintojai: "Cigarečių pakuočių suvienodinimas tik padidins kontrabandą". https://www.lrytas.lt/verslas/rinkos-pulsas/2018/11/02/news/tabako-gamintojai-cigareciu-pakuociu-suvienodinimas-tik-padidins-kontrabanda%2D%2D8078976/. Accessed 16 Apr 2020
Kazakevičius K (2018) Rūkalų kontrabanda: skaičiai disonuoja. https://www.lzinios.lt/Lietuva/rukalu-kontrabanda-skaiciai-disonuoja/261510. Accessed 16 Jan 2020
Sinkevičius D (2015) Niekam neprilygstančios gaujos byla: patyrė milijoninius nuostolius. https://www.delfi.lt/news/daily/crime/niekam-neprilygstancios-gaujos-byla-patyre-milijoninius-nuostolius.d?id=67321544. Accessed 16 Apr 2020
Steniulienė I (2019) Karaliaus kontrabandos byla: prašo priteisti per 4,8 mln. eurų muitinei. https://www.delfi.lt/news/daily/law/karaliaus-kontrabandos-byla-praso-priteisti-per-4-8-mln-euru-muitinei.d?id=80919381. Accessed 16 Apr 2020

Gintaras Švedas Ph.D., is Professor of criminal law at the Faculty of Law of the University of Vilnius, Lithuania. He has been Head of Criminal Justice Department of Law Faculty of Vilnius university (from 2003), Professor of law at Law Faculty of Vilnius university (from 2009); Vice-Dean for Planning and Sciences of Law Faculty of Vilnius university (from 2006); Member of the Committee of the Criminal Code Supervision under the Ministry of Justice (from 2012); Contact point for Lithuania in the European Criminal Law Academic Network (ECLAN) (from 2006) and Member of Management Committee of ECLAN (from 2018); Member of the Committee on Legal Reform in Ukraine (from 2019). As a Lithuanian national expert, he took part in numerous international scientific projects. Professor Švedas has held many public offices. He was Vice-Minister of Justice of Lithuania in the years 1993–2006, Agent of the Government of the Republic of Lithuania to the European Court of Human Rights (1995–2003), Member of the Management Board of Fundamental Rights Agency (2007–2010), Public Adviser to the Minister of Justice in the fields of criminal law, enforcement of punishments, implementation of the EU law (2012–2016). Professor Švedas authored and coauthored 9 monographs, 85 scientific articles, 21 manuals, textbooks and educational works, 11 compendiums. He also was involved in preparation of, among others, the Criminal Code, Code of Punishment Enforcement and Code of Criminal Procedure of the Republic of Lithuania.

Legal and Practical Challenges of Combating Illicit Trade of Tobacco in Poland

Konrad Buczkowski and Paweł Dziekański

Contents

K. Buczkowski (✉)
Institute of Law Studies, Polish Academy of Sciences, Department of Criminology, Warsaw, Poland
e-mail: k.buczkowski@inp.pan.pl

P. Dziekański
Institute of Law Studies, Polish Academy of Sciences, Department of Criminal Law, Warsaw, Poland
e-mail: p.dziekanski@inp.pan.pl

C. Nowak (ed.), *Combatting Illicit Trade on the EU Border*,
https://doi.org/10.1007/978-3-030-51019-0_6

Abstract This chapter focuses on the analysis of four main criminal aspects of smuggling in Poland. The first part presents criminal law regulations including regulations on fiscal offences. It was necessary to show criminal reacquisition measures as a result of this kind of crimes. Next, the issues procedural rules with very important matter like international cooperation between authorities to combat global illicit trade. The last part allow to understand the phenomenon of illicit trade of tobacco products, modus operandi and provide basic data on smuggling in Poland.

1 Introduction

The *WHO Framework Convention on Tobacco Control* (hereinafter FCTC) defines the concept of illicit trade in cigarettes and other tobacco products indicating that it means any practice or conduct prohibited by law relating to manufacture, shipment, receipt, possession, distribution, sale or purchase, including any practice or conduct intended to facilitate such activity (Article 1(a) FCTC).

The FCTC Convention focuses on international cooperation to reduce tobacco use by emphasising its harmful effects on health. However, this act contains regulations concerning the area of criminal law. It is assumed that the fight against illicit trade in tobacco products reduces the supply of such products. This thesis, however, stemming directly from the FCTC, needs further investigation and an answer to the question of whether existing criminal law instruments contribute to reducing the demand for cigarettes and other tobacco products. Two situations should be distinguished. Criminal law provisions can be an important factor in the fight against the grey market in tobacco products and can lead to an effective reduction in the volume of products derived from illegal production or smuggling.

The illicit tobacco market is the result of, on the one hand, a desire to avoid the high tax burdens that are imposed on such products. It is estimated that the tax on the price of one pack of cigarettes oscillates around 80%. This is one of the reasons why criminal activity in this area is so lucrative. It is also pointed out that economic crime related to the extortion of tax on goods and services, evasion of excise duty and customs duty is, alongside the production and trafficking in narcotics, one of the most profitable activities of criminal groups. On the other hand, in view of the high prices of cigarettes and other tobacco products, products from illegal sources are popular because of their competitiveness. It should be noted here that available studies show a trend that regular cigarette smoking is more common among people with poor material circumstances (37% of men, 23% of women smokers), while the highest percentage of regular smokers is among the unemployed (53% of men, 41% of women). For comparison, among people with good material status, the number of men who smoke regularly is 23%, while that of women is 21%.[1] Criminal repressive

[1] Trząsalska et al. (2017), p. 11.

measures, however, are not, and cannot even be, an instrument for reducing the need to use this type of product. Such an objective should be pursued through educational campaigns to raise public awareness in promoting healthy lifestyles and to highlight the harm caused by smoking cigarettes or other tobacco products. Although, in the light of the same studies, respondents indicated that one of the most important factors limiting smoking was increasing the price of cigarettes (65% of respondents), doubts were raised as to whether it was effective. The share of the grey tobacco market in Poland is at a high level, much higher than in the European Union as a whole. Criminal law instruments should therefore be designed in such a way that they can lead to the elimination or significant reduction in the grey market in tobacco products, for which organised crime is largely responsible. Only the elimination of much of the grey tobacco market, i.e. the unavailability of illegal products, can make the price of a pack of cigarettes or other tobacco products a real factor in reducing the supply of cigarettes or other tobacco products.

The smuggling of cigarettes and other tobacco products is facilitated by the huge differences in cigarette prices across the European Union. This difference can be as much as four times. The differences occur mainly between the eastern and western countries of the EU. This also indicates the direction of cigarette smuggling. However, differences, although slightly lower, also exist in cigarette prices between countries such as Spain, Italy, and the UK, Ireland, France. For example, in 2017 the highest retail price of a pack of 20 cigarettes (converted into British pounds) was recorded in the UK at £9.91, the lowest in Bulgaria at £2.32. In Poland, the amount was £2.81, in Spain £3.93, Italy £4.37, Ireland £9.15, and France £5.67.[2]

Polish criminal law provisions with respect to the issues addressed in this paper are not focused on the notion of illicit trade in cigarettes and other tobacco products. Although the comprehensive collection of individual provisions and the determination of their normative scope allow us to state that the Polish legislator provides for sanctions for the overwhelming majority of activities falling within the definition of illicit trade in the FCTC Convention (Article 1(a)), it does so with the fiscal perspective of the State Treasury and the European Union in mind. The provisions therefore mainly address the issue of the avoidance of the tax that would occur if the goods were legally traded. This approach of the legislator is understandable in the light of the fact that tens of billions of zloty in tobacco excise tax is received annually by the state budget. These products occupy a leading position in the structure of excise revenues.[3] However, this does not mean that existing fiscal offences legislation is an effective instrument in the prevention of criminal phenomena linked to the illicit manufacture of, or trade in, cigarettes or tobacco products. The concept of illicit trade, as defined in the FCTC, is not transferable to criminal law. It is

[2] www.statista.com/statistics/415034/cigarette-prices-across-europe/. (Retail price of a premium pack of 20 cigarettes in selected European countries in 2017).

[3] For example, in 2017, tobacco excise revenues amounted to 18.8 billion PLN (compared to 68.8 billion PLN of total excise revenues), which gave second place in the structure of excise revenues (only motor fuels reached a higher level); see Szajner (2018), p. 3.

characterized by a high degree of ambiguity. There is also a lack of clear criteria for linking individual behaviours to illicit trade, and for determining at what stage it is already possible to talk about such trade.

In systematizing Polish criminal law regulations concerning the illicit trade in cigarettes or tobacco products, their smuggling, or illegal production, we can distinguish: (1) regulations on fiscal offences regarding excise tax and VAT; (2) regulations on fiscal offences regarding customs law; (3) criminal regulations concerning the illegal manufacture of tobacco products; (4) criminal law regulations. This is because it cannot be ruled out that the perpetrators of acts related to the illicit trade in cigarettes or other tobacco products may carry out the elements of crimes stipulated in the Criminal Code. Of course, this classification has been developed for the purposes of this report and has been prepared on the basis of the types of crimes that are related to the illicit activities in question. In making this distinction and in citing and presenting specific crimes in the next section, the theoretical assumptions and available or acquired empirical data were taken into account.

2 Legal Aspects of the Fight Against the Smuggling of Cigarettes and Other Tobacco Products

2.1 The Penal Fiscal Code

2.1.1 General Characteristics

In Poland, penal fiscal law is a part of the criminal law system, but it retains its autonomy. The act referred to above confirmed the specific concept of separating crimes and offences related to the areas of tax law and customs law. There is no space for an historical analyses in this study. However, it seems that a glance into the past shows the gradual development of the concept in Polish legislation that penal fiscal law is an autonomous field of criminal law. Like any theory, this one also has its opponents. The systematisation of crimes against the fiscal interests of the state in a single act took place before the Second World War (the act of 2nd August, 1926). This kind of solution is rare in other legal systems. This is because criminal provisions detrimental to the financial interest of the state are included in individual acts regulating tax and customs law. This type of legislative technique consisting of introducing criminal provisions into acts regulating specific areas of law (so-called industry acts) is known to the Polish legal system, but it is not applicable in the penal fiscal area. An example of such solutions can also be encountered in relation to the issue which is the subject of this report (e.g. the provisions concerning the illicit manufacture of tobacco products are contained in a so-called industry act, which in the following section is included in the second group of the proposed system in the previous paragraph). Without going into detailed considerations referring to the concept adopted by the Polish legislator, it should be stated that penal fiscal law is a specific, separate field of Polish criminal law, in particular it does not constitute non-statutory criminal law.[4] This should be adopted in the light of the nature of the regulations of the Penal Fiscal Code. Examples illustrating the above thesis will be provided later in this study. The legislator himself, in the justification of the draft to the Penal Fiscal Code, indicated that the separateness of this legal act is dictated by tradition and the financial object of the regulation's character.[5] However, it will be necessary to critically evaluate the effectiveness of such a solution by posing the question whether the Penal Fiscal Code really meets the challenge of taking into account the financial specificity of the institutions concerned, the construction of individual taxes, the specificity of activities, and economic turnover in a given field. For obvious reasons, the analyses in this respect will be limited to excise duties on tobacco products, or possibly to selected issues related to VAT.

The Polish Penal Fiscal Code[6] (hereinafter: PFC) encompasses the material, legal, procedural and executive aspects. The first of these best expresses this separate character of the regulations. The principles of criminal liability for fiscal offences have been developed independently of the Criminal Code[7] (hereinafter: CC). This is confirmed by the provision of article 20, § 1 of the PFC, stating that the provisions of the general part and Chapter XXXVIII of the Criminal Code (general provisions concerning soldiers) do not apply to fiscal offences, except for the provisions expressly indicated in Article 20, § 2 of the PFC. The aforementioned Article 20, § 1 of the PFC in fact excludes the application of the provisions of the general part of the Criminal Code which, in accordance with the principle in article 116 of the CC, applies to other acts providing for criminal liability, unless these acts expressly exclude their application. The provision of article 20, § 1 of the PFC performs such a function. At this point, it must become clear that, unlike general criminal law offences, fiscal crimes or offences are not found in other laws. The Penal Fiscal Code stipulates all fiscal offences and misdemeanours. On the one hand, the complexity of codification can be considered an important advantage. On the other hand, however, there are some doubts as to whether the types of fiscal offences take into account the specificity of excise tax, and generally also other tax constructions, including changes in excise tax regulations. The assumption is that the Penal Fiscal Code is to take into account the specificity of its normative scope, and adopt tax and civil law constructions. In addition, it is to change the approach to punishment placing the main emphasis on the penalty of a fine, the financial nature of criminal repression. However, in practice there are many problems that call into question the thesis that the assumptions of the Penal Fiscal Code quoted above have been fulfilled or are even accurate. Some of them will be indicated in the further sections of this study.

---

[4]See also: Prusak and Skowronek (2018), pp. 7–9.

[5]Justification to the government's bill on the Penal Fiscal Code, Sejm of the 3rd term, print No. 1146, http://orka.sejm.gov.pl/Rejestrd.nsf/wgdruku/1146/$file/1146.pdf.

[6]The act of 10th September, 1999—Penal Fiscal Code (i.e. Journal of Laws of 2020, item 19, as amended).

[7]The act of 6th June, 1997—the Criminal Code (Journal of Laws of 2019, item 1950, as amended).

In article 46 of the PFC the assumption was adopted that the provisions of the general part of the Code of Administrative Offences shall not apply to fiscal offences.[8] In this case, the Penal Fiscal Code does not make any breakthrough in the principle of autonomy, as it was done in the area of fiscal offences by allowing appropriate application of certain provisions of the general part of the Criminal Code, which was mentioned earlier. Such a solution can be justified on at least two grounds. Firstly, for fiscal offences, certain provisions on liability for fiscal offences will apply. The provisions of the general part included in Chapter 1 "Preliminary provisions", Chapter 2 "Refraining from punishing an offender" (article 1–19 of the PFC) are applicable to fiscal offences and, obviously, Chapter 3 "Fiscal offences" (article 46–52 of the PFC). Secondly, the nature of fiscal offences should be highlighted. The overwhelming majority of them refer to the features describing the causal activity of particular fiscal crimes. In such cases, the determination of whether we are dealing with a crime or a fiscal offence is limited to the amount of tax liable to be depleted. If it does not exceed the statutory threshold, i.e. five times the minimum remuneration at the time of committing the act (article 53, § 6 of the PFC in conjunction with article 53, § 3 of the PFC), the act constitutes an offence. The second, smaller, part of offences in the Penal Fiscal Code is no longer determined by the aforementioned limit, but by a clear statutory indication. In accordance with article 53, § 3 *in fine* of the PFC, a fiscal offence is also any another act if the Code so provides.

2.1.2 Penal Fiscal Offences Related to the Illicit Trade in, or Smuggling of, Tobacco or Other Tobacco Products

The provision of article 54, § 1 of the PFC states that a taxpayer who evades taxation and fails to disclose to the competent authority the subject or taxable base or does not submit a declaration, thus exposing the tax to depletion, is subject to the penalty of a fine of up to 720 daily rates or the penalty of deprivation of liberty, or both these for a privileged type of crime described above. The perpetrator is more leniently liable—the act is punishable only by a fine of up to 720 daily rates, if the amount of tax liable to depletion is small. However, in article 54, § 3 of the PFC we find a penalties jointly. This act constitutes a fiscal offence. This is the basic type of tax evasion offence, where the subject or taxable base is not disclosed or a tax return is not filed. Article 54, § 2 of the PFC provides for a fiscal offence consisting of the execution of the elements of the act described in article 54, § 1 of the PFC, but the exposure to tax depletion does not exceed the statutory threshold. A consequence of being included in the elements of a crime under article 54 of the PFC is therefore a symptom which allows one to distinguish the type of a privileged crime, as well as a fiscal offence. This type of construction falls under the jurisdiction of the Polish Penal Fiscal Code,

[8]The act of 20th May, 1971—the Code of Administrative Offences (i.e. Journal of Laws of 2019, item 821, as amended).

which has already been noted. This provision, although it does not refer anywhere to the phenomenon of illicit trade in cigarettes, tobacco and excise duties, is often used to combat crime associated with the activity in question. The behaviour of a taxpayer who evades taxation or does not submit a return, thereby exposing the tax to depletion, will relate to those situations in which he markets or transports cigarettes or other tobacco products. Nonetheless, due to the fact that the structure of excise duty includes situations where no tax liability arises in the Republic of Poland, while simultaneously a person is involved in illicit trade in illicit cigarettes or other tobacco products, in the light of article 54 of the PFC, it must be established each time that a specific person is subject to a tax obligation resulting from a specific tax act (article 7, § 1 of the Tax Code), as this results from the legal definition of a taxpayer under the Penal Fiscal Code (article 53, §30 of the PFC and article 53, §30a of the PFC). The indicator of a taxpayer used in article 54, § 1 of the PFC is a generalised indicator. Its determination requires not only finding the source of the tax obligation, but also stating that in this particular factual state this obligation existed (there are certain doubts in this respect in the case of the procedure for the suspension of excise duty collection). If the procedural authorities fail to prove this, criminal liability for the above mentioned act will not be possible.

Notwithstanding the fact that there are problems with the fact that not every person involved in the illicit trade in cigarettes or tobacco may be considered a taxable person, there are also situations where the taxable person within the meaning of the aforementioned provisions is not a natural person but a legal person. In such a case, the fiscal liability may be incurred only in the case described in article 9, § 3 of the PFC. It shall apply to a person who, on the basis of a provision of law, a decision of a competent authority, a contract or actual execution, deals with economic matters, in particular financial matters, a natural person, a legal person or an organisational unit without legal personality. These circumstances require evidence to be established. Within the framework of the analysed type of crime, very often, especially within the framework of organised crime, we are dealing with the creation of fictitious legal entities, involving random persons, a so-called "front man", who takes on (often unconsciously or not knowing about the essence or size of the criminal activity) the functions associated with certain obligations in the tax sphere. This makes it impossible or very difficult in reality to capture and prosecute the actual perpetrators.[9]

The question is whether the subject of taxation within the meaning of article 54, §1 of the PFC are products derived from illegal activities. Similar doubts apply to article 56 of the PFC. Both these provisions may give rise to fiscal liability for activities connected with the smuggling of cigarettes or other tobacco products. These crimes are commonly referred to as tax fraud. They concern both value added tax and excise tax.

---

[9]Buczkowski, Przestępstwa skarbowe jako czyny bazowe w konstrukcji prania pieniędzy (2013), pp. 1117–1152.

The provision of article 56, § 1 of the PFC stipulates that a taxpayer who, by submitting a declaration or statement to the tax authority, other authorised body or payer, gives untrue information or conceals the truth or fails to fulfil the obligation to notify about a change of data covered by it, thus exposing the tax to depletion, is subject to a fine of up to 720 daily rates or a penalty of deprivation of liberty, or both these penalties jointly. Similarly to article 54 of the PFC, the following paragraphs of article 56 of the PFC, i.e. § 2 and § 3 introduce, respectively, a privileged type of fiscal crime consisting of exposure to low value tax depletion and a fiscal misdemeanour concerning such exposure to tax depletion if it does not exceed the statutory threshold. Additionally, article 56, § 4 of the PFC provides for a fiscal offence consisting of not submitting a tax return or declaration on time to the tax authority or payer or in breach of the obligation not to submit them by electronic means of communication. The provision of article 56, § 4 of the PFC provides for the same penalty as for an offence under article 56, § 3 of the PFC. In the case of excise tax, it is the case that a taxpayer submits a number of declarations to the tax authority (article 21 of the Excise Tax Act) in cases where tax liabilities arise in the event of the existence of the events specified in the act (such is indicated in article 8 of the Excise Tax Act).[10] A taxpayer is obliged to identify and declare the amount of tax liabilities on its own. In such a state of affairs, the provision of article 56 of the PFC is a standard securing the execution of tax liabilities. There is no doubt that it refers to taxpayers who make fraudulent reporting procedures with respect to the extent of their obligations under the Excise Duty Act. The Constitutional Tribunal ruled on the compatibility of the article with the Constitution of the Republic of Poland, while commenting on the proportionality and the need for the functioning of this provision, indicating that the establishment of sanctions for breach of record-keeping obligations is not only allowed, but necessary to ensure equality and universality of taxation.[11] It should be remembered that acts under article 56 of the PFC are material crimes. In order to bring the perpetrator to justice it is not sufficient to establish the behaviour of the taxpayer in terms of one of the modal features, but it is necessary to establish the effect of exposure to a reduction in tax.

At this point, it is necessary to make a few remarks concerning the act described in article 76 of the PFC. It can be seen as a complement to the crime under article 56 of the PFC, which, due to the way its constituent elements are formulated, does not refer to facts including annoying criminal practice related to obtaining a tax refund. In practice, there are often cases in which an important issue is the issue of separating whether the perpetrator commits a crime under article 56 of the PFC or article 76 of the PFC. The decisive factor in this respect is the assessment of the party concerned. The provision of article 76, § 1 of the PFC states that anyone who, by providing data inconsistent with the actual state of affairs or concealing the actual state of affairs, misleads the competent authority by exposing it to undue tax refund

[10] The act of 6th December, 2008, on Excise Duty (i.e. Journal of Laws of 2020, item 722).

[11] Judgement of the Constitutional Court of 12th September, 2005, Case No. SK 13/05, LEX No. 165330.

of public-law receivables, in particular input tax within the meaning of the provisions on value added tax, excise tax, refund of overpayment or its crediting towards tax arrears or current or future tax liabilities, is subject to a fine of up to 720 daily rates or a penalty of deprivation of liberty, or both these penalties jointly. Article 76, § 2 of the PFC introduced a type of privileged offence, if the amount exposed to undue tax refund is of low value, the perpetrator of the prohibited act specified in article 76, § 1 of the PFC is subject to a fine of up to 720 daily rates. Article 76, § 3 of the PFC stipulates that an offence shall be punishable by a penalty. According to the construction already discussed, if the amount exposed to undue tax refund does not exceed the statutory threshold, the perpetrator of the prohibited act specified in article 76, § 1 of the PFC is subject to a penalty as for a fiscal offence.

The problem indicated in the introduction to the discussion on articles 54 and 56 of the PFC, on whether illegal activities or activities related to such products may be subject to taxation, is of significant importance for the issue to be addressed in the study. The Supreme Court in its decision of 22nd November, 2011, file ref. No. IV KK 270/11,[12] indicated that the Excise Duty Act does not introduce any additional requirements for obtaining the status of an excise tax payer. It has been pointed out that article 8 of the same act, when calculating the activities subject to excise duty, does not make distinctions for two situations: their execution "legally" or "illegally". It was considered that this argument already demonstrates that each of these behaviours is subject to excise duty. This is related to the specific nature of excise duty. Its construction entitles one to make the thesis that anyone who performs certain activities giving rise to tax liability is a taxpayer. Therefore, if an activity—even a criminal activity—corresponds in its content to an activity that is subject to excise duty, then a tax obligation arises. The position, also presented in the aforementioned ruling, is correct, namely that while procedures involving, for example, drug trafficking or prostitution cannot be taxed, those activities that were illegal, but could be carried out as legal, should be subject to taxation. An analogous position is clearly expressed in the case law of the Court of Justice of the European Union, which draws attention to a very important aspect of the problem—the competitiveness of products. In several judgements, the Court has pointed out that no distinction can be drawn between activities carried out lawfully or illegally if they are capable of competing on the market.[13] This is the case, for example, with cigarettes that have been legally placed on the market and counterfeit cigarettes from illegal production or smuggling. Although the CJEU rulings relate to value added tax, these considerations should also apply to excise duty. Taking the opposite view would lead to better treatment of products coming from illegal sources and the avoidance of fiscal liability by the persons who, in fact, carry out the activities that create the tax obligations.

[12] Legalis No. 509576.

[13] Judgement C-3/97 of 28th May, 1998 in J.C. Goodwin and E.T. Unstead, CELEX No. 61997CJ0003; judgement C-455-98 of 29th June, 2000 in Karpo Salmets and Others, CELEX No. 61998J0455.

2.1.3 Excise Fraud

We will now move on to a discussion of the group of fiscal offences and crimes known as excise offences. So far, crimes related to all taxes have been described, including naturally excise taxes and VAT. One of the significant problems of Polish criminal law in relation to the problem raised is the fact that a range of crimes has been foreseen which potentially relate to the issue of illegal production, smuggling or trade in tobacco products. We are referring here to a particularly large group of excise offences in the Penal Fiscal Code, which may concern various behaviours occurring at various stages of the procedure under discussion. However, in practice these provisions are not used, often confining themselves to the use of the discussed article 54 of the PFC. The issue of criminal activities related to the illicit trade in tobacco products is thus reduced solely to the issue of tax evasion. Regardless of this approach, a group of excise offences must be presented in this study as the bulk of them relate to this type of crime, especially if we accept the definition of the FCTC or recognise the need for a broad understanding of the concepts of illicit trade, smuggling, or illicit manufacture.

The provision of article 63, § 1 of the PFC stipulates that whoever, contrary to the provisions of the act, issues excise goods in relation to which the excise duty suspension procedure has been completed, without prior marking with excise duty markings, shall be subject to the penalty of a fine of up to 720 daily rates or the penalty of deprivation of liberty for up to 2 years, or both of these penalties jointly. This provision contains a clause referring to the Excise Duty Act. Only conduct that violates the individual provisions of the Tax Act is subject to criminal liability. Tobacco products are one of the basic categories of excise goods (article 2, paragraph 1, point 1 of the Excise Duty Act). The source of the definition of tobacco products is Directive 2011/64/EU (merging Directives 95/59 EC, 92/79/EEC, and 92/80/EEC).[14] Article 98 of the Excise Duty Act contains the list of tobacco products. Excise duty suspension arrangements are defined in article 4, point 7 of Directive 2008/118//EEC as "a tax arrangement applicable to the production, processing, holding or movement of excise goods not placed under a customs suspensive procedure or arrangement where excise duty is suspended".[15] This definition has been transposed into national law. In accordance with article 2, paragraph 1, point 12 of the Excise Duty Act, it means a procedure applied during the production, storage, handling and movement of excise goods, during which, when the conditions set out in the provisions of the Excise Duty Act and in the implementing acts issued on its basis are fulfilled, no tax liability arises from a tax obligation. Excise duty becomes due at the time of release for consumption (article 7 of Directive 2008/118//EEC). Thus, under a duty suspension arrangement, the tax is levied and collected in

[14]Council Directive 2011/64/EU of 21st June, 2011, on the structure and rates of excise duty applied to tobacco products, OJ L 176/24 of 5/07/2011.

[15]Council Directive 2008/118/EC of 16th December, 2008 concerning the general principles of excise duty and repealing Directive 92/12/EEC, OJ L 9/12 of 14/01/2009.

the EU Member State where the product is intended for consumption. The main assumption of the procedure is therefore to shift the obligation to pay the tax in such a way that it does not take place during production but at the moment of release for consumption and in the country where the product is released for consumption. The excise duty suspension procedure applies to so-called community goods. The end of the excise duty suspension arrangement actually means release for consumption. The provisions of article 42, paragraph 1 and article 44, paragraph 1 of the Excise Duty Act provide an exhaustive list of cases in which the procedure is terminated. Excise markings are markings specified by the minister in charge of public finances, used to mark excise goods subject to the obligation to be marked, including: excise tax markings, which confirm payment of the amount constituting the value of excise tax markings; legalisation excise tax markings, which confirm the right of an entity obliged to mark excise goods with excise tax markings, to designate those goods for sale (article 2, paragraph 1, point 17 of the Excise Duty Act). Cigarettes, tobacco for smoking, cigars and cigarillos and dried tobacco are products subject to the obligation to bear excise duty markings (article 114 of the Excise Duty Act and Annex 3 thereto). Excise goods that have not been marked, are incorrectly marked or marked with incorrect markings cannot be marketed (see the obligations to mark contained articles 116 and 117 of the Excise Duty Act). Therefore, this provision of the Penal Fiscal Code sanctions such a ban and this is important for the correctness of the suspended excise duty procedure. It should be noted that activities related to the movement of excise goods, including under the suspended excise duty procedure, are subject to administrative control of the state and are subject to a number of administrative obligations. The criminal law norm not only secures the fact of paying fiscal debts, but also the fact that the product on the market is a fully legal product, released for consumption. Any behaviour involving a change of location or movement of excise goods should be considered as the release of excise goods.[16] In accordance with article 63, § 2 of the PFC, a penalty specified in the discussed article 63, § 1 of the PFC is imposed on anyone who, contrary to the provisions of the act, imports excise goods into the territory of the country without prior marking with excise tax markings. The term "imports" covers two groups of behaviours referred to in the Excise Duty Act: (1) importation into the territory of the Republic of Poland of excise goods from countries which are not members of the European Union, i.e. import (article 2, paragraph 1, point 7, subpoint b of the Excise Duty Act); (2) movement of excise goods from the territory of a Member State of the European Union other than the Republic of Poland to its territory, i.e. intra-Community acquisition (article 2, paragraph 1, point 9 of the Excise Duty Act). A discussion of the provision of article 63, § 3 of the PFC will be omitted as it does not apply to tobacco products. Article 63, § 4 of the PFC stipulates that the same penalty as in article 63, § 1 of the PFC is imposed on a person who removes excise goods from a tax warehouse without prior marking with excise duty stamps on the basis of a permit to remove excise goods from someone else's tax warehouse as a taxpayer

---

[16] Łabuda (2017), pp. 721–722.

outside the excise duty suspension procedure. Within the meaning of that provision, removal is to be understood as the physical change in the location of a product constituting an excise product. The procedure of permitting the removal of products from a third-party warehouse is governed by article 54 of the Excise Duty Act. The result is a change of taxpayer. It is no longer the person who runs the tax warehouse, but the person who obtained a decision of an authority allowing it to remove products from someone else's warehouse and it is they who are responsible for obligations secured by the criminal norm resulting from article 63, § 4 of the PFC. In accordance with article 63, § 5 of the PFC, the penalty specified in article 63, § 1 of the PFC is also imposed on a person who commits the behaviours specified in article 63, § 1–4 of the PFC in relation to excise goods which have been marked incorrectly or with inappropriate excise duty markings, in particular with damaged, destroyed, counterfeited, forged or invalid markings. The rules and procedure for applying excise markings are laid down in the Excise Duty Act (see article 120) and the ordinance of the Minister of Finance of 7th June, 2019, on the marking of excise goods[17] with excise markings issued pursuant to article 122 of this act. In view of these regulations, placing a marking in such a way that its removal or opening does not cause damage to the marking, which thus allows its reuse, should be considered as incorrect marking with excise tax markings. It is not appropriate to mark excise goods with excise markings which are not intended for a given excise product. Article 131, paragraph 7 of the Excise Duty Act specifies that damaged excise duty markings are those in which a permanent and visible violation of the physical properties allows identification of markings with respect to their originality, type, name, dimensions, series, registration number and date of manufacture. Article 131, paragraph 8 of the act indicates that the damaged markings are original excise duty markings in which permanent and visible violations of physical properties make it impossible to identify the marking as to its type, name, series, identification number and date of manufacture. Excise duty markings may turn out to be invalid in the event of the introduction of a new design for an excise marking. In such a case, in accordance with article 134, paragraph 1 of the Excise Duty Act, entities holding existing markings are obliged to return the unused markings to the issuing entity within 30 days of the date of the introduction of the new design. In addition, markings affixed before the introduction of the new design are valid for a period of 12 months from the date of the introduction of the new marking (article 134, paragraph 2 of the Excise Duty Act). The notion of counterfeiting and falsification should be given the meaning which these terms have in the Criminal Code (see article 270, § 1 of the Criminal Code). Thus, counterfeit excise duty markings should be considered to be those imitating an authentic marking, coming from an issuer who is not entitled to issue it. Alteration of an excise tax marking relates to changes made to an authentic marking and assumes that the content of the marking will be different

[17]Journal of Laws of 2019, item 1147; the ordinance came into force on 19th June, 2019, and replaced the previous ordinance on this subject of 23rd December, 2015, Journal of Laws of 2015, item 2283, as amended.

from the original one. Unlike counterfeiting, alteration does not have to have the characteristics of permanence and non-removability of the changes made.[18] The provision of article 63, paragraph 6 of the PFC provides for a privileged type with reference to all acts described in § 1–5 of article 63 of the PFC. If the excise duty due is of low value, the perpetrator of the offence is liable to a fine of up to 720 daily rates. However, if the excise tax does not exceed the statutory threshold, the perpetrator of the prohibited act specified in § 1–5 of article 63 of the PFC is subject to a fine for a fiscal offence. Due to an error by the legislator, it is not possible to order forfeiture in regards to all fiscal offences under article 63 of the PFC, types of privileged fiscal offences under article 63 of the PFC, or other fiscal offences if the subject is an excise product incorrectly marked or inadequately marked with excise tax markings with respect to acts committed in the period from 17th October, 1999 (date of entry into force of the Penal Fiscal Code) up to 29th July, 2010 (on 30th July, 2010, the error resulting from the amendment of the Penal Fiscal Code made in the act dated 25th July, 2010, amending the act on tax inspections and certain other acts[19]). Forfeiture in the Penal Fiscal Code is adjudicated if the Code provides for this, while the court may pronounce forfeiture only in the cases provided for in the Code (article 30, § 1 of the PFC, article 49, § 1 of the PFC). As regards the acts referred to, prior to 30th July, 2010, there was no provision allowing for a forfeiture decision (optional or obligatory).

Not all crimes under article 64 of the PFC will be related to tobacco products. The offences in § 2–5 of this article shall not apply to such offences. In this study, only those that are related to the issues under study will be indicated. The provision of article 64, § 1 of the PFC states that anyone who, without written notification within the time limit of the competent authority, removes excise goods not marked with excise markings from a tax warehouse for the purpose of making their intra-community supply or export shall be subject to a fine of up to 720 daily rates. In article 118, paragraph 5 of the Excise Duty Act is the main source of the obligation to notify the competent authority about the removal of excise goods not marked with excise markings from a tax warehouse. In the Excise Duty Act, this situation is understood as an exemption from the obligation to use markings, which applies to specific excise goods and is subject to a written notification to the competent head of the tax office. The cases of exemption from that obligation are indicated not only in article 118 of the Excise Duty Act, but also in the Ordinance of the Minister of Finance of 20th August, 2010, on the exemption of excise goods from the obligation to mark excise goods with excise[20] markings, which concerns tobacco products, issued pursuant to article 119 of the Excise Duty Act. The provision of article 64, § 6 of the PFC states that the penalty specified in article 64, § 1 of the PFC is also imposed on a person who, without written notification to the competent authority,

[18]See with respect to the term of alteration, falsification of a document: (Wróbel and Zoll 2017), pp. 695, 699.

[19]Journal of Laws of 2010, No. 127, item 858.

[20]Journal of Laws of 2019, item 2427, as amended.

places excise goods not marked with excise markings, intended for sale in commercial units located there, in a duty free zone without a written notification. The provision of article 64, § 7 of the PFC indicates that if the offences specified in § 1–6 of the same article constitute a minor case, they are fiscal offences. The Penal Fiscal Code defines a legal definition of a minor case in article 53, § 8 of the PFC.—it is a prohibited act as a fiscal offence, which in a specific case, due to its special circumstances—both subjective and objective—contains a low degree of social harmfulness of the act, in particular when the public-law debt depleted or exposed to depletion does not exceed the statutory threshold (article 53, § 6 of the PFC), and the manner and circumstances of committing the prohibited act do not indicate a gross disregard by the perpetrator of the financial and legal order or prudential rules required in given circumstances, or the perpetrator of the prohibited act, where the subject is of low value, does this for reasons that should be taken into consideration. The characteristic of removal should be understood in the same way as in relation to article 63 of the PFC.

Article 65 of the PFC typifies a prohibited act known as the illicit handling of excise goods. In accordance with article 65, § 1 of the PFC: whoever acquires, stores, transports, sends or transfers excise goods being the subject of a prohibited act specified in articles 63, 64, or 73 or assists in their disposal, or accepts or assists in their concealment of these excise goods, shall be subject to the penalty of a fine of up to 720 daily rates or the penalty of deprivation of liberty for up to 3 years, or both of these penalties jointly. In article 65, § 2 of the PFC we find an unintentional type of this crime ("...of which on the basis of accompanying circumstances one should and may presume that they are the subject of a prohibited act as specified in article 63, 64, 73..."), punishable by a fine of up to 720 daily rates. § 3 refers to the type of privileged fiscal crime. If the amount of tax at risk of depletion is low, the perpetrator of the offence specified in § 1 is subject to a fine of up to 720 daily rates. However, if the amount of tax at risk of depletion does not exceed the statutory threshold, the perpetrator of the prohibited act specified in § 1 (intentional handling of excise goods) or § 2 (unintentional handling of excise goods) shall be liable to a fine for a fiscal offence. The act of committing the illicit handling of excise goods was defined very broadly, much more broadly than in the case of the crime of receiving stolen goods (article 291 of the CC, article 292 of the CC). It is expressed in the following characteristic verbs: purchases, stores, transports, sends, transfers, moves, assists in disposal, accepts, assists in concealing. In order to commit an offence of handling excise goods, it is sufficient for the perpetrator to carry out one of the above elements. It cannot be ruled out that the perpetrator will satisfy more of them with his behaviour. These characteristics refer to the illegal acts listed by the legislator, which is a closed list. With respect to the problem of illicit trade in tobacco products, the provision of article 65 of the PFC will not be effective, in particular with respect to activities related to purchasing, storing, transporting, sending, transferring, assisting in disposal, receiving, assisting in concealing cigarettes and other tobacco products derived from illegal production. A person dealing with such a procedure does not fulfil the characteristics of any of the offences listed in article 65, § 1 or 2 of the PFC, and therefore it is not possible to recognise on the basis of the provision in question that such objects originate from a crime. Although it cannot be excluded that tobacco products may be the subject of certain crimes under articles 63, 64 and 73 of the PFC, these cases are not frequent, all the more so as some of the crimes referred to in these articles concern other excise goods, as already mentioned. However, article 65 of the PFC is not an instrument for combating trade in tobacco products originating from illegal production or smuggling.

The crime of defective marking of a product with excise tax markings has been stipulated in article 66 of the PFC. In accordance with § 1, a fine of up to 720 daily rates is imposed on anyone who incorrectly or inappropriately marks excise goods, in particular with damaged, destroyed, counterfeited, altered or invalidated markings. In cases of lesser significance, the perpetrator of this act is subject to a fine as for a fiscal offence (§ 2). The concepts and basic provisions of the Excise Duty Act in the field of marking of excise goods were discussed earlier in dealing with a crime under article 63, § 5 of the PFC. This act did not concern the issue of marking of excise goods, but the undertaking of one of the enforcement activities listed in article 63, § 1–4 of the PFC with respect to incorrectly marked excise goods. The presented understanding of the notions of damaged, destroyed, counterfeited, falsified, altered and invalid markings should also be referred to article 66 of the PFC.

It is a criminal offence to falsify excise markings. Whosoever forges or alters an excise marking or authorization to collect an excise marking shall be subject to the penalty of a fine of up to 720 daily rates or the penalty of deprivation of liberty, or both of these penalties jointly (article 67, § 1 of the PFC). The usage of the verbs forge or alter have been discussed in the analysis of article 63, § 5 of the PFC. The authorisation to collect excise duty markings is issued by the head of the tax office competent in matters related to excise tax markings (article 128, paragraph 2 of the Excise Duty Act). Such authorisation shall be preceded by a corresponding decision on the issuing of excise tax markings. The provision of § 2 criminalises obtaining or adapting measures in order to commit the fiscal offence specified in article 67, § 1 of the PFC. This is liability for preparing for a fiscal crime. This act is punishable by a fine of up to 240 daily rates or by imprisonment for up to 2 years or both jointly. Article 67, § 3 of the PFC provides for a special case of active grievance (special with regard to article 16 of the PFC and the requirements stipulated therein): there is no penalty for a fiscal offence defined in article 67, § 2 of the PFC for a perpetrator who withdrew from its execution, in particular, destroyed or prevented the acquired or adopted measures or prevented their use in the future. The provision of article 67, § 4 of the PFC stipulates that cases of minor importance, the perpetrator of a prohibited act specified in article 67, § 1 or 2 of the PFC is subject to a fine for a fiscal offence.

In accordance with article 68, § 1 of the PFC, anyone who fails to fulfil the obligation to draw up a list and present it for confirmation to the competent authority in the event of unspecified excise goods marked incorrectly or improperly with excise markings, in particular damaged, destroyed, forged, altered, counterfeited or invalid in circulation outside the excise duty suspension procedure, shall be subject to a fine of up to 720 daily rates. This criminal standard is another one, which is connected with the violation of obligations resulting from the specific nature of the trade in excise goods. The provision of article 116 of the Excise Duty Act specifies the entities obliged to mark their products with excise duty markings, and also indicates certain additional obligations, such as the obligation to prepare a list and present it for confirmation to the competent head of the tax office in the event of the possession of unmarked excise goods, excise goods marked incorrectly or excise goods with inappropriate markings. The source of the obligation secured with a punitive sanction under article 68, § 2 of the PFC is the provision of article 116, paragraph 3 of the Excise Duty Act. The penalty specified in article 68, § 1 of the PFC is imposed on a person who does not fulfil the obligation to mark excise goods with legalization excise markings. Article 68, § 3 of the PFC states that in cases of minor importance, the perpetrator of a prohibited act specified in article 68, § 1 or 2 of the PFC is subject to a fine for a fiscal offence.

The provision of article 69 of the PFC is very important in the fight against the illicit trade in tobacco products. It concerns such behaviours as: undertaking activities directly related to the production, import or trade in excise goods, as well as their marking with excise markings without official verification (§ 1); providing false information on the characteristics of manufactured excise goods (§ 2); removing excise goods from the place of production, processing, consumption, storage or during transport (§ 3). For each of these acts, the perpetrator is liable to a fine of up to 720, 360 and 240 daily rates, respectively. Compared to the offences previously discussed, the legislator has not provided for their privileged types or for a case of minor importance constituting an offence. This distinguishes this prohibited act in terms of the assessment of its degree of social harmfulness, of course, in an abstract way. Moreover, article 69, § 4 of the PFC stipulates punishment for attempting the acts specified in article 69, § 2 or 3 of the PFC. "Attempting" in penal fiscal law is punishable by a penalty not exceeding two-thirds of the upper limit of the statutory threat provided for the given fiscal offence (article 21, § 2 of the PFC). The official verification is carried out by an institution specified in the act of 16th November, 2016, on National Treasury Administration,[21] which belongs to the competence of the head of the customs and fiscal office. It is carried out in the cases and to the extent specified in article 106 of the aforementioned act. Activities related to the production, import and marketing of tobacco products, as well as to their marking, must be carried out within a tax warehouse (Article 47, paragraph 1 of the Excise Duty Act) with the exception of dried tobacco (Article 47, paragraph 1, point 8 of the Excise Duty Act) and the production of excise goods on which advance payment of excise duty has been paid (Article 47, paragraph 1, point 1 of the Excise Duty Act). This means that, with the exception of two exceptions, it is mandatory to carry out an official check.

The act under article 69, § 2 of the PFC is related to obligations concerning customs and fiscal control. In the Act on National Treasury Administration (hereinafter: NTA), entities operating in the field of production, import and trade in tobacco products are subject to a number of information obligations (see e.g. article 74 of the

[21]Journal of Laws of 2020, item 505, as amended.

NTA Act), article 69, § 2 of the PFC criminalises only those behaviours which concern the transfer of data on the quantity and quality of excise goods. It follows from the provision in question *expressis verbis* that a causative act does not include an omission, but concerns only an act—the provision of false data. This means data that does not correspond to the actual state of affairs. In legal doctrine, a situation in which the perpetrator does not provide data to his disadvantage, i.e. leads to an overstatement of the tax due, is resolved differently. The realisation of the elements of the offence in question may result in a reduction of excise duty or in its undue reimbursement. If we support the view that the Penal Fiscal Code applies the rules of excluding multiple assessments, then in the case of depletion of excise tax only article 56, § 1–3 of the PFC will have to be applied, and in the case of improper reimbursement of excise tax—article 76, § 1–3 of the PFC. Otherwise, the crimes described (article 69, § 2 of the PFC will be in concurrence with article 56, § 1–3 of the PFC or article 76, § 1–3 of the PFC) will remain in real concurrence with fiscal offences. In the event that the perpetrator provides untrue data to his disadvantage, which means that it leads to an increase in his tax liability or an understatement of his tax refund, the execution of the elements of article 56, § 1–3 of the PFC or article 76, § 1–3 of the PFC should be excluded. In such cases, the lack of liability for the act of article 69, § 2 of the PFC is explained by the lack of an impact on the legal good.[22] However, in the authors' opinion, consideration should be made on how legal goods subject to protection under the Penal Fiscal Code are understood. On the grounds of various fiscal crimes, commentators basically distinguish one legal good—property of the State Treasury, sometimes of the European Union, because the income from taxes goes to the national and European budget. However, the scope of criminalization determined at least by the crimes discussed makes one wonder whether it is correct to reduce the regulations of the Penal Fiscal Code to the protection of legal property consisting solely of the fiscal interest, and also whether it is not possible to distinguish a further and closer subject of protection. Another common view justifying the thesis that the perpetrator is not responsible for providing untruths which leads to a tax overstatement is the concept that the social harmfulness of such an act is negligible.[23] Assuming that the property of the Treasury is the sole legal asset subject to protection of article 69, § 2 of the PFC, the first of the aforementioned views should be supported. Nonetheless, the provision in question should be amended. It should not be reduced solely to a question of tax assessment and the possible reduction of the amount of tax due. It performs a function related to the correctness of the customs and fiscal control, and not to the issue of the amount of tax liability. The application of the Excise Duty Act and the regulations issued on its basis, as well as the regulations issued on the basis of the Act on National Treasury Administration, give rise to many obligations related to the transfer of data on the type, quantity or quality of excise goods. The crime under article 69, § 2 of the PFC refers to manufactured excise goods, thus the act cannot

[22]Wilk, Komentarz do art. 69 Kodeksu karnego skarbowego (2018a), article 69.

[23]Konarska-Wrzosek et al. (2013), p. 280.

refer to situations related to processing, transport, storage, or destruction of excise goods. The crime in question therefore sanctions the provision of false data only at the stage of the manufacture of excise goods.

The generalised approach expressed in the provision of article 69, § 3 of the PFC refers to the ordinance of the Minister of Finance of 10th May, 2017, on customs and fiscal control of certain excise goods.[24] Tobacco products are covered by the material scope of that regulation (§ 1, paragraph 1, point 1b, third indent of that regulation). The provision is a consequence of the fact that the activity connected with production, import, or trade in tobacco products, and their marking requires conducting in a tax warehouse, and is subject to, customs and fiscal control. Therefore, the regulation is intended to ensure the correctness of the marking of excise goods, and control of their storage, processing, destruction and transport. All these issues are addressed by the ordinance. However, the causative act concerns only the removal of excise goods from the locations specified in the ordinance, and not a number of other obligations related to customs and fiscal control of excise goods.

The excise duty suspension procedure is one of the basic institutions of tax law, important for the marketing of goods. Its significance has been explained earlier. The provision of article 69a, § 1 of the PFC states that whoever, contrary to the provisions of the act, violates the conditions for applying the excise duty suspension procedure, produces, stores or trans-ships excise goods outside a tax warehouse shall be subject to a fine of up to 720 daily rates or deprivation of liberty for up to 2 years, or both of these penalties jointly. In cases of lesser weight, the perpetrator of the prohibited act specified in § 1 shall be subject to the penalty of a fine for a fiscal offence. With regard to this provision, it is pointed out that it erroneously uses the clauses "contrary to the provisions of the law", "in breach of the conditions for the application of the excise duty suspension arrangement".[25] It is enough to leave the second one. Currently, the suspended excise duty procedure is not applied to products manufactured outside a tax warehouse. This applies to all products.

In this part of the study it is worth noting that the construction of the provision of article 69a of the PFC is not correct and it is worth considering legislative changes to this element. All the elements expressed in the verbs used in the act: "produces", "stores", "trans-ships" are covered by the clause "in breach of the conditions for the application of the excise duty suspension arrangement". If such a procedure applies, performing the aforementioned activities outside a tax warehouse is contrary to the provisions of the Excise Duty Act (see article 47 of the Excise Duty Act). It seems that the legislator's intention was to limit the punishability of a violation of the suspension of excise duty procedure to the strictly defined behaviours referred to in article 69a, § 1 of the PFC. However, it is worth considering both the form of this provision and the possible extension of criminalisation related to infringements within the scope of the excise duty suspension procedure. It is important not only

[24] Journal of Laws of 2020, item 262.

[25] Łabuda (2017), p. 750.

from the point of view of the fiscal obligations of taxable persons, but also from the point of view of control of tobacco products since the excise duty suspension procedure is connected with numerous information obligations of the entity applying it. Within the meaning of article 8, paragraph 1, point 1 of the Excise Duty Act, production is subject to excise duty. In the case of tobacco products, the act provides a legal definition of tobacco production. In accordance with article 99, paragraph 1 of the Excise Duty Act, the production of tobacco products within the meaning of the act is the manufacture, processing and packaging of tobacco products. In addition, the production of cigarettes is also the manufacturing of cigarettes, including by the consumer, using machinery for the manufacture of cigarettes (article 99, paragraph 1a of the Excise Duty Act). The production of cigarettes by a consumer by hand at home shall not be considered as the manufacture of cigarettes. It seems that such a definition should be transferred to the Penal Fiscal Code, although it should be noted that the issue of the definition of cigarette production—its very broad scope—raises doubts in the doctrine of tax law.[26] The jurisprudence of administrative courts has a broad interpretation.[27] This is how the legislative changes made in the Excise Duty Act are understood (the addition of the cited article 99, paragraph 1a and 1b of the Excise Duty Act), i.e. the intention of the legislator to give the concept of "manufacture of cigarettes" the broadest possible scope.

The provisions of article 69b and 69c of the PFC reveal the problem of the proper process of law making, which has recently been particularly intense in Poland. This is because there are legitimate doubts as to the procedure for their adoption (they were introduced within the framework of amendments at the final stage of legislative work, without going through the prescribed procedure for adopting the provisions). Moreover, it is incorrect that both in the explanatory memorandum and in the doctrine that these provisions are viewed only through the prism of value added tax and the specific practice of crime on the fuel market.[28] There may be an impression that this is the scope of the regulation of these provisions. Such an impression arises from the fact that these regulations were developed within the framework of amendments to tax acts (the VAT Act and the Excise Duty Act) in order to solve specific problems occurring in practice in the application of taxes and combating large-scale fraud. This view is erroneous because the legislation in question applies to all excise goods in the context of intra-Community acquisition or supply. It should be noted at this point that there are reservations as to whether the act under article 69b, § 1 of the PFC complies with all the directives resulting from the principle of legality of an act under criminal law. There are many obligations arising from intra-Community acquisitions or intra-Community supplies. It seems that article 69b, § 1 of the PFC concerns tax obligations related to the determination and performance of a tax obligation.

[26]Zimny (2017), pp. 775–776.

[27]Judgement of the Voivodship Administrative Court of 21st July, 2016, case ref. No. WSA Kr I SA/KR 336/16, LEX No. 2120499.

[28]Łabuda (2017), pp. 754–756.

In accordance with article 69b, § 1 of the PFC, anyone who, contrary to the provisions of the act, makes an intra-Community supply or intra-Community acquisition of excise goods is subject to a fine of up to 720 daily rates or a penalty of imprisonment, or both. § 2 of the same provision provides for a fiscal offence punishable by a fine. It consists of the implementation of the elements of article 69, § 1 of the PFC, with the proviso that the perpetrator's act meets the conditions of a case of lessor significance. The relationship between the provisions of article 69a, § 1 of the PFC and article 54, § 1 of the PFC, article 56, § 1 of the PFC and article 76, § 1 of the PFC is puzzling. Making an intra-Community supply or acquisition gives rise to certain obligations in the field of value added tax and excise duty. Intra-Community acquisition is directly listed as an activity subject to excise duty (article 8, paragraph 1, point 4 of the Excise Duty Act). Intra-Community acquisitions also give rise to VAT obligations. It is therefore the case that article 69a, § 1 of the PFC in fact shifts the field of criminalisation—in relation to article 54, § 1 of the PFC, article 56, § 1 of the PFC, article 76, § 1 of the PFC—to an earlier stage. The question is only whether procedural authorities are already in a position to effectively implement this provision at this stage. The fact is that the mechanisms referred to in article 69a, § 1 of the PFC are very often used by perpetrators who intend to avoid taxation, on the other hand their control at this stage (making an intra-Community acquisition, intra-Community supply) is difficult. It is established that such activities are performed in practice at a later stage, at which evasion should be considered (article 54, § 1 of the PFC, article 56, § 1 of the PFC—tax evasion, article 76, § 1 of the PFC—extortion of undue tax refund).

In accordance with article 69c, § 1 of the PFC, a person who, in breach of his or her obligation, moves excise goods from the territory of one Member State to the territory of another Member State through the territory of the country without a simplified accompanying document, or a commercial document replacing a simplified accompanying document, or without printing an e-AD with an assigned reference number, or another commercial document containing an e-AD reference number in the System, or a document replacing an e-AD, or, on the basis of these documents containing data inconsistent with the actual state of affairs, is subject to a fine of up to 720 daily rates, or a penalty of imprisonment, or both. As stated in § 2 of the same article, in the case of a minor offence, the perpetrator of the offence referred to in § 1 shall be liable to a fine for a fiscal offence. Movement of excise goods is a frequent activity associated with the production and marketing of tobacco products. In relation to article 69c, § 1 of the PFC, it concerns only such a movement of excise goods that is connected with the need to hold a specific document used in this type of activity. Article 2, paragraph 1, point 15 of the Excise Duty Act defines the "e-AD" as an electronic administrative document on the basis of which excise goods are moved under the excise duty suspension procedure. It should be pointed out here that the excise duty suspension procedure applies in the situation described in article 69c, § 1 of the PFC because, according to article 40, paragraph 2 of the Excise Duty Act, the procedure applies if excise goods are moved from a tax warehouse on the territory of a Member State through the territory of the country to a customs authority in the territory of another Member State which supervises the actual removal of the goods from the territory of the European Union (point 5 of the same), through the territory of the country between tax warehouses in the territory of Member States (point 8 of the same); through the territory of a country from a tax warehouse to the territory of a Member State to a purchase in the territory of a Member State which is an entity authorised by the applicable tax authorities of this European Union Member State to receive excise goods under the excise duty suspension procedure or to entities covered by the exemption from excise duty resulting from article 31, paragraph 1 of the Excise Duty Act (point 9 of the same). Pursuant to article 2, paragraph 1, point 15a of the Excise Duty Act, a document replacing e-AD is a document on the basis of which excise goods are moved under the excise duty suspension procedure when the EMCS System is unavailable, containing the same data as e-AD. According to article 2, paragraph 1, point 16 of the Excise Duty Act, a simplified accompanying document is a document on the basis of which excise goods listed in Annex 2 to the Excise Duty Act, which are outside the excise duty suspension procedure, and ethyl alcohol fully denatured with substances permitted to denature ethyl alcohol under Commission Regulation (EC) No 3199/93 of 22 November 1993 on the mutual recognition of procedures for the complete denaturing of ethyl alcohol for the purposes of exemption from excise duty, are moved within the framework of an intra-Community supply or acquisition.[29] The movement of excise goods is subject to customs and fiscal control. In principle, every movement of excise goods requires the completion of procedures defined by tax law and the possession of appropriate transport documentation. Failure to do so will result in criminal liability.

Under article 69c, § 1 of the PFC, the issue of an entity bearing criminal liability is problematic. It is pointed out that the crime is of an individual nature and may be committed by a person, on whom the obligation rests.[30] A situation in which the transport organizer, the person ordering the transport, does not bear liability under article 69c, § 1 of the PFC should be considered as an error. Transports of goods are commissioned to shipping companies, so there is doubt as to whether the construction of a penal fiscal provision, which leads to punishment of drivers of vehicles transporting excise goods, is correct, particularly as there is no obligation resting on the party accepting the transport order, or the driver to verify the goods in transport and the formal requirements to be met by its transport. At the same time, there is no liability for ordering such transport without fulfilling the conditions stipulated by law.

The acts referred to in article 70–72 and article 75 of the PFC constitute fiscal crimes and offences related to the use of excise tax markings. Excise duty markings have already been discussed. The provisions of the Excise Duty Act formulate a number of obligations and prohibitions concerning excise duty markings. Generally speaking, it should be pointed out that free circulation of excise markings is not

[29]OJ EC L 288 of 23/11/1993, p. 12, as amended, EU OJ Polish Special Edition, chapter 9, vol. 1, p. 249, as amended.

[30]Łabuda (2017), p. 762.

allowed (see article 130, paragraph 1 of the Excise Duty Act), they must be recorded, stored, and transported in a prescribed manner (article 131 of the Excise Duty Act), there is an obligation to settle the excise markings transferred (articles 132 and 135 of the Excise Duty Act), and procedures are provided for in case of loss, damage or destruction of excise markings (article 138 of the Excise Duty Act). The provisions of the Penal Fiscal Code in the provisions of the paragraph referred to in the introduction secure some of these obligations taking into account the functions performed by excise tax markings (legalization, protection, and a fiscal function[31]). Thus, article 70, § 1 of the PFC stipulates that whoever, contrary to the provisions of the act, sells or otherwise transfers excise tax markings to an unauthorised party shall be subject to the penalty of a fine of up to 720 daily rates or the penalty of deprivation of liberty for up to 2 years, or both of these penalties jointly. Criminal liability will also be borne by the purchaser of such markings, because according to article 70, § 2 of the PFC, the penalty specified in article 70, § 1 of the PFC is subject to whoever purchases or otherwise accepts excise tax markings from an unauthorized party in order to use or put them into circulation. In addition, the person who removes them from the excise goods in order to reuse or circulate them will also be liable. The attempt to commit the aforementioned crimes is punishable. Pursuant to article 70, § 4, the penalty specified in § 1 shall also be imposed on a person who, without being authorised to do so, possesses, stores, transports, sends or transfers excise duty markings. The provision of article 70, § 5 of the PFC introduces liability for misconduct in relation to the behaviour described in article 70, § 1, 2, and 4 of the PFC if it constitutes a case of lesser significance. Article 71 of the PFC stipulates that whoever, by a gross violation of the regulations on transport or storage of excise tax markings, exposes them to direct danger of theft, destruction, damage or loss, shall be subject to a fine of up to 480 daily rates. Another article concerns non-accounting for excise tax markings. Pursuant to article 72 of the PFC, anyone who, in breach of the obligation, fails to account on time with the competent authority for the usage of excise tax markings, in particular does not return unused, damaged, destroyed or invalid markings, is subject to a fine of up to 360 daily rates. Moreover, pursuant to article 75 of the PFC, an importer, an entity making an intra-Community acquisition and a tax representative who does not fulfil the obligation to obtain from an entity established outside the territory of the country for the settlement of the excise duty markings transferred to it is subject to a fine of up to 180 daily rates.

There are cases in which certain excise goods or excise goods under certain conditions or status are exempted from the obligation to mark them with excise tax markings. Of course, such an exemption must be clearly indicated by law. This is done in article 118 of the Excise Duty Act. Moreover, article 119 of the Excise Duty Act constitutes a statutory delegation for the minister in charge of public finances to grant an exemption—by way of a regulation—from the obligation to mark certain excise goods with excise duty markings if: (1) this is justified by an important interest of the state or entities obliged to mark excise goods with excise duty

[31]On the functions of excise tax markings, see more broadly: (Zimny 2017), pp. 824–825.

markings; (2) it results from the provisions of European Union law or international agreements; (3) it indicates that certain excise goods are intended for use in the form of samples for scientific, laboratory or quality research. Cigars and cigarillos are covered by such exemption until 31st December, 2020, pursuant to § 2 of the ordinance of the Minister of Finance of 20th August, 2010, on exemptions of excise goods from the obligation to mark them with excise markings.[32] In addition, excise goods produced outside the national territory and intended for use at exhibitions, fairs, exhibitions and similar events may benefit from an exemption under the conditions laid down in the ordinance. Article 73 of the PFC provides for liability for acts related to the existence of exemptions from marking excise goods with excise markings. Pursuant to article 73, § 1 of the PFC, anyone who, in the use of an excise product, changes the purpose for which it is intended or fails to observe another condition, on the basis of which the exemption from the obligation to mark excise duty with excise markings on excise goods is subject to a fine of up to 720 daily rates. The provision of article 73, § 2 of the PFC introduces liability for a fiscal offence if the uncollected excise duty does not exceed the statutory threshold. It is doubtful whether the perpetrator can be held liable for the above act in the case of the exemptions provided for in the ordinance cited above. The provision of article 73, § 1 of the PFC clearly indicates that the objectives and conditions for exemption from excise duty on excise goods must be provided for by law.

2.1.4 Customs Offences

The crime of smuggling is stipulated in article 86 of the PFC. Paragraph 1 of this states that anyone who, in breach of his customs obligation, imports or exports goods abroad without presenting them to customs or without a customs declaration, thereby rendering the customs debt liable to depletion, shall be liable to a fine of up to 720 daily rates or deprivation of liberty, or both. Paragraph 2 stipulates that the same penalty shall be imposed on a perpetrator if the customs smuggling relates to goods traded with foreign countries subject to non-tariff regulation. § 3 provides for the type of privileged offence described in § 1 and 2, which consists of the fact that the amount of customs duty exposed to depletion or value of goods traded with foreign countries subject to non-tariff regulation is of low value. In this case, the offender is only liable to a fine of up to 720 daily rates. An offence under article 86, § 1 and 2 of the PFC shall be a situation where the amount of customs duty at risk of depletion or the value of goods in foreign trade, which is subject to non-tariff regulation, does not exceed the statutory threshold.

That provision is referred to as customs smuggling because it is described as consisting of the failure of the person concerned to fulfil a customs obligation. This obligation is related to the import or export of goods from a third country to an EU Member State. These obligations are twofold. They are defined in the EU Customs

[32]Journal of Laws of 2019, item 2427, as amended.

Code (hereinafter: UCC).[33] The presentation of goods to customs bodies means notification of the customs authorities of the arrival of goods at a customs office or at any other place designated or approved by the customs authorities and of the availability of these goods for customs controls (article 5, point 33 of the UCC). However, a customs declaration shall be the act whereby a person indicates in the prescribed form and manner his intention to place goods under a given customs procedure, specifying, where appropriate, any particular arrangements to be applied. At present, such notifications are made in electronic form (article 6, paragraph 1 of the UCC[34]). These two obligations, taken as an alternative because it is the customs rules that determine when it is sufficient to present the goods to customs and when the customs declaration has to be made, remain essential for the recognition of the liability of the offender. However, it cannot be equated with the creation of a customs debt. It is true that such a procedure will most often arise in the event of failure to fulfil the obligations under article 86, § 1 of the CC (in particular in the case of the import and export of goods discussed in this study). However, not every failure to fulfil the obligation to present the goods or its customs declaration to the customs authority gives rise to a customs debt within the meaning of article 5, point 18 of the UCC. The existence of a customs duty which the perpetrator exposes to depletion (apart from failing to fulfil his obligations) is a necessary condition for attributing a crime to the offender under article 86, § 1 of the PFC. This provision is another example of a regulation which requires *in contrecto* determination of the obligations incumbent on the offender, their scope, whether there is in fact a customs debt, and thus the recourse to customs legislation, and the proper assessment of those standards.

The European Union is a customs union. This means that the exchange of goods throughout the territory between Member States may not be subject to import and export duties or other equivalent charges. However, there are different rules and restrictions on tobacco products. Limits are set at Union level (800 cigarettes, 400 cigarillos, 200 cigars, 1 kg of tobacco). States may provide for higher thresholds than those set, which is also the case. Exceeding such limits in the movement of goods between EU countries will not, however, constitute a crime under article 86, § 1 of the PFC. The position is correct that as of the date of Poland's accession to the European Union, the acts which depenalysed the characteristics of the crimes specified in articles 85–96 of the Code of the PFC in relation to trade in goods with countries belonging to the European Union were depenalyzed.[35] Violation of tax obligations related to exceeding the above limits should therefore be sought in

[33]Regulation (EU) No. 952/2013 of the European Parliament and of the Council of 9th October, 2013, laying down the Union Customs Code, EU OJ L 269, hereinafter referred to as "UCC".

[34]The detailed terms and conditions are specified in the ordinance of the Minister of Finance of 8th September, 2016, on customs declarations, Journal of Laws of 2018, item 2262.

[35]Decision of the Supreme Court of 22nd November, 2006, case ref. No. V KK 247/06, LEX No. 202287.

completely different fiscal norms (the acts referred to in Chapter 6 on excise duty should be considered here).

The fundamental principle of the EU is a common customs tariff in its relations with third countries. The Union's Customs Code, as mentioned above, is a key Union act in this area. To a certain extent, it is complemented by EU regulations and national legislation. The import or export of goods must be identified with this act within the customs union (EU), which in turn gives rise to a customs obligation and failure to comply with it leads to the fulfilment of the constituent element of the crime in question. International agreements, domestic laws and regulations may contain exemptions from the principle that every carriage or export gives rise to a customs obligation. Such exceptions, of course, apply. The crime of customs smuggling is one of the most frequently committed customs crimes. At present, tobacco products are not subject to non-tariff regulation. Therefore, this concept will not be discussed in this study. The crime of customs smuggling may be cumulative in relation to other crimes under the Penal Fiscal Code. The collection of customs duty is not the only receivable that can be linked to the import or export of a product. Smuggling itself may also be related to the failure to fulfil other obligations and be subject to criminal liability or to the depletion or exposure to depletion of tax other than excise duty, e.g. value added tax. In jurisprudence the opinion has been expressed that the object of a fiscal tort under article 86, § 1 of the PFC may be goods legally purchased abroad, not by way of crime, because the perpetrator of a crime cannot be subject to the obligation of self-denunciation. Moreover, it was also indicated that only the goods for which Poland is a destination country may be the subject of this act.[36] Commentators discussing this provision cite the decision of the Court of Appeal in Poznań,[37] in which it did not justify the thesis presented. A wider commentary is also lacking in studies referring to this judicature. However, the thesis of this ruling is not justified. First of all, it should be noted that Poland was not a member of the European Union at the time of committing the offence and the decision of the Court of First Instance in the aforementioned judgement. There are no grounds whatsoever for assuming that it may only relate to goods for which Poland is a destination country, mainly due to the fact that currently the territory of Poland is in the area of the customs union. The entire area of the European Union is therefore protected, so that there are no illegal imports or exports from the European Union. It does not matter what their destination country is. From the point of view of proceedings for acts under article 86, § 1 of the PFC, it is more important to make determinations regarding the origin of goods. For example, if the goods are not stopped at the border (the EU's external border), then liability under the aforementioned article will only be possible if it is shown that the goods originate from a non-EU country. The same will apply to exports. Another controversial thesis is that the perpetrator cannot be held criminally liable in the case of goods of illegal origin

[36]Judgement of the Court of Appeal in Poznań of 6th November, 2000, Case No. II Aka 430/00, Legalis No. 54145.

[37]Wilk, Komentarz do art. 86 Kodeksu karnego skarbowego (2018b), article 86, thesis 5.

being the subject of smuggling. We have already analysed the problem of differentiation in the taxation of goods of legal and illegal origin. It seems that the theses presented in this respect in the earlier part of the study should also refer to the crime of customs smuggling discussed here. To sum up, the object of a customs offence under article 86, § 1 of the PFC may be goods of illegal origin, as well as goods whose destination is a country other than Poland.

Article 87 of the PFC stipulates a crime known as customs fraud. In this case, the entity fulfils the obligations resulting from article 86, § of the PFC and relevant customs regulations, but at the same time misleads the authority authorised to conduct customs control. The offender undertakes this action in order to avoid payment of the customs duties. A crime can therefore be committed intentionally only with direct intent.[38] The perpetrator's action consists in causing the customs authority to make an assessment, inconsistent with the objective state of affairs, of the relevant circumstances constituting the tax (duty) assessment, which, for example, may relate to any calculation prerequisites related to the application of the relevant customs tariff.[39] In relation to this crime, it is noted in the literature that this crime may be committed exclusively through an action (contrary to the crime of fraud under article 286, § 1 of the PFC).[40] Accordingly, the offender shall not be liable to prosecution if the customs authority erred in fact or in law and the person subject to the procedure makes use of it. The authorities authorised to conduct customs inspections are the authorities of the National Treasury Administration. In actual fact, this will be an officer authorised to carry out inspections. It should be emphasised that an officer must be misled, i.e. the mere provision of erroneous data by the perpetrator is not sufficient, as a necessary condition is that a specific officer who performs the inspection has an erroneous idea of the factual or legal situation in his/her awareness. If a public officer, despite defective data, is not misled, the offence under article 87, § 1 of the PFC will not be in the form of an act of execution. In such a case, the liability for attempting to act pursuant to article 87, § 1 of the PFC should be considered.

Pursuant to article 87, § 1 of the PFC, whosoever, by misleading the authority authorised to conduct customs inspections, exposes the customs receivable to depletion is subject to a fine of up to 720 daily rates or deprivation of liberty, or both. Article 87, § 2 of the PFC refers to the same executive activity with respect to goods or services in foreign trade, which are subject to non-tariff regulation. The criminal liability is the same as in § 1. The provision of article 87, § 3 of the PFC is a privileged type of crime under article 87, § 1 or 2. The perpetrator is liable to a fine of up to 720 daily rates if the amount of customs duty liable to depletion or value of goods or services in foreign trade, which are subject to non-tariff regulation, is of low value. However, the provision of article 87, § 4 of the PFC introduces liability for an

[38]Otherwise: (Prusak and Skowronek 2018), p. 154.

[39]Decision of the Supreme Court of 28th January, 2005, case ref. No. V KK 377/04, LEX No. 146256.

[40]Magnuszewska (2016), p. 71.

offence if the amount of customs duty liable to depletion or value of goods or services in foreign trade, which are subject to non-tariff regulation, does not exceed the statutory threshold.

A crime similar to the act under article 87, § 1 of the CC is the act stipulated in article 92 of the PFC, and occasionally this latter act is termed customs fraud. It consists of defrauding the repayment of a customs debt or the remission of a customs debt. Pursuant to article 92, § 1 of the PFC: whosoever, by providing data inconsistent with the actual state of affairs or by concealing the actual state of affairs, misleads the competent authority by exposing it to the risk of undue repayment of the customs debt or remission of the customs debt due to be paid, is subject to a fine of up to 720 daily rates or deprivation of liberty, or both. The privileged type of this offence is provided for in § 2, which indicates that the perpetrator is subject to a fine of up to 720 daily rates if the amount exposed to undue repayment or remission of customs duty is of low value. However, if this amount does not exceed the statutory threshold, the perpetrator of the prohibited act is liable to a fine for a fiscal offence. The EU Customs Code lays down the rules for the repayment or remission of customs duties (see article 116–118 of the UCC). The point is, of course, that the sums unduly and unlawfully collected are to be refunded. However, this does not apply to conscious action. Repayment or remission shall be made upon request. In most cases, the moment of its submission should be tied to the implementation of the prerequisites by the perpetrator. Misrepresentation should be understood as specified in the aforementioned article 87, § 1 of the PFC. The crime under article 92, § 1 of the PFC includes another form of causal action—concealment of the actual state of affairs, i.e. concealment, the conscious omission of the essential elements for performing repayment or remission. The repayment or remission of the customs debt is not required for committing this crime.

The provision of article 90, § 1 of the PFC criminalises the removal of goods or means of transport from customs supervision. This crime is punishable by a fine of up to 720 daily rates, or by imprisonment for up to 3 years, or both. Pursuant to article 90, § 2 of the PFC, the same penalty is imposed on anyone who destroys, damages or removes a customs seal without the consent of an authorised authority. In cases of lesser significance, the perpetrator of the prohibited act specified in § 1 or 2 shall be subject to the penalty of a fine for a fiscal offence. Customs supervision means action taken by the customs authorities to ensure that customs legislation and, where appropriate, other provisions applicable to goods subject to such action are observed (article 5, point 32 of the UCC). In the case of an offence under article 90, § 2 of the PFC, the principles arising from article 134 of the UCC are applicable. Firstly, goods are subject to customs supervision from the moment they enter the customs territory of the Union. Secondly, goods must remain under customs supervision for as long as necessary to determine their customs status and are not taken up without the approval of the customs authorities. The means of transport referred to in article 90, § 1 of the PFC is defined in article 53, § 18 of the PFC as an object for the transport of persons or goods, in particular a road vehicle, rail transport, a trailer, a semi-trailer, a vessel or an aircraft. The concept of "customs seal" is an example of a situation where the legislator fails to ensure the coherence of the system. The issue of incorrectly used wording may be removed pursuant to article 53, § 32 of the PFC. This provision introduces the rule that the meaning of certain terms should be determined in accordance with the meaning given to them in specific tax acts, and the determination of the law actually referred to by the legislator allows the adoption of an appropriate term and its meaning. However, we should postulate that the legislator should properly and precisely define the characteristics of a prohibited act. In customs law and proceedings there is no "customs seal" but an "official seal" (article 65 of the law on the NTA). The regulations specify the conditions under which an official seal may take place; this is not required and applied in all cases. In principle, the authorities of the National Treasury Administration (the head of the customs and tax office or a person authorised by him/her) have the power to remove official seals. The terms removes, destroys and damages were discussed in an earlier part of this study. The provision of article 94 of the PFC is related to customs supervision. Failure to provide oral or written explanations relevant to customs controls or failure to provide access to the required documents concerning foreign trade in goods or services shall be criminally liable. The penalty for this fiscal crime is a fine of up to 720 daily rates (§ 1). According to § 2, a person who in some other manner frustrates or hinders a person authorised to conduct customs inspections or supervision activities shall be liable to the penalty, in particular, whosoever refuses to carry out preparatory acts for a customs inspection without complying with the obligation to deliver the goods immediately to the place designated by the customs authority. In cases of lesser significance, the perpetrator of the above acts shall be subject to a penalty for a fiscal offence. The construction of article 94 of the PFC could be simpler, even if one wanted to calculate examples of behaviour that would hamper the performance of customs control activities. It is precisely only customs inspection that should be included in the constituent elements of this crime. The use of the expression "customs supervision" makes the act described in article 94, § 1 of the PFC of an indefinite nature and thus violates the basic principles of criminal law (the principle of determination of a prohibited act). The source of the obligation, the non-fulfilment of which is subject to criminal liability, can be found in article 72 of the NTA Act. The scope is very extensive. In criminal law (under the Criminal Code), the term "prevent" has long been understood not only as a complete impossibility of any action, but also as a hindrance to it. The wording of article 94, § 2 of the PFC would suggest a slightly different meaning.

Another provision of article 91 of the PFC typifies customs goods handling. Pursuant to article 91, § 1 of the PFC, whosoever purchases, stores, transports, moves or transfers goods being the subject of a prohibited act specified in article 86–90, § 1 of the PFC or assists in its sale or accepts or assists in its concealment, shall be subject to a fine of up to 720 daily rates or deprivation of liberty for up to 3 years, or both of these penalties jointly. This is an intentional crime. The aforementioned provision refers to article 86 of the PFC (customs smuggling), article 87 of the PFC (customs fraud), article 88 of the PFC (violation of the temporary admission procedure), article 89 of the PFC (violation of the conditions for customs exemption), and article 90, § 1 of the PFC (removal of goods or means of transport from customs supervision). Some of these provisions have been discussed. The others are not even potentially applicable to the problem of illegal smuggling. The crime of customs goods handling will relate to goods originating from strictly defined criminal offences. It is therefore necessary to establish evidence as to the origin of the goods.[41] The provision of article 91, § 2 of the PFC deals with inadvertent customs goods handling. It is committed by someone who purchases, stores, transports, sends or moves goods which, on the basis of accompanying circumstances, should and can be assumed to be the subject of a prohibited act specified in article 86–90, § 1 of the PFC, or assists in its sale, or accepts the product or assists in its concealment. The perpetrator of this act is liable to a fine of up to 720 daily rates. In the provision of article 91, § 3 of the PFC, the legislator provided for a privileged type of act under article 91, § 1 of the PFC. The perpetrator is liable to a fine of up to 720 daily rates if the amount of customs duty or the value of goods in foreign trade, which is subject to non-tariff regulation, is of low value. If this value does not exceed the statutory threshold, the perpetrator of the prohibited act specified in § 1 or 2 is liable for a fiscal offence (article 91, § 4 of the PFC). The elements of article 91, § 1 and § 2 of the PFC defining a causal activity are presented alternatively. It is obvious that for the existence of a crime it is sufficient to realize one of these verbal characteristics. These terms should be given the same meaning as they are commonly understood. We are not going to discuss here each of the wordings used in this provision.

The provision of article 93, § 2 of the PFC concerns the proper functioning of a customs free zone or a customs warehouse.[42] According to it, anyone who grossly violates the customs legislation on the conditions of operation of a customs free zone or a customs warehouse is liable to a fine of up to 240 daily rates. Pursuant to article 93, § 3 of the PFC, the penalty specified in § 2 shall also be imposed on any person who grossly violates the provisions on the conditions of temporary storage. The creation and operation of a customs free zone are defined in the Union Customs Code. The Member States are authorised to designate customs free zones (article 243 of the UCC). Examples of behaviours that may constitute an act under article 93, § 2 of the PFC are violations of the rules related to the functioning of such an area, e.g. the introduction or removal of goods from it (see article 243–249 of the UCC), its control, notification to customs authorities, performance of commercial, industrial and service activities contrary to the provisions of customs law. The Union Customs Code also defines a customs warehouse as referred to in article 93, § 3 of the PFC. The customs warehousing procedure allows non-Union goods to be stored in places approved by the customs authorities for this procedure and under customs supervision. The provisions of the Union Customs Code lay down the rules for the operation of such a warehouse and there is a risk of criminal liability for violation of them. In both offences, the legislator used the term "grossly". The term is generalised

[41] Judgement of the Court of Appeal in Szczecin of 25th February, 2016, Case No. II AKa 226/15, LEX No. 2025614.

[42] The provision of § 1 was repealed in connection with Poland's accession to the EU.

in nature and in practice may cause difficulties in determining which infringements are of such a nature, i.e. serious, unambiguous and glaring.

Pursuant to article 95, § 1 of the PFC, anyone who, contrary to the obligation, fails to keep documents relevant for customs control is subject to a fine of up to 180 daily rates. In accordance with article 92, § 2 of the PFC, in cases of lesser significance, the perpetrator is liable as for a fiscal offence.

The closing regulations of chapters 6 and 7 of the PFC are analogous in content. The difference is limited solely to the scope of the legislation to which each of the following provisions applies. Pursuant to article 84, § 1 of the PFC, anyone who does not fulfil the obligation to supervise the observance of rules binding in the activity of an entrepreneur or other organisational unit, allows, even if unintentionally, a prohibited act specified in this chapter to be committed (this means chapter 6, the acts referred to in articles 54–83 of the PFC), is subject to a fine for a fiscal offence. Pursuant to article 84, § 2 of the PFC, the provision of § 1 shall not apply if the act of the perpetrator satisfies the features of another fiscal offence or fiscal misdemeanour specified in this chapter or if the failure to fulfil the duty of supervision is a part of their characteristics. As has already been stated, the provision of article 96 of the PFC is constructed in the same way: § 1 typifies the liability of a person who, without fulfilling the obligation to supervise the observance of the rules binding in the activity of a given entrepreneur or other organisational unit, allows, even if only unintentionally, a prohibited act specified in this chapter to be committed (this means chapter 7, the acts referred to in articles 85–95 of the PFC). In such a case, a fine for a fiscal offence shall be imposed. However, in accordance with § 2 of the provision, § 1 shall not apply if the act of the perpetrator satisfies the features of a different fiscal offence or fiscal misdemeanour specified in this chapter or if the failure to fulfil the duty of supervision belongs to their features. Both provisions (article 84 and 96 of the PFC) extend criminal liability (although it is only liability for an offence) to conduct that does not result from the violation of certain norms of tax law, but from the fact that the offence was committed by another person as a result of a lack of supervision over compliance with the rules applicable to the business of the entrepreneur or other organisational unit. It is a specific form of perpetration in the Penal Fiscal Code, outside the traditional forms of perpetration (article 9, § 1 and 2 of the PFC) and the principle resulting from article 9, § 3 of the PFC. It should be noted that failure to comply with supervision obligations must be intentional. However, inadvertence may include the commission of an offence as defined in chapter 6 or chapter 7, as appropriate.

2.2 *The Illicit Manufacture of Tobacco Products*

The illicit production of tobacco products in Poland is another phenomenon, which must be tackled in order to eliminate the crime discussed in this study. The external border of the European Union is located in the territory of Poland. It is one of the longest. It is 1163 km long, of which 535 km is the border with Ukraine, 418 km with Belarus, and 210 km with Russia (Kaliningrad Oblast). The smuggling of cigarettes and other tobacco products across the external borders of the European Union is a major risk. It results from the strengthening of the border, active operations of the Border Guard service in combating all forms of illegal transport of goods, and equipping the border with advanced devices for detecting smuggling. The illicit production of cigarettes for distribution within the country and for transport to other Schengen countries reduces the risks mentioned above, while still remaining a lucrative activity for criminal groups.[43]

The act of 2nd March, 2001, on the manufacture of ethyl alcohol and the manufacture of tobacco products[44] states in article 12a, paragraph 1, that whosoever, without the required entry in the registers referred to in article 3, paragraph 2, manufactures tobacco products shall be subject to a fine, restriction of liberty or deprivation of liberty for up to 1 year. Economic activity related to the manufacture of tobacco products is a regulated activity within the meaning of the act of 6th March, 2018, the Law on Entrepreneurs.[45] This means that the production of tobacco products requires registration in the register of tobacco producers, which is preceded by an administrative procedure and the fulfilment of legal conditions. The next paragraph of article 12a provides for a qualified type consisting of permitting the act in question in respect of high-value tobacco products. High-value should be considered as a value exceeding 200,000 PLN (article 115, § 5 of the CC in conjunction with article 116 of the CC). In such a case, the penal sanction is slightly higher, the penalty of deprivation of liberty may be pronounced for up to 2 years, while the possibility of imposing a fine or penalty of restriction of liberty remains. Moreover, if the perpetrator has made the perpetration of the crimes in question a permanent source of income, then, pursuant to article 14 of the act on the production of ethyl alcohol and manufacture of tobacco products, the perpetrator shall be liable to incur higher criminal penalties, i.e. up to 3 years of imprisonment, while the legislator has not provided for other alternative penalties (fines, imprisonment). Article 14a of the act on the production of ethyl alcohol and manufacture of tobacco products provides for the possibility to order the forfeiture of items being the subject of crime or intended for its perpetration, even if it is not the property of the perpetrator. In article 14a of the aforementioned act, the legislator should use precise definitions and those adopted on the basis of the Criminal Code. This article uses the term "object of crime". It should be assumed that the article in question *de facto* concerns the forfeiture of an object derived directly from a criminal offence. It is not correct that under the act on the production of ethyl alcohol and production of tobacco products, the forfeiture of items originating from crime is optional, whereas in the Criminal Code the ruling on the same items is obligatory. Another inconsistency is that, in principle, article 44, § 2 of the Criminal Code, concerning the forfeiture of objects used or intended to be used for committing a crime, has been

[43]These issues are discussed in more detail in the criminological part of the study.

[44]Journal of Laws of 2018, item 2352.

[45]Journal of Laws of 2019, item 1292 as amended.

repeated in article 14a of the act on the manufacture of ethyl alcohol and manufacture of tobacco products, which makes this measure optional. The regulation of article 14a of the aforementioned act would make sense only in such a way, if an obligatory forfeiture of objects used or intended for committing a crime was introduced. The provision of article 14 of the act on the production of ethyl alcohol and production of tobacco products is also unnecessary, as article 65 of the Criminal Code would be sufficient. The introduction of the aforementioned provisions concerning forfeiture and increasing criminal liability, took place in isolation from the provisions of the general part of the Criminal Code. The solutions adopted are irrational. If one assumes that a different regulation of a specific issue is already sufficient grounds to exclude the application of the provision of the general part of the Criminal Code pursuant to the provision of article 116 of the Criminal Code,[46] then articles 12a, 14, 14a of the act on the manufacture of ethyl alcohol and tobacco products exclude the application of the provisions of the general part of the Criminal Code in such a way that: (1) a decision on the confiscation of objects directly originating from a crime is only optional, whereas in the Criminal Code it is always obligatory; (2) the penalty of imprisonment for a perpetrator who has made committing these crimes a permanent source of income for himself is more lenient than would be the case on the basis of article 65, § 1 of the Criminal Code. Doubts may arise as to whether the provision of article 65, § 2 of the Criminal Code is to be applied. Although it should be pointed out that making article 14a stricter eliminates penalties not limiting freedom (a fine, or penalty of restriction of liberty), which is not done by article 65, § 1 of the Criminal Code. The ethyl alcohol and tobacco products act also raises the question of whether article 12a of the act applies to persons producing cigarettes and other tobacco products for their own use. The Supreme Court answered the question concerning the production of alcohol in the affirmative in the resolution of 30th November, 2004, case ref. No. I KZP 23/04.[47] The construction of article 12a, paragraph 1 of the act on the manufacture of ethyl alcohol and the manufacture of tobacco products equates the manufacture of alcohol with the manufacture of tobacco products, so it could be argued that this position of the Supreme Court could also apply to the manufacture of cigarettes for personal use. Notwithstanding the fact that the above resolution should be critically analysed[48] and consequently disagree with the Supreme Court, a number of inconsistent regulations should be considered with respect to the problem of cigarette or other tobacco products, including Polish tax regulations (the Excise Duty Act), EU regulations, and administrative provisions on tobacco production. Their comprehensive analysis, determining which of them is of decisive importance for determining the normative content of the characteristics of an act under article 12a, paragraph 1 of the act on the manufacture of ethyl alcohol and manufacture of tobacco products may only lead

[46]Raglewski, Stosunek przepisów części ogólnej nowego kodeksu karnego do innych ustaw przewidujących odpowiedzialność karną (1998), p. 27. Otherwise: (Wojciechowski 2002), p. 232.

[47]LEX No. 132570.

[48]See aptly: (Warylewski 2005), p. 139 et seq.

to certain results.[49] In this study there is no place for a detailed presentation of the issue raised. Only a conclusion will be presented. Currently, the manual production of tobacco products, in a home-made way, without the use of machines, remains fully legal. Such a person should not be held criminally liable under article 12a, paragraph 1 of the aforementioned act.

The provisions criminalising the illicit manufacture of tobacco products should be amended. First, a clear distinction needs to be made between the production of a significant quantity of tobacco products, production in order to obtain a financial, personal and marketing advantage, and the manufacture of products for personal use. Under the current legislation, not only does the problem of determining the scope of liability under article 12a, paragraph 1 of the act on the manufacture of ethyl alcohol and manufacture of tobacco products, described above, arise, but above all, there is no clear increase in the penal sanction for behaviours involving large-scale illegal manufacture of tobacco products. Secondly, the forfeiture of objects used to commit a crime, i.e. machinery and equipment used for illegal tobacco production, should be subject to mandatory confiscation. Thirdly, the provision of article 14a of the act on the manufacture of ethyl alcohol and tobacco products should be deleted. As already mentioned, the provision of article 65 of the Criminal Code is sufficient. Moreover, it will remove any doubts as to which of these provisions should be applied in criminal cases under the act. In addition, the terminology used in criminal legislation in the ethyl alcohol and tobacco products act should be clarified. Fourthly, it is worth considering the introduction of criminal preparation for the crime of illicit manufacture of tobacco products. A further remark concerns the application of the criminal law provisions of the act on ethyl alcohol production and the manufacture of tobacco products. The interpretation of the constituent elements of individual offences should take into account tax regulations, in particular the Excise Duty Act and its definitions of tobacco products and the production of tobacco products.

2.3 The Criminal Code

As can be seen from the previous part of the study, the provisions of the Criminal Code, its general part will be applied in a very limited scope (resulting from article 20, § 2 of the PFC) to cases related to crime involving the illegal production and trade in tobacco products, decided on the basis of the Penal Fiscal Code. It will be slightly different in cases concerning the illegal production of tobacco products due to article 116 of the Criminal Code and the fact that this aspect is regulated by another act (the act on the manufacture of ethyl alcohol and tobacco products). Selected provisions of the general section of the Criminal Code were commented on in the part devoted to crimes under this act. No provision was selected from the

[49] See more on the scope of criminalisation under article 12, paragraph 1 of the act on the production of ethyl alcohol and tobacco products: (Zontek 2019), pp. 66–81.

catalogue of articles of the Criminal Code referred to in article 20, § 2 of the PFC, which would require a detailed presentation within the framework of this study because of its importance for combating crime related to the illicit trade in tobacco products. Therefore, it was confined solely to signalling that in practice, in cases concerning the discussed type of crime, the enumerated provisions of the Criminal Code will be applied.

It is obvious that criminal activity related to illicit trade in tobacco products may consist of the perpetrator's compliance with the prohibited acts provided for in the Criminal Code, the Penal Fiscal Code or the act on the manufacture of ethyl alcohol and tobacco products. This will be decided by specific factual arrangements and the nature of the perpetrators' activities. Therefore, as in the previous sections, the individual offences of the Criminal Code will not be discussed here, also due to the fact that they do not show such a direct connection with crime related to the illegal trade in tobacco products as the acts stipulated in the Penal Fiscal Code or the act on the production of ethyl alcohol and tobacco products.

However, two points will be noted. In the provision of article 258 of the Criminal Code, the Polish legislator, irrespective of the restriction of criminal liability resulting from article 65 of the Criminal Code, and article 37, § 1, point 2 and 5 of the PFC, criminalises participation in an organised criminal group. In accordance with article 258, § 1 of the Criminal Code, whosoever participates in an organised group or association aiming at committing a crime or fiscal offence shall be subject to the penalty of deprivation of liberty for a term of between 3 months and 5 years. The qualified types of this offence are further specified. Thus, in § 2, criminal liability will be more severe, with a penalty of imprisonment from 6 months to 8 years, if the criminal group or association referred to in article 258, § 1 of the Criminal Code are of an armed nature or are aimed at committing a crime of a terrorist nature. § 3 provides for a higher sanction, i.e. from 1 year to 10 years, for anyone who establishes or manages a group or association referred to in article 258, § 1 or 2 of the Criminal Code. The latter type of qualification consists of setting up or directing a group or association with the aim of committing a terrorist offence. This act is punishable with imprisonment for 3 years or more. Therefore, regardless of the liability for other crimes committed or fiscal offences, the perpetrator will also be liable for their very participation in a criminal group (association), their establishment and management. Moreover, to incur liability under article 258 of the Criminal Code it is not necessary to commit another offence. The traits of this act are fulfilled when a person belongs to a criminal group, occupies a place in its structure, carries out orders, tasks, etc. Individuals belonging to criminal groups involved in the illicit trade in tobacco products should be held accountable for their involvement in such organisations. The provision of article 259 of the Criminal Code specifies the premises for not punishing a case for an offence under article 258 of the CC. This will be the case if the offender who voluntarily withdrew from participation in a criminal group or association and disclosed to a law enforcement authority all the relevant circumstances of the act committed, or if the offender who voluntarily withdrew from participation in a criminal group or association and prevented the commission of the intended offence, including a fiscal offence. The purpose of this provision is to create instruments to combat organised crime and to encourage members of groups to break links with such an organisation.[50] It is not the only institution of this type in Polish law. Since 1997, the so-called Minor Crown Witness Act has been in force.[51] In the Criminal Code we also find the institutions of the so-called minor crown witness. The provision of article 60, § 3 of the Criminal Code states that the court applies an extraordinary leniency of the sentence, and may even conditionally suspend its execution in relation to the offender cooperating with other persons in committing the crime, if he discloses to an authority appointed to prosecute crimes information concerning the persons participating in committing the crime and important circumstances regarding its commission. Although these institutions are controversial, they are an essential instrument in the fight against organised crime. Remember that such groups are hermetic, operate in a very professional manner, and are difficult to detect. Obtaining a repentant offender by authorities can sometimes be the only way of prosecuting those involved in managing and setting up criminal groups, as well as recovering and confiscating money from them. The sense of the functioning of these institutions should not be called into question. They require further development and professionalization, in particular in such a way that the services are able to attract in a wider manner the members of criminal groups in their hierarchy. Furthermore, the evidence (frequently very extensive) obtained as a result of explanations/statements from a crown witness should be precisely recorded in the course of proceedings.

Studies and analyses carried out in the course of the project[52] show that, despite the preliminary study on increasing the imperviousness of the European Union's external border and the trend towards relocating illegal factories to the Schengen area, criminal groups are still trying to smuggle goods across the border.[53] As already indicated, this is due to the high profits from smuggling and, at the same time, the relatively low losses resulting from the detection of smuggling. Officers from the Police Central Investigation Bureau estimate that the loss resulting from the detection of illegal cigarette transport is compensated for by another—second or third successful smuggling. The organisers of such transports very often remain elusive because they do not undertake activities directly related to the preparation and implementation of the transports. In most cases, the driver is not aware that he or she is transporting illegal tobacco products. All the more so as the ways of hiding smuggled goods are many and often changed. The information obtained shows that criminal groups are interested in obtaining and corrupting officers of the Border Guard. Such cases are not common, but it is necessary to take action to monitor this phenomenon, conduct research into its occurrence and place great emphasis on its

[50]Flemming and Kutzmann (1999), p. 88.

[51]The Act of 25th June, 1997, on Crown Witnesses, Journal of Laws of 2016, item 1197.

[52]Based on discussions with representatives of state authorities responsible for prosecuting and combating crime related to illegal smuggling and production of tobacco products.

[53]See (Laskowska 2017); also: (Buczkowski, Cudzoziemcy jako sprawcy przestępstw gospodarczych – wyniki badań aktowych 2017).

prevention. In this respect, the Polish Criminal Code provides for liability for the crime of passive bribery (article 228, § 1 of the Criminal Code), i.e. acceptance of a material or personal benefit in connection with the performance of public functions; active bribery (article 229, § 1 of the CC) consisting of granting or promising a material or personal benefit to a person performing a public function in connection with the performance of this function; and paid protection (article 230, § 1 of the CC, article 230a, § 1 of the CC). In connection with corrupt practices, liability for abuse of power or failure to perform duties by a public official may also be applicable. Officers of the Border Guard and the National Treasury Administration are public officers and persons performing public functions within the meaning of the provisions of the Criminal Code.

2.4 *Sanctions*

2.4.1 Penalties

As results from the descriptions of particular crimes presented above in the Penal Fiscal Code, the penalty of a fine plays a crucial role. It may be pronounced for any of the aforementioned crimes, including in many cases imprisonment. Such a solution should be considered correct due to the financial nature of the crimes covered by the Penal Fiscal Code. A fine measured in daily rates is applicable to fiscal offences. Pursuant to article 23, § 1 of the PFC, unless the Code provides otherwise, the lowest number of rates is 10, the highest number is 720. It is for the court to determine the number of daily rates for the fine and the amount of one daily rate for a fine. One daily rate depends on the minimum remuneration. It is established in an ordinance of the Council of Ministers. From 1st January, 2020, the minimum remuneration shall be 2,600.00 zloty.[54] The daily rate may not be lower than one thirtieth of the minimum remuneration (86.67 zloty) or exceed four hundred times its value (1,040,000 zloty). The maximum fine may therefore reach 748,800,000 zloty. When determining the daily rate, the court takes into account the offender's income, personal and family conditions, property relations and income opportunities (article 23, § 3 of the PFC).

For offences, the fine is imposed in a different way. In the Polish legal system it has been assumed that this is done in terms of amounts (so there are no daily rates). The fine for a fiscal offence (article 48, § 1 of the PFC), unless the Code provides for an exception, may range from one tenth of the minimum remuneration (260 zloty) to twenty times the minimum remuneration (52,000 zloty). Similarly as in the case of imposing a fine for a fiscal offence, and also determining the amount of the fine for

[54]The ordinance of the Council of Ministers of 10th September, 2019, on the minimum remuneration for work and the minimum hourly rate in 2020, Journal of Laws of 2019, item 1778.

committing an offence, the court takes into account the financial and family relations of the perpetrator, his or her income and earning potential (article 48, § 4 of the PFC).

The construction of the fine under the Criminal Code is similar to that of the Penal Fiscal Code. For offences, fines are also imposed at daily rates, but the limits of the rates and their levels are different. Thus, the lowest number of rates is 10, while the highest number is 540 (article 33, § 1 of the CC), the daily rate for the fine cannot be lower than 10 zloty nor exceed 2000 zloty (article 33, § 3 of the Criminal Code). Similarly to the Penal Fiscal Code fine, a court, when imposing a fine for a crime, takes into account the offender's income, personal and family conditions, property relations and property possibilities. In practice, some difficulties may arise in this respect, in particular with regard to perpetrators of criminal groups, perpetrators who rely on criminal activity for their livelihood. Their actual income is not documented, and they are often employed on low wages as unskilled workers. Moreover, they do not have any assets, they state they lack education, they do not document their professional career, they show financial burdens, and they show dependants.

An important institution in the Criminal Code is the so-called independent fine. Pursuant to article 33, § 2 of the Criminal Code, the court may impose a fine in addition to the penalty of imprisonment imposed for a crime, if the perpetrator committed an act in order to obtain a material benefit or if the perpetrator obtained a material benefit. Therefore, this institution will be very important in the case of committing acts under the Criminal Code and other criminal laws. We are well aware that activities related to the illegal production of tobacco products, for example, generate significant profits for the perpetrator. Therefore, in the case of imposing a sentence of imprisonment for acts under the act on the manufacture of ethyl alcohol and manufacture of tobacco products, the possibility of imposing a fine under article 33, § 2 of the CC is very important.

As a rule, the penalty of deprivation of liberty in the Penal Fiscal Code lasts at its shortest 5 days, and at its longest 5 years. It is measured in days, months and years (article 27, § 1 of the PFC). The Penal Fiscal Code provides for the penalty of restriction of liberty. However, it is not mentioned in the individual provisions of the detailed section of the Penal Fiscal Code. The provision of article 26, § 1 of the Penal Fiscal Code states that if a fiscal offence is punishable by a penalty of deprivation of liberty, a court may instead impose the penalty of restriction of liberty, in particular if a penalty mentioned in article 22, § 2, points 2–6 is simultaneously pronounced. The imposition of a custodial sentence shall not preclude the imposition of a fine for that offence in addition to a custodial sentence. The penalty of restriction of liberty consists of the obligation to perform unpaid, controlled work for social purposes or in deducting from 10% to 25% of remuneration for work on a monthly basis for a social purpose indicated by the court. This penalty can be imposed from 1 month to 2 years. The penalty of restriction of liberty will be imposed as in the Criminal Code, as the provision of article 26, § 4 of the PFC refers to articles 34 and 35 of the Criminal Code. Thus, it also presented what the penalty of restriction of freedom under the Criminal Code is and how its length is established. The penalty of restriction of liberty has no significant practical significance in cases of fiscal offences. No penalty of arrest is envisaged for fiscal offences (in the case of common offences, such a penalty is provided for by the Polish Code of Administrative Offences), nor the penalty of restriction of liberty. The only penalty for a fiscal offence is a fine (article 47, § 1 of the PFC). In the Criminal Code the penalty of deprivation of liberty lasts at its shortest for a month, and at its longest for 15 years (article 37 of the Criminal Code). For the crimes described in this study, the Criminal Code does not provide for penalties of any kind other than those discussed above.

2.4.2 Penal Measures

Sanctions for offences are not limited to fines only. The criminal liability of the offender for criminal offences should also be determined to a large extent on the basis of penal measures. The list of these should be as broad as possible. Contemporary research should be carried out to search for new forms of criminal law responses. It is not possible to discuss at this point the problem indicated, or the system of penalties and measures in Polish criminal law. The penal measures of the most importance for combating the practices discussed in this study are: forfeiture of objects (article 22, § 2, point 2 of the PFC), recovery of the monetary equivalent of forfeiture of objects (article 22, § 2, point 3 of the PFC), forfeiture of financial benefits (article 22, § 2, point 4 of the PFC), collection of the monetary equivalent of forfeiture of financial benefits (article 22, § 2, point 4a of the PFC), prohibition on conducting a specific business activity, performing a specific profession or taking a specific position (article 22, § 2, point 5 of the PFC). Penalties have been calculated for aspects of a financial nature. This is in line with the research findings, in particular with regard to the fight against organised crime, where the most important issue remains the application of criminal reaction measures that will permanently deprive offenders of the financial resources to engage in illegal activities, sanctions that will make them unprofitable or at high risk of engaging in such activities.

The forfeiture of objects has such a function. In accordance with article 29 of the PFC, the forfeiture of objects includes: (1) objects directly derived from a fiscal offence; (2) tools or other movable property used or intended to be used to commit a fiscal offence; (3) packaging and objects connected with the subject of a fiscal offence in such a way that they cannot be disconnected without damaging any of these items; (4) objects whose manufacture, possession, circulation, storage, transport, transfer or shipment is prohibited. So, as can be seen from this list, the range of forfeiture is extensive. It includes the fruits of a fiscal crime (such as smuggled cigarettes) and the tools used to commit the crime. This category includes the means of transport by which tobacco products are smuggled. A specific category of items subject to forfeiture under the provisions of the Penal Fiscal Code covers the packaging listed in point 3. The reasonableness of such a decision is confirmed by the example resulting from the subject matter discussed in this paper. Namely, the specificity of excise goods—cigarettes and tobacco—requires that confiscation also apply to the packaging in which they are contained. The more so, because false excise tax markings are often applied to such packaging. The last category is obvious. The goods listed in point 4 should not be in circulation, therefore the ruling on this category of confiscation restores the lawfulness of the condition. This will apply to smuggled cigarettes, for example. The provision of article 30, § 1 of the PFC introduces a rule that a court may order the forfeiture of objects only in cases provided for in the Penal Fiscal Code (optional forfeiture). A forfeiture is obligatorily pronounced if the Penal Fiscal Code so provides. The same article clarifies the offences for which forfeiture is pronounced. The provision of article 30, § 2 of the PFC enumerates the offences in respect of which the forfeiture of objects specified in article 29, points 1 to 3 of the PFC may be ordered. The provision of article 30, § 3 of the PFC specifies offences in respect of which a decision on forfeiture is obligatory in the case of the objects referred to in article 29, points 1–2 of the PFC, and in the case of the objects referred to in article 29, point 3 of the PFC, forfeiture is optional. In relation to the offences discussed in this study, mandatory forfeiture refers to the offences in Chapter 7 (offences against customs obligations and rules on foreign trade in goods and services) and items constituting the rewards of crime, tools and other objects used or intended to be used to commit the offence; otherwise, the forfeiture is optional. Nevertheless, the forfeiture of items whose manufacture, possession, circulation, storage, transport or shipment is prohibited (article 29, point 4 of the PFC) is, in the case of the crimes referred to in article 29, § 2–4 of the PFC, obligatory (article 30, § 6 of the PFC). The rule is also that the court may decide, and in cases where the ruling is mandatory, the court shall decide on the forfeiture of objects: those directly originating from a fiscal offence (article 29, point 1 of the PFC); packaging and objects connected with the subject of a fiscal offence in such a way that they cannot be disconnected without damaging any of these items (article 29, point 3 of the PFC); objects whose manufacture, possession, circulation, storage, transport, transfer or transmission is prohibited (article 29, point 4 of the PFC) even if they are not owned by the perpetrator. An exception is a situation in which the perpetrator obtained the objects by way of a prohibited act—a crime or an offence (article 31, § 3 of the PFC). In relation to objects which are not the property of the perpetrator and which are tools or other objects constituting movable property used or intended to be used to commit a fiscal offence (article 29, point 2 of the PFC), the court can order their forfeiture if their owner or another authorised person anticipated that they could be used or intended to be used to commit a fiscal offence or could have foreseen it with due care required in given circumstances (article 31, § 1a of the PFC). Article 31, § 3 of the PFC provides for conditions under which a forfeiture decision is not possible. The first situation is that a forfeiture order would be disproportionate to the seriousness of the fiscal offence committed. The second is the fact of whether the public and legal fees were paid for the items at risk of forfeiture. However, forfeiture will be able to be ordered (will be ordered) if the public-law receivable is disproportionately low to the amount of the monetary equivalent of the forfeiture of objects or the forfeiture concerns objects that are tools or other items constituting movable property which served or was intended to commit a fiscal offence (article 29, point 4 of the PFC), or objects which were specially adapted to commit a prohibited act. The provisions of article 31, § 6 of the PFC stipulate that the enforcement of a decision on forfeiture of tobacco products shall be effected by destroying them. Pursuant to article 31, § 7 of the PFC, the costs of destroying objects for which forfeiture has been ordered are charged to the perpetrator.

The penal measure which is to replace the forfeiture of objects is the collection of the monetary equivalent of the forfeiture of objects (article 22, § 2, point 3 of the PFC). This will be the case where it is not possible to order partial or total forfeiture. Pursuant to article 32, § 1 of the PFC, if it is impossible to make a decision in whole or in part on the forfeiture referred to in article 29 of the PFC, if the object has been destroyed, lost, hidden or cannot be acquired for other factual or legal reasons, the court shall order a penal measure to recover the monetary equivalent of the forfeiture of the object, unless the forfeiture concerns the objects specified in article 29, point 4 of the PFC. This provision indicates the cases in which it is impossible to pronounce a forfeiture decision. It should be stressed, however, that this list catalogue is open in the sense that it may refer to any situation (with the exception of the objects referred to in article 29, point 4 of the PFC) in which a forfeiture decision is impossible. For example, if the objects belong to a third party and the court does not pronounce a forfeiture, it is possible or necessary to apply article 32, § 1 of the PFC. The literature shows that the measure discussed is subsidiary in nature.[55] This is confirmed by the comments made so far. In addition, it is worth noting that if the forfeiture decision is mandatory, the decision to recover the monetary equivalent of the forfeiture is also mandatory.[56] The provision of article 32, § 2 of the PFC indicates that if the monetary equivalent of the forfeiture of objects cannot be determined precisely, it is approximated, and if several persons participated in the commission of a fiscal offence, they are jointly and severally liable for the payment of the monetary equivalent of the forfeiture of objects. It is not satisfactory that the provision of article 32, § 1 of the PFC excludes the possibility of recovering the monetary equivalent of forfeiture in the case of items whose manufacture, possession, turnover, storage, transport, transfer or shipment is prohibited. If the justification for this is that there may be difficulties in estimating the value of such objects in relation to such objects,[57] then this is not a sufficient argument. Such a solution as in article 32, § 1 *in fine of the PFC* should concern not every case, but only those in which there is no possibility of making estimates or factual findings regarding such objects. However, if the facts show that the perpetrator had such objects at his disposal, it is also possible to estimate their value. Measures of fiscal repression must very restrictively implement the objective of depriving perpetrators of crimes, fiscal offences of benefits from committed acts, financial resources used to organise their unlawful practices.

Such an objective is to be achieved by further penal measures provided for in the Penal Fiscal Code. The provision of article 33, § 1 of the PFC stipulates that if the perpetrator obtained, even indirectly, a material benefit from committing fiscal

[55]Postulski and Siwek (2004), pp. 301–302.

[56]Judgement of the Court of Appeal in Białystok of 19th March, 2015, case ref. II AKa 28/15, LEX 1663035.

[57]Such motives are indicated by: J. Raglewski, see: Raglewski (2007), p. 181.

offences which is not subject to forfeiture of objects specified in article 29, point 1 or 4 of the PFC, the court (obligatorily) decides on a penal measure in the form of forfeiture of the material benefit. On the other hand, in the event that such a judgement cannot be made, a penal measure in the form of recovering the monetary equivalent of the forfeiture of material benefit is pronounced. The legal definition of a material benefit under article 53, § 13 of the PFC, that a material or personal benefit is a benefit both for oneself and for someone else, does not in fact reflect the complexity of this concept and the significance it assumes in relation to individual taxes. It is not a definition that meets the assumptions of the code's regulations and the provision, which aims to determine the meaning of a given term on the basis of a given act. In fact, the provision of article 53, § 13 of the PFC is an interpretative rule defining only the subjective scope of the concept, and not its meaning. The concept of material benefit (in article 33, § 1 of the PFC there is talk only of such a benefit) should be determined in relation to each case, including criminal tax cases, and it is necessary to refer to tax regulations. Recovering the monetary equivalent in the case of a material benefit is possible (similarly as in the case of article 32, § 1 of the PFC) only after it has been established that the forfeiture of the material benefit is impossible. Article 33 introduces two presumptions. They are intended to ensure more effective implementation of the measures in question. They may be refuted by evidence to the contrary, which may be provided by the perpetrator or person concerned. The first is defined in paragraph 2 in such a way that in the case of a conviction for a fiscal offence, from which the perpetrator obtained, even indirectly, a material benefit of high value[58] or a fiscal offence, from which the perpetrator obtained or could have obtained, even indirectly, a material benefit, threatened by a penalty of imprisonment, the upper limit of which is higher than 3 years, or committed in an organised group or association aiming at the commission of a fiscal offence for the benefit obtained from the commission of the offence, is considered to be property which the perpetrator took possession of (ownership, co-ownership, possession, lease) or with respect to which he obtained any title in a period of 5 years prior to committing the fiscal offence until the issue of even a non-binding judgement, unless the perpetrator or other interested person presents contrary evidence (article 33, § 2 of the PFC). The second presumption stems from paragraph 3 of this article and concerns a situation in which the perpetrator transferred property to a natural or legal person or an organisational unit without legal personality, in fact or under any legal title. Following the adoption of such a regulation, property in the sole possession of a person or entity and his or her property rights shall be regarded as belonging to the perpetrator, unless it could not be presumed from the circumstances

[58]High value is considered by the Penal Fiscal Code to be a value which at the time of committing a prohibited act exceeds five hundred times the minimum remuneration—see article 53, § 15 of the PFC). Since 1st January, 2020, the minimum remuneration amounts to 2600 PLN, which gives the amount of 1,300,000 PLN as corresponding to a high value under the Penal Fiscal Code. The minimum remuneration for the work shall be established by way of a regulation of the Council of Ministers.

surrounding their acquisition that the property, even indirectly, was derived from a criminal offence.

Similar regulations concerning forfeiture of objects, forfeiture of material benefits or equivalent are provided for in the relevant provisions of the Criminal Code.[59] They will not be discussed here, because in relation to proceedings concerning crimes related to the illicit trade in tobacco products, the fiscal regulations are important in this respect. However, when discussing offences under the act on the manufacture of ethyl alcohol and production of tobacco products, attention was drawn to fundamental issues concerning forfeiture and differences introduced by the act.

The Penal Fiscal Code provides for a penal measure in the form of a ban on conducting specific business activity. Article 34, § 2 of the PFC refers to the offences for which it may be pronounced, and also indicates that this measure may be pronounced in the event of an extraordinary restriction of the penalty (article 38, § 1 and 2 of the PFC). This prohibition may last from 1 to 5 years (article 34, § 4 of the PFC). This prohibition may fulfil its functions, with the proviso, however, that the decision on such a measure shall not affect persons operating on the grey market or organised crime. This measure can play a role, including in particular the prevention of phenomena such as also conducting illegal activities alongside legitimate activities connected with the manufacturing and marketing of tobacco products. In the course of the research carried out, such procedures were revealed. In such cases, the measure may be of great importance. An analogous measure is provided for in the Criminal Code (article 39, point 2 of the Criminal Code, article 41, § 2 of the Criminal Code).

3 Procedural Rules

Criminal procedural law in Poland does not provide for separate procedures or rules for proceedings strictly related to combating smuggling of cigarettes or other tobacco products. There are no specialised bodies to deal with such cases. As was already mentioned at the beginning of the study, the Penal Fiscal Code, on the basis of which most behaviours related to the issues discussed in the report are penalized, is a special proceeding concerning acts of a financial nature that is outside normal provisions. The special modes of a criminal trial are not clearly stated in Poland and they have also been subject to many changes, which have modified their original assumptions. It is possible to distinguish special modes, which are so directly defined by the Criminal Code and proceedings which, although not so called, are different in

[59]See (Buczkowski, Skuteczność odzyskiwania korzyści majątkowych uzyskanych przez sprawców przestępstwa – analiza przepadków orzeczonych na podstawie art. 45 k.k., 2010), pp. 221–263, also: (Buczkowski, Przepadek korzyści majątkowej po nowelizacji kodeksu karnego z 13 czerwca 2003 r. Wyniki badań aktowych 2007), pp. 26–42.

nature. They should also be considered as special modes. The latter include proceedings in cases of fiscal offences and fiscal misdemeanours. This procedure also includes special modes in the first of the meanings cited here. Apart from the ordinary procedure, the Penal Fiscal Code provides for the following procedures: (1) with regard to granting permission for voluntary submission to liability; (2) mandatory; (3) with regard to absent persons; (4) a mandated procedure (it should not be equated with a ruling; the first three procedures and the ordinary procedure belong to judicial procedures).

Criminal proceedings in cases of fiscal offences and fiscal misdemeanours are regulated in Title II of the Penal Fiscal Code (Chapters 11–20, articles 113–177). Only in passing will it be noted that the Code also contains provisions concerning enforcement proceedings in cases of fiscal offences and fiscal misdemeanours (title III, chapters 21–24, articles 178–191). Some authors classify enforcement proceedings as criminal proceedings, hence the existence of the provisions of article 178–191 of the PFC. However, it should be assumed that such regulations maintain a high degree of separation from criminal proceedings. For these reasons, they will not be discussed in this report nor in the section on procedural issues.

Article 113, § 1 of the PFC indicates that in proceedings in cases of fiscal offences and fiscal misdemeanours the provisions of the Code of Criminal Procedure apply accordingly.[60] It follows from this principle that the fiscal procedure is not a separate procedure.[61] The legislator only excluded the application of certain provisions of the Code of Criminal Procedure (article 113, § 2 and 3 of the PFC). Thus, the provisions concerning an injured party and mediation (article 113, § 2, point 1 of the PFC), article 325f of the Code of Criminal Procedure (article 113, § 2, point 2 of the PFC) are not applicable, while in cases of fiscal offences the provisions concerning preventive measures, searching for the defendant and an arrest warrant (article 113, § 3, point 1 of the PFC) and enumerated provisions (article 113, § 3, point 2 of the PFC) are not applicable. In cases of fiscal offences, the Code of Conduct for Infringements does not apply,[62] but only the provisions of the Code of Criminal Procedure. Thus, the model of proceedings in cases concerning fiscal offences and fiscal misdemeanours is based on the Code of Criminal Procedure with certain modifications, which may be of two types: (1) resulting from an explicit provision contained in title II of the PFC, which regulates a given institution differently; (2) resulting from the manner in which a given provision of the Code of Criminal Procedure will be applied due to the fact that we are dealing with a statement that the

[60]The act of 6th June, 1997, Code of Criminal Procedure, Journal of Laws of 2020, item 30, as amended.

[61]Unlike the repealed Fiscal Act of 1971 (the Act of 26th October, 1971, Journal of Laws of 1984, No. 22, item 103), which provided for a completely opposite principle, i.e. the application of the provisions of the Code of Criminal Procedure only in cases of an explicit referral. However, it cannot be omitted that there were many such references, and therefore, de facto the provisions of the Code of Criminal Procedure were applied.

[62]The Act of 21st August, 2001—the Code of Conduct on Misdemeanours, Journal of Laws of 2019, item 1120, as amended.

provisions are applied appropriately. The latter may mean: (1) application of provisions directly (without any change); (2) application of provisions with modifications resulting from the nature of the fiscal regulation; (3) non-application of provisions due to lack of such possibility, e.g. due to their contradiction with the fiscal regulation. The rules discussed here reveal a dilemma about how to regulate special proceedings. On the one hand, it is understandable that the aim is to harmonise the standards of criminal procedure. This is the way to read the solution adopted by the legislator in the current Penal Fiscal Code. On the other hand, it seems that the solutions consisting of (the simultaneous): (1) exclusion of certain provisions from application; (2) the introduction modifications in the standards resulting from given regulations; (3) referring directly to specific provisions of the Code of Criminal Procedure—this is done irrespective of the principle resulting from article 113, § 1 of the PFC, and may cause doubts concerning the application of a specific provision. There will be problems concerning the scope of the relevant application of a provision. As a consequence, it results in a requirement each time or relatively frequently to undertake an analysis of what regulations and to what extent they will be applied in proceedings concerning acts typified in the Penal Fiscal Code. This, in turn, not only prolongs the workload, but also causes interpretational difficulties, leads to inconsistencies in jurisprudence and even errors in the application of the law. The research carried out under the project shows that the long duration of criminal proceedings is a weakness in combating the illicit trade in tobacco products. Undoubtedly, the codified solutions discussed here are not conducive to the speed of proceedings and may be one of the factors extending them and affecting their effectiveness.

The provision of article 114, § 1 of the PFC expresses the purpose of proceedings in cases of fiscal offences and fiscal misdemeanours consisting of the fact that the provisions of the code are aimed at shaping the proceedings in cases of fiscal offences and fiscal misdemeanours in such a way that the objectives of the proceedings in terms of compensating for the financial loss to the State Treasury, local government unit or other eligible entity caused by such an act are achieved. In the case of fiscal proceedings, this is an additional purpose in relation to those resulting from the applicable article 2, § 1 of the Code of Criminal Procedure. In view of this directive, we may risk the thesis that the legislator has opted for the enforcement of debts which should be paid by the perpetrator, and to a lesser extent it is a matter of repression. This is one of the elements which was supposed to distinguish criminal proceedings in cases of common crimes from fiscal proceedings. The separate procedure—allowing voluntary submission to liability and the wider possibilities of using this type of institution, slightly broader institutions than under the Criminal Code, institutions of refraining from punishing the perpetrator, caution under article 114, § 2 of the PFC (the body conducting the proceedings is to instruct about the rights of the perpetrator in the event of compensation for the financial damage caused) are an expression of this objective. It also results from the nature of a large number of acts detrimental to the fiscal interest, but it cannot be omitted, which also results from the previous part of the study, that in the Penal Fiscal Code we will find acts that do not consist of the depletion of public and legal receivables. It seems that Polish fiscal law has not developed a clear concept as to whether the emphasis should be on the enforcement of public-law debts or on repression.

Polish criminal proceedings consist of two main stages: (1) preparatory proceedings and (2) court proceedings (this procedure consists of two instances). Chapter 14 of the Penal Fiscal Code (article 133–135) deals with the competence of preparatory proceedings authorities. The bodies of preparatory proceedings are listed in article 118, § 1 and 2 of the PFC. These are: the head of the tax office, the head of the customs and tax office, the Head of the National Treasury Administration, the Border Guard service, the police, the Military Police, the Internal Security Agency, and the Central Anti-Corruption Bureau. The public prosecutor wasn't included in this list. However, it should be included in the bodies of preparatory proceedings in view of the provisions of the Code of Criminal Procedure, which will be discussed later. The jurisdiction of the organs is presented in casuistic terms, i.e. to a large extent, it has been listed which crimes are dealt with by which individual authorities.

Pursuant to article 133, § 1 of the PFC, preparatory proceedings are conducted by: the heads of customs and tax offices, the heads of tax offices, the Head of the National Treasury Administration. These bodies are referred to as financial bodies in the pre-trial phase. These authorities form the National Treasury Administration. It is included in the structure of the Ministry of Finance, the Head of the National Treasury Administration reports to the Minister of Public Finance. As a general rule, with respect to offences related to the illicit trade in tobacco products, proceedings will be conducted by the heads of customs and tax offices. The Head of the National Treasury Administration may conduct any proceedings in cases of fiscal offences and fiscal misdemeanours disclosed within the scope of his activity, unless he transfers them to the authorities competent for such proceedings due to the subject of the act (article 133, § 1, point 3 of the PFC). Both the head of the tax office and the head of the customs and treasury office may also initiate proceedings which do not fall within their competence. However, in such cases, once the evidence has been preserved, the authority is obliged to transfer the case to the competent authority for further prosecution.

The second group of authorities conducting preparatory proceedings, the so-called non-financial bodies of preparatory proceedings, are: the Border Guard service with respect to selected fiscal crimes and fiscal offences (article 134, § 1, point 1 of the PFC); and also with respect to crimes disclosed within the scope of its activity: the police (article 134, § 1, point 2 of the PFC); the Internal Security Agency (article 134, § 1, point 3 of the PFC); and the Central Anti-Corruption Bureau (article 134, § 1, point 5 of the PFC). The Penal Fiscal Code introduces an obligation to exchange information on pending proceedings between authorities, in particular non-financial and financial authorities. In practice, in relation to crimes related to illicit trade in tobacco products, preparatory proceedings are conducted by the Border Guard service and the police. It is worth noting that the police have a Central Investigation Bureau of the Police, which deals with combating organised crime. This unit is therefore intended to combat criminal groups that are engaged in activities such as illicit production and trade in tobacco products. An authority in preparatory proceedings for treasury cases also includes a prosecutor, who can conduct preparatory proceedings in cases concerning fiscal offences and fiscal misdemeanours in any case (article 134a of the PFC, article 298, § 1 of the Code of Criminal Procedure in connection with article 113, § 1 of the PFC). If a prosecutor does not conduct preparatory proceedings, he or she shall supervise them (article 326 of the Code of Criminal Procedure in connection with article 113, § 1 of the PFC, article 151c, § 2 of the PFC). In practice, preparatory proceedings are usually conducted by the authorities indicated in article 133 of the PFC (financial bodies of preparatory proceedings), article 134 of the PFC (non-financial bodies of preparatory proceedings), and the prosecutor supervises such proceedings, performs activities reserved for him/her by law (e.g. filing motions for provisional detention, issuing a security decision).

Court proceedings in cases of fiscal offences and fiscal misdemeanours fall within the jurisdiction of district courts. In the second instance, district courts decide. Pursuant to article 121, § 1 of the PFC, apart from the prosecutor, the public prosecutor in court is the body that makes and supports the indictment. The competence to do so is granted by the provision of article 121, § 2 of the PFC, but only in cases of fiscal offences. The prosecutor is responsible for filing and supporting a bill of indictment in cases of fiscal offences. The provision of article 122, § 1 and 2 of the PFC defines the financial powers of the bodies of preparatory proceedings. The aforementioned provision determines the powers provided for the prosecutor to be vested in the bodies of preparatory proceedings.

In cases concerning crimes under the Criminal Code or other penal acts, as a rule, preparatory proceedings are conducted by a prosecutor or the police. The powers of the police are also vested in other bodies within the scope of their competence (the Border Guard service, the Internal Security Agency, the National Treasury Administration, the Central Anti-Corruption Bureau, the Military Police and other bodies, if such a special provision provides for such). Court proceedings in criminal cases belong to the jurisdiction of the regional court or the district court in the first instance. The provisions of the Code of Criminal Procedure shall determine the material jurisdiction. Generally, the jurisdiction of a regional court ruling in the first instance includes cases of serious crimes. The decisions issued by the district court are subject to appeal to the regional court, and the decisions issued by the regional court in the first instance to the court of appeal. The regional court as the court of first instance will adjudicate in criminal tax cases in such a procedural arrangement where the indictment includes crimes falling within the jurisdiction of the district court (there will be a group of fiscal crimes and fiscal offences here) and the jurisdiction of the regional court (common crimes reserved for consideration by this court). The provisions on joint cases will apply in such cases.

In criminal cases of a financial nature, the use of a security on property as a measure is of significant importance. Such an institution is known to the Code of Criminal Procedure as well as the Penal Fiscal Code. The purposefulness of adjudicating on security on property is justified by the fact that such security, at an early stage of preparatory proceedings, may in many cases be the only possibility of recovering property derived from crime, subject to forfeiture or other penal measures. Compared to the security which may be applied under the Code of Criminal Procedure, the security under the Penal Fiscal Code has a wider scope of subject matter. Pursuant to article 131, § 1 of the PFC, in the event of a fiscal offence, the following penal measures may be secured: forfeiture of objects (article 22, § 2, point 2 of the PFC), collection of the monetary equivalent of forfeiture of objects (article 22, § 2, point 3 of the PFC), forfeiture of material benefits (article 22, § 2, point 4 of the PFC), collection of the monetary equivalent of forfeiture of objects (article 22, § 2, point 4a of the PFC), the obligation to return financial benefits and the obligation to pay public law dues that have been reduced due to a prohibited act. A prerequisite for a securing order is a well-founded fear that, without such a securing order, the enforcement of the securing order in respect of the said institutions will be impossible or significantly impeded. The provision of article 291, § 1 of the Code of Criminal Procedure (this provision is also applied in the fiscal procedure) allows for securing: a fine, forfeiture, cash benefit, compensatory measure, return to the wronged party or other entitled entity of the financial benefit that the perpetrator has obtained from the committed offence, or its equivalent. The Penal Fiscal Code also allows security to be made on the property of an entity held liable for an auxiliary penalty of a fine, recovery of the monetary equivalent of the forfeiture of objects, forfeiture of a material benefit, recovery of the monetary equivalent of the forfeiture of a material benefit, and the obligation to return a material benefit (article 131, § 3 of the PFC).

The police, the National Treasury Administration, the Border Guard service, as well as special services such as the Internal Security Agency and the Central Anti-Corruption Bureau may conduct operational and exploratory activities. The powers to do so are determined by individual acts regulating the activities of the aforementioned services and bodies. There is no room for quoting all these regulations in this paper. The concept of operational and exploratory activities is not defined by law. It should be understood as a non-confidential, non-procedural activity of authorised services, which is aimed at ensuring public order and state security.[63] The functions of such activities remain important. They are as follows: the exploratory function, i.e. the investigation of criminal environments and criminogenic phenomena; the discovery function, i.e. the disclosure of offences and the identification of perpetrators; the evidentiary function; the preventive function, i.e. the prevention of offences and threats.[64] Operational and exploratory activities may be implemented after certain statutory conditions have been met and, if required by law, after obtaining the consent of the competent authorities. The aforementioned functions make operational and exploratory activities very important and sensitive to the work of the services. Sometimes they are very complex operations that are legally and technically demanding. There is no definitive list of operational activities. We may distinguish operational activities such as, but not limited to: operational control; use of technical means such as tapping or monitoring; correspondence control;

[63]Czeczot and Tomaszewski (1996), p. 67.

[64]Tarach (2006), p. 17.

collaboration with information sources; controlled purchases; controlled acquisition or handing over; submission of proposals for the giving or receiving of a financial benefit; controlled delivery; secret agent; or special operation. The issue of operational and exploratory activities is very broad. It also gives rise to controversy as to the legality of evidence obtained using certain operational and exploratory methods. However, particularly in the fight against organised crime, as is the case with this problem, the use of operational and exploratory methods is an indispensable part of the services and must, in principle, remain a fundamental instrument in the fight against organised crime of this nature. In the course of the research conducted, it was established that in the assessment of the services, the scope of the subject matter of operational and exploratory methods is set at a satisfactory level. What is needed, however, is to provide better and better equipment and resources to carry out such activities. It is, of course, a reflection of what has already been pointed out that criminal groups use very advanced, modern technical means. Therefore, the services must have adequate technical resources. Human resources and the preparation of such operations in legal terms are also important, so that the information and evidence obtained can be used in a legal process in the future and constitute a complete body of evidence.

4 Cooperation Between State Authorities

A very important practical element, noticed in research interviews conducted with officers of the Central Investigation Bureau of the police and the National Treasury Administration, is cooperation between services. As can be seen from the procedural issues presented above, the proceedings concerning the issue discussed may in fact be conducted by several authorities. In the course of the research, attention was paid to whether it does not cause difficulties in prosecuting fiscal crimes or fiscal offences. The answer to this question is negative. The authorities competent for conducting pre-trial investigations share their specific competence. For example, the Central Investigation Bureau of the police is responsible for combating organised crime, the Border Guard service is responsible for crimes committed in connection with crossing the border, the Voivodship Police Headquarters conducts, among others, cases concerning the marketing of illegal tobacco products in the country, customs and tax offices examine strictly tax-related issues. Respondents argue that cooperation between these services is progressing well and that there is no need to introduce changes in this respect, in particular to consolidate the powers to conduct proceedings to combat crime involving illicit trade in tobacco products. In the course of the research, the need to develop and improve cooperation with the prosecutor was pointed out. As mentioned above, the prosecutor supervises ongoing preparatory proceedings. Less frequent are situations in which the prosecutor conducts an investigation, and even if a significant scope of activities is entrusted to other bodies (e.g. heads of customs and tax offices, the police, etc.). There are no procedural or organisational rules on what the prosecutor's supervision over the proceedings conducted should look like. It cannot be precluded that the problem revealed should constitute an encouragement to reflect on how the prosecutor's supervision over conducted proceedings in the scope of the crime in question should be shaped and performed, and what tasks (apart from those explicitly reserved for him by the provisions of the Code of Criminal Procedure) the prosecutor should perform. Aspects of international cooperation in combating crime related to illicit trade in tobacco products were also analysed. The conclusion is that there are instruments in place to ensure a general level of cooperation, i.e. primarily the legal basis. There is no need to create an organisation to coordinate such cooperation. However, there is a need (taking into account the experience of Polish authorities) to develop operational cooperation between services of different countries, the exchange of information at such a level, and the integration of communities and joint training. The aim is to ensure the possibility of direct cooperation between officers from units in different countries, which is supposed to lead to quick action.

5 Criminological Issues

5.1 Introduction

Poland, as a country with one of the longest external borders of the European Union in the east of the Community, is particularly exposed to crime associated with the smuggling of goods. The eastern border of Poland, which is at the same time the eastern border of the European Union, is threatened with high levels of smuggling, production and distribution of tobacco products. The removal of stationary border controls on the Polish section of the internal EU/Schengen border and the persisting disproportion in excise prices between countries of origin and destination have resulted in an increase in the production and smuggling of tobacco products on a large scale by organised criminal groups.

5.2 Categories of Crime Linked to the Trade in Tobacco Products

Crime in the broader context of trade in tobacco products can generally be divided into three categories:

- acts related to the smuggling or illegal import of cigarettes into Poland without Polish excise tax markings for the purpose of their distribution in Poland or export to other countries;
- acts relating to the illegal manufacture of cigarettes, their marking with counterfeit trademarks and excise duties, and the trade in such cigarettes;
- acts related to the illegal trade in tobacco.

All of the above categories are primarily linked to financial losses incurred by the state as a result of lost tax revenues.

The former leads to a reduction in excise duty primarily as a result of the fact that tobacco products imported into Poland are not marked with excise tax markings. In addition, other public law liabilities, in particular VAT and customs duties, are depleted.

The second category covers illegal tobacco factories, where production takes place without quality control, as well as without any of the formal permits required for this type of activity. These acts include not only counterfeiting of tobacco products but also counterfeiting of the external appearance of the product, including in particular tobacco product packaging, cigarette trademarks and the failure to mark products with excise duty markings or the use of counterfeit markings.

The third category is linked to a change in the rules governing the production and purchase of raw tobacco in member states of the European Union. This has resulted in an increase in the illegal trade in unprocessed tobacco leaves (loose tobacco).

5.3 *Statistical Data*

An analysis of data is hampered by the fact that statistics maintained by police, prosecutors, courts, customs officers and border guards do not distinguish illegal trade in tobacco products as a separate category of offences. Such acts fall into larger categories such as: smuggling, handling, failure to mark products with excise stamps; the production, import or trade in excise goods without official verification; the manufacture of tobacco products without the required entry in registers; or a reduction in VAT or customs duties due. Therefore, an analysis can only be based on data provided by these individual authorities or services and as such the data used does not have the attributes of data enabling an estimation of the scale of the phenomenon for the whole country (Table 1).

In addition, the personal data of the perpetrators of crimes related to the illegal trade in tobacco products is not collected separately, and therefore it will not be possible to analyse this data within the framework of this study.

In Poland, from 500 million to almost 800 million illegal cigarettes are uncovered each year as a result of inspections carried out by tax inspectors, the police, border guards and customs officers.

The upward trend in seizures of cigarettes began in 2013 and continued until 2016, which was a record year in terms of the number of illegal cigarettes discovered by the services. In the following years (2017–2018), the number of cigarettes seized decreased significantly: in 2017, from about 10% for the police to 30% for the National Tax Administration (NTA), while in 2018, the trend was even worse, from over 26% for the NTA to almost 40% for the police.

In the case of tobacco and dried tobacco seizures, the peak period was 2015, when more than 2,500,000 kg of these goods were seized, followed by a significant

Table 1 Preparatory proceedings initiated by the Border Guard Service in relation to a violation of the provisions of the Penal and Fiscal Code in the years 2011–2018

Year	2011	2012	2013	2014	2015	2016	2017	2018	Total
Number of preparatory proceedings instituted	3186	2463	2342	1948	2541	2190	2124	1730	18,524
Including:									
In conjunction with organised crime	25	32	16	14	18	19	22	18	164
In conjunction with the act on Industrial Property Law	3	0	6	15	5	5	5	4	43
In conjunction with the act on the Production of Ethyl Alcohol and Manufacturing of Tobacco Products	5	0	8	7	4	14	10	13	61

Source: Border Guard Service

decrease in seizures in subsequent years (2016–2017), amounting to as much as 54% in 2017 in the case of the Border Guard Service.

However, it should be stressed that this data does not indicate a decrease in the effectiveness of activities undertaken by services involved in combating tobacco-related crime (police, Border Guard Service, National Treasury Administration), but rather indicates a certain trend resulting from the tightening of the eastern border of Poland (which is also the eastern border of the European Union/Schengen) and the relocation to the south of Europe (primarily to the Balkan countries: Bulgaria, Romania, Greece and the Mediterranean countries) of the main routes for the smuggling of tobacco products manufactured in eastern European countries (Belarus, Russia, Ukraine) (Fig. 1).

A similar trend can be observed with illegal cigarette production in factories in Poland, where domestic production is gradually being exported from Poland to western European countries, although according to statistics, 36 illegal cigarette factories were discovered and shut down in Poland in 2018, compared to only 18 in 2015.

In 2016, the public prosecutor initiated 2672 preparatory proceedings concerning crimes related to the illegal trade in cigarettes, in which:

- charges were brought against 3496 suspects,
- 178 people were temporarily arrested,
- 1796 indictments were filed,
- 2573 people were charged and subsequently convicted,
- 1471 cases were concluded with judgements,
- 430 proceedings were discontinued.

The total value of public and legal receivables at risk of depletion in cases concluded in 2016 with bills of indictment amounted to 3,117,050,003 PLN (approximately 718,000,000 EUR).

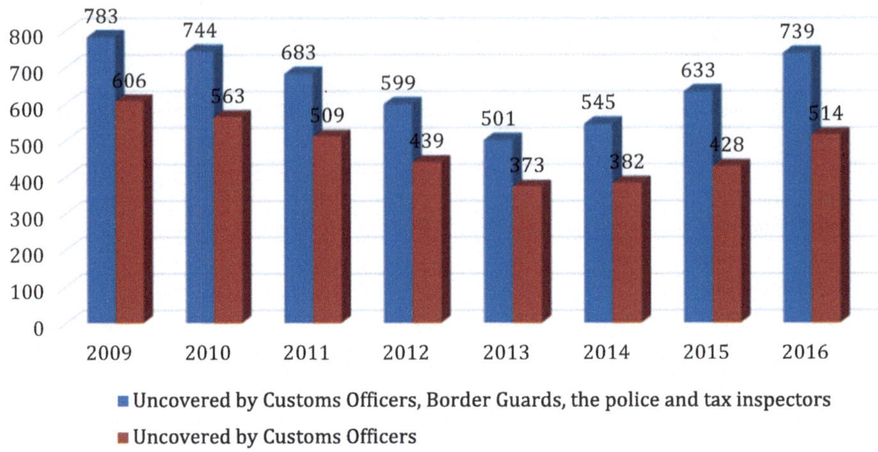

Fig. 1 The number of illegal cigarettes discovered in Poland in 2009–2016 (in millions of cigarettes). Data source: Report on the state of national security 2016, Warsaw, Ministry of Internal Affairs and Administration

For comparison, it should be noted that in 2010 in all public prosecutor's offices there were 1984 preparatory proceedings concerning crimes related to tobacco products (smuggling, handling of stolen goods, the illegal production of tobacco products), of which:

- 1130 proceedings were concluded with a bill of indictment,
- 1722 people were charged,
- 274 cases were dismissed,
- 20 proceedings were concluded with a refusal to initiate proceedings,
- 472 cases were concluded in some other manner (suspension of proceedings, transfer to customs officers, etc.).

The total value of public and legal receivables at risk of depletion and damages suffered by other entities in all cases concluded in 2010 with bills of indictment amounted to 541,635,018 PLN (approximately 135,280,238 EUR).

It should be noted that there has been a steady decline in the share of illegal cigarettes in the domestic tobacco market since 2015. It is estimated that in the second quarter of 2015 it amounted to 19%, while in the third quarter of 2018 it fell to just over 11%.

As a result, the number of legally available tobacco products increased and the state budget's excise tax revenue increased despite the fact that the excise tax rates applied remained unchanged (Fig. 2).

Due to the widespread use of modern methods of smoking involving the use of heating devices, the cartridges for these devices may also be smuggled, mainly from the territory of Ukraine, where the factories are located, and at least three times more money on the smuggled cartridges can be made on the difference in price between

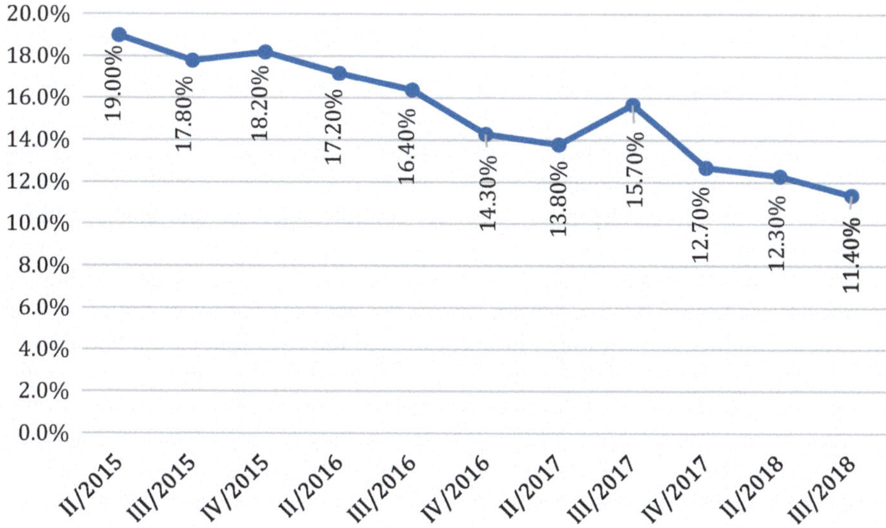

Fig. 2 The share of illegal cigarettes in the domestic tobacco market between 2015 and 2018 (%). Data source: The Ministry of Finance

the Ukrainian and Polish markets. When smuggling them to western European countries, a smuggler's profit may be even higher.

The data for 2010–2013 shows that when Poland was a destination country for smuggled tobacco products, the source of their origin (the place from which they came to Poland) was primarily Belarus, Ukraine, Russia, but also Lithuania, Latvia and China. When Poland was a country from which tobacco products were smuggled to other countries, the main destinations were Germany, Italy, the United Kingdom, the Czech Republic and Sweden. However, when Poland was a transit country for smuggled products from Ukraine, Russia, Lithuania and Latvia, the destination countries were Germany, the Czech Republic, the United Kingdom, Belgium and Italy.

It should be noted that in connection with the sealing of Poland's eastern border (e.g. through the use of goods scanners and new technical surveillance measures on the border), an increase in illegal production of tobacco products has been observed in the country for several years. This is connected with the lower costs for the organisers (mostly organised crime groups) than is the case for smuggling from neighbouring countries. Production in domestic factories is mostly directed to western European markets, in particular the German and British markets, where—due to differences in tobacco prices—the profitability of the whole process is very high.

5.4 Modus Operandi

The specific nature of the eastern border of Poland and the European Union means that the main route for tobacco smuggling into the territory of the Community is by land. Polish border crossing points with Belarus, Ukraine or Russia are used for this purpose (on the Polish-Lithuanian border, due to the presence of both countries in the Schengen structures, there are no border controls although, and this should be noted, there are still some discoveries of illegal cigarettes) and the so-called "green border" in the mountainous areas of the Bieszczady mountains on the border between Poland and Ukraine, where, due to the physical terrain of the area, it is difficult to conduct very thorough inspections, and the river Bug on the border.

It should be emphasized that tobacco products are imported mainly from over the eastern border of Poland and the target countries for this type of smuggling are the countries of western Europe: Germany, Belgium, Italy, and the United Kingdom). Prior to 2010 tobacco products were mainly smuggled from the territory of Ukraine, however since 2011 Belarus has become the dominant country for this type of criminal activity. According to data from 2018, as much as 54% of the tobacco products seized by Polish customs officers were smuggled from Belarus, 29.4% from Ukraine and the remaining 16.6% were mainly from Russia, China and the United Arab Emirates.

The mechanisms used to smuggle tobacco products include road transport, including lorries, rail transport, petty smuggling by private individuals (smugglers commonly referred to as "ants") carrying tobacco products across borders or transporting them using their private cars. A commonly used method for cigarette smuggling at road border crossings is to transport cigarettes in structural and non-structural compartments of cars and vans (e.g. in a converted fuel tank, the floor or other elements of a vehicle's fixtures and fittings).

Tobacco smuggling in private cars accounted for more than 82% of the tobacco products discovered and confiscated by Polish customs officers in 2018. In the case of lorries, confirmed smuggling accounted for less than 2% of all confiscated tobacco products and for more than 5% in the case of buses.

The Polish Customs and Border Protection Services points to a reduction in the risk of smuggling of tobacco products concealed in railway wagons (in 2018 it accounted for only 1.8% of confiscated tobacco products). However, the Border Guard Service still uncovers cases of smuggling of such products hidden in the technological elements of wagons and in bulk and general cargo being transported. The discovery of tobacco products smuggled on a freight train results means there are no persons who can be held criminally or fiscally liable.

Smuggling through mountainous areas on the border between Poland and Ukraine, due to the terrain, makes it impossible to use road transport on a larger scale; therefore, the smuggling of tobacco products using this means of transport is quantitatively smaller, although in recent years—due to the tightening of controls at border crossings—there has been an increase in reported cases of smuggling through the so-called "green border" of the two countries indicated above. The river Bug is also used for smuggling. Tobacco smuggling is carried out with the use of both lightweight floating equipment and by swimmers and persons pulling bags behind them.

Tobacco smuggling across the “green border” is becoming increasingly popular among organised crime groups and is a channel that is increasing being used. This may be evidenced by the excise goods discovered by border guards, prepared for transport in the vicinity of specific border marks. It cannot be ruled out that organised crime groups, through the identification of convenient transit points across the state border, will later use them as proven mechanisms for the smuggling of narcotic substances or weapons, for example.

Small flying objects (microlights, drones) are also used for tobacco smuggling. This is the fastest means of transport and, furthermore, it does not require the involvement of many people in the whole process. In the case of microlights, cigarettes are dropped from a low height and then recovered by smugglers. Up to 10,000 packs of cigarettes can be dropped at a time using this means of transport. Since 2013, the use of small aircraft has been one of the most common ways of smuggling tobacco products on the Polish-Ukrainian section of the state border among criminal groups. Flights are usually performed at night, in good weather conditions, with no rainfall, no cloud cover, very little wind and good visibility.

The removal of stationary border controls on the Polish sections of the internal border of the European Union/Schengen and the persistent disproportion in the prices of excise goods between countries of origin and destination, as well as the introduction of visa fees for third country nationals and the restrictions on the importing of cigarettes up to 40 cigarettes, resulted on the one hand in a reduction in smuggling by private individuals and on the other hand in an increase in the production and smuggling of tobacco products by organised crime groups operating in Poland.

The procedures for the transit of goods through Poland are also used for the purposes of tobacco smuggling. This involves their removal from customs supervision and fictitious confirmation of their export to the European Union. As a result, tobacco products which are listed in customs systems as having left the Polish customs territory actually remain in the country, from where they can be smuggled into another country. This type of smuggling is used primarily by organised criminal groups, as it requires significant financial resources (e.g. to pay for two methods of transport or payment for falsifying transport documents or vehicle registration documents) and good logistics.

Organised crime groups are also involved in the illegal production of tobacco products in Poland. Their involvement results from the specific nature of this type of crime requiring the existence of a structure involving many people, incurring specific financial outlays (purchase of dry tobacco leaves, payment of employees, the rental of buildings) and providing appropriate technical resources (machines for the production of products, packaging, and means of transport). Illegal tobacco product factories are often located close to major transport routes, which facilitates their distribution, and also close to legally operating entities, which enables the concealment of increased traffic in their vicinity. The machinery for the production of illegal tobacco products is sourced from bankrupt factories in Bulgaria together with their machine operators. One novelty is the use by organised groups of mobile mini factories organised in truck trailers, which makes it difficult for law enforcement authorities to detect them.

6 Conclusions

As can be seen from the above analysis, the legal regulations that may address the issue of illicit trade in tobacco products are very extensive. This concerns both the area of criminal law and tax regulations, an analysis of which is an indispensable element of making arrangements for the criminal liability of perpetrators for the crimes discussed. The provisions of the specific part of the Penal Fiscal Code, in which particular crimes were penalised, should be reviewed by the legislator in terms of their usefulness for the effectiveness of combating specific crimes. As it has been shown above, in the category of tax crimes and tax misdemeanours one can find such acts, which in fact contain (absorb) others. In addition, tax and fiscal law should not be subject to such frequent changes. Moreover, the legislator must remember that when amending the provisions of the latter, it is necessary to introduce appropriate changes to the Penal Fiscal Code, so as not to lead to inconsistent regulations.

The question arises here whether such a shaping of the model of responsibility for fiscal offences is appropriate. Questions also need to be asked as to whether the system is coherent. Responsibility for minor acts (low depletion/exposure to depletion, low value of goods/services committed by natural persons not linked to the activities of criminal groups) and liability for formal crimes (violation of tax law obligations) is not clearly separated from responsibility for acts of high social harmfulness (very high depletion/exposure to depletion, high value of goods/services, crimes committed by organised criminal groups, crimes committed in recidivism). Criminal repression for this type of crime should increase significantly in such a way as to make it unprofitable for perpetrators to carry out large-scale activities. While there are criminal reaction measures in place to deprive offenders of the benefits of criminal activity, an improvement should take place in terms of obtaining information and searching for assets hidden by offenders. In addition, it is necessary to use the institution of securing property. The only postulate for changes in this respect is that the criminal measure in the form of recovering the monetary equivalent of the forfeiture should include the objects referred to in article 29, point 4 of the PFC (objects whose manufacture, possession, marketing, storage, transport, transfer or shipment is prohibited).

We also see, on the basis of the analyses made, that the problem of illegal trade, production, smuggling of cigarettes or other tobacco products is perceived by the legislator and law enforcement authorities only as a phenomenon of a fiscal nature, detrimental to the legal rights and interests of the state, or the interests of the European Union of such a nature. However, this problem should also be seen in the light of how it affects the health, life of citizens and the functioning of the economy (i.e. a broader aspect than just taxation should be taken into account).

The aspects relating to the conduct of proceedings should be examined in greater depth. It cannot be ruled out that such research would lead to the conclusion that serious systemic changes are necessary with regard to the conduct of proceedings in cases concerning fiscal offences. Reasonable questions arise about the effectiveness and economics of proceedings in frequently occurring agreements where tax proceedings are conducted, and then (most often as a result of irregularities found in the proceedings) fiscal proceedings are initiated. The scope of the two proceedings overlaps to a large extent. Solutions should be sought in which a single procedure would be conducted in the area of fiscal liability and tax liability. The more so as the tax authorities are also in many cases competent to conduct proceedings for fiscal offences and fiscal misdemeanours.

Looking at the operational powers of the authorities, it should be said that this is set at an appropriate level. However, it is necessary to undertake actions related to effective use of operational and exploratory measures in the technical aspect (equipping the authorities of proceedings with the necessary technologically advanced equipment, corresponding to the measures used by perpetrators of crimes), logistic aspect (creating good working conditions for officers, ensuring appropriate human resources to perform tasks), and organisational and legal aspects. Operational and exploratory methods are very important in the fight against organised crime. At the same time, cooperation between the services of the Member States of the European Union should be developed at the level of operational cooperation, as well as with the services of other countries neighbouring Poland.

Among the most serious difficulties related to combating tobacco-related crime, it is worth mentioning the following:

- the cross-border nature of the activities of organised crime groups;
- the dispersal of criminal activity into different locations at different stages of the activity: preparation, production and distribution of criminal products (different locations for the collection and production (factories) and different locations for storage facilities);
- the non-unified legal norms at the level of EU Member States as regards to the classification of crimes related to the production and smuggling of excise goods and specific activities (non-unified penal and fiscal policy);
- the simultaneous participation of persons conducting legal economic activity related to the production and trade in excise goods in the practice (e.g. conducting legal tax warehouses, customs warehouses, and using them to store goods from an illegal source or production of tobacco products outside supervision in a legal factory).

Combating the illegal trade in tobacco products would make it easier:

- to strengthen international and cross-border cooperation, with particular emphasis on intensifying contacts with the services responsible for combating excise crime,

- to cooperate with tobacco companies—primarily for training purposes, with a view to increasing specialist knowledge in tobacco labelling and traceability,
- to introduce more effective legal solutions to combat excise crime.

It should be pointed out that criminal liability for cigarettes, unlike for the manufacture and trade in narcotics, is also disproportionately low in relation to the profits, which encourages this type of criminal activity. Such criminal activities are generally not seen as highly socially harmful, which is also reflected in the low penalties imposed for offences related to the illegal trade in tobacco products.

Finally, it is worth noting that combating crime of the character discussed requires significant financial outlays, investments in human resources (posts, training, working conditions and wages) and tools for the implementation of demanding tasks. Crime related to the illicit trade in tobacco products is very well organised. Criminal groups have large financial resources, advanced techniques, and are able to adapt quickly to the prevailing conditions, especially in terms of modifying their methods of action in case of detection by the services (this is evidenced by the variety ways used for smuggling, production, and concealing criminal activity).

At the same time, it is also worth taking action to raise citizens' legal awareness and develop a negative attitude towards products from illegal production and smuggling. For the crime in question, social consent to the phenomena is not without significance. Of course, this is not about the phenomenon of organised crime, because it is not accepted by society, but about the phenomenon of purchasing products on the grey market, which is already receiving much more lenient views.

References

Buczkowski K (2007) Przepadek korzyści majątkowej po nowelizacji kodeksu karnego z 13 czerwca 2003 r. Wyniki badań aktowych. Biuletyn Polskiego Towarzystwa Kryminologiczny im. prof. Stanisława Batawii 16:26–42

Buczkowski K (2010) Skuteczność odzyskiwania korzyści majątkowych uzyskanych przez sprawców przestępstwa – analiza przepadków orzeczonych na podstawie art. 45 k.k. In: Siemaszko A (ed) Prawo w działaniu, vol 8. Oficyna Naukowa, Warszawa

Buczkowski K (2013) Przestępstwa skarbowe jako czyny bazowe w konstrukcji prania pieniędzy. In: Rzepliński A, Rzeplińska I, Niełaczna M, Wiktorska P (eds) Pozbawienie wolności – funkcje i koszty. Księga Jubileuszowa Profesora Teodora Szymanowskiego. Wolters Kluwer Polska, Warszawa

Buczkowski K (2017) Cudzoziemcy jako sprawcy przestępstw gospodarczych – wyniki badań aktowych. In: Klaus W, Laskowska K, Rzeplińska I (eds) Przestępczość cudzoziemców. Aspekty prawne, kryminologiczne i praktyczne. Wydawnictwo Naukowe Scholar, Warszawa

Czeczot Z, Tomaszewski T (1996) Kryminalistyka ogólna. Comer, Toruń

Flemming M, Kutzmann W (1999) Przestępstwa przeciwko porządkowi publicznemu. Rozdział XXXII kodeksu karnego. Komentarz. C. H. Beck, Warszawa

Konarska-Wrzosek V, Oczkowski T, Skorupka J (2013) Prawo i postępowanie karne skarbowe. Wolters Kluwer Polska, Warszawa

Łabuda G (2017) Kodeks karny skarbowy. In: Kardas P, Łabuda G, Razowski T (eds) Komentarz. Wolters Kluwer Polska, Warszawa

Laskowska K (2017) Granica państwa jako miejsce popełniania przestępstw przez zorganizowane grupy przestępcze z udziałem cudzoziemców. In: Klaus W, Laskowska K, Rzeplińska I (eds) Przestępczość cudzoziemców. Aspekty prawne, kryminologiczne i praktyczne. Wydawnictwo Naukowe Scholar, Warszawa

Magnuszewska J (2016) Oszustwo zwykłe a oszustwo celne – podobne czy zupełnie inne czyny zabronione? In: Dziembowski R, Pieńkowska M, Oplaksa A (eds) Prawo karne skarbowe - wybrane zagadnienia teorii i praktyki. Olszty

Postulski K, Siwek M (2004), Przepadek w polskim prawie karnym. Zakamycze, Kraków

Prusak F, Skowronek G (2018) System Prawa Karnego. Szczególne dziedziny prawa karnego. In: Bojarski M (ed) Prawo karne wojskowe, skarbowe i pozakodeskowe. C.H. Beck, Warszawa

Raglewski J (1998) Stosunek przepisów części ogólnej nowego kodeksu karnego do innych ustaw przewidujących odpowiedzialność karną. Przegląd Sądowy 7–8:19–28

Raglewski J (2007) Penal fiscal code. Commentary. In: Bogdan G, Nita A, Raglewski J, Światłowski AR (2007) Kodeks karny skarbowy: Komentarz. Arche, Gdańsk, p 181

Szajner P (2018) Rynek wyrobów tytoniowych. Stan i perspektywy, Warszawa

Tarach A (2006) Czynności operacyjno-rozpoznawcze. Aspekty kryminalistyczne i prawnodowodowe. Wydawnictwo Uniwersytetu Marii Curie-Skłodowskiej, Lublin

Trząsalska A, Staszyńska M, Krassowska U (2017) Report from a nationwide survey on attitudes towards tobacco consumption, Kantar Public dla Głównego Inspektoratu Sanitarnego. Kantar Public, London

Warylewski J (2005) Wyrób alkoholu na własny użytek. Glosa do uchwały SN z dnia 30 listopada 2004 r., I KZP 23/04. Gdańskie Studia Prawnicze – Przegląd Orzecznictwa 1–2:139–144

Wilk L (2018a) Komentarz do art. 69 Kodeksu karnego skarbowego. Legalis, electronic version, access date: 2019-07-09

Wilk L (2018b) Komentarz do art. 86 Kodeksu karnego skarbowego. Legalis, electronic version, access date: 2019-07-09

Wojciechowski J (2002) Kodeks karny. Komentarz. Piśmiennictwo. Orzecznictwo. Librata, Warszawa

Wróbel W, Zoll A (2017) Kodeks karny. Część szczególna. Komentarz do art. 212-277d, vol. 2. Wolters Kluwer Polska, Warszawa

Zimny M (2017) Akcyza. Komentarz. C. H. Beck, Warszawa

Zontek W (2019) Papierosy domowej produkcji – odpowiedzialność karna w obliczu paralelnej i niespójnej regulacji. Palestra 6:66–82

Reports

Report on the state of national security 2016, Warsaw, the Ministry of Internal Affairs and Administration

Report on the state of national security 2010, Warsaw, the Ministry of Internal Affairs and Administration

Transcrime. European Outlook on the Illicit Trade in Tobacco Products. Trento: Transcrime – Università degli Studi di Trento, 2015

Country Report 2017 – Poland, Task Group Cigarettes 2018

Country Report 2018 – Poland, Task Group Cigarettes 2019

Report from a nationwide survey on attitudes towards tobacco consumption. Kantar Public for the Chief Sanitary Inspectorate, 2017. https://gis.gov.pl/wp-content/uploads/2018/04/Postawy-Polaków-do-palenia-tytoniu-Raport-2017.pdf

Other

Justification to the government's bill on the Penal Fiscal Code, Sejm of the 3rd term, print No. 1254, http://orka.sejm.gov.pl/Rejestrd.nsf/wgdruku/1146/$file/1146.pdf
www.statista.com/statistics/415034/cigarette-prices-across-europe/

Konrad Buczkowski Ph.D., is Assistant Professor at the Institute of Law Studies, Polish Academy of Sciences, Poland. His main research interest is criminology, however in addition he has a vast experience in the field of economic criminal law, especially: economic crime, insurance fraud, money laundering, white-collar crime and cybercrime. He is a member of the European Society of Criminology and the Member of the Board of the Polish Society of Criminology.

Paweł Dziekański a Kozminski University graduate, works as a research assistant at the Department of Criminal Law at the Institute of Law Studies of the Polish Academy of Sciences. Previously he was a teaching assistant at the Kozminski University. His research interests focus on criminal procedure. He is an attorney at law, actively working at the private practice.

A Complex Legal Framework for a Lack of Legal Certainty: Case Study of Romania

Sergiu Bogdan

Contents

The research for the present chapter included both legal framework and case-law analysis (cc. 400 court sentences).
Note: Translated into English by George Zlati and Andra Maria Coţ.

S. Bogdan (✉)
Faculty of Law, University Babeş-Bolyai, Cluj-Napoca, Romania
e-mail: sbogdan@law.ubbcluj.ro

C. Nowak (ed.), *Combatting Illicit Trade on the EU Border*,
https://doi.org/10.1007/978-3-030-51019-0_7

Abstract The chapter deals with Romanian legal framework related to illicit trade in tobacco products, both in criminal and administrative law. Criminological data as well as preventive measures on illicit trade in tobacco products in Romania are also presented. In addition, various aspects of cooperation matters concerning control and prevention of the illicit trade of tobacco products in Romania, which due to its geographical location deals with significant flows of illegal cigarettes from non-EU Member States.

1 National Legal Framework Related to Illicit Tobacco Trade/Smuggling

1.1 Substantive Law Issues: Criminal Offenses

1.1.1 Law No. 86/2006 on the Customs Code of Romania

The notion of "smuggling" does not have a legal definition in the Romanian legal system. However, the illicit trade or smuggling of tobacco is an offense according to a variety of criminal provisions that will be discussed below.

Article 270 of Law no. 86/2006 [Customs Code][1] is the most relevant and the most frequently used criminal provision in regard to illicit trade and smuggling of tobacco products.

The offense stipulates in para. (1) that *the introduction into or removal from the country, by any means, of goods or merchandise through places other than those established for customs control constitutes a smuggling offense and is punishable by imprisonment from 2 to 7 years and the prohibition of certain rights*. In this case the criminal deed (introduction into or removal from the country of goods and merchandise) must take place in any other place than those established for customs control. The scope of article 270 is not narrowed to illicit trade of tobacco products, as it applies to goods of merchandise subject to excise duties. Smuggling tobacco products through the places established for customs control also constitute an offense, only under para. (2) of art. 270. This criminal provision stipulates that it also constitutes an offense the following: (a) *introduction into or removal from the country through the places established for customs control by removal from customs control of the goods or goods to be placed under a customs procedure if the customs value of the goods or stolen goods is greater than 20,000 lei [cc. 4,200 euro - note] for products subject to excise duties and more than 40,000 lei [cc. 8,400 euro - note] for other goods or commodities*; *(b) the introduction into or removal from the country, twice in any one year, through the places laid down for customs control, by removal from customs control of the goods or goods to be placed under a customs procedure if the customs value of the goods or stolen goods is less than 20,000 lei for products subject to excise duty and less than 40,000 lei for other goods or commodities; (c) the alienation of goods in customs transit in any form.*

Nonetheless according to article 270 para. (3) the act of collecting, possessing, producing, transporting, taking over, storing, handing over, disposing of and selling

---

[1]Article 270 of Law no. 86/2006: "(1) The introduction into or removal from the country, by any means, of goods or merchandise through places other than those established for customs control constitutes the smuggling offense and shall be punished by imprisonment from 2 to 7 years and the prohibition of certain rights.

(2) It also constitutes a smuggling offense and is punished according to par. (1):

(a) the introduction into or removal from the country through the places established for customs control by removal from customs control of the goods or goods to be placed under a customs procedure if the customs value of the goods or stolen goods is greater than 20,000 lei [cc. 4,200 euro - note] for products subject to excise duties and more than 40,000 lei [cc. 8,400 euro - note] for other goods or commodities;

(b) the introduction into or removal from the country, twice in any one year, through the places laid down for customs control, by removal from customs control of the goods or goods to be placed under a customs procedure if the customs value of the goods or stolen goods is less than 20,000 lei for products subject to excise duty and less than 40,000 lei for other goods or commodities;

(c) the alienation of goods in customs transit in any form.

(3) They are assimilated to the smuggling offense and shall be punished according to par. (1) collecting, possessing, producing, transporting, taking over, storing, handing over, disposing of and selling the goods or merchandise to be placed under a customs procedure knowing that they are smuggled or intended to be smuggled."

the goods or merchandise to be placed under a customs procedure knowing that they are smuggled or intended to be smuggled are assimilated to the smuggling offense.

This offense can be committed both by individuals or legal entities, and it has the purpose to protect the social good consisting in the "customs regime". By smuggling tobacco products, the state suffers a damage consisting of the value of taxes and excise duties that are not paid by the perpetrator to the public budget.

The notion of "smuggling" was up the debate in a preliminary judgement (decision no. 32/2015[2]) of the High Court of Cassation and Justice [Înalta Curte de Casație și Justiție]. At the origin of the preliminary judgement was a reference made by Alba Iulia Court of Appeal. The question raised by the Alba Iulia Court of Appeal in regard to article 270 para. (3) of the Law no. 86/2006 was the following: If the notion of "smuggling" used by the legislator in the provisions of art. 270 par. (3) of the Law no. 86/2006 in the phrase "knowing that they come from smuggling" refers to the offense of smuggling in the sense defined by art. 270 par. (1) and (2) of Law no. 86/2006 or the notion of "smuggling" in a broad sense; if it is established that the text provided by art. 270 par. (3) of the Law no. 86/2006 on the Customs Code of Romania refers to the offense of smuggling, which of the two ways is to be considered: that provided by art. 270 par. (1) or that provided by art. 270 par. (2) of the Law no. 86/2006 on the Customs Code of Romania.

In answering this question the High Court of Cassation and Justice emphasized that the notion of "smuggling" used by the legislator in the provisions of art. 270 par. (3) of the Law no. 86/2006 on the Customs Code of Romania in the phrase "knowing that they come from smuggling" concerns the smuggling of the goods or merchandise to be placed under a customs regime in places other than those established for customs control or introduction in the country of these goods or merchandise through the places established for customs control by evading customs control.

Below a relevant case law in regard to article 270 of Law no. 86/2006 is being cited. In one of the cases, during the period February-March 2019, the defendant had smuggled cigarettes, and on March 21, 2019, he owned and transported the quantity of 2111 packets of smuggled cigarettes, in a car having a specially arranged compartment.[3] The defendant received a sentence of imprisonment of 1 year and 4 months, the execution of which was suspended under supervision. The assessed damage was to the amount of 23.111 lei. The cigarettes were all seized.

In another case, on 15.01.2019, a search was carried out at the defendant's home, on which occasion, in the kitchen of the building, were identified 5120 unmarked cigarette cartridges, for which he could not present documents of origin.[4] The defendant received a sentence of imprisonment of 2 years, the execution of which

[2]Available at the following link: https://www.scj.ro/1093/Detalii-jurisprudenta?customQuery%5B0%5D.Key=id&customQuery%5B0%5D.Value=126163. Accessed on 19 April 2020.

[3]Cluj Court of Appeal, criminal section, decision no. 1413/2019. www.rolii.ro/hotarari/5de71f01e49009581600004e. Last accessed on 20 April 2020.

[4]Timișoara Court of Appeal, criminal section, decision no. 1215/2019. www.rolii.ro/hotarari/5de71f42e49009780400003f. Last accessed on 20 April 2020.

was suspended under supervision. The assessed damage was to the amount of 65.538 lei. The cigarettes were all seized.

A different defendant was found, holding at the point of work of the individual enterprise a number of 1005 of cigarette packages, different brands, without stamp or with a stamp issued in the Republic of Moldova.[5] The defendant received a sentence of imprisonment of 1 year and 3 months, the execution of which was suspended under supervision. The assessed damage was to the amount of 11.224 lei.

In the market, a defendant was found on 16.12.2016 and 20.06.2017, having in his possession 480 packs of cigarettes (in his car), respectively 19 packages of cigarettes, all having stamps from Republic of Moldova.[6] The defendant received a sentence of imprisonment of 1 year and 10 months, the execution of which was suspended under supervision.

Another defendant transported, along with another person, the quantity of 2990 packs of Winston cigarettes and 88 packs of Viceroy cigarettes, having stamps issued by Republic of Moldova.[7] The defendant received a sentence of imprisonment of 3 years, the execution of which was suspended under supervision.

The offense stipulated under article 272 of Law no. 86/2006 [Customs Code][8] is also important in regard to illicit trade and smuggling of tobacco products. This criminal provision has the legal nature of a preparatory criminal deed (an inchoate offense) in relation with the offense of smuggling provided by article 270 of Law no. 86/2006. It covers the deed of using deceptive documents [e.g. documents issued for other goods or merchandise] in front of customs authority. From a conceptual point of view this offense is similar to traditional fraud [article 244 of the Criminal Code] by using deceptive documents with the purpose to obtain an illicit gain.

This offense can be concurrent with the offense provided under article 270 of Law no. 86/2006.[9] It was held by the Court that during 2014, the defendant, in order to complete the customs formalities for importing a container with 3560000 unmarked cigarettes, used customs and transport documents (electronic document of import, certificate of origin of goods, external invoice, Packing List related to Invoice, letter of authority regarding the correction information sent by the consignor to the Romanian customs authority etc.), documents referring to goods and quantities other than those actually presented in customs.

---

[5] Galați Court of Appeal, criminal section, decision no. 1344/2019. www.rolii.ro/hotarari/5de087a0e490093809000044. Last accessed on 20 April 2020.

[6] Iași Court of Appeal, criminal section, decision no. 801/2019. www.rolii.ro/hotarari/5dd74cf1e49009881a000042. Last accessed on 20 April 2020.

[7] Galați Court of Appeal, criminal section, decision no. 1027/2019. www.rolii.ro/hotarari/5dae5cd9e49009582100002d. Last accessed on 20 April 2020.

[8] Article 272 of Law no. 86/2006: "Using in front of customs authority of transport or commercial documents relating to other goods or merchandise or to other quantities of goods or merchandise than those presented to customs constitutes the offense of using deceptive documents and is punished by imprisonment from 2 to 7 years and the prohibition of certain rights".

[9] See Timișoara Court of Appeal, criminal section, decision no. 1089/2015. www.rolii.ro/hotarari/58951a26e490096c25000b4b. Last accessed on 20 April 2020.

Article 273 of Law no. 86/2006[10] is similar to article 272 but covers the deed of using falsified documents in front of customs authority.[11] This offense does not cover the forgery of the documents used in front of customs authority. As a consequence, the forgery of the documents in question can also raise a criminal liability under articles 320–322 of the Criminal Code [offenses regarding counterfeiting of documents]. In a Court decision

Article 274 of Law no. 86/2006[12] covers an aggravating circumstance—when the deed provided under article 270–273 is being committed by one or more armed individuals or by two or more individuals together. In a Court decision it was stated that "*this [aggravated] circumstance applies when two persons jointly own or transport together or produce together or trade together, etc. these quantities of cigarettes. This [aggravated] circumstance does not apply, however, when one person delivers and another takes the same quantity of cigarettes, or one person transports and another deposits the same quantity, or one person markets and another holds after purchasing the same quantity*".[13]

An armed individual does not need to use the weapon if it consists in a tool, device or part of a device declared as such by the law [see article 179 para. 1 of the Criminal Code[14]]. If an object is used for attack in order to commit an offense then such an object will be considered a weapon according to the law [see article 179 para. 2 of the Criminal Code[15]].

A brief analysis of the case law concerning the offense under article 270 of Law no. 86/2006 shows that the offense is mostly committed by two or more persons together.[16]

---

[10]Article 273 of Law no. 86/2006: "Using in front of customs authority of forged customs documents related to transport or merchandise constitutes the offense of using falsified documents and is punished by imprisonment of 3 to 10 years and the prohibition of certain rights".

[11]See Iași Court of Appeal, criminal section, decision no. 513/2016. www.sintact.ro/#/jurisprudence/529929532/1/decizie-penala-nr-513-2016-din-30-iun-2016-curtea-de-apel-iasi-infractiuni-la-regimul-vamal-legea...?keyword=Decizia%20513~2F2016&cm=SREST. Last accessed on 20 April 2020.

[12]Article 274 of Law no. 86/2006: "The deeds provided under article 270-273, committed by one or more armed persons or by two or more persons together, shall be punished by imprisonment from 5 to 15 years and the prohibition of certain rights."

[13]Iași Court of Appeal, criminal section, decision no. 482/2018. www.rolii.ro/hotarari/5b853746e49009881f00002f. Last accessed on 20 April 2020.

[14]Article 179 para. 1 of the Criminal Code: "Weapons mean tools, devices or parts declared as such by legal stipulations".

[15]Article 179 para. 2 of the Criminal Code: "Any other objects likely to be used as weapons and which have been used for attacks shall be assimilated to weapons".

[16]See High Court of Cassation and Justice, criminal section, decision no. 614/2013. www.scj.ro; Suceava Court of Appeal, criminal section, decision no. 338/2016. www.rolii.ro/hotarari/5899f8ffe49009e83e001622. Last accessed on 20 April 2020; Oradea Court of Appeal, criminal section, decision no. 141/2017. www.rolii.ro/hotarari/58d6790de49009f41b00003a. Last accessed on 20 April 2020; Suceava Court of Appeal, criminal section, decision no. 152/2017. www.rolii.ro/hotarari/58bfc4c8e49009d41a000073. Last accessed on 20 April 2020; Suceava Court of Appeal, criminal section, decision no. 2336/2012; Suceava Court of Appeal, criminal section, decision

Article 275 of Law no. 86/2006 stipulates that the attempt to commit the offenses provided under articles 270–274 is also punishable. For example, there is an attempt to commit the smuggling offense under article 270 para. 1 of Law no. 86/2006 when an individual does not succeed to introduce into the country tobacco products through places other than those established for customs control, being caught by the authorities. Also, there is an attempt to commit the smuggling offence under article 270 para. 3 of Law no. 86/2006 if an individual is trying to transport or sell tobacco products to the final consumer but is caught in the process.

1.1.2 Law No. 227/2015 Regarding the Romanian Tax Code

Article 452 of Law no. 227/2015 covers different behaviours that can be related to the illicit trade/smuggling of tobacco products. According to article 452 the following deeds are considered to be an offense:

- the production of excise goods covered by the warehousing procedure outside a fiscal warehouse authorized by the competent authority;
- the marking with falsified marks of the excisable products subject to the marking or the possessing in the fiscal warehouse of the marked products;
- the refusal to offer access to the competent authorities with control duties to performing unannounced checks in the fiscal warehouses;
- the possession outside the fiscal warehouse or sale on Romanian territory of excisable products subject to marking without being marked or badly marked or with false markings above the limit of 10,000 cigarettes, 400 cigarettes of 3 g, 200 cigarettes of more than 3 g or over 1 kg of smoking tobacco.

In a Court decision it was held that the defendant produced during December 2016 until January 2017, outside the authorized fiscal warehouse, respectively in the building located in Bucov, Prahova county, the quantity of 38,740 cigarettes, which he intended to transport in other counties with the purpose of selling the products for the amount of 5 lei/pack of 20 cigarettes and 25 lei/box of 200 cigarettes.[17]

1.1.3 Law No. 241/2005 on Tax Evasion

Article 7 para. 1 of Law no. 241/2005 makes it an offense to place into circulation, without right, the stamps, banders or standardized forms used in the tax field, with a special regime. It is also an offense to knowingly print, use, possess or put into

no. 3009/2013; Suceava Court of Appeal, criminal section, decision no. 245/2012. www.sintact.ro/#/jurisprudence/528076833/1/decizie-nr-245-2012-din-12-mar-2012-curtea-de-apel-suceava-infractiuni-la-regimul-vamal-legea-141...?cm=SREST). Last accessed on 18 April 2020.

[17]See Ploiești Court of Appeal, criminal section, decision no. 1197/2017. www.rolii.ro/hotarari/5a0e4ecae49009f824000042. Last accessed on 20 April 2020.

circulation of falsified stamps, banders or standardized forms, used in the tax field [art. 7 para. 2].

This offense is relevant in regard to illicit trade/smuggling of tobacco products because the deeds stipulated under article 270 of Law no. 86/2006 (see above) can be committed using falsified stamps in order to hide the origin of the tobacco products.

1.2 Substantive Law Issues: Administrative Law

We must emphasize that in the Romanian legislation there are many—and varied—administrative fines relevant for the illicit trafficking in tobacco.

1.2.1 Government Decision No. 707/2006 for the Approval of the Regulation in Regard to the Application of the Customs Code of Romania

Article 651 of Government Decision no. 707/2006 stipulates that the following deeds are punishable by an administrative fine of 500 lei (cc. 100 euro) to 1500 lei (cc. 400 euro):

- failure by the carrier [transporter - note] or his representative to fulfil the obligation to submit to the border customs office the accompanying documents of the means of transport engaged in international traffic and the documents regarding the goods transported with them;
- failure by the master, shipowner or agent of the ship to submit a statement of ship's stores within the time limits;
- failure by the postal authorities to declare and submit to the customs authority parcels and postal items which, according to the law, are subject to customs control;
- non-fulfilment by the postal bodies of the obligation to present the list of postal bags to the border customs office;
- failure by the carrier, at the request of the customs authority, to present the documents related to the means of transport for the goods transported in international traffic;
- non-compliance by any person with the obligation to make the customs authorities designated by the customs authority available to customs control;
- the transfer of the goods which have been the subject of a summary declaration in other cases and places than those established by the customs authority;
- failure by the owner of the commercial operation or his representative to oblige to apply within the legal term for the goods entered in the summary declaration, a customs destination;

- non-fulfilment of the obligation to ensure the integrity of the seals or markings by the carrier or the unsecured operator, except in case of force majeure or force majeure;
- non-compliance by the holder of a mandatory information with the obligation to declare to the customs authorities, when carrying out customs formalities, that he is in possession of mandatory information relating to the goods in question;
- non-fulfilment by the holder of an authorization issued by the National Customs Authority of the obligation to notify the customs authority of any change after its granting;
- the lodging of a customs declaration containing incomplete or inaccurate data where this does not affect the determination of import duties and other legally owed duties representing taxes and duties to be imposed when goods are released for free circulation but which has effects on the application of the measures trade policy or other provisions established by special regulations.

Article 652 of Government Decision no. 707/2006 stipulates that the following deeds are considered to be a contravention punishable by a fine of 1500 lei (cc. 400 euro) to 3000 lei (cc. 700 euro):

- the failure by the transport manager to fulfil the obligation to stop at the specific formal signal of the authorized customs personnel;
- the mooring of ships or the landing of aircraft at places other than the control points where the customs authority operates, except in the event of force majeure, force majeure or serious illness on board;
- the failure to present documents of any kind and any support requested in the framework of customs control, as well as non-observance of the deadline established by the customs authority for the submission of documents;
- the non-fulfilment by natural persons crossing the border of the obligation to declare and present for the customs control the goods for which this obligation is stipulated;
- the provision by an applicant of erroneous or incomplete information on the basis of which a decision favourable to him was adopted by the customs authority;
- the exercise of any commercial, industrial or service activity in a free zone, free warehouse or free port, without complying with the conditions laid down in customs regulations and without prior notification by the customs authority;
- the transfer of the rights and obligations of the holder of an economic regime to other persons who do not fulfil the conditions laid down in order to benefit from the regime in question.

Article 653 of Government Decision no. 707/2006 stipulates that the following deeds are considered to be a contravention punishable by a fine of 3000 lei (cc. 700 euro) to 8000 lei (cc. 1700 euro):

- the removal from customs control of any goods or merchandize which are to be placed under a customs procedure. In this case, the goods are confiscated;
- unloading from ships, loading on ships or transhipment of goods or merchandize subject to customs clearance without customs clearance or without the consent of

the customs authority; in this case the quantity of goods loaded, unloaded or transhipped shall be confiscated;
- the submission of the customs declaration and proof of origin containing erroneous data on the origin of the goods;
- the lodging of the customs declaration and accompanying documents containing incomplete or incorrect data on the customs value of the goods or merchandise;
- filing the customs declaration and accompanying documents containing erroneous data on the quantity of the goods if the act does not constitute an offense under the Customs Code. Where the determination of import duties and other legally owed duties representing taxes and duties to be charged by the customs authority on release for free circulation of goods is affected, the goods found in addition to those entered in the customs declaration shall be seized;
- exercising the activity of commissioner in customs without authorization; revenue from unauthorized activity is seized;
- filing the customs declaration and accompanying documents containing erroneous data on the type of goods. If this fact is influenced by the establishment of import duties and other legally owed duties representing taxes and duties to be charged by the customs authority when goods are released for free circulation, the goods found in addition to those entered in the customs declaration shall confiscate. The type of goods means the variety, type or those defining characteristics.
- non-fulfilment by the natural persons crossing the border of the obligation stipulated in art. 3 of Regulation (EC) No. 1.889/2005 of the European Parliament and of the Council declaring in writing to the Customs Authority the cash in foreign currency and/or national currency equal to or exceeding the limit set by the Regulation in their means of transport or in luggage accompanied or unaccompanied, as well as in parcels. Any unrecognized cash in excess of the limit set by the Regulation shall be confiscated.

If the deeds provided in art. 653 letter (a)–(c), where the goods are no longer identifiable, the offender shall be obliged to pay an amount equal to their customs value, to which shall be added the import duties and other legally owed duties representing taxes and duties fixed at the release for free circulation of the goods.

This measure has the same legal effect as the seizing of goods in respect of the extinction of the customs debt.

Article 653^1 of Government Decision no. 707/2006 stipulates that if the deeds provided for in art. 651–653 are perpetrated by using modified means of transport for the purpose of dissimulation of goods or merchandize, the customs authority has, in addition to the other sanctions provided for contravention in question, the possibility to seize the modified means of transport.

Because at least some of the deeds provided under articles 651–653 of the Government Decision no 707/2006 can also constitute an offense, art. 655 stipulates that a contravention is applicable only if the deed in question is not committed in such a way as to constitute, under criminal law, an offense. This is a subsidiarity clause that is problematic taking into consideration the ultima ratio principle.

1.2.2 Law No. 227/2015 on Tax Code

Article 449 of Law no. 227/2015 provides that the retail sale excisable products from the fiscal warehouse, with the exceptions provided by the law, according to art. 362 par. (6) (the exceptions concern alcoholic beverages, beer, etc.) is to be considered a contravention unless it can also be considered an offense.

According to article 362 the production, processing and possession of excise goods, where the excise duty has not been levied, is allowed only in a fiscal warehouse. Any exception from this rule can only be provided by the law. It is forbidden to possess an excisable product outside the fiscal warehouse if the excise duty on that product has not been levied. Possession of excisable products outside the fiscal warehouse, for which no proof of excise duty can be obtained, entails the obligation to pay them.

According to article 367 any authorized warehouse keeper must submit to the competent authority, by the 15th of the month following the reporting date, the reporting situations provided for in the methodological norms. If the warehouse keeper fails to comply such a deed constitutes a contravention. A similar provision exists for the registered consignee—article 375 of Law no. 227/2015.

Also, article 449 provides that the following deeds constitute a contravention:

- failure to notify the competent authority in the case of deterioration of the seals applied according to the law;
- the carriage of excise goods under suspension of excise duty which is not covered by the electronic administrative document or, where applicable, by another document used for the procedure provided by the law, or by non-compliance with the procedure if the computerized system is unavailable to the expedition according to the tax law provisions;
- possession for commercial purposes, by failing to fulfil the condition provided by the law in regard to excise goods which have already been released for consumption in another Member State.

Another contravention is found in article 414 of Law no. 227/2015 which covers possessing outside the fiscal warehouse or the selling on the territory of Romania the excisable products subject to marking, without being marked or marked inappropriately or with false markings, as well as carrying out the wholesale trading of alcoholic beverages and manufactured tobacco.

1.2.3 Law No. 12/1990 on the Protection of the Population Against Illicit Production, Trade and Services

Article 1 of Law no. 12/1990 stipulates that it constitutes illicit commercial activities and constitute a contravention or can raise criminal liability, as the case may be, to those who have performed activities of production, trade or provision of services, as the case may be, with goods whose provenance is not proven, according to the law.

Documents of origin must accompany the goods, no matter where they are, during transport, storage or sale. Documents of origin means, as appropriate, the tax invoice, the invoice, the consignment note, the customs documents, the external invoice or any other documents established by law.

1.2.4 Fiscal Responsibility for Illicit Trade

From the fiscal point of view, such a responsibility refers to the customs debt and the excise duties.

In regard to the customs debt, it consists in the amount of money needed to pay for the import or export duties. It becomes relevant when goods are being imported: (i) by illegally introducing the goods subject to import duties on the Romanian customs territory. It is also considered an illegal introduction if they are taken out of a free zone or free warehouse located on the territory of Romania; (ii) by non-fulfilment of one of the obligations which results, in regard to goods which are subject to import duties, from their temporary storage or from the use of their customs regime under which they are placed; (iii) by the consumption or use in a free zone or free warehouse of goods subject to import duties, in other conditions than those provided by the law.

It becomes relevant when goods are being exported by removing the goods subject to export duties from the customs territory of Romania without a customs declaration; or by failing to comply with the conditions under which goods were allowed to leave the customs territory of Romania with total or partial relief from export duties.

When goods are being imported, the following individuals are liable to pay the customs debt:

- the person illegally entering the goods in question;
- any person who participated in the illegal introduction of the goods and who knew or ought to have known that such an introduction was illegal;
- any person who bought or owned the goods in question and who knew or ought to have known, when purchasing or receiving the goods, that they had been illegally introduced.
- the person who stole the goods under customs supervision;
- any person who participated in such a deed and who knew or ought to have known that the goods had been taken out of customs supervision;
- any person who bought or held the goods in question and who knew or ought to have known, at the time of purchase or receipt of the goods, that they had been removed from customs supervision;
- the person who is required to fulfil his obligations with regard to goods subject to import duties following their temporary storage or use of the customs procedure under which they were placed;
- the person who was required to comply with the conditions governing the placement of goods under that regime.

- the person who consumed or used the goods and any person who participated in such consumption or use and who knew or ought to have known that the goods had been consumed or used under conditions other than those provided for by law.

On the other hand, when goods are being exported, the customs duties are to be paid by: (i) the person who removed the goods and any person who participated and who knew or ought to have known that no customs declaration had been filed, although this should have been lodged at the customs authorities; (ii) in the event of non-compliance with the conditions under which the removal of the goods was allowed, the debtor is the declarant. In the case of indirect representation, the person on whose behalf the declaration is made is also a debtor; (iii) the amount of the customs debt shall be determined on the basis of the chargeable elements from the time a customs debt started to exist. The moment of the customs debt is the moment when the goods are illegally introduced/removed or when an equivalent fact takes place. Compensatory interest may be applied in order to avoid a financial gain by postponing the date of birth of the customs debt or entry in the accounts and the cases and conditions under which it is applicable shall be determined by the customs regulation.

Excise goods (manufactured tobacco) are subject to excise duty at the time of their production, including or when they are imported into the territory of the European Union. Such goods become chargeable at the time of release for consumption. The conditions of chargeability and the level of excise duty applicable shall be those in force on the date on which the excise duty becomes chargeable in the Member State in which the release for consumption takes place.

The release for consumption is considered to be:

- the exit of excise goods, including an irregular one, from a suspensive regime of excise duties;
- the possession of excise goods outside a suspensive regime of excise duty for which excise duty has not been levied;
- the production of excisable products, including with irregularities, outside a suspensive regime of excise duties;
- the importation of excise goods, including with irregularities, except where excise goods are placed, immediately after import, under a duty suspension arrangement;
- the use of excisable products inside the fiscal warehouse other than as raw material.
- the commercial possession by a person of excise goods which have been released for consumption in another Member State and for which excise duty has not been collected in Romania.
- in the case of an excise goods for which the excise duty was not previously due, release shall be considered for consumption when the excise goods are held in a fiscal warehouse for which the authorization was revoked or cancelled.
- in the case of an excise goods for which the excise duty was not previously due, release shall be deemed to be release for consumption when the excise product is

held in a fiscal warehouse for which the authorization has expired and a new authorization has not been issued.
- in the case of an excise product entitled to be exempted or exempt from excise duty, use for any purpose not in accordance with the exemption, that is to say, the exemption entails the obligation to pay the excise duty.

In principle, the individuals responsible for committing offenses or contraventions are also liable to pay excise duties. In regard to the exit of excise goods from a suspensive arrangement of excise duty, the person responsible is the authorized warehouse keeper, the registered consignee or any other person who issues the excise goods under the excise duty suspension arrangement or on whose behalf such release is made and, in the event of an irregular departure from the fiscal warehouse, any other person who participated in that exit. In the event of an irregularity in the course of a movement of excise goods under a duty suspension arrangement, as defined in Art. 412 par. (1), (2) and (4) of the Tax Code, the person responsible is the authorized warehouse keeper, the registered consignor or any other person who has guaranteed excise duty in accordance with art. 348 par. (1) and (2) of the Tax Code, as well as any person who participated in the irregular departure and who was or would have been aware of the irregular nature of such an exit;

In regard to the possession of excise goods, the person who possess the excise goods or any other person involved in their possession.

In regard to the production of excise goods, the person who produces the excise goods or, in the case of unauthorized production, any other person involved in their production;

In regard to the import of excise goods, the person who declares the excise goods or on whose behalf the products are declared at the time of import or, in the case of irregularities to the import, any other person involved in their import;

When more than one person is required to pay the same excise duty, they are required to pay that debt jointly and each of these people can be tracked for the entire debt.

We also must emphasize that IQOS or electronic cigarette products are due to non-amortized excises (see Articles 439–441 of the Tax Code).

1.3 Relation Between Criminal and Administrative/Fiscal Responsibility

The fact that the participant in the offense is liable to pay the customs debt and the excise duties does not raise problems from the perspective of the *ne bis in idem* principle, because in such a context it is considered a reparation and not a criminal sanction.

The *ne bis in idem* principle is applicable only in situations where the same deed is punished both as a contravention (administrative fine) and as a criminal offense (criminal fine or imprisonment).

However, the legislator attempted to resolve such an overlap by imposing a series of obligations in behalf of the authorities. More specifically, by Government Ordinance no. 2/2001, it established the following (see article 30): *If the person empowered to impose the sanction considers that the deed was committed under such conditions as to constitute a criminal offense, according to the criminal law, it shall notify the competent prosecution body* [Article 30 par. (1)]. Taken into consideration this provision, the custom authorities will not impose an administrative/ fiscal liability if the deed in question also consists in a criminal offense. But if the custom authorities impose an administrative sanction for a particular deed, no criminal liability can raise for the same deed.

Article 30 also provides that *if the act was prosecuted as an offense and subsequently it was determined by the prosecutor or the court that it could constitute a contravention, the act of notification or the finding of the deed, together with a copy of the resolution, the ordinance or, as the case may be, from the court order, the law body shall be immediately informed of the offense, in order to take the necessary measures according to the law.*

1.4 Relations Between Criminalisation of Illicit Trade of Tobacco and Other Types of Economic Crimes

Because there are many overlaps between different criminal provisions relevant in the context of illicit trade of tobacco products, it must be established if different offenses can be committed in concurrence or not.

1.4.1 The Relationship Between the Smuggling Offense (Article 270 (3) of Law No. 86/2006 on the Customs Code of Romania) and the Offense Provided by Article 452 Letter d) of Law No. 227/2015 (Tax Code)

The relationship between art. 270 para. (3) of Law no. 86/2006 and art. 452 letter d) of Law no. 227/2015 was clarified by the High Court of Cassation of Justice [Înalta Curte de Casație și Justiție] after different points of view emerged in the jurisprudence.

By a preliminary judgement, namely by Decision no. 17/2013[18] (published in the Official Gazette, Part I no. 35 of 16.01.2014) the High Court of Cassation and Justice concluded that the act of possessing excisable goods subject to marking, without marking, or marked inappropriately, outside the tax warehouse, knowing that they come from smuggling, constitutes only the offense provided by art. 270 para. (3) of

[18] Available at the following link: www.scj.ro/1093/Detalii-jurisprudenta?customQuery%5B0%5D.Key=id&customQuery%5B0%5D.Value=86231. Last accessed on 15 April 2020.

Law 86/2006 on the Customs Code of Romania. We must emphasize that a preliminary judgement from the High Court of Cassation and Justice is mandatory for the courts.

Basically, the High Court of Cassation and Justice stated that the offense provided under art. 270 para. (3) of Law no. 86/2006 has a complex nature and it includes also the deed provided by art. 452 letter d) of Law no. 227/2015.

1.4.2 The Relationship Between the Smuggling Offense (Article 270 of Law No. 86/2006) and the Offense of Tax Evasion (Article 9 Para. 1 of Law No. 241/2005)

The High Court of Cassation and Justice stated in decision no. 1145/2013 that the possession and transport of goods or merchandize to be placed under a customs procedure such as cigarettes, knowing that they come from smuggling for the purposes of sale without payment of customs duties, excise duties and value added tax [VAT], by removing them from the payment of their obligations tax, is covered by the offense provided in art. 270 par. (3) of the Law no. 86/2006, and not the elements of the offense of tax evasion provided in art. 9 par. (1) lit. a) of Law no. 241/2005. The rationale of the court emphasized the fact that the offense provided under Art. 270 para. (3) of the Law no. 86/2006 consists in a specific deed of avoiding the payment of tax liabilities of goods or goods illegally introduced into the country.

1.4.3 The Relationship Between the Smuggling Offense (Article 270 of Law No. 86/2006) and the Money Laundering Offense (Article 49 Para. 1 c) of Law No. 129/2019)

The relationship between the two offenses raises problems from the perspective of para. (3) of art. 270 of Law no. 86/2006, which states that the deeds of collecting, possessing, producing, transporting, taking over, storing, handing over, disposing of and selling the goods or merchandise to be placed under a customs procedure knowing that they are smuggled or intended to be smuggled are assimilated to the smuggling offense and are punished according to par. (1).

The relationship between the two is solved according to the rule of special norm-general norm. Para. (3) of article 270 of Law no. 86/2000 would be the special norm, and article 49 para. (1) c) of Law no. 129/2019 would be the general norm. Also, according to article 49 para. (1) c) of Law no. 129/2019 the deed of acquisition, possession or use of goods must be perpetrated by another person than the one committing the offense from which the goods are originating. In other words, the person who commits a smuggling offense cannot be found criminal liable also for a money laundering offense, in regard to the same goods. The narrow scope of the mentioned money laundering offense is due to Decision no. 625/2018 of the Constitutional Court.

1.4.4 The Relationship Between the Smuggling Offense (Article 270 of Law No. 86/2006) and Organized Crime Offense (Article 367 of the Criminal Code)

According to article 367 para. 6 of the Criminal Code an "organized criminal group" means a structured group, made up of three or more persons, which exists for a certain period of time and acts in a coordinated manner for the purpose of perpetrating one or more offenses. The criminal offense stipulated under article 367 of the Criminal Code consists is a deed of initiating or creating an organized crime group or of joining or supporting such a group in any way.

If the smuggling offense was committed by an organized criminal group, both offenses will be taken into consideration as a concurrence of offenses. A problem arises in such a context because of the aggravated circumstance of the offense provided by art. 274 of Law no. 86/2006—when the smuggling is perpetrated by two or more individuals together. The legal literature, in relation to the relationship between the general aggravating circumstance—committing the deed by three or more individuals together—and the offense of an organized criminal group, it was stated that although the aggravating circumstance could not be held altogether with the offense of an organised criminal group, such a restriction does not apply for offenses committed by the group.

The same conclusion was reached in the jurisprudence regarding the relationship between the aggravated form of the smuggling offense (Article 274 of Law no. 86/2006) and the offense of an organized criminal group, namely that both of them are applicable.[19]

1.4.5 The Relationship Between Illicit Trade of Tobacco and Corruption

If the illicit trade of tobacco products includes bribery (art. 290 of the Criminal Code) or an act of influence peddling (art. 292 of the Criminal Code) there will be a concurrence of offenses. The basic argument for such a solution is that any offense in regard to corruption protects a completely different social good than the one protected by an offense that covers the deed of illicit trade of tobacco.

[19]See High Court of Cassation and Justice, criminal section, decision no. 129/2016. www.scj.ro. Last accessed on 20 April 2020; High Court of Cassation and Justice, criminal section, decision no. 146/2016. www.scj.ro. Last accessed on 19 April 2020; Timişoara Court of Appeal, criminal section, decision no. 1071/2019. www.rolii.ro/hotarari/5dc4d81de490098019000031. Last accessed on 20 April 2020; Oradea Court of Appeal, criminal section, decision no. 141/A/2017. www.rolii.ro/hotarari/58d6790de49009f41b00003a. Last accessed on 20 April 2020; Galaţi Court of Appeal, criminal section, decision no. 477/A/2016. www.rolii.ro/hotarari/5898bbd1e490095834001a4c. Last accessed on 20 April 2020.

Relevant in this contest is a decision from Oradea Court of Appeal[20] in which the Court concluded that the defendants asked the Ukrainian citizens to illegally introduce cigarettes in Romania and communicated the date, time and location by which they were going to do so, with one of the defendants waiting for them in that place. It also turned out that one of the defendants repeatedly contacted a border police officer and offered him money for not fulfilling his duties.

In this context it must be emphasized that two of the first, biggest and most notorious corruption scandals in Romania were related to the illicit trade of tobacco. These cases were named by the media "Cigarette 1" and "Cigarette 2".

"Cigarette 1" broke out in the media in 1993 when in a warehouse belonging to the Romanian Armed Forces were discovered cases of cigarettes, which were smuggled across Romanian borders. The cigarettes were delivered by a contractual partner of Romtehnica (Romanian company in National Defence Industry), allegedly as a partly payment for weaponry delivered by Romtehnica. Members of the Armed Forces were convicted, including the general director of Romtehnica.

"Cigarette 2" first appeared in the media in April 1998. Two Romanian newspapers received an anonymous information about a Ukrainian plane landing on Otopeni Military Airport, caring on board 4275 master cases of smuggled cigarettes. There were 19 people indicted, out of which 15 convicted, including members of the Romanian Armed Forces and of the Romanian Protection and Guard Service (secret service, with tasks in the field of national security).

1.4.6 The Relationship Between Illicit Trade of Tobacco and Organised Crime

In this context the relevant the offense is the one provided by article 367 of the Criminal Code which stipulates the following:

(1) The act of initiating or creating an organized criminal group or of joining or supporting such a group in any way shall be punishable by no less than 1 and no more than 5 years of imprisonment and a ban on the exercise of certain rights.
(2) When the offenses included in the purpose of an organized crime group are punished by life imprisonment or by a term of imprisonment exceeding 10 years, it shall be punishable by no less than 3 and no more than 10 years of imprisonment and a ban on the exercise of certain rights.
(3) If the acts set out in par. (1) and par. (2) were followed by the commission of an offense, the rules on multiple offenses shall apply.
(4) No penalty shall apply to the individuals who committed the acts set out in par. (1) and par. (2) if they report the organized crime group to the authorities before it was discovered and before the commission of any of the offenses included in the purpose of the group.
(5) If the perpetrator of one of the acts referred to in par. (1) - (3) facilitates, during the criminal investigation, discovery of the truth and the prosecution of one of more

[20]See Oradea Court of Appeal, criminal section, decision no. 430/2015. www.rolii.ro/hotarari/589a3734e49009742f001c3f. Last accessed on 20 April 2020.

members of the organized crime group, the special limits of the penalty are reduced by one-half.

(6) An "organized crime group" means a structured group, made up of three or more persons, which exists for a certain period of time and acts in a coordinated manner for the purpose of perpetrating one or more offenses.

Taken into consideration article 367 para. 3 of the Criminal Code, if a person initiates, creates, joins or supports in any way an organized criminal group and such criminal deeds are then followed by the commission of a smuggling offense, such a person will be found criminal liable for both offenses (see above).

1.5 Sanctions

1.5.1 Aggravating Circumstances

In this context is relevant the aggravating circumstance provided by art. 274 of Law no. 86/2006—the smuggling is committed by two or more persons together. If the smuggling offense provided by article 270 of Law no. 86/2006 is committed in this aggravating circumstance then the criminal sanction is imprisonment from 5 to 15 years and the prohibition of certain rights.

Regarding the situation in which the criminal activity meets the elements of multiple offenses, the criminal sanctions will be merged according to article 39 of the Criminal Code: when only penalties of imprisonment have been established, the heaviest penalty shall be applied, which can be increased by one-third of the total of all the other penalties handed down.

In regard to contraventions (administrative fines) both negligence and intention can raise liability. No strict liability is allowed by the law in the context of contraventions but negligence is sufficient to raise liability.

In regard to all the offenses which covers illicit trade or smuggling of tobacco products it must be emphasized that liability can only be raised if the prosecution can prove the intent to commit the criminal deed in question. The intent can be a direct one or an indirect one (*dolus eventualis*).

1.5.2 Sanctions Applicable for Illicit Trade of Tobacco Products with Regard to Individuals

The basic form of the smuggling offence [see article 270 of Law no. 86/2006] is punishable by 2 to 7 years of imprisonment and the aggravating form [see article 274 of Law no. 86/2006] is punishable by 5 to 15 years of imprisonment. In the Tax Code (Law no. 227/2015), for certain deeds the punishment is imprisonment from 1 to 5 years [e.g. Article 452 para. 1 letters e) and h)], for the other offenses being between 2 and 7 years.

In our research we have found that for the offence provided under art. 270 parag. 3 of Law no. 86/2006 (collecting, possessing, producing, transporting, taking over, storing, handing over, disposing of and selling the goods or merchandise to be placed under a customs procedure knowing that they are smuggled or intended to be smuggled), if the quantity of the smuggled goods is relatively low, a minimum imprisonment punishment is the most common penalty, the sentence being suspended. In contrast, in cases were the offenses are committed by an organized criminal group the sentence it is not suspended, and the courts tend to establish punishments close to the statutory maximum. Still, it must be emphasized that there is no available data in regard to the penalties applied by the courts for criminal offenses relating to illicit trade.

The prohibition of certain rights—this constitutes a complementary [ancillary]/ accessory criminal sanction, that is mandatory in the case of the offenses provided by Law no. 86/2006 [regarding smuggling] and Law no. 241/2005 [regarding tax evasion], except for the ones provided by the Tax Code.

According to article 66 of the Criminal Code complementary [ancillary] penalty consists in a ban, for one to five years, on the exercise of one or several of the following rights:

a) right to be elected to the ranks of public authorities or any other public office;
b) right to take a position that involves exercise of State authority;
c) right of a foreign citizen to reside on Romanian territory;
d) right to vote;
e) parental rights;
f) right to be a legal guardian or curator;
g) the right to take the position, exercise the profession or perform the activity they used in order to commit the offense;
h) the right to own, carry and use any category of weapons;
i) the right to drive certain categories of vehicles as established by the Court;
j) the right to leave Romanian territory;
k) the right to take a managerial position with a public legal entity;
l) the right to be in certain localities as established by the Court;
m) the right to be in certain locations or attend certain sports events, cultural events or public gatherings, as established by the Court;
n) the right to communicate with the victim or the victim's family, with the persons together with whom they committed the offense or with other persons as established by the Court, or the right to go near such persons;
o) the right to go near the domicile, workplace, school or other locations where the victim carries social activities, in the conditions established by the Court.

Both for contraventions and offenses, confiscation [seizing] is mandatory. Regarding to this subject there is also a preliminary judgement of the High Court of Cassation and Justice (decision no. 11/2015) in which it was stated that in the case of the smuggling offense provided by Law no. 86/2006 on the Customs Code of Romania, it is necessary to apply the criminal provisions on special confiscation of the goods or merchandize illegally entered in the customs territory of Romania, at the same time as obliging the defendants to pay the amounts representing the customs debt only if they have passed the first customs office located in the customs territory of the Community without having been presented to customs and transported to that customs office.

Also, according to article 449 para. 3 of Law no. 227/2015, in case of a criminal deed that has the nature of a contravention, without making a difference between the individual or the legal entity (although some measures are applicable only to legal entities), the following measures are provided:

a) the confiscation of the products and, if sold, confiscation of the proceeds of the sale,
b) seizure of tanks, containers and means of transport used in the transport of excise goods
c) suspension of trading of excisable products for a period of 1–3 months in the case of wholesale and/or wholesale traders;
d) stopping the production of excisable products by sealing the plant, in the case of producers;
e) suspension, upon proposal of the control body, of the fiscal warehouse permit, registered consignee, registered consignor or authorized importer, as the case may be, for the situations stipulated in paragraph (1) lit. j) and par. (2) lit. g) and m).
f) the revocation, on the proposal of the control body, of the fiscal warehouse permit, registered consignee, registered consignor or authorized importer, as the case may be, for the situations stipulated in paragraph (1) lit. b), d) and e).
g) also, the competent control body may order the stopping of the activity, the sealing of the plant in accordance with the technological closure procedures of the plant and the submission of the control act to the tax authority that issued the authorization with the proposal to suspend the fiscal warehouse authorization.

1.6 Legal Responsibility of Legal Entities

According to article 135 of the Criminal Code a legal entity can be found criminal liable under following conditions: if the offense is being committed in the performance of the object of activity of legal entities or in their interest or behalf (article 135 para. 1 of the Criminal Code). For example, this criminal provision could apply if a legal entity that sells tobacco products starts to sell or transport smuggled tobacco products.

The criminal liability of legal entities does not exclude the criminal liability of the individual participating in the commission of the criminal deed. For example, in a decision from the Craiova Court of Appeal[21] it was also held that the defendant is the owner of an Individual Enterprise, whose main activity is retail trade in non-specialized stores, with a predominant sale of food, beverages and tobacco. Considering that the defendant collected and detained cigarettes and alcoholic beverages, in accomplishing the object of activity of the legal entity, it was found that the Individual Enterprise is also guilty of the offense provided under article 270 para. (3) of Law no. 86/2006.

It must be emphasized that in our research we have identified very few cases in which legal entities were convicted for criminal offenses related to illicit trade of tobacco. Also, there is not any official data available in this regard. Still, this does not mean that a legal entity cannot be found criminal liable for any of the offenses which covers illicit trade of tobacco products.

In the case of an offense, the principal, complementary and accessory criminal sanctions are provided by article 136 of the Criminal Code, as well as the confiscation measure.

In the case of the offenses provided by the Tax Code (Law no. 227/2015), after the facts have been established, the competent control body may order the closure of the activity, the sealing of the plant in accordance with the technological closure procedures of the installation and the forwarding of the control act to the tax authority that issued the permit, to suspend the tax warehouse authorization.

According to article 136 of the Criminal Code, the criminal sanctions applicable to legal entities can consist in a criminal fine and different complementary (ancillary) penalties. The main penalty that can be imposed to a legal entity is a criminal fine, which is the sum of money that the legal entity is ordered to pay to the State. The criminal fine is established according to article 137 of the Criminal Code. The amount of the fine is determined based on the fine-days system. The amount corresponding to the fine-days, varying between Lei 100 and 5000, shall be multiplied by the number of days subject to the fine (between 30 and 600 days). The court shall decide on the number of days subject to the fine considering the general criteria for the customization of penalty. The amount of the fine-days is determined by taking into account the turnover (in case of for-profit legal entities), and the value of assets (in case of the other legal entities), as well as other obligations of the legal entity.

When the offense committed by legal entity was intended to the obtaining of a monetary benefit, the special limits of the fine-days provided by law for the committed offense may be increased by one-third, without exceeding the general maximum of the fine. When determining the fine, the value of the monetary benefit obtained or sought shall be considered.

The complementary (ancillary) penalties consists in the following:

[21] See Craiova Court of Appeal, criminal section, decision no. 333/2013. www.sintact.ro/#/jurisprudence/526739783/1/decizie-penala-nr-333-2013-din-18-feb-2013-curtea-de-apel-craiova-infractiuni-la-regimul-vamal...?cm=SREST. Last accessed on 13 April 2020.

- winding-up of legal entities;
- suspension of the activity or of one of the activities performed by the legal entity, for a term between three months and three years;
- closure of working points of the legal entity for a term between three months and three years;
- prohibition to participate in public procurement procedures for a term between one and three years;
- placement under judicial supervision;
- display or publication of the conviction sentence.

In the case of contraventions, the sanction is an administrative fine. Other measures may also be taken, such as: the confiscation of the products and, if sold, confiscation of the proceeds of the sale; the seizure of tanks, containers and means of transport used in the transport of excise goods; the suspension of trading of excisable products for a period of 1–3 months in the case of wholesale and/or wholesale traders; the stopping the production of excisable products by sealing the plant, in the case of producers; suspension, upon proposal of the control body, of the fiscal warehouse permit, registered consignee, registered consignor or authorized importer, as the case may be, for the situations stipulated in paragraph (1) lit. j) and par. (2) lit. g) and m); the revocation, at the proposal of the inspection body, of the fiscal warehouse permit, registered consignee, registered expeditor or authorized importer, as the case may be, for the situations stipulated in paragraph (1) lit. b), d) and e).

The competent control body may also discontinue the activity, sealing the plant in accordance with the technological closure procedures of the installation and submitting the control act to the tax authority that issued the permit with the proposal to suspend the fiscal warehouse permit.

1.7 Disposal or Destruction of Confiscated Tobacco Products

The Customs Code (Law no. 86/2006) stipulates that the rules are laid down in a customs regulation, but there no reference in the customs regulations in force in regard to the destruction of goods.

The Tax Code (Law no. 227/2015) provides for the following under article 431:

(1) By way of derogation from the legal provisions in the field regulating the manner and conditions for the capitalization of assets legally seized or admitted, according to the law, private property of the state, processed tobacco seized or entered, according to the law, in the private property of the state, by the body which ordered confiscation, for destruction, authorized warehousekeepers, registered consignees or importers authorized by such products as follows:

(a) the varieties appearing in the product nomenclature of authorized warehousekeepers, registered consignees, registered consignors or authorized importers shall be surrendered in their entirety;

Table 1 Assets recovery in relation to illicit trade of tobacco products

Year	2017	2018	2019
Quantity of seized cigarettes	149,097,768 pcs.	112,964,175 pcs.	137,833,307 pcs.
Total value of the seized cigarettes	90,934,411 lei (cc. 20 million euros)	49,913,172 lei (cc. 10.7 million euros)	71,753,182 (cc. 15 million euros)

Source: www.stopcontrabanda.ro (The aggregate presented figures are from the official reports of the Romanian Police and the Border Police and from other official communications)

(b) the varieties which do not appear in the nomenclatures stipulated in letter a) are handed over to custodial authorities by authorized bodies for the production and/or storage of manufactured tobacco.

(2) The distribution of each batch of confiscated manufactured tobacco, the taking over of the manufactured tobacco by the authorized warehouse keepers, the registered consignees and the authorized importers, as well as the destruction procedure shall be performed according to the provisions of the methodological norms.
(3) Each authorized warehouse keeper, registered consignee and authorized importer shall ensure at his own expense the taking over, transporting and storing the quantities of products in the confiscated consignment which he has been assigned to.

1.8 Asset Recovery Related to Illicit Trade of Tobacco Products

There are no relevant statistics regarding assets recovery in relation to illicit trade of tobacco products. The only available relevant data refers to the number of seized cigarettes (Table 1).

1.9 The Impact of the WTO FCTC and the 2012 Protocol to the FCTC on the National Law

Romania ratified the Convention in 2005 by Law no. 332/2005. In regard to the 2012 Protocol, until now Romania has not ratified it. Even so, in 2016 the Romanian legislator adopted a law that would, in principle, constitute the implementation of the protocol.

It should also be emphasized that the European Union has made a statement on the Protocol, stating that aspects regarding its exclusive competence are adopted by the Protocol, and on the other matters it is up for the member states to decide.

The national legislation is at some extend in compliance with the provisions of the Protocol. In regard to behaviours considered to be illegal under the Protocol, they are also mostly considered to be illegal under the national law, being criminalized either as an offense or as a contravention.

The correspondence between the illicit deeds provided under art. 14 of the Protocol and the national legislation can be found in the table below.

(a) Manufacturing, wholesale, brokerage (acting as agent for others, such as negotiating contracts, purchases or sales, in exchange for a remuneration or a commission), selling, transporting, distributing, storing, shipping, importing or the export of tobacco, tobacco products or manufacturing equipment that contravenes the provisions of this Protocol (it is required, in principle, that persons involved in the distribution chain be authorized and comply with certain due diligence, in order to prevent illicit trade).	These acts under Romanian law would constitute either a criminal offense, either a contravention. Offenses: – art. 270, art. 272 and art. 273 from Law no. 86/2006 (see the references made above, I.1). – art. 452 from Law no. 227/2015 (Tax Code)—the holding by any person outside the fiscal warehouse or the marketing on the territory of Romania of excisable products subject to marking, according to the present title, without being improperly marked or marked or with false markings above the limit of 10,000 cigarettes, 400 cigarettes of 3 grams, 200 sheet cigarettes larger than 3 g, over 1 kg smoking tobacco, ethyl alcohol over 40 litters, spirits over 200 litters, intermediate products over 300 litters, fermented beverages, other than beer and wines, over 300 litters. Contraventions (administrative fines): –art. 652 letter g) from Ordinance no. 707/2006 for the approval of the Regulation applying the Romanian Customs Code—transfer of the rights and obligations of the holder of an economic customs regime to other persons who do not fulfil the conditions provided to benefit from the regime in question; – art. 449 para. (1) letter b) of Law no. 227/2015 (Tax code)—retail sale of excisable products from the fiscal warehouse; – art. 449 para. (2) of Law no. 227/2015 (Tax code).[a] – art. 1 of Law no. 12/1990 – art. 23 of Law no. 201/2016 contains provisions which would transpose the protocol regarding the track & tracing system. Violations of the provisions in question are considered to be a contravention punishable by an administrative fine. In conclusion, the distribution, storage, shipping etc. of manufacturing equipment are not covered by the legal provisions.
(b) (i) manufacture, wholesale, brokerage, sale, transport, distribution, storage, shipment, import or export of tobacco, tobacco products or manufacturing equipment without payment	In principle, the same texts as in the previous section and also art. 7 of Law 241/2005, which states that it is a criminal offense to possess or to put into circulation, without right, the

(continued)

of applicable taxes, taxes and other taxes or without the application of stamps tax, unique identification markings or any other necessary markings or labels; (ii) any other acts of smuggling or attempted smuggling of tobacco, tobacco products or manufacturing equipment that are not covered by point (b) (i); (c) (i) any other form of illicit manufacture of tobacco, tobacco products or tobacco manufacturing equipment or packaging bearing tax stamps, unique identification markings or any other necessary markings or labels forged; (ii) wholesale, brokerage, sale, transport, distribution, storage, shipment, import or export of illicitly manufactured tobacco, illicit tobacco products, products with tax stamps and/or other necessary markings or labels or counterfeit equipment; illicit manufacturing;	stamps, banders or standardized forms used in the tax field, with a special regime and to knowingly print, use, possess or put into circulation falsified stamps, banders or standardized forms, used in the tax field. These actions are not criminalised with regard to the manufacturing equipment.
(d) *mixing tobacco products with other types of products along the supply chain, in order to hide or hide tobacco products.* *(e) mixing of tobacco products with other types of products, in violation of Article 12 (2) of this Protocol (mixing of tobacco products with other types of products in a single container or any other similar transport unit at the time is prohibited exit from free zones).*	These acts do not seem to be covered by the law, but they could be considered as a preparatory act in order to commit another offense.
(f) using Internet-based sales methods, telecommunications or any other new technology for marketing tobacco products in violation of the Protocol (which imposes the same obligations as any other trader).	These acts are covered by the law in the same way as a regular sale.
(g) obtaining by the holder of an authorization, in accordance with Article 6, tobacco, tobacco products or manufacturing equipment from a person who should hold an authorization in accordance with Article 6, but who does not hold such an authorization;	The person who does not have authorization would commit a crime (either smuggling or producing excisable products, incriminated by art. 452 Tax Code), consequently, it would be smuggling/stealing/money laundering. There are no incrimination rules in relation to manufacturing equipment.
(h) obstruction of a public official or an authorized official in the performance of his duties related to the prevention, deterrence, detection, investigation or elimination of illicit trade in tobacco, tobacco products or manufacturing equipment;	It is incriminated both as an offense (art. 452 paragraph 1, letter e fiscal code), as well as a contravention by the Regulation applying the Romanian Customs Code (see Government decision no. 707/2006).
(i) (i) any false, misleading or incomplete material statement or failure to provide the information requested by a public official or authorized officer in the performance of his or her duties related to the prevention, deterrence,	Such deeds are considered to be offenses under art. 272 and art. 273 of Law no. 86/2006, even if the traditional offenses regarding the forgery of documents could also apply. The contravention regime stipulated by the Regulation

(continued)

detection, investigation or elimination of illicit trade in tobacco, tobacco products or manufacturing equipment, when this does not contravene the right not to incriminate oneself; *(ii) false statements made in official forms in relation to the description, quantity or value of tobacco, tobacco products or manufacturing equipment or any other information provided in the protocol for the purpose:* *(a) to evade payment of the applicable taxes, duties and other charges; or* *(b) to prejudice any control measures to prevent, deter, detect, investigate or eliminate the illicit trade in tobacco, tobacco products or manufacturing equipment;* *(iii) refusal to set up or keep records covered by this Protocol or to keep false records;*	applying the Romanian Customs Code also applies, when it comes to incorrect or inaccurate data. Also, by Law no. 201/2016 it is sanctioned as a contravention the violation of the provisions regarding the keeping of the records, in case such a behaviour does not constitute an offense.
(l) the laundering of the proceeds of illicit deed established as an offense under paragraph 2	It is considered to be a money laundering offense under art. 49 of Law no. 129/2019

[a]Article 449 para. (2) of Law no. 227/2015: "a) the sale by any person of cigarettes for which retail prices have not been established and declared according to art. 343 para. (9);b) the sale of cigarettes by any person at a price that exceeds the retail price declared according to art. 343 para. (10);c) the sale of cigarettes by any person to natural persons at a price lower than the retail price declared according to art. 343 para. (11);d) capitalization of excisable products in a fiscal warehouse for which the authorization has expired, has been revoked or cancelled, without payment of excises to the state budget, according to art. 344 para. (2);e) non-observance of the provisions of art. 356 paragraph (2) and art. 357;f) non-observance of the provisions of art. 362 para. (1) and (7);g) failure of the competent authority in case of deterioration of the seals applied according to art. 367 para. (1) lit. c);h) failure to comply with the provisions of art. 397 para. (3);i) the transport of excisable products under suspension of excise duty which is not covered by the electronic administrative document or, as the case may be, by another document used for this regime, provided for in this title, or with the failure to comply with the procedure if the computerized system is unavailable upon shipment according to the provisions of art. 402 paragraph (1) and art. 406 paragraph (1);j) holding for commercial purposes, failing to fulfil the condition provided in art. 414 para. (1), of excise goods that have already been released for consumption in another Member State;k) holding outside the fiscal warehouse or marketing on the territory of Romania excisable products subject to marking, according to the provisions of art. 421 para. (3), without being marked or improperly marked or with false markings below the limits provided in art. 452 para. (1) lit. h);l) non-observance of the provisions of art. 428 para. (3);m) non-observance of the provisions of art. 435 paragraph (1);n) non-observance of the provisions of art. 435 paragraph (2);o) carrying out the wholesale marketing of alcoholic beverages and processed tobacco and the wholesale and / or retail marketing of energy products - gasoline, diesel, lamp oil, liquefied petroleum gas, and biofuels, with non-compliance with the obligations set out in art. 435 paragraph (3) and (4);p) acquisition of excisable products from persons carrying out wholesale distribution and marketing activities of alcoholic beverages and processed tobacco, respectively wholesale marketing of energy products - petrol, diesel, lamp oil and liquefied petroleum gas, as well as biofuels and non-fuels. respects the conditions or obligations provided in art. 435 paragraph (3) and (4)"

1.10 Procedural Law Issues

1.10.1 Institutional Framework

In the case of offenses, the institutions involved would be criminal investigation bodies (police, including Border Police) and the Public Ministry—investigating offenses. The Directorate for Investigating Organized Crime and Terrorism [DIICOT], which is a specialized prosecution body attached to the High Court of Cassation and Justice prosecution body. If the offenses regarding the illicit trade of tobacco products are being committed by a criminal organization (defined by article 367 of the Criminal Code) DIICOT is the competent body for the criminal investigation in question (see in this regard article 11 from the OUG [Government Ordinance] no. 78/2016). Also, ANAF (National Agency for Fiscal Administration) is responsible for the recovery of the damage or the notification of the criminal investigation bodies. Secret services are not competent to investigate smuggling offenses, but may report to the criminal investigation bodies if they have relevant information.

In the case of contraventions, the competent authority to apply the sanction for contraventions established by the customs regulation is the customs authority [National Agency for Fiscal Administration and the subordinated structures], namely the person empowered by the customs authority. If the customs offenses are found by the police or other bodies responsible for control in places other than the premises of the customs and where operations are under customs supervision, they are required to present once documents attesting to the customs authority closest to the goods subject to the offense (Article 280 of Law no. 86/2006). In the case of contraventions provided by the Tax Code, the competent bodies within the Ministry of Public Finance, through ANAF [National Agency for Fiscal Administration], are found and sanctioned. and its subordinated units, except sanctions on the suspension or revocation of the authorization of tax warehouse, registered consignee, registered consignor or authorized importer, which has competent authority on the proposal of the control. For contravention stipulated by Law 12/1990, establishing offenses and penalties are carried out by officials from the mayor's specialized apparatus, Fiscal Antifraud Directorate General, financial control bodies and the staff of the Romanian Police and Police Romanian Border.

A cooperation protocol was concluded between ANAF and the Public Ministry in 2013, which is still in force. It provides for mutual support regarding the relevant information and data resulting in relation to the possible perpetration of criminal provisions that constitute customs offenses. The protocol also created the framework for setting up of joint teams under the supervision of a prosecutor.

At the same time, the protocol stipulates that anti-fraud inspectors will carry out their activity within the prosecutor's offices, on positions of economic-financial specialists.

Nonetheless, ANAF has the legal obligation to notify the criminal prosecution bodies in case it finds out of a deed that could constitute an offense.

Concerning the effectiveness of cooperation, as can be seen from the mentioned criminological data, it is difficult to assess the magnitude of the phenomenon in Romania. As a consequence, the efficiency of the authorities in combating illicit trade of tobacco products cannot be determined, since the collection of these data has not been systematically and annually carried out by the authorities.

The main problem for the authorities is to determine the chain travelled by tobacco products from the introduction into the country to the final consumer, so that all the persons involved in the illicit trade of tobacco can be held accountable. This is the hard task because such products go through different intermediaries.

Moreover, the introduction of tobacco products is sometimes carried out by citizens of the neighbouring states. As such, the investigation becomes more difficult in the absence of effective cooperation with the neighbouring states.

At the same time, another problem encountered in combating illicit trafficking with tobacco is the lack of personnel and, correlatively, the increase in the volume of work/person related to the cases of illicit trafficking notified, which leads to a longer time to complete the investigations, and thus the effect the deterrent to punishment is diminished.

In view of the problems identified above, the increase of the number of civil servants, the increase of the funds allocated to fight illicit trade, as well as a better cooperation between Romania and the neighbouring states, from which the smuggling cigarettes are being imported into the country, would increase the efficiency of the authorities, consequently reducing the level of illicit trade in tobacco products.

1.10.2 Procedural Rules

The criminal prosecution bodies can proceed *ex officio*, or as a result of a notification from ANAF or any other person. In case of a notification from ANAF, the administrative procedures are suspended, in order to avoid infringing the *ne bis in idem* principle. The next phase is the investigation stage *in rem*, in which criminal investigation is carried out to establish the deed and the person who committed it. The next step is to begin the criminal investigation *in personam*, at which point an individual is officially notified that he is a suspect.

Investigations are still being carried out, and if the evidence shows a reasonable suspicion that an offense has been committed by that particular individual he will be indicted.

Thereafter, the indicted individual has the possibility to conclude a plea-agreement with the prosecutor. In the event that such an agreement is not conclude, the prosecutor will proceed to trial.

The prosecutor, the preliminary chamber judge or the court, can take different preventive measures in order to avoid the concealing, destroying or alienating goods that may be seized or which can serve to guarantee the execution of the fine or the legal expenses or to repair the damage caused by the offense in question (as set forth in article 249 and article 254 of the Criminal procedure code).

The only authority that would have a special competence in prosecuting offenses related to illicit trafficking would be the Border Police. In OUG [Government Ordinance] no. 104/2001, it is stipulated under art. 21 letter u) that it is the Border Police that carries out the criminal investigation activities and, through the criminal investigation bodies of the judicial police within the Romanian Border Police, carries out investigations in connection with them, according to the law, but only in its area of competence.

The area of competence is the area of the national territory consisting of the border area, the surface and the buildings of the airports and ports located inside the country, opened for international traffic, as well as the contiguous area and the exclusive economic zone of Romania, where the Romanian Border Police performs its duties provided by law; as well as the entire territory of the national territory, only for fulfilling the tasks related to the prevention and combating of illegal migration.

There are no specific criminal intelligence activities undertaken by national authorities with regard to investigating illegal trade of tobacco. Even in the pre-trial phase the prosecution body can ask a judge to authorize a special surveillance method consisting in access to a computer system, intercepting communications, phone tapping etc.

Article 138 of the Criminal Code of Procedure provides for the following special surveillance or research methods: (a) intercepting communications or any kind of remote communication; (b) access to a computer system; (c) video, audio or video surveillance; (d) location or tracking by technical means; (e) obtaining data on a person's financial transactions; (f) detention, surrender or search of postal items; (g) use of undercover investigators and collaborators; (h) authorized participation in certain activities; (i) supervised delivery; (j) obtaining traffic and location data processed by providers of public electronic communications networks or providers of publicly available electronic communications services. All these can be used as special investigative techniques in order to obtain evidence in regard to illegal trade of tobacco.

2 Criminological Data

2.1 Offenses

In these annual activity reports no distinction is made between illicit trade of tobacco products and smuggling of other products (e.g. alcohol). Taken into consideration these general official data we cannot conclude in regard to the total number of cases of illicit trade of tobacco products per year (Tables 2 and 3).

Concerning the cases of illicit trade/smuggling of tobacco products following data is available (Tables 4 and 5).

It is worth mentioning that an indictment act may include more than one individual.

Table 2 Criminological data in regard to the number of solved smuggling criminal cases

Year	2011	2012	2013	2014	2015	2016	2017
Number of solved criminal cases regarding smuggling offenses	1657	1766	1774	1908	No available data	No available data	2472

Source: Annual activity reports of the Prosecutor's Office attached to the High Court of Cassation and Justice (Available at http://www.mpublic.ro/ro/content/raport-de-activitate. These annual activity reports are available starting with 2011)

Table 3 Criminological data in regard to the number of pending smuggling criminal cases

Year	2010	2011	2012	2013	2014	2015	2016	2017
Number of pending criminal cases (old cases and new cases)	1052	695	435	463	563	788	588	667

Source: Annual activity reports of the Directorate for Investigating Organized Crime and Terrorism—DIICOT

Also, it must be emphasised that DIICOT investigates offenses regarding illicit trade/smuggling of tobacco products only if they were committed by an organized criminal group (art. 367 of the Criminal Code). According to the 2017 and 2018 annual activity reports of the DIICOT, investigations regarding organized criminal groups who commit crimes related to illicit trade/smuggling of goods represent 3% in 2017 and 2% in 2018 of the total number of investigations conducted by them.

In regard to the estimated financial impact of illicit trade, in particular smuggling, of tobacco products the data is presented in Table 6.

There is no conclusive data available on conviction for illicit trade/smuggling of tobacco products. The only data available is relating to the number of people incarcerated, who were convicted for criminal offenses stipulated in the Romanian Customs Code, but this data in not conclusive because a person might be convicted for illicit trade/smuggling of tobacco and not be serving the sentence in prison, as it was suspended.

Taken into consideration the available data from the annual activity reports of the Directorate for Investigating Organized Crime and Terrorism [DIICOT] we can conclude that customs offenses (provided in Law no. 86/2006) are most often committed in concurrence with the organized criminal group offense (article 367 of the Criminal Code).

The only data available in this regard is relating to the number of people incarcerated, who were convicted for criminal offenses stipulated in the Romanian Customs Code (Law no. 86/2006). There is no data available for any suspended prison sentences or any other penalties or measures applied in regard to perpetrators (Table 7).

There is no available data on the subject of convictions of legal entities.

Also, there is no available data on characteristics of perpetrators of illicit trade of tobacco products.

Table 4 Criminological data in regard to the number of indictment acts and plea-bargains in smuggling criminal cases opened by the Prosecutor's Office attached to the High Court of Cassation and Justice

Year	2009	2010	2011	2012	2013	2014	2015	2016	2017	2018
Number of cases that resulted in an indictment act or a plea-bargains	No available data	No available data	376	383	394	422	No available data	No available data	554	No available data
No. of indicted persons for the offense provided under art. 270 of Law no. 86/2006	123	275	727	879	764	960	1263	1154	1017	1077

Source: Annual activity reports of the Prosecutor's Office attached to the High Court of Cassation and Justice

Table 5 Criminological data in regard to the number of indictment acts and plea-bargains in smuggling criminal cases opened by the Directorate for Investigating Organized Crime and Terrorism - DIICOT

Year	2010	2011	2012	2013	2014	2015	2016	2017	2018
Number of cases that resulted in an indictment act or a plea-bargains	63	42	25	15	24	40	17	25	27
Number of indicted persons	190	223	277	149	162	330	212	237	193

Source: Annual activity reports of the Directorate for Investigating Organized Crime and Terrorism—DIICOT

2.2 *Financial Impact of Illicit Trade*

In the Reports of the Prosecutor's Office attached to the High Court of Cassation and Justice, the damage caused by offenses prosecuted in 2014 was estimated at 51.904.671 lei (cc. 11.7 million euros) and 56.329 euros. The damage caused by offenses prosecuted in 2013 was estimated at 8.000.073 lei (cc. 1.8 million euros), to which is added about 135 million euros.

There is no available data concerning asset recovery related to illicit trade of tobacco products. In the Reports of the Prosecutor's Office attached to the High Court of Cassation and Justice the following data is available:

- in 2017, goods amounting to 58.739.248 lei (cc. 12,9 million euros) were seized and preventive measures were instituted in regard to goods worth 5.000.000 euros;
- in 2014, preventive measures were instituted in regard to goods worth 11.788.763 lei (cc. 2.6 million euros).

In regard to 2015–2016, there is no specific data, and for 2011–2013, the numbers are not broken down for each offense (they also include money laundering, tax evasion etc.).

The annual performance reports of the National Agency for Fiscal Administration [ANAF] specify the following:

- in 2018 were seized 45.3 million pcs. of cigarettes and 609.7 kg of tobacco.
- in 2017 were seized 61.8 million pcs. of cigarettes and 7056.58 kg of tobacco.
- in 2015 were seized 69,531,890 pcs. of cigarettes and 2.53 tons of bulk tobacco.
- in 2014 were seized 62,604,599 pcs. of cigarettes and 10.9 tons of bulk tobacco.

Table 6 Criminological data in regard to smuggling volume quota

Month/Year	Volume quota/smuggling
August 2008	15.8
November 2008	19.6
February 2009	18.2
April 2009	22.2
July 2009	20.1
January 2010	36.2
March 2010	33.9
May 2010	26.8
July 2010	21.3
September 2010	24.4
November 2010	22.8
January 2011	22.5
March 2011	14.7
May 2011	11.8
July 2011	15.7
September 2011	11.8
November 2011	15
January 2012	13
March 2012	13.4
May 2012	13.3
July 2012	12.9
September 2012	14.2
January 2013	15.4
March 2013	13.1
May 2013	12.6
July 2013	11.8
September 2013	15
November 2013	14.1
January 2014	15.7
March 2014	15.8
May 2014	16.1
July 2014	17
September 2014	15.4
November 2014	15.4
January 2014	19.2
March 2015	15.2
May 2015	14.1
July 2015	15.3
September 2015	14.8
November 2015	17.5
January 2016	17.8
March 2016	14.6
May 2016	16.9

Source: Novel Research (Available on https://www.novelresearch.ro/comertul_ilicit/)

3 Exemplary Case of Illicit Trade

A relevant decision is from the Cluj Court of Appeal.[22] The case is exemplary because it illustrates the route of cigarettes from the introduction into the country to the final consumer. Thus, a number of 15 individuals were sent to court and convicted for committing the smuggling offenses [art. 270 para. (1) and (3) with the application of art. 274 of Law 86/2006]. From the total of 15 accused individuals, 7 of them were also accused for being part of an organized criminal group (article 367 of the Criminal Code).

The criminal activity of the defendants is presented in 3 different stages. At Stage 1, an introduction of tobacco products into the country takes place. The first category of defendants is represented by those involved with the introduction of the cigarettes into the country. Thus, the leader of the criminal group was a citizen from a locality near the border (A), a Ukrainian-speaking person, who was traveling to Ukraine and buying cigarettes from Ukrainian citizens. The cigarettes were actually carried across the border by Ukrainian citizens, the defendant along with another person (B), also accused and convicted, ensuring only the safeguard of the route that the Ukrainian citizens were to follow. Cigarettes were transported to B's home. From B's house, part of the cigarettes was subsequently moved to A's house, each of them having to deal with their subsequent distribution. In principle, cigarettes were sold in larger quantities to people who in turn resold them. However, they also sold cigarettes in smaller quantities to final consumers, specifically to people living in the same city as them.

Stage 2 refers to the sale of tobacco products to the first buyers. The second category of defendants is represented by the first buyers of cigarettes, who took them from the defendants A and B, and then wholesale them at a higher price to different other people. In this activity were involved people who only deal with the transport of cigarettes from one location to another, persons also accused and convicted.

Stage 3 consists in the sale of tobacco to the final consumers. The third category of defendants is represented by those who bought the cigarettes from the defendants of the second category, and then they marketed them to the final consumers. These people either traded cigarettes in markets or traded them through the grocery stores they owned.

4 Methods and Other Phenomenological Details Related to Illicit Trade of Tobacco Products

On the website of the Romanian Border Police[23] there is a brief presentation regarding methods of smuggling and the relation to the organised crime.

[22] See Cluj Court of Appeal, criminal section, decision no. 122/2016. www.rolii.ro/hotarari/589b6e14e490095c2f001557. Last accessed 21 April 2020.

[23] See Romanian Border Police website. www.politiadefrontiera.ro. Last accessed 20 April 2020.

Table 7 Criminological data in regard to the number of incarcerated individuals

Month/Year	December 2016	March 2017	December 2018	November 2019
Number of individuals incarcerated for crimes stipulated in the Romanian Customs Code	286	299	258	273

Routes used for smuggling are identifies as follows. At the northern border (Maramureş, Suceava, Satu Mare counties), cigarettes of Ukrainian origin are prevalent, smugglers being organized into real criminal groups, with segments abroad, at the border and inside the country. They are trying to pass the packages of cigarettes over the "green" border, especially at night. At the eastern border (Galaţi, Vaslui, Iaşi, Botoşani counties), cigarettes of origin from the Republic of Moldova are predominant (lower quality cigarettes—Plai, Doina, Plugarul, MT), their introduction into the country being made through border points, either in large quantities, in specially arranged means of transport, or in small quantities individuals. In the south-western counties of the country (Caraş-Severin, Mehedinţi, Timiş), generally, medium and superior quality cigarettes, purchased from duty-free shops and transported across the border, in small quantities by individuals.

In addition, the following methods used for smuggling are identified by the Romanian Border Police. The first one is called "cap" method. It consists in concealing cigarette packages among other categories of goods, legally transited through the border crossing points. Second one is "proofing" of cars with cigarettes, consisting of hiding the packages in their various component parts (tires, side rails, doors, etc.) or the use of double walls. Perpetrators also use concealment of cigarettes in clothing or glued on the body, in other food packaging or in double-bottomed bags. The "cable" method is used in the area of the river border; it involves the passage of cigarette bottoms on a cable fixed on the two banks of the watercourse. In addition, the perpetrators transit the mountainous border area with horse drawn trailers, taking advantage of the difficult accessible mountainous terrain, which makes it difficult for authorities to check the routes. They also use flight devices—moto-hang gliders, or gliders or drone, which are modified for transport of cigarettes across the border.

5 Preventive Measures

The aspects regulated by the Convention and even by the Protocol of 2012 are transposed by Law no. 201/2016 and by Law no. 47/2004. The track & tracing system is in conformity with the protocol and has entered into force as of October 31, 2019. Advertising for tobacco products is prohibited, as stipulated in the Convention, being allowed only in publications exclusively intended for professionals in the trade of tobacco products and in publications that have not been published or printed in Romania or in a Member State of the Union. They are neither European nor intended mainly for the Romanian or the Community market.

The appearance of cigarette packages is regulated in detail, being mandatory to present the warning messages on them (e.g.: smoking kills, etc.), and from this perspective the Romanian legislation being in accordance with the Convention.

The efficiency of the measures is relevant, first of all, from the fact that the appearance of the cigarette package (the fiscal stamp, the language in which the warning messages are played, etc.) can raise the consumer's suspicions about its origin, which would—in theory—discourage him from purchasing such a product. Since there is no retail market, illicit tobacco traffic would be significantly reduced.

But the problem is that although these preventive measures are effective in terms of determining the origin of the cigarettes, they do not discourage people interested in purchasing smuggled products, as they are aware of their source. The main reason they want to buy them is the reduced cost.

In regard to the track and tracing system, being recently implemented (2 months ago), we cannot assess its effectiveness.

The main way to prevent illicit trade of tobacco products is to carry out customs controls, as well as to protect the borders in order to prevent the introduction of products through places other than those established for customs control.

At the same time, the national institutions started a series of national campaigns to fight smuggling and illicit trade, through which citizens were informed about the legal consequences of the purchase/sale of smuggled products, but also about the negative impact on the national economy.

6 Cooperation

In the field of prevention, the relevant national institutions would be the National Agency for Fiscal Administration [ANAF] and Border Police.

As far as ANAF is concerned, the regional customs offices and the customs offices as subordinate units thereof, referred to as customs authorities, are established. The main task of the customs authorities is to carry out customs control of goods imported or removed from the country. Customs control shall be carried out at customs offices and customs posts by the customs authority, under the direction and control of the regional customs directorates and the National Agency for Fiscal Administration.

ANAF has the competence to establish the customs debt as well as to find contraventions and apply the sanctions in question.

According to OUG [Government Emergency Ordinance] no. 104/2001, the Border Police is a part of the Ministry of Administration and Interior and is the specialized institution of the state exercising its powers regarding the supervision and control of the state border crossing, the prevention and combating of illegal migration and the specific facts of cross-border crime committed to the area of competence, respecting the legal regime of the state border, passports and aliens, ensuring the interests of the Romanian state, the contiguous area and the exclusive economic zone, and public peace in the area of competence, under the law.

Between ANAF and the Public Ministry a cooperation Protocol was signed in 2013, which is still in force. It provides for mutual support in relation to relevant information and data on possible deeds which could constitute customs offenses and the establishment of joint teams to act on the basis of action plans under the direction and the coordination of prosecutors.

At the same time, the protocol provides that anti-fraud inspectors will carry out their activity in the prosecutor's offices, as economic and financial specialists.

The ANAF also has the obligation to notify the criminal investigating authorities when it finds that they committed a crime that could constitute an offense.

Concerning the Border Police, the OUG [Government Emergency Ordinance] no. 104/2001 states that annual cooperation protocols can be concluded between the authorities of the local public administration and the territorial units of the border police in order to prevent and combat antisocial deeds. The Border Police General Inspectorate cooperates with central public administration authorities, judicial bodies, other central bodies and institutions of the state, as well as representatives of civil society. On a territorial level, the structures subordinated to the Border Police General Inspectorate cooperate with the local public administration authorities, the judicial bodies, the other state bodies and institutions, the decentralized ministries, as well as representatives of the civil society. Border Police General Inspectorate collects, stores, processes, exploits and exchanges data and information, under the conditions established by the law for the Romanian Police, in order to exercise its legal attributions, with the interested public authorities, on a protocol basis.

The cooperation between the Romanian Border Police and the other structures of the Ministry of Administration and Interior for securing the state border and combating cross-border crime is carried out on the basis of the order of the Minister of Interior.

Concerning ANAF, the Tax Procedure Code provides in article 71 that based on international conventions, tax authorities must cooperate with similar tax authorities in other states. But in the absence of a convention, the tax authorities may grant or may require the collaboration of another tax authority in another State on the basis of reciprocity. ANAF, as an authorized representative of the Ministry of Public Finance or, as the case may be, of the Minister of Public Finance, is the competent authority in Romania to exchange information for fiscal purposes with the states with which Romania has committed itself by a legal instrument international law, other than the Member States of the European Union, for the information provided by those legal instruments of international law.

Concerning the Border Police, the OUG [Government Emergency Ordinance] no. 104/2001 states that the Border Police has the task of concluding treaties, through the General Inspectorate of Border Police, and international cooperation documents with similar authorities from other states in the specific fields of activity, in compliance with the relevant national legislation and relevant international law. Also, the Border Police organizes and carries out cooperation, in the specific fields of activity, with similar bodies of neighbouring states, other states or communities of states, according to bi- or multilateral agreements to which Romania is a party;

Concerning the cooperation with EU Member State institutions, the Customs Code only stipulates that the National Agency for Fiscal Administration is designated as the competent authority to apply to Romania at the date of accession to the European Union the provisions of the Convention on the Use of Information Technology by Customs and the Convention on Mutual Assistance and Cooperation between customs administrations.

Furthermore, Border Police cooperates with the Frontex Agency for securing the external borders of the European Union. In this respect, in OUG [Government Emergency Ordinance] no. 104/2001 it is specified that the Romanian Border Police cooperates with the other structures of the Ministry of Administration and Interior and with other institutions in the system of defence, public order and national security in order to ensure the logistic resources and personnel for the participation to joint operations/activities organized by the Frontex Agency (European Institution) to secure the external borders of the European Union, as required by the mission (see article 25^1).

7 General Issues

A first factor contributing to the illicit trafficking of cigarettes in Romania is the low income, the gross minimum wage being about 300 euros/month, while the incomes from the illicit trafficking of cigarettes are much higher, which corroborated with the lack of jobs in rural areas and especially those close to the borders determine the increase in the level of illicit traffic.

At the same time, in Romania the consumption of tobacco among the population over the age of 15 is 28% (According to Eurobarometer 2017, made by the European Commission and published on the occasion of the World Day without Tobacco), which, again, corroborated with the low incomes, determines people to buy cigarettes from smuggling, because of their lower price.

Concerning the general political and institutional factors which may contribute to the illicit trade of tobacco products in Romania, lack of funds and staff, as well as high corruption both in neighbouring countries and in Romania should be pointed out.

There are some geographical circumstances, which must additionally be mentioned. The first factor contributing to the illicit trafficking of cigarettes in Romania is its geographical positioning, with Romania having longer borders with the states that are not members of the European Union, namely Ukraine, Moldova, Serbia. A second factor is the opening to the Black Sea, through the port of Constanța which is also used to illegally import cigarettes into the country.

The available statistical data indicates that most cigarettes were seized in the South-east area (Constanța port), and North-east and North-west (border with Ukraine and Moldova) as well as in the West zone (border with Serbia).

8 Conclusions

The Romanian legal framework for illicit tobacco trade/smuggling is a complex one. There are a variety of offenses and a problematic partial overlap with the administrative liability. The fact that in some situations the same deed can raise a criminal or an administrative liability puts into question the lack of legal certainty.

Sergiu Bogdan Ph.D., is Professor at the Babeş-Bolyai University, he teaches the following courses: *Criminal Law – Special Part, Business Criminal Law* and *Criminology*; he is also doctoral supervisor in the field of criminal law. He wrote numerous scientific papers in the field of criminal law. Prof. Bogdan is also the founder and leading partner lawyer at "Sergiu Bogdan & Associates" law firm, specialised in criminal law. He is a member of European Criminal Policy Initiative (www.crimpol.eu) and co-author of the Manifesto on European Criminal Policy (first published in ZIS 2009, pp. 697–747, updated in EuCLR 2011, pp. 86–103), the Manifesto on European Criminal Procedure Law (first published in ZIS 2013, pp. 412–446) and the Harmonisation of Criminal Sanctions in the European Union (Herausgegeben von Prof. Dr. Helmut Satzger, Nomos Publishing, 2020).

Prevention and Repression of Illicit Trade in Tobacco Products: Experience of Slovakia

Libor Klimek

Contents

Abstract Illegal smuggling with tobacco products as well as trafficking in drugs are crucial problems of modern society, including the Slovak Republic. The chapter deals with the theoretical and applicable issues of the Illegal smuggling with tobacco products in the Slovak Republic. It is divided into three sections. The first section is focused on national legal framework related to illicit trade in tobacco products.

L. Klimek (✉)
Matej Bel University, Faculty of Law, Department of Criminal Law, Criminology, Criminalistics and Forensic Disciplines, Banská Bystrica, Slovak Republic
e-mail: libor.klimek@umb.sk

C. Nowak (ed.), *Combatting Illicit Trade on the EU Border*,
https://doi.org/10.1007/978-3-030-51019-0_8

While the second section is focused on criminological data, the last third section is focused on preventive measures.

1 National Legal Framework Related to Illicit Trade in Tobacco Products

1.1 Substantive Law Issues

1.1.1 Combatting Illegal Smuggling of Tobacco Products

Illegal smuggling of tobacco products as well as trafficking in drugs are crucial problems of modern society, including the Slovak Republic.[1] Combatting the illegal smuggling of tobacco products in the Slovak Republic is a threefold system—the application of tax law, the application of criminal law and the application of administrative law. At the outset, it should be noted that the reality shows that illegal smuggling of tobacco products is investigated in major cases according to tax law by customs officers as an administrative offence under Act No. 106/2004 Coll. on Excise Duty on Tobacco Products (details below).

1.1.1.1 Tax Law (Applicable in the Majority of Cases)

The special law regulating taxes in the area of tobacco products is Act No. 106/2004 Coll. on Excise Duty on Tobacco Products.[2] This Act regulates excise taxation on tobacco products; moreover, it regulates special provisions on administrative offences.

Illegal smuggling of tobacco products is prohibited under Articles 40 and 41a of the Act No. 106/2004 Coll. on Excise Duty on Tobacco Products.

Under Article 41 entitled "Administrative offenses", an administrative offense is committed by a person authorised to do business if this person (among others):

- is not in a position to demonstrate, in accordance with the law, the origin or method of acquiring the tobacco products found in his/her possession, whether or not he/she handles tobacco products as his/her own;
- is unable to demonstrate, in accordance with that law, the origin or method of acquiring the tobacco raw material found in his/her possession, whether or not it is in its own right, whether or not he/she handles tobacco raw material;
- produces tobacco products without permission to operate a tax warehouse.

[1]Holcr et al. (2008), p. 294.

[2]Slovak: Zákon Národnej rady Slovenskej republiky č. 106/2004 Z. z. o spotrebnej dani z tabakových výrobkov v znení neskorších predpisov.

In all cases the Customs Office shall impose a fine for this offense from €100 to €1,000,000. In determining the amount of the fine, the Customs Office shall take into account the seriousness, duration and consequences of the illegal conduct.

Under Article 41a entitled "Offenses", an offense is committed by a natural person who is not entitled to do business if he/she (among others):

- sells, offers for sale, stores or transports consumer packaging of tobacco products that are not marked in accordance with this Act and special law (i.e. the Decree of the Ministry of Finance of the Slovak Republic No. 254/2014 Coll., laying down the particulars, preparation and price of a control mark intended for labelling consumer packaging of tobacco products[3]);
- marks consumer packaging of tobacco products with counterfeit control marks;
- is not in a position to demonstrate, in accordance with the law, the origin or mode of acquisition of tobacco products found in his/her possession, whether or not he/she handles tobacco products as his/her own;
- is unable to demonstrate, in accordance with the law, the origin or method of acquiring the tobacco raw material found in his/her possession, whether or not it is in its own right, whether or not he/she handles tobacco raw material;
- is not able to demonstrate, in accordance with that law, the origin or method of acquiring a smokeless tobacco product found in his/her possession, or whether or not it is a smokeless tobacco product.

For the above-mentioned offenses, the Customs Office shall impose a fine from €50 to €50,000. Similarly, in determining the amount of the fine, the Customs Office shall take into account the seriousness, duration and consequences of the illegal conduct.

1.1.1.2 Criminal Law

Illegal smuggling of tobacco products is addressed by the Criminal Code No. 300/2005 Coll.[4] Illegal smuggling of tobacco products is prohibited under Article 279 of the Criminal Code entitled "Violation of Regulations on State Technical Measures on Marking Goods", which stipulates that any person with control marks, control tapes or other technical control measures to identify goods for tax purposes or for other purposes stipulated by law shall, in contravention of the generally binding legal regulations, intend to cause other damage or to obtain for themselves or others an unlawful benefit or who, in a manner inconsistent with generally binding legal regulations, imports, exports, transports, puts into circulation

---

[3]Slovak: Vyhláška Ministerstva financií Slovenskej republiky č. 254/2014 Z. z., ktorou sa ustanovujú náležitosti, vyhotovenie a cena kontrolnej známky určenej na označovanie spotrebiteľského balenia tabakových výrobkov.

[4]Slovak: Zákon Národnej rady Slovenskej republiky č. 300/2005 Z. z., Trestný zákon v znení neskorších predpisov.

or stores goods without control marks, control tapes or without other technical control measures for its labelling for tax purposes or for other purposes stipulated by law shall be punished with imprisonment of 6 months to 3 years. This crime can by committed only intentionally.[5]

Further, the offender shall be subject to a term of imprisonment of 1–5 years if he/she commits the above-mentioned offense in special circumstances, namely if he/she caused greater damage,[6] or with a specific motive, or by a more serious procedure.

Furthermore, the offender shall be liable for a term of imprisonment of 3–8 years if he/she commits the above-mentioned offence causing large-scale damage, or as a member of a dangerous group.

1.1.1.3 Administrative Law

Measures combatting illegal smuggling of tobacco products by administrative law are rarely applicable, but possible some cases. This is stipulated by Act No. 372/1990 Coll. on Offences (i.e. Act on Administrative Offences).[7] Illegal smuggling of tobacco products is prohibited under Article 30(1) of the Act No. 372/1990 Coll. on Offences (i.e. on Administrative Offences) entitled "Offenses in the Area of Protection Against Alcoholism and Other Toxicants", which stipulates that an offense has committed by the offender if he/she:

(a) sells, facilitates or otherwise allows the consumption of alcoholic beverages to a person who is clearly affected by an alcoholic beverage or other addictive substance, a person under the age of eighteen, or a person who knows that he or she will engage in labour or any other activity that could endanger human health or property;
(b) sells, facilitates or otherwise allows another person to engage in the harmful use of an addictive substance other than alcohol;

[5]Klátik et al. (2018), p. 179; Ivor et al. (2017), p. 257.

[6]Under Article 124 of the Criminal Code for criminal law purposes the term *damage* shall mean damage to property or a real loss of property or rights of the injured party, or any other damage that is causally related to the offense, regardless of whether it is damage to property or rights. Moreover, damage shall mean also obtaining a benefit in a causal relationship with a criminal offense. In addition, damage shall mean also damage to profits which would otherwise be injured or otherwise justified by the circumstances. Under Article 125 of the Criminal Code *minor damage* means damage exceeding €266; *larger damage* is an amount of at least ten times that amount; *significant damage* shall mean an amount of at least 100 times that amount; *large-scale damage* shall mean an amount of at least five times that amount. These considerations apply equally to determining the amount of the benefit, the value of the case and the extent of the act. If, in a particular part, the Criminal Code requires damage to be caused as a material fact/material consequence of the offense and does not state its amount, it shall be deemed to be at least *minor damage*.

[7]Slovak: Zákon Národnej rady Slovenskej republiky č. 372/1990 Zb. o priestupkoch v znení neskorších predpisov.

(c) is not subject to a measure affecting the excessive consumption of alcoholic beverages or the use of other addictive substances;
(d) deliberately produces spirit or distillate without permission, or delivers or puts into circulation spirit or distillate produced without authorization;
(e) deliberately allows an alcoholic drink or other addictive substance to be consumed by a person under the age of eighteen if it is threatening that person's physical or moral development;
(f) consumes an alcoholic beverage or another addictive substance, even though he/she knows that he/she will be engaged in labour or any other activity that could endanger human health or damage property;
(g) performs the activity referred to in point (f) upon consumption of an alcoholic beverage or the use of another addictive substance;
(h) in a state of intoxication which he/she has brought about by consuming an alcoholic beverage or by using another addictive substance, he/she performs the activity referred to in point (f).

For an offense under sections (a)(b)(c)(d)(f), a fine may be imposed of up to SKK 3000 (approx. €100); for (e)(g) a fine of up to SKK 5000 (approx. €166) and for an offense under paragraph 1(h) a fine of up to SKK 10,000 (approx. €333); a ban on activities up to 6 months may be imposed for an offense under paragraph 1(f), a ban on activities up to 1 year for an offense under paragraph 1(g) and a ban on activities up to 2 years for the offense referred to in paragraph 1(h).

1.2 Application of ne bis in idem *Principle*

The principle of *ne bis in idem* is applicable at both national and international (European) level.[8] The decision of which law is applicable in an administrative or criminal investigation is a matter for the competent officers. In principle, if somebody has been investigated under the administrative law system, there is no possibility to investigate that person for the same act under the criminal law system; if somebody has been investigated under the criminal law system, there is no possibility to investigate that individual for the same act under the administrative law system. This principle is applicable only in the same case, but in a new case an alternative system can be applied.

If the perpetrators of illicit trade of tobacco products are investigated under criminal law rules, they may be investigated as well for fraud, corruption, possession of proceeds obtained from crime, association in an organised criminal group, money laundering, or unauthorised business.

Naturally, each case is individual. One could not state that all perpetrators of illicit trade in tobacco products are investigated for the above-mentioned crimes, but in

[8]Ivor et al. (2013), p. 132; Klimek (2017), p. 130.

individual cases it is possible. For example, the perpetrators bribe customs officers, or they are members of an organised criminal group.

1.2.1 Legal Responsibility

1.2.1.1 Legal Responsibility of Individuals: Administrative Law Perspective

Administrative law responsibility of individuals in the case of illegal smuggling of tobacco products is set out by the Act No. 372/1990 Coll. on Offences. This act is a general act (*lex generalis*) regulating the responsibility of individuals for administrative offences, since it is a general law regulating conditions for the commission of all administrative offences defined in this Act, as well as in all special acts defining other administrative offences. In comparison to criminal law, where all crimes are defined only in the Criminal Code, in administrative law Act No. 372/1990 Coll. on Offences is the general act, and in addition to this Act there exist many special administrative acts defining special administrative offences; all special acts—including the Act No. 106/2004 Coll. on Excise Duty on Tobacco Products, which provides for administrative offences—follow the rules on administrative responsibility of individuals as defined in the Act No. 372/1990 Coll. on Offences.

As regards individuals, according to the Act No. 372/1990 Coll. on Offences, there are two conditions for committing an administrative offence under all administrative acts in the Slovak Republic:

- the age of 15 years or above; and
- competency (i.e. competency at the time of commission of the offence).

Responsibility for administrative offense is assessed under the law effective at the time of the commission of the offense; it can be considered under a later law only if that law is more favourable for the offender (the same principle applies in the criminal law system). Under the Act No. 106/2004 Coll. on Excise Duty on Tobacco Products, negligence is a satisfactory condition for responsibility for the above-mentioned offences.

1.2.1.2 Legal Responsibility of Individuals: Criminal Law Perspective

Criminal law responsibility of individuals in respect of illegal smuggling of tobacco products is set out by the Criminal Code No. 300/2005 Coll. The Criminal Code is the only national law defining all crimes and criminal responsibility of individuals in the Slovak Republic.

As regards individuals, according to the Criminal Code, there are two conditions for committing crime under Article 279 of the Criminal Code, i.e. Violation of Regulations on State Technical Measures on Marking Goods:

- the age of 14 years or above; it should be noted that a juvenile younger than 15 years of age who, at the time of the offense, has not attained a level of intellectual and moral maturity sufficient to recognise the illegality of or exercise control over his/her conduct is not responsible for his/her act; and
- competency (i.e. competency at the time of commission of the act).

In comparison to other crimes in the Criminal Code, the above-mentioned conditions are applicable to all crimes, except for one entitled Sexual Abuse (the Criminal Code requires the age of 15 years or above).[9]

Responsibility for a crime is assessed under the law effective at the time of the commission of the act; it can be considered under a later law only if that law is more favourable for the offender (the same principle applies in the administrative law system). The Criminal Code requires intentional commission of the crime defined in Article 279.

1.2.1.3 Legal Responsibility of Legal Persons: Administrative Law Perspective

In general, administrative responsibility of legal persons exists in the legal system of the Slovak Republic. A legal person is responsible for the conduct of its employees, members, statutory representatives, etc. within the scope of its tasks. This applies to all administrative delicts, including the above-mentioned administrative delicts. The condition for administrative responsibility of legal persons is delinquency, which is associated with its establishment and existence.

There is a practical problem. Any legal person, in particular commercial companies, may deliberately avoid responsibility for committed administrative offenses, and in consequence avoid sanctions. It can convert, for example, in the form of a merger. It may be the case that the same or partially same circle of persons (owners, shareholders, persons in statutory bodies) continues to operate with the same property as a new legal entity.

1.2.1.4 Legal Responsibility of Legal Persons: Criminal Law Perspective

In general, criminal responsibility of legal persons exists in the legal system of the Slovak Republic (the Slovak Republic was one of the last European Union Member States to introduce it). As stated above, their criminal responsibility is regulated by a special law—the Act No. 91/2016 Coll. on Criminal Responsibility of Legal Persons.[10] This act contains a list of crimes under the Criminal Code for which legal persons as well can be responsible under criminal law. However, the list does not

---

[9]Klátik et al. (2018), p. 105; Ivor et al. (2017), p. 135.

[10]Záhora and Šimovček (2019), p. 17.

include Article 279 of the Criminal Code, i.e. Violation of Regulations on State Technical Measures on Marking Goods. Indeed, in the Slovak Republic, responsibility for the above-mentioned crime in the case of legal persons is not possible; it only applies in the case of individuals.

1.2.2 Disposal or Destruction of Confiscated Tobacco Products

Destruction of confiscated tobacco products is simple—the Slovak Republic employs incineration (burning out) of confiscated tobacco products in so-called incineration houses.

Seized tobacco products shall be incinerated (burned out) in special incineration houses under the control of a special committee. One such house is located in Košice (the second largest city in the Slovak Republic). For example, in October 2016, customs officers in Košice burned out over 430,000 seized cigarettes with a total weight of 570 kg and valued at €66,244. The seized cigarettes were mostly the subject of smuggling, revealed by customs officers in the exercise of customs supervision.

On the other hand, there are many problems. For example, some officers "steal" seized tobacco products and smoke them, or even sell them.

1.3 Slovak Republic and WTO Framework Convention on Tobacco Control and the 2012 Protocol to the Framework Convention on Tobacco Control

The Slovak Republic is a party to the Framework Convention on Tobacco Control of 2003. It was signed on 19 December 2003 and ratified on 4 May 2004. It is established in national law as Decree No. 84/2005 Coll.

As regards the Protocol to the Framework Convention on Tobacco Control of 2012, the President of the Slovak Republic signed accession to the Protocol on 19 July 2017. The Protocol was opened for signatures from 10 January 2013 to 9 January 2014 and was signed by 53 States as well as the European Union. The Slovak Republic did not sign the protocol within the set deadline, but pursuant to Article 44(1) of the Protocol "it shall be open for accession from the day after the date on which the Protocol is closed for signature". The protocol was ratified by the Slovak Republic on 25 September 2017. It is established in national law as Decree No. 255/2018 Coll.

It should be noted that according to Article 7(4) of the Constitution of the Slovak Republic No. 460/1992 Coll.,[11] the Framework Convention on Tobacco Control of

[11]Slovak: Zákon Slovenskej národnej rady č. 460/1992 Zb., Ústava Slovenskej republiky v znení neskorších predpisov.

2003 as well as the Protocol to the Framework Convention on Tobacco Control of 2012 are international treaties, the implementation of which requires national law, and therefore in accordance with Article 86(d) of the Constitution they were subject to the approval of the National Council of the Slovak Republic and subsequent ratification by the President of the Slovak Republic.

In principle, Slovak national law is aligned with the requirements set forth in the above-mentioned documents. Since the Protocol to the Framework Convention on Tobacco Control of 2012 is ratified as international treaty, its provisions are recognised in Slovak national law, including definitions stipulated in Article 14 entitled "Unlawful conduct including criminal offences". On the other hand, Slovak national practice accepts, primarily, only definitions of crimes as set out in the Criminal Code. However, the Criminal Code does not follow (i.e. does not "copy") the provisions contained in Article 14 of Protocol to the FCTC of 2012.

2 Procedural Law Issues

2.1 General Overview

The most important body in the Slovak Republic combatting illicit trade in tobacco products is the Financial Administration of the Slovak Republic.[12]

The main task of the Financial Administration of the Slovak Republic is to efficiently collect and administer customs duties and taxes in the Slovak Republic and to protect the economic interests of the State. Its special tasks are based on the programme of the Government of the Slovak Republic, the Program Declaration of the Government of the Slovak Republic and the strategic intentions of the Ministry of Finance of the Slovak Republic. The Financial Administration of the Slovak Republic shall:

- perform the tasks arising from the main mission of financial administration, in particular, in the area of ⍰⍰customs and tax avoidance,
- supervise compliance with generally binding EU legislation and international agreements to ensure the implementation of trade policy, customs policy, tax policy and common agricultural policy in the circulation of goods in contact with third States;
- perform customs supervision of goods within the customs territory of the EU, in the field of indirect tax administration, tax supervision of excise goods;
- perform mutual international assistance and cooperation in the management of customs and taxation and in the recovery of financial claims;

[12]Slovak: Finančná správa Slovenskej republiky.

- perform tasks in the areas of customs tariffs, customs value, nomenclature classification of goods, origin of goods, statistics of trade with third countries and trade between EU Member States; and
- perform other tasks laid down by specific regulations.

The Financial Administration of the Slovak Republic was established on 1 January 2012 by merging the former customs administration and tax administration. Its establishment was preceded by approval of the reform of the customs administration and the tax administration with a view to unifying the collection of taxes, customs and insurance contributions through the UNITAS program, which was initiated in 2008 by the adoption of the Resolution of the Government of the Slovak Republic No. 285/2008 of 7 May 2008 on the Concept of Tax and Customs Reform.

The legal basis of the Financial Administration of the Slovak Republic is the Act No. 333/2011 Coll. on State Administration Bodies in the Area of Taxes, Fees and Customs.[13] Under this Act, the Financial Administration of the Slovak Republic ensures the performance of tasks in accordance with: first, the Act No. 333/2011 Coll. on State Administration Bodies in the Area of Taxes, Fees and Customs and Act No. 479/2009 Coll. on State Administration Bodies in the Field of Taxes and Fees; second, the Act No. 652/2004 Coll. on State Administration Bodies in Customs; third, other generally binding legal regulations; and, fourth, international agreements by which the Slovak Republic is bound.

The Financial Administration of the Slovak Republic is structured thus:

- the Financial Directorate of the Slovak Republic—whose headquarters is in Banská Bystrica (a city in the central part of the Slovak Republic); its statutory body is the President, which is its director/manager, and he/she is responsible to the Minister of Finance of the Slovak Republic;
- Customs Offices;[14]
- Tax Offices;[15] and
- the Criminal Office of the Financial Administration. It is headquartered in Bratislava (the capital of the Slovak Republic). The Director is in charge of the Criminal Office—he/she is responsible to the President of the Financial Administration of the Slovak Republic.

According to Article 5 of the Act No. 333/2011 Coll. on State Administration Bodies in the Area of Taxes, Fees and Customs the competences Criminal Office of the Financial Administration are (among others):

[13]Slovak: Zákon Národnej rady Slovenskej republiky č. 333/2011 Z. z. o orgánoch štátnej správy v oblasti daní, poplatkov a colníctva v znení neskorších predpisov.

[14]See list of all Customs Offices available online <https://www.financnasprava.sk/sk/kontakt/kontakty-na-urady>.

[15]See list of all Tax Offices available online <https://www.financnasprava.sk/sk/kontakt/kontakty-na-urady>.

- it shall execute the tasks of a central coordination unit and other tasks deriving from international agreements,
- it shall execute tasks in the fight against the illicit import, export and transit of narcotic drugs, psychotropic substances, their precursors, protected plant species, animals and specimens, against the illicit transport of radioactive materials and other highly hazardous materials, if the detection of persons are in any way involved in offenses committed in the field of narcotic drugs, psychotropic substances, their precursors and protected species of plants, animals and specimens in connection with their import, export or transit;
- it shall execute customs supervision in agreement with the authorities of other States, with escorts or other classified means of surveillance, if it is reasonable to assume that the consignment contains narcotics, psychotropic substances, their precursors, tobacco, tobacco products, protected plant species, animals and specimens for which there is no relevant authorisation or other possession of which special permission is required, goods suspected of being involved in the commission of a tax or customs offense, items intended to commit an offense or a criminal offense, or where international contact is necessary in order to identify persons who are involved in the handling of the shipment; if the information thus obtained is to serve as evidence in criminal proceedings, it is based on the rules of international cooperation of judicial authorities in criminal matters;
- it shall execute cross-border surveillance and cross-border persecution to the extent and under the conditions laid down by a special regulation and international treaty;
- it shall execute tasks in the field of detection and investigation of crimes committed in connection with violations of value added tax legislation on imports and excise duties or customs regulations and the detection of their perpetrators;
- it shall ensure the safety of the transport of seized goods, perform escorts of detained or remanded persons suspected of committing a crime.

2.2 *Real Work*

Every fourteenth cigarette in the Slovak Republic is illegal. Indeed, the Financial Administration of the Slovak Republic and its bodies have too much work to do.

As regards illicit trade in tobacco products, while it was only 1% in 2014, it increased to 6% in 2018. Consumers in the Slovak Republic do not realise that it is precisely this kind of source that criminal groups use to fund their illegal activities.

According to information collected by the Financial Administration of the Slovak Republic on the fight against illegal cigarettes, more than 2.2 million cigarettes were seized directly at the eastern border with Ukraine in 2015—worth €66,000. These are just cigarettes from Ukraine without EU valid stamps. In 2016 it was considerably less—1.2 million cigarettes worth €38,000. Since the beginning of 2019, over 400 cases on the eastern border with Ukraine have been identified, in which officers have seized more than 1.3 million illegal cigarettes. "We know from practice that cigarettes are the most common commodity. In the east of Slovakia they are a smuggling classic", explained Tomáš Prochocký, General Director of the Customs Financial Administration. He added that "customs officers in the field are confronted with truly inventive smuggling shelters, in tires, bicycle frames, pastries, juices, wooden boards, metal pipes . . . but with years of experience and convenient modern technology, we can uncover these hiding places. Especially on the eastern border our work is very important, because we protect the security and interests of the citizens of the whole EU".[16]

However, the fight against illegal cigarettes is not just about smuggling cigarettes from Ukraine to Slovakia. In fact, the Slovak Republic has already identified several cases of illegal production in Slovakia. "We have had a number of successful interventions against illegal cigarette production. Only this year [2019] we prevented almost 30 million illegal cigarettes, 30 tons of tobacco and thousands of cigars from reaching the European market. In addition, we also made raids in two factories and seized complete cigarette production lines. Indeed, we destroyed the perpetrators' illegal business" said Ľudovít Makó, Director of the Criminal Office of the Financial Administration. He also explained: "The Slovak Republic is a transit country for illegal cigarettes. Most illegal cigarettes go further to Europe – to the UK, Germany, Poland or the Czech Republic."[17]

In addition, even the illegal production of cigarettes in the Slovak Republic with the use of illegally imported tobacco is not exceptional. For example, in 2016 customs officers seized more than 2 tonnes of tobacco, from which 2.3 million cigarettes could be produced. The tax evasion would have amounted to €170,000. Such cigarettes are generally more dangerous than regular cigarettes.

2.3 Specific Procedural Issues Regarding Investigation and Prosecution of Illegal Trade in Tobacco

The competent body for investigations in the majority cases is the Financial Administration of the Slovak Republic—its Criminal Office of the Financial Administration.

The Act No. 333/2011 Coll. on State Administration Bodies in the Area of Taxes, Fees and Customs does not regulate special provisions on procedural rules and investigations; in Article 8, it "only" states that investigator(s) shall respect the Constitution of the Slovak Republic, national law, ratified international agreements,

[16]Až každá štrnásta cigareta na Slovensku je nelegálna [online] (translation – Every fourteenth cigarette in Slovakia is illegal). Available <https://www.financnasprava.sk/sk/pre-media/novinky/archiv-noviniek/detail-novinky/_fejky-cig-ts>.

[17]Nelegálne cigarety [online] (translation – Illegal Cigarettes). Available <https://www.szzv.sk/az-kazda-strnasta-cigareta-na-slovensku-je-nelegalna-na-vychodnom-dokonca-kazda-tretia/>.

etc. Special rules are regulated by so-called "internal law", i.e. law adopted by the Financial Administration of the Slovak Republic for its own "internal" purposes.

The Criminal Office of the Financial Administration has special investigators, i.e. investigators of the Criminal Office of the Financial Administration. In accordance with Article 10(b) of the Criminal Proceedings Code, he/she is a customs officer who has been appointed as a financial administration investigator by the Minister of Finance of the Slovak Republic. Such investigators carry out investigations into crimes committed in connection with violations of customs or tax regulations within the scope of customs administration, as well as offenses committed in connection with customs or tax violations.

The Criminal Office of the Financial Administration can set up a special group called an *itinerant group*. This is a special group working with technical means. Its mission encompasses urgent actions and one-off cases. The group's exercises are carried out continuously, according to planned schedules for a period of 1 month.

Criminal intelligence activities in the Slovak Republic are connected to combatting illegal smuggling of tobacco products. They are performed by the Slovak Information Service (hereinafter SIS). The SIS is regulated by the Act No. 46/1993 Coll. on the Slovak Information Service.[18] This Act regulates official provisions on its establishment, tasks, structure, etc., however, there is no operational or procedural information about how it works.

The annual reports of the SIS provide information on results for specific years, but almost all information is vague (no detailed information, no reference numbers of cases, no detailed figures, etc.). As regards illicit trade in tobacco, in the Annual Report of the Slovak Information Service of 2018,[19] we can find the following statements:

- The SIS informed recipients about the distribution of cigarettes produced on illegal routes in western Slovakia. As part of the detection of crime related to the distribution of non-taxed cigarettes, the SIS also received information on the import of smuggled cigarettes into the territory of the Slovak Republic from Ukraine and Hungary.
- The SIS sent information to the relevant national authorities on tax fraud organisers who avoided value added tax (VAT) and corporate income tax through a network of interconnected companies or unduly benefited from excessive VAT deductions. It also involved cigarette smuggling, illegal production and sale of non-taxed spirits, cigarettes and mineral oils.

The SIS also examined suspicions of corruption in the police, courts and financial administration. The relevant knowledge concerned, for example, members of the Police corps who allegedly cooperated with organised crime groups in smuggling

[18]Slovak: Zákon Národnej rady Slovenskej republiky č. 46/1993 Z. z. o Slovenskej informačnej službe v znení neskorších predpisov.

[19]Správa o činnosti SIS za rok 2018, Bratislava, 2019. Available online <http://www.sis.gov.sk/pre-vas/sprava-o-cinnosti-2018.html>.

goods through the Slovak-Ukrainian border in exchange for bribes, provided official information to unauthorised persons and engaged in activities aimed at obstructing related criminal investigations.

2.4 Special Investigative Techniques Which May Be Used with Regard to Investigations of Illegal Trade in Tobacco

In practice, electronic surveillance is used, especially along the eastern border with Ukraine, because it is an external border of the Schengen area—the only external border on Slovak territory. However, at night it is difficult to "see" the movement of smugglers. Officers use also special radars.

Many times controlled deliveries have been used, for example in cases of smuggling from Ukraine to the Slovak Republic through the eastern (Slovak-Ukrainian) border. Moreover, it has been used many times in the Schengen area, for example in cooperation with Hungary.

2.5 Preventive Measures That Are Applied in Criminal Proceedings with Regard to Perpetrators of Illicit Trade

Under the Criminal Proceedings Code, the taking of funds (money) in bank account (s) is possible; the Code uses the terminology "seizure" (rather than "freezing"). The procedure is regulated by Article 95, which stipulates that if the facts indicate that the funds in an account at the bank or at the branch of a foreign bank or other funds are intended or have been used to commit an offense, or are proceeds of commission of a crime, a judge may issue an order to the prosecutor that the funds shall be seized. The order described in the preceding sentence may also apply to additional funds received to the account, including of accessories, if the reason for detention also applies to them. Seizure cannot apply to funds that are necessary to satisfy the basic living needs of the accused or the person from whom they were seized, to meet the living needs of a person whose upbringing or maintenance they are responsible for, or the person from whom the funds are secured is required by law to look after them.

If there are no longer grounds for seizing the funds, the seizure is revoked. If there are no longer grounds for seizing a specified amount of funds, the seizure shall be limited. The judge and the prosecutor shall decide on the revocation or limitation of the seizure by order.

Seized funds may only be disposed of after the prior written consent of the judge and in the pre-trial proceedings of the prosecutor. If the seizure continues, all legal acts and claims against secured funds are ineffective. The person whose funds were seized has the right to request the revocation or limitation of the procedure. The judge and the prosecutor shall rule without delay on such a request. A complaint is admissible against this decision. If the application is rejected, the person whose funds have been seized may, if he/she does not provide other reasons, resubmit it 30 days after the date on which the decision on the previous application entered into force.

Moreover, under the Criminal Proceedings Code it is possible to order a house search. The procedure is regulated by Articles 99 and 100. They stipulate that a house search can be carried out if there is reason to believe that there is a matter of importance in the apartment or other housing serving or in the premises belonging thereto, or that a person suspected of having committed the crime is hiding there, or the securing of movable property to satisfy the injured party's claim for damages. The house search shall be ordered by the judge in pre-trial proceedings on its own initiative or at the request of the prosecutor. The house search shall be carried out without delay by the authority which ordered it, or by a police officer at the authority's command.

In addition, the Criminal Proceedings Code allows for the search of other premises and parcels of land. The procedure is regulated by Article 101, which stipulates that either a judge or the prosecution with the consent of a police officer may order the search of other premises and parcels of land. The order must be issued in writing and must be justified. It shall be delivered to the owner or user of the premises or land or to his/her staff during the search. The search of other premises or land shall be carried out without delay by the authority which ordered it or by a police officer at the authority's command. Without an order or consent, a police officer may only search other premises or land if the order or consent cannot be obtained in advance and the matter cannot be delayed, or if the person is caught in the commission of a criminal offense, or there is an arrest warrant for the person, or the person is believed to be hiding in these areas.

3 Criminological Data

In the Slovak Republic there is no free, publicly available database containing criminological information regarding illicit trade in tobacco products.

For example, in 2014 customs officers seized a total of 19,481,493 smuggled cigarettes; the total financial loss for 2014 was calculated at €1,941,440.85.

The most problematic situation is on the eastern border with Ukraine. In the past, smugglers created a hidden tunnel almost 700 m long—they dug it without approval underneath the border. All kinds of customs goods were transported, including tobacco products. The tunnel was used for 2 years. The newest method used by smugglers are drones (flying machines) carrying smuggled products across borders.

As regards the characteristics of perpetrators of illicit trade in tobacco products in the Slovak Republic, smugglers come from all social "levels". Many smugglers on the Slovak-Ukrainian border have simple strategies, for example:

- Groups of friends behave like tourists taking a walk in nature. They cross borders with touristic backpacks, buy tobacco products in Ukraine and walk back to Slovakia through the forest. This is a common procedure.
- Many smugglers have renovated cars to add special compartments for cigarettes. They legally cross the border from Slovakia to Ukraine, legally buy customs goods and then claim that they were shopping for cheaper products in Ukraine. The reality is that they are smuggling hidden tobacco products. This is a common procedure.

Even the husband of a Ukrainian diplomat smuggled tobacco products by car, and at border stated that the car enjoyed diplomatic immunity; indeed, it was not possible to search it. The Slovak authorities contacted Ukrainian central authorities, who allowed to search him and his car, where almost 60,000 packages of cigarettes from Ukraine were found worth approx. €30,000.

4 Preventive Measures

Restrictions on tobacco advertising are regulated by Article 6(1) of the Act No. 147/2001 Coll. on Advertising,[20] which stipulates that the advertising of tobacco products shall be prohibited:

- on all types of informational media;
- through distribution of tobacco products to the public;
- on non-smoking advertising media which are distributed to the public, other than advertising distributed at points of sale of products;
- through tobacco product sponsorship;
- through indication of the trademark, emblem, name or other significant feature of a tobacco product aside from its presentation at points of sale of tobacco products.

As a result, in the Slovak Republic there is almost zero commercial advertising of tobacco products. This approach is welcomed. Supervision of compliance with the cited provisions is carried out by the Slovak Trade Inspection.[21]

Since 2017, special markings of packages are used in the Slovak Republic, i.e. special pictures on packages of cigarettes. They replaced earlier simple written warning on packages, such as "Smoking can kill!". However, even though the packages have disgusting pictures, many people ignore them.

The Financial Administration of the Slovak Republic (details about this body are presented above) initiated the project *Don't Smoke Fakes* and made the relevant information available online at <https://nekurfejky.sk>. It adapted the language on the site to a younger audience so that all information was given clearly and

---

[20]Slovak: Zákon Národnej rady Slovenskej republiky č. 147/2001 Z. z. o reklame v znení neskorších predpisov.

[21]Slovak: Slovenská obchodná inšpekcia.

comprehensibly. The creators of the idea chose the name "Don't Smoke Fakes" ("*Nekur fejky*") intentionally to attract attention and also because the problem of illegal cigarettes concerns primarily eastern Slovakia, where, according to analyses of the Financial Administration of the Slovak Republic, almost every third package of cigarettes is illegal.

Moreover, the Slovak Republic adopted legislation protecting non-smokers—the Act No. 377/2004 Coll. on the Protection of Non-smokers.[22] This Act regulates, first, the conditions for protecting people from becoming addicted to nicotine as an addictive and harmful ingredient found in tobacco and tobacco products, from the harmful effects of smoking, and from other uses of tobacco products that harm the health of smokers who are directly exposed to smoke; and second, conditions for protecting people against products intended for smoking and not containing tobacco.

According to Article 7 of the Act No. 377/2004 Coll. on the Protection of Non-smokers smoking is prohibited:

- in public airports, in public passenger rail vehicles, in passenger transport vehicles, in station and stopping areas, waiting rooms, shelters and stops, covered platforms and closed public spaces related to such traffic for passengers, on open platforms within four meters of the defined platform area;
- in health establishments other than reserved smoking areas in psychiatric wards;
- in primary schools, secondary schools and school facilities, pre-school establishments and playgrounds;
- in universities and student hostels;
- in social services establishments other than smokers;
- in theatres, cinemas, exhibition halls, museums, galleries and other cultural establishments, sports facilities and shops;
- in official buildings other than reserved smoking areas;
- in department stores, except in areas that are structurally separate so that no harmful substances from tobacco products nor their smoke and tar from smoking and/or non-tobacco products enter nor pollute publicly accessible department stores;
- in mass catering facilities other than those which have at least 50% of space reserved for non-smokers in an area that is structurally separate from the smokers' compartment, so that no harmful substances from tobacco products or smoke or tar, nor from products that are intended to be smoked and do not contain tobacco are introduced into the smoke-free area, while the non-smoking area must be located at the entrance to the facility;
- in health care facilities; and
- in areas where juveniles are in custody or serving a custodial sentence.

On top of all the above-mentioned provisions, the Slovak Republic has also implemented European Union legal measures, for example:

---

[22]Slovak: Zákon Národnej rady Slovenskej republiky č. 147/2001 Z. z. 377/2004 Z. z. o ochrane nefajčiarov v znení neskorších predpisov.

- Council Directive 2008/118/EC concerning the general arrangements for excise,[23]
- Council Directive 2011/64/EU on the structure and rates of excise duty applied to manufactured tobacco,[24]
- Council Directive 2007/74/EC on the exemption from value added tax and excise duty of goods imported by persons travelling from third countries[25] and
- Council Directive 2006/79/EC on the exemption from taxes of imports of small consignments of goods of a non-commercial character from third countries.[26]

All of the above-mentioned directives have been implemented into the Act No. 106/2004 Coll. on Excise Duty on Tobacco Products.

As stated above, the most important body in the Slovak Republic combatting illicit trade in tobacco products is the Financial Administration of the Slovak Republic. There is no special body or institution responsible for prevention of illicit trade in tobacco products, but the Government of the Slovak Republic is the main authority creating strategic prevention plans. It should be noted, as regards the education of youth, the National Institute for Education operates in the Slovak Republic.[27] Its mission is to continually enhance curricula development based on the results of pedagogical research and the latest scientific knowledge. It provides children and young people with opportunities for their personal development so that they have the cognitive, personal and social skills necessary for their future life and also for lifelong learning. In 2011, it published a prevention-focused book for youth entitled Towards Prevention at School.[28] The majority of this book is focused on smoking prevention.

[23]Council Directive 2008/118/EC of 16 December 2008 concerning the general arrangements for excise duty and repealing Directive 92/12/EEC, as amended by the Directive 2010/12/EU of 16 February 2010. Official Journal of the European Union, L 9/12, 14 January 2009.

[24]Council Directive 2011/64/EU of 21 June 2011 on the structure and rates of excise duty applied to manufactured tobacco. Official Journal of the European Union, L 176/24, 5 July 2011.

[25]Council Directive 2007/74/EC of 20 December 2007 on the exemption from value added tax and excise duty of goods imported by persons travelling from third countries. Official Journal of the European Union, L 346/6, 29 December 2007.

[26]Council Directive 2006/79/EC of 5 October 2006 on the exemption from taxes of imports of small consignments of goods of a non-commercial character from third countries (codified version). Official Journal of the European Union, L 286/15, 17 October 2006.

[27]Slovak: Štátny pedagogický ústav.

[28]Slovak: K prevencii v škole. The book is available online <http://www.statpedu.sk/files/sk/metodicky-portal/metodicke-podnety/k-prevencii-skole.pdf>.

5 Cooperation

Slovak Customs Offices cooperate with law enforcement authorities, in particular with police officers. As stated above, the most problematic is the Slovak-Ukrainian border. Indeed, Slovak officers cooperate with Ukrainian officers.

Slovak national institutions cooperate with OLAF (European Anti-Fraud Office), which is a body of the European Union protecting its financial interests.

6 General Issues

Young people in particular are of the opinion that smoking cigarettes is a lifestyle question. The majority of them do not have much money. As a consequence, they have a small budget for smoking. Smuggled tobacco products are accessible for them, because they are cheaper. They are a target group for smugglers.

As for adults, many are addicted to smoking—due to stress, social behaviour in groups, etc. Despite the fact that a large selection of cigarette brands offer high-quality products on legal markets in shops, there are still people looking for cheaper cigarettes. They are a target group for smugglers as well. On the other hand, the number of people using electronic cigarettes is increasing. In recent years, former "classic smokers" have become "vapers". However, the majority of smokers are still "classic smokers".

In the eastern part of the Slovak Republic the unemployment rate is the highest in the country. People living/residing near the Slovak-Ukrainian border have good access to Ukraine. Taking into account the fact that they have a low standard of living, since they are poor, there is a possibility to "earn" extra money. Of course, not only poor people smuggle illegal tobacco products. There are organised groups specialising in this kind of "undertaking". They "run" a business, but without official approval, since for "smuggling" it is not possible to apply for registration of a commercial company.

The Slovak Republic is one of the smallest Member States of the European Union, and as such, it is only a minor destination for large European organised smuggling groups. Due to the relatively low price of cigarettes compared to Western Europe, organised groups with cigarette contraband mostly transit through the Slovak Republic to markets in Western Europe. For example, while in the Slovak Republic 1 package of cigarettes costs approx. €3.50, the same costs €6–7 in Germany. Indeed, if a large number of cigarette packages are smuggled from Ukraine to the Slovak Republic, which is the point of entry to the Schengen area, it is very easy to transport them to any other Schengen state because of the absence of control at internal borders.

7 Conclusion

A legal framework related to illicit trade in tobacco products exists. Its objective is to combat this phenomenon. However, reality shows that there is much more work to do, since the legal regulation itself is not satisfactory. As we have seen, many people have reasons to buy and use illicit tobacco products.

The best results in combatting illicit trade in tobacco products are achieved by the Financial Administration of the Slovak Republic, in particular the Criminal Office of the Financial Administration. Its work is effective; however, it will never be perfect. Smugglers have effective means of performing their illegal activities, and contrary to the Financial Administration of the Slovak Republic, they are not bound by law. European states, including the Slovak Republic, are aware that their cooperation is of crucial importance. In the case of Slovakia, the most important cooperation is with Ukraine. The Slovak-Ukrainian border is a gateway to the European Union, since the Slovak Republic is often a transit state for illegal cigarettes—most illegal cigarettes go further into Europe.

References

Až každá štrnásta cigareta na Slovensku je nelegálna [online] [transl.: Every fourteenth cigarette in Slovakia is illegal]. <https://www.financnasprava.sk/sk/pre-media/novinky/archiv-noviniek/detail-novinky/_fejky-cig-ts>.

Holcr K et al (2008) Kriminológia [transl.: Criminology]. Iura edition, Bratislava, 403 pp

Ivor J, Klimek L, Záhora J (2013) Trestné právo Európskej únie a jeho vplyv na právny poriadok Slovenskej republiky [transl.: Criminal Law of the European Union and its impact on the legal order of the Slovak Republic]. Eurokódex, Žilina, 888 pp

Ivor J, Polák P, Záhora J (2017) Trestné právo hmotné II – Osobitná časť [transl.: Substantive criminal law II – special part]. Wolters Kluwer, Bratislava, 648 pp

Klátik J et al (2018) Trestné právo hmotné – Osobitná časť [transl.: Substantive criminal law – special part]. Vydavatelství a nakladatelství Aleš Čeněk, Plzeň, 422 pp

Klimek L (2017) Základy trestného práva Európskej únie [transl.: Fundamentals of the European Union criminal law]. Wolters Kluwer, Bratislava, 265 pp

Nelegálne cigarety [online] (transl.: Illegal cigarettes). <https://www.szzv.sk/az-kazda-strnasta-cigareta-na-slovensku-je-nelegalna-na-vychodnom-dokonca-kazda-tretia/>

Správa o činnosti SIS za rok 2018, Bratislava, 2019. <http://www.sis.gov.sk/pre-vas/sprava-o-cinnosti-2018.html>

Záhora J, Šimovček I (2019) Zákon o trestnej zodpovednosti právnických osôb. In: Komentár, vol 2. Wolters Kluwer, Bratislava

Zákon Národnej rady Slovenskej republiky č. 372/1990 Zb. o priestupkoch v znení neskorších predpisov

Zákon Národnej rady Slovenskej republiky č. 46/1993 Z. z. o Slovenskej informačnej službe v znení neskorších predpisov

Zákon Národnej rady Slovenskej republiky č. 147/2001 Z. z. o reklame v znení neskorších predpisov

Zákon Národnej rady Slovenskej republiky č. 147/2001 Z. z. 377/2004 Z. z. o ochrane nefajčiarov v znení neskorších predpisov

Zákon Národnej rady Slovenskej republiky č. 106/2004 Z. z. o spotrebnej dani z tabakových výrobkov v znení neskorších predpisov

Zákon Národnej rady Slovenskej republiky č. 300/2005 Z. z., Trestný zákon v znení neskorších predpisov

Zákon Národnej rady Slovenskej republiky č. 333/2011 Z. z. o orgánoch štátnej správy v oblasti daní, poplatkov a colníctva v znení neskorších predpisov

Libor Klimek Ph.D., is Associate Professor at the Department of Criminal Law, Criminology, Criminalistics and Forensic Disciplines and director of the Criminology and Criminalistics Research Centre at the Faculty of Law, Matej Bel University, Banská Bystrica, Slovak Republic. Prof. Libor Klimek is Visiting Professor at the Faculty of Law, Leipzig University, Germany. He is advisor of the Constitutional Court of the Slovak Republic and author and member of editorial boards of legal journals *EU Law Journal* and *Štát a právo* (State and Law). He has published over 150 publications.

Part III
Conclusions

Conclusions: Criminal Policy on Illicit Tobacco Trade Between Scylla of Health Concerns and Charybdis of Fiscal Interests

Konrad Buczkowski and Celina Nowak

Abstract This chapter summarizes the research findings presented in the chapters on national criminal policies above in this volume. It also puts forward some recommendations to national policy makers aimed at improving national criminal policies on illicit tobacco trade.

This volume presents a comprehensive analysis of criminal policies that govern the illicit tobacco trade and that have been adopted by six of the Member States of the European Union. This comparative chapter identifies common features of these policies and summarizes the research to prepare for deeper examination and to support practical application by national policymakers.

The research on national systems confirms the preliminary presumption underlying the research that on the national level, the fight against the illicit trade of tobacco products is primarily conducted through the enforcement of criminal law. It issues from the chapters above that administrative (tax or fiscal) law play a secondary, subsidiary role with regard to the criminal legal framework.

The main goals of any national criminal law are to prevent crime (primarily by deterrence), bring offenders to justice and enforce sanctions. Effectiveness of criminal law is very difficult to assess, as evaluation criteria (such as for instance a decrease of the number of committed offences or the increase of the number of convictions) are fluent and, even if agreed upon by researchers, they change over time. However, attempting to pinpoint "an effective way to fight against illicit

K. Buczkowski (✉)
Institute of Law Studies, Polish Academy of Sciences, Department of Criminal Law, Warsaw, Poland
e-mail: k.buczkowski@inp.pan.pl

C. Nowak
Institute of Law Studies, Polish Academy of Sciences, Warsaw, Poland
e-mail: cnowak@inp.pan.pl

C. Nowak (ed.), *Combatting Illicit Trade on the EU Border*,
https://doi.org/10.1007/978-3-030-51019-0_9

tobacco trade", we should first emphasise the following goals in tackling this type of crime: to reduce the consumption of tobacco (as required by the WHO FCTC), decrease the volume of tobacco products illegally distributed in states and secure steady fiscal revenue for the state's budget.

The countries must translate these goals into legislation while taking a variety of factors into account. First, there are serious health considerations related to tobacco use. However states decide to shape their criminal law, the issue of health remains of utmost importance and constitutes a primary concern.

Additionally, states must fulfil their international obligations as well as their obligations to the EU legal instruments. These instruments, as mentioned previously, articulate a variety of measures to reduce the demand and supply of tobacco. Those measures may be repressive, regulatory or preventive. Repressive measures establish a catalogue of unlawful behaviours in national policy and enforce them with effective, proportionate and dissuasive criminal or non-criminal sanctions, including monetary sanctions. Regulatory measures establish fiscal policies that comply with respective EU instruments, as well as establish a track and trace system. Preventive instruments mainly govern advertising, packaging and the labelling of tobacco products.

Furthermore, as mentioned above, national criminal policy on the illicit tobacco trade is just an element of the general national criminal policy. Therefore, it must conform to a state's response to other types of criminality. Thus, the criminal policy regarding illicit tobacco trade must be compatible with the general legal rules of the national law, most significantly rules referring to criminal law and criminal procedure.

Finally, criminal law never occurs in a void. It is created by states situated in different geographical locations with, therefore, different histories and legal backgrounds. These geographical, economic, political and social circumstances impact states' experiences with the illicit tobacco trade and on how they cope with this phenomenon.

The studies presented in this collection are proof of the fact that, to different extents and in different ways, the six states examined here struggle to find an effective response to the illicit tobacco trade.

The states presented in this volume have very diverse circumstances. Four states: Lithuania, Poland, Slovakia and Romania, which are the newer EU Member States, are all located on the Eastern EU border. Lithuania has a small population but shares a long land border with much poorer countries, such as Belarus and Russia. Poland is the largest of the four states, in terms of both population and territory. It has a long land border with non-EU countries, most notably with Belarus and Ukraine. Both Lithuanian and Polish eastern borders are easily accessible—they cross flat plains and woods and occasional rivers are their only natural obstacles. Slovakia's eastern neighbour is Ukraine, and their shared border is more difficult terrain, especially in the mountains. The borders of Romania on the east are long. Parts thereof are somewhat difficult to cross because of the mountains, but the Romanian border with Moldova is fluvial, following the river Prut. Also, all these counties struggle with their post-communist heritage, one of the element of which are rather difficult economic situations of their populations. Large groups of inhabitants have emigrated over the years to richer states in the west and north of the continent.

Germany has the strongest economy of the examined states. Also, it has a more convenient geographical location than any of the examined states. It is situated in the middle of the continent. Italy, on the other hand, may be richer than the four Eastern states, but is in the south of the continent and has a long waterfront border.

The economic situation of citizens also greatly influences the size of the illicit tobacco trade. The poorer populations east of the EU, who often have strong personal ties with people living across the EU eastern border, are more likely to buy cheaper illegal cigarettes or to contribute to illegal trade than populations from western EU countries. They may, for instance, be more inclined to take bribes from individuals involved in this illegal activity. Also, general social attitudes toward crime, including corruption, are important.

The research shows that the practices used to illicitly trade tobacco products are similar in all examined states. The criminals still use individual, small-scale smugglers, as they had been over the years, or organize and engage in large criminal operations. In addition, in recent years smugglers have been using modern technologies, such as drones, to pursue their illegal activities. With the improvement of detection techniques on the Eastern border of the Union, more organized crime groups have given up smuggling and started opening factories inside these states to avoid having to pass through borders. They manufacture illicit cigarettes and then sell them inside a given country or push them further to the West, to gain more profit as prices of legal cigarettes are higher on the West.

All national policymakers in the examined states rely upon criminal law instruments to combat the illicit tobacco trade. Therefore, in all these states this activity is recognised as a crime. As stated in Art. 15 WHO FCTC, the phrase 'illicit tobacco trade' covers a variety of activities, such as smuggling, tax evasion, manufacturing and counterfeiting. The research shows that—from the point of view of criminalisation—in all the examined countries all of the features of illicit tobacco trade enumerated in Art. 15 WHO FCTC are covered. However, in some countries (Germany, Italy, Lithuania) due to the particularities of their respective national legal systems and the hierarchy of legal goods covered by criminal law, when the value or volume of illicitly traded tobacco products remains under a specified threshold, the activity is usually covered by administrative law. The latter solution implies financial sanctions, but not custodial sanctions, which are applied only with regard to perpetrators of crimes. Criminal law thus refers to more serious cases, more detrimental to the fiscal interests of the state. In other countries the criminal liability and administrative liability are independent and may be applied in parallel. In Poland and Romania, aside from administrative liability, depending upon the value of the damage to the public finances, perpetrators may be held liable for offences or for contraventions, the latter constituting a lesser form of criminal liability. Despite these rather complicated typologies of prohibited acts under respective national laws, interestingly, in general the ne bis in idem principle does not constitute an obstacle for states in prosecuting illicit tobacco trade, as the legal systems provides for some, even if imperfect, collision rules.

The overall positive assessment of the level of criminalisation of the illicit tobacco trade in the examined legal systems is diminished by the realization that in some examined countries sanctions on the illicit tobacco trade, which always depend upon the role and specific activity of the perpetrator, are less severe than for violent crimes (Poland, Germany). In other countries though the sanctions are quite severe in comparison to the other examined legal systems (Lithuania, Romania), amounting up to several years of imprisonment, although these systems present a general higher level of punitiveness, which is symptomatic for post-communist countries.

Overall, the illicit tobacco trade is often perceived as less serious criminal activity—and an occasional severity of applied sanctions is a result of general punitiveness of national criminal policy. The general perception, although stereotypical, is that this is a victimless violation of complicated financial rules that are incomprehensible for the average citizen. The crime is considered even less harmful than other types of economic crimes. Especially in Eastern Europe, where remnants of Soviet mentality and distrust towards authorities are still present, perpetrators of this type of criminality are met with limited social reprehension. They are lauded for outsmarting and gaining profit from a fiscal system that is unfavourable to ordinary people.

The effectiveness of the system of sanctions gives room for improvement in all the examined countries. In particular the application of financial penalties and forfeiture should be more effective. Sadly, enforcement of fines as well as asset recovery seem to be a challenge throughout. Criminals are not prevented from hiding their assets, and the sanction becomes void, when there is nothing to forfeit.

It is interesting to note that in all the examined states the national law provides for the responsibility of individuals, as well as legal persons for the said offences, with the notable exception of Germany. Germany does not allow for criminal liability of legal persons and only recognises some administrative liability of corporations. Yet, when provided, liability of legal persons for offences is only symbolic, hardly ever applied in practice.

The illicit tobacco trade in all its forms is usually an activity undertaken by a group of individuals. As mentioned above, a tendency is observed that organized crime groups have gotten more involved in the illicit tobacco trade in recent years. Sanctions for the illicit trade of tobacco products are less severe than, for instance, for drug offences. The risks are generally lower, due to the ambiguous social image of illicit tobacco manufacturers and smugglers. It is therefore important to note than in some of the examined legal systems (Germany, Italy, Romania) the fact that the illicit trade involved more than one person, or it involved organized crime, may warrant an increase in sanctions. It is therefore recommended to all other states to consider commission of illicit tobacco trade by more than one person, especially as part of activities of organized crime groups, an aggravating circumstance in the process of sentencing.

To sum up, we recommend a thorough assessment of the system of criminal and administrative sanctions and penalties that deter engagement in the illicit tobacco trade. We does not advocate for a general introduction of severe sanctions but recommend for the states to consider introducing a penalty of imprisonment or higher financial sanctions for more serious cases of illicit tobacco trade. The enforcement of financial penalties and forfeiture, as well as asset recovery should be more effective.

Also, the inevitability of sanctions seems crucial, so it must be recommended to conduct criminal proceedings in an expedite manner, especially with regard to less serious cases of illicit tobacco trade. In addition, national systems of liability of legal persons should be revised and made efficient in order to deter legal persons from encouraging or participating in illicit tobacco trade.

The national criminal policies that govern the illicit tobacco trade have some of the weaknesses as criminal policies adopted with regard to other types of crime. The level of criminalisation and sanctions are satisfactory, but the enforcement of the provisions needs improvement.

National enforcement is the domain of specialised law enforcement institutions, such as the financial police. Different agencies usually share the task of fighting the illicit tobacco trade on a national level. They cooperate, but at times this cooperation could be better. All enforcement agencies experience the same problems. Lack of resources has been pointed out as an issue; not enough funds, not enough trained staff, who are not paid well enough to abstain from taking an occasional bribe. It should be mentioned that the *modus operandi* of organised crime groups evolves. Law enforcement institutions face creative perpetrators operating more and more advanced technologies and thus, evading detection. Therefore, the material situation of investigative agencies should definitely be improved.

Still, more importantly, effective cooperation is not just about money. Lack of communication and exchange of experiences with partners inside and outside the country seem more troublesome than the lack of appropriate resources. The different law enforcement stakeholders should be cooperating and swiftly communicating with one another, instead of disputing over competencies or jurisdiction. We must consider the difficulties of conducting investigative operations of the organised crime groups involved in the illicit tobacco trade. These investigations are rarely supported by local communities. Coordination of law enforcement activities aimed at preventing and combating illicit tobacco trade should be a priority for national policymakers and the law enforcement authorities themselves, this is undoubtedly one of the most important recommendations resulting from the study at hand.

Another recommendation, based on the research presented in this collection, refers to the availability of data on the illicit tobacco trade. As observed by the research team and mentioned in the chapters above, no detailed and comprehensive data on criminality related to illicit tobacco trade are systematically collected in any of the examined states. If they exist, such data are part of data collected about general categories of related crimes, such as smuggling, tax evasion or lack of excise tax labels. Therefore, it is impossible to single out the data on tobacco-related crime. For this reason, such data are unavailable (Italy, Slovakia, Romania). Furthermore, pertinent data are often collected by more than one institution. Sometimes they are included in statistical data gathered in databases run by different institutions (fiscal administration, border guards), which assesses the real scope of the phenomenon (Poland, Germany). For the abovementioned reasons, evaluation of the so-called "dark number" of tobacco-related crimes is extremely problematic. The lack of detailed data will flaw all estimates, and the margin of error will be large. For the sake of future research on this topic, national law enforcement authorities should collect detailed and systematic data on the illicit tobacco trade and tobacco-related crimes. Without such data, conducting criminological studies in this field will be difficult.

All the examined states have implemented at least some preventive measures aimed at reducing tobacco demand, such as bans on advertising tobacco products or rules related to the packaging and labelling of tobacco products. Some countries adopt new methods to combat illicit trade, for instance in Italy authorities may prohibit access to web pages through which foreign tobacco products are illegally sold or advertised, which is a good solution limiting access to illegal products and must be recommended to be more widely adopted.

Also, EU Member States, as of 20 May 2019, have all adopted the EU track and tracing system of cigarettes, stipulated in Art. 15 and 16 of the Tobacco Products Directive 2014/40/EU.

Yet, states cannot easily find remedies to the uneven cigarette prices, which is the main contributor to the illicit tobacco trade, across EU Member States, as well as UE Member States and non-EU Member States. Smokers, notably in the eastern regions of Lithuania, Poland, Slovakia and Romania, as well as poorer smokers in other parts of these countries and smokers in Western states, tend to smoke illicit cigarettes, be it in the form of so-called illicit whites (local Eastern brands, usually produced with raw materials of lesser quality) or counterfeited western brands of cigarettes, because they are considerably cheaper than legal cigarettes.

There may be ways to change this landscape of varying prices, but none of them is satisfactory and each would certainly have unwanted ramifications. Prices in the different EU Member States could all be equalized, lowered to the current lowest legal level or increased to the current highest level. Neither of these scenarios is good though. Prices that are too high would push smokers to the dark market, which would be bad for their health, as well as bad for national public revenues. On the other hand, prices that are too low would make cigarettes so affordable they would undermine national health policies on tobacco.

Similar considerations apply to national criminal policies on the illicit tobacco trade. Total prohibition of tobacco, basically the criminalisation of tobacco, like the criminalisation of street market drugs, would turn smokers into criminals and consequently, encourage them to participate in the dark market. Subsequently, there would be no tax revenue for the state; worse quality products would further harm the health of users and underfunded law enforcement and eventual increase in crime levels would place huge burdens on society.

On the other hand, total decriminalization of tobacco, as well as waiving the excise tax on tobacco is also unthinkable; mainly due to health concerns, but also because of national fiscal needs.

As mentioned in this study, national criminal policy is always a result of an effort to combine a variety of factors in a comprehensive manner. National criminal policy on illicit tobacco trade is a good example of such a struggle. Given the results of the comparative study conducted in this volume, we must appreciate that the makers of the national criminal policy on illicit tobacco trade are between Scylla of health concerns and Charybdis of their own fiscal interests. There is no good solution, no one perfect criminal policy, or rather, there are no better criminal policies than states currently have. They are striving to find a delicate balance between health concerns and states' fiscal needs, considering requirements of the national legal systems and national criminal policies in general, as well as particular social and economic circumstances in the country, mainly related to pricing tobacco products, as well as in other countries. But there is no doubt that as long as there is no tobacco-free world, there is a need for a comprehensive and well-designed criminal policy on illicit tobacco trade.

Konrad Buczkowski Ph.D., is Assistant Professor at the Institute of Law Studies, Polish Academy of Sciences, Poland. His main research interest is criminology, however in addition he has a vast experience in the field of economic criminal law, especially: economic crime, insurance fraud, money laundering, white-collar crime and cybercrime. He is a member of the European Society of Criminology and the Member of the Board of the Polish Society of Criminology.

Celina Nowak Ph.D., is Associate Professor and Head of the Institute of Law Studies of the Polish Academy of Sciences. She holds a Ph.D. and habilitation in law, as well as a postgraduate diploma of Université de Paris I—Panthéon–Sorbonne in criminal law and criminal policy in Europe. Her research refers to criminal law, with focus on international, EU and comparative criminal law. In addition, she has extensive experience as an academic teacher at the Kozminski University and the Warsaw University. Prof. Nowak has taken part in a number of comparative law projects, in the national and EU context, either as a project leader, or as a national expert. She has authored 2 monographs, edited and co-edited 10 books. She has written more than three dozen articles and chapters in Polish, English and French, published in Poland and internationally.